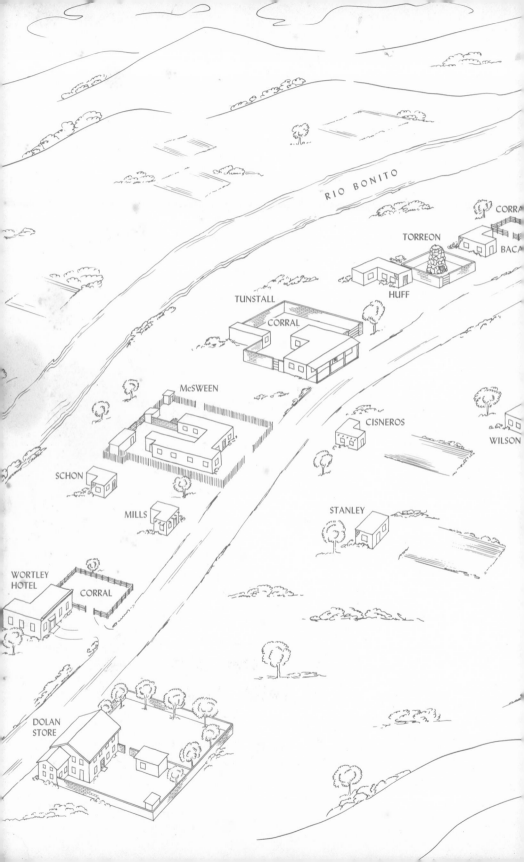

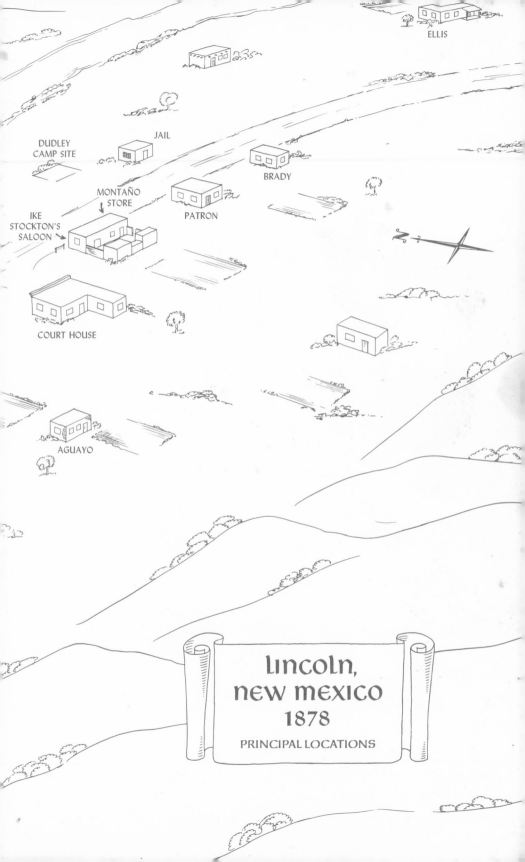

ELLIS

DUDLEY
CAMP SITE

JAIL

MONTAÑO
STORE

BRADY

PATRON

IKE
STOCKTON'S
SALOON

COURT HOUSE

AGUAYO

lincoln,
new mexico
1878

PRINCIPAL LOCATIONS

Colonel Maurice Garland Fulton
1877–1955

Maurice Garland Fulton's

HISTORY OF THE

LINCOLN COUNTY WAR

Edited by
ROBERT N. MULLIN

THE UNIVERSITY OF ARIZONA PRESS
Tucson, Arizona

COLONEL MAURICE GARLAND FULTON over a period of years
acquired a remarkable collection of interviews, photographs,
maps, documents, and other source materials which established
him as the foremost authority on Lincoln County, New Mexico,
and its celebrated era of 19th-century violence. Although he
began drafting the manuscript of this volume long before
publishing his annotated edition of Pat Garrett's *Authentic
Life of Billy the Kid*, Fulton's tireless pursuit of minute detail
as well as over-all truth prevented him from completing the
Lincoln County manuscript before his death. This task fell to
his friend, collaborator, and literary executor of the Fulton
estate, ROBERT N. MULLIN, Western historian and collector,
who has skillfully preserved the Fulton standards for meticulous
detail and authenticity in bringing the project to completion.

Third printing 1980

THE UNIVERSITY OF ARIZONA PRESS

S. B. N. 8165-0052-5
L. C. No. 68-13544

Contents

ILLUSTRATIONS

Introduction:

The Narrator of the Story

"THE DEFINITIVE HISTORY of the Lincoln County War and the career of the Kid has not yet appeared. Colonel Maurice G. Fulton has labored long in the preparation of such a history, fully documented. When it is completed it should place the Kid in his proper niche in the history of New Mexico and put an end to the legend. But folklore is seldom restrained by documented fact, and it is probable the legend will go right on growing. . . . As far as I am concerned, Colonel Fulton is the leading scholar of the Lincoln County War and its participants." So wrote the outstanding authority on Lincoln County War bibliography, J. C. Dykes, in his *Billy the Kid, the Bibliography of a Legend*, published by the University of New Mexico Press in 1952.

Assessments such as that of Dykes were well earned. Maurice Garland Fulton came from a family where scholarship was a way of life. Born December 3, 1877, he was the son of Robert Burwell Fulton, a professor and later chancellor of the University of Mississippi at Oxford, where he grew up in an atmosphere of study and inquiry. After graduating from the University of Mississippi, he took graduate work at the University of Michigan, and later taught there as well as at the University of Illinois for a year. In 1905 he became professor of English at Centre College of Kentucky and from 1909 until he entered the army in World War I he was professor at Davidson College in North Carolina. After military service in 1919, he resumed his career, this time at Indiana University. When problems of health required a move to a milder climate in 1922, he was quick to accept an invitation to

[1]

teach at the New Mexico Military Institute at Roswell, New Mexico.

Before coming to New Mexico Colonel Fulton was best known as the author of several textbooks for college use, including (in collaboration with Raymond George Bressler and Glenn Hawthorne Mullin) a student manual on the English language. Among the books he edited was the Macmillan edition of Viscount James Bryce's commentaries on American democracy. For the same publisher he had edited, with introduction and notes, Theodore Roosevelt's *Winning the West*.

Such was the background and training which Fulton brought with him when he reached the Southwest in 1922. Almost immediately he became intrigued by the history, tradition, and legend of New Mexico. He plunged into study and research but it was not until fifteen years later that he felt qualified to write his definitive monograph, *Roswell in Its Early Years*. In that same year, 1937, appeared the book, *New Mexico's Own Chronicle, Three Races in the Writings of Four Hundred Years*, prepared in collaboration with his friend Paul Horgan. Four years later the University of Oklahoma Press published *The Diary and Letters of Josiah Gregg* with an interpretive introduction by Maurice Garland Fulton.

When the Macmillan Company published *The Authentic Life of Billy the Kid* by Pat F. Garrett in 1927, Colonel Fulton was asked to edit and annotate the work, although his studies of the subject then represented but a small part of the information he was later to develop. His persistent ferreting out of information from pioneer residents and from private and public records had won him such recognition in the Pecos country that when John W. Poe's *The Death of Billy the Kid* was being readied for publication in 1933 Mr. Poe's widow insisted that Fulton was the one person qualified to write the introduction.

Colonel Fulton's search for the true facts in the Lincoln County troubles extended over a period of some thirty-three years and continued almost to the day of his death. Early in February, 1955, he had started by bus from Roswell to El Paso where he expected to meet his brother, Harry R. Fulton of Washington, D.C., and this editor, and to look into some recently discovered evidence concerning one of the men involved in the Lincoln County War. Stricken with what proved to be a heart attack, he stopped at Ruidoso where his friend and fellow student of early-day New Mexico matters, Mrs. Eve Ball, arranged for his return to Roswell. Here his death occurred on February 12. Even at the last his concern was that his work had been interrupted.

The passing of Fulton, with his work unfinished, was the cause of deep regret among students of Southwestern frontier history and left a niche which may never again be quite filled. The blunt candor with which he expressed (not always diplomatically) his impatience at superficial conclusions left abiding scars in some quarters. But among those who knew him best he was recognized for his personal and intellectual integrity, his modesty, and his openness of mind. Above all, he will probably be best remembered for the kindness and generosity he extended to all who came to him for information, advice, and encouragement. Coloradoan John J. Lipsey, respected authority on Western books, wrote in the *Brand Book* of the Chicago Corral of The Westerners, in the summer of 1955:

> Colonel Fulton was the greatest authority on the history of Lincoln County, N. M., and especially that of the Lincoln County War . . . He, I think, carried in his head more New Mexico history than many collectors have in their libraries.
>
> One reason why he was unable to complete his books was the constant flow of visitors to his home, visitors who wanted his advice and help in writing their own books. He never denied them . . . Correspondents pestered him for information and he wrote them long letters. . . . He lived in a tiny, crowded house where he had no space to spread out his treasures and to write about the time and the land he knew and loved.
>
> But the citizens of Roswell knew and loved him, too. I saw them, on the streets and in restaurants, greet him with respect and affection. His published works are monuments to his knowledge and ability, but they are small compared with what they might have been if he had not had such a great heart. His influence in Western historical writing is tremendous and continuing, but the remembrance by his countless friends and the beneficiaries of his generosity may be the monuments this great, kind, gentle man would have preferred.

The Lincoln County War manuscript, many times revised, had been nearly completed when Colonel Fulton was overtaken by his final illness. Completion of the work was not difficult, thanks to the availability of the author's original notes as well as several hundred letters he wrote this editor over a period of years. The sparsity of footnotes in the manuscript confronted the editor with something of a problem, particularly in documenting situations where Fulton's findings and conclusions run contrary to oft-repeated versions. Perhaps he expected to append additional footnotes before submitting the manscript for publication; however, he disliked footnotes in general and felt strongly that in matters requiring documentation the sources should be given in the text. Having observed the thoroughness of Fulton's research and analysis before reaching final conclusions, the editor is inclined to accept the author's statements whether sources are identified or not.

Colonel Fulton, for example, was not content to accept at face value the newspaper accounts of Governor Lew Wallace's activities and observations relating to the New Mexico disturbances, and he made a sustained effort to find the original Wallace papers. It was the good fortune of the editor to locate these for the Colonel; thus, in many cases, but by no means in all, the manuscript names the Wallace papers as the author's source of information. Another indication of the Fulton concern with accuracy of detail was his study of geography — he felt that without a knowledge of the "lay of the land" one could not properly assess the validity of reports of crucial happenings. Maps, he often said, were essential to a clear understanding, but he was not content merely to pore over old maps and diagrams. On various occasions he guided the editor to the scenes of most of the Lincoln County War activities: the place where John Tunstall was murdered, the sites of the two Tunstall ranches, L. G. Murphy's Carrizo Spring ranch, the two Brewer farm locations, the site of the notorious Shedd ranch, old Fort Sumner, Taiban, White Oaks, and Seven Rivers, among others. At practically all of the locations visited the Colonel's familiarity with the surroundings gave ample evidence of his previous inspections and study. It was while walking in Blackwater Canyon, where Morton, Baker, and McCloskey had been killed, that Fulton explained a cardinal principle of his writing, saying that in order to understand a man's actions, he always tried to put himself in that man's place under the circumstances which confronted him.

Maurice Fulton had a unique faculty for securing information where others had failed. Some experienced researchers have said that in trying to get information from people reluctant to divulge their information, the best way to start is with the ordinary trick of salesmanship, a bit of ego-building flattery: "Assuring a man what a great authority he is, deferring to his judgment or admiring his remarkable memory, is a sure-fire way of breaking down resistance," is the advice of one very successful interviewer. Fulton scorned all such tactics. Quietly, but directly, he came to the point. Strangely enough, many who had consistently refused to express themselves on controversial matters talked freely and frankly with him, perhaps disarmed by the straightforward simplicity of the man.

Among those consulted by Colonel Fulton in person or by correspondence were Mr. A. N. Blazer and his son Paul, Mr. Robert Brady, Mr. Will J. Chisum, Mr. Frank Coe, Mr. George W. Coe, Miss Ruth R. Ealy, Mr. W. C. Foor, Mrs. Lilly Casey Klasner, Mrs.

George W. Barber (Mrs. Sue E. McSween), Mr. John P. Meadows, Mr. Jim Miller, Mr. José Montaño, Mr. Juan Peppin, Mr. John W. Poe, Mrs. Sophie A. Poe, Mrs. Sally Chisum Robert, Mr. Francisco Trujillo, Mr. Gregorio Wilson, and Mrs. Caroline Dolan Vorwerk. The author's examination of public and private records included such places as Mesilla, Las Cruces, Carrizozo, Las Vegas, and Santa Fe. At Silver City he not only searched the newspaper files and court records but interviewed many informants, including Mr. Anthony B. Conner and Mr. Louis Abraham, both one-time schoolmates of Henry McCarty. Particularly rewarding were his conversations with A. M. ("Gus") Gildea of Pearce, Arizona, whom he met by appointment at Douglas. Gildea, who had known Billy the Kid in Arizona before the Lincoln County War days and who had later been a fighting man in the Dolan forces during that struggle, greatly amplified the information given in his letters to Colonel Fulton. In 1931 Colonel M. Behrens, John Tunstall's nephew in England, sent the author originals of some and copies of others of Tunstall's letters to his family, as well as letters from Alex McSween, Sam Corbet, and John Middleton, all participants in the Lincoln County War.

Perhaps the greatest single source of information acquired by interview was the former Mrs. McSween. In addition to the extensive correspondence with her, Colonel Fulton visited that lady in White Oaks on many occasions; here, in addition to long question-and-answer sessions, Mrs. Barber's collection of old letters and papers proved exceptionally valuable. Mr. George Coe was another principal source of information. The accounts of the native New Mexicans being, like those of Mrs. Barber and the Coes, generally unfavorable to the Murphy-Dolan-Riley-Catron element, Colonel Fulton made a special effort to obtain also the views of those who were sympathetic to the Dolan faction. However, while giving full consideration to the accounts given him by individuals, Fulton accorded special weight to the recorded testimony of court proceedings such as the grand jury records and the testimony of both factions at the Military Court of Inquiry dealing with the so-called Five-Day Battle.

In the murder of Tunstall, Colonel Fulton's final conclusion was that Tunstall's companions were not guilty of such a cowardly performance as that with which many writers have charged them. This was based not only on Mrs. Barber's account, gained from persons involved, but largely upon the author's analysis of the twenty-two affidavits included in the report made to the United States Attorney General at Washington by federal investigator Judge Frank Warner Angel.

The Fulton account of the ambush-killings of William Brady and George Hindman varies in one important detail from the customary versions. The editor finds it difficult to document thoroughly the basis for Colonel Fulton's conclusion, although the latter appears quite logical. The only reference found is that the information came from "one of Lincoln's oldest residents who, as a boy, had witnessed the shooting," and from what Mrs. Barber told the author she had learned from persons who had been present.

Several versions of the killing of A. L. Roberts and Richard Brewer have appeared; for example, the account given Mrs. Eve Ball by Paul Blazer, grandson of Dr. Joseph H. Blazer, which appeared in the Autumn, 1964, issue of *Arizona and the West*, differs in some details from the Fulton account. The author's version was derived from a number of sources, including Paul Blazer's father, Almer, who had been an actual witness, and the Coes, who had been participants. Colonel Fulton's final conclusions were based primarily on the Court of Inquiry held at Fort Stanton immediately after the event.

Some excellent accounts of the Lincoln County troubles, as well as a great many accounts not so dependable, have appeared over the years, but in this book Maurice Garland Fulton may well have succeeded in presenting the final, most accurate, and most complete account of the Lincoln County War.

Introduction:

The Background of the Story

THE CONFLICT known as the Lincoln County War may be said to have commenced with the murder of John H. Tunstall, February 18, 1878, and have ended five months later with the killing of Alexander McSween on July 19, at the close of the so-called Five-Day Battle.

Actually, however, the struggle did not end with the death of McSween, and it had its beginnings long before either Tunstall or McSween reached Lincoln County.

Not even at the beginning could the Lincoln County War properly be called a cattle war or a range war, though cattle-stealing and range rights frequently played some part. Nor was this a feud in the usual sense of the word, since it was not a vendetta born primarily of personal hatreds between families or clans, although in the course of the conflict many bitter personal enmities naturally developed.

The Lincoln County War was essentially a struggle for economic power. In a land where hard cash was scarce, federal government contracts for the supply of provisions, principally beef, for the military posts and for the Indian reservations, were the grand prize. The competition for these contracts was bitter and frequently ruthless. Since the early 1870's Lawrence Gustave Murphy had been the Lincoln County sub-contractor for William Rosenthal and the political clique at Santa Fe which enjoyed a near-monopoly in supplying the government with beef, even though neither Rosenthal nor Murphy himself then raised or owned any significant number of cattle. They were challenged by John H. Chisum, owner of the largest herds of cattle in the territory, who declined to do business through Rosenthal but instead bid direct on the beef contracts. Thus began Chisum's struggle with Murphy and his successors along with their backers at Santa Fe — a struggle out of which grew the Lincoln County War.

When John Tunstall came to Lincoln County, he aligned himself with Chisum, McSween, and others opposing James J. Dolan, who had succeeded Murphy as economic and political boss of upper Lincoln County. Tunstall's ranching venture posed no great threat to the entrenched interests, but when he established a mercantile business at Lincoln he brought matters to a head. This was the first serious competition encountered by the old Murphy-Dolan-Riley store, The House. And the activities of The House were the keystone in the party's economic and political power structure.

When the competitive struggle resulted in a fighting war, the opposing forces were numerically about equal. The Dolan organization commanded the support of many through political favors granted and through credit extended at the store. Too, many of the small cattlemen in lower Lincoln County resented Chisum's pre-emption of grazing land of the public domain in the Pecos Valley and so aligned themselves with Murphy and later with Dolan. On the other hand, the McSween faction found strong support among small farmers and ranchers, particularly those in the Ruidoso valley, who felt that they had been mistreated by The House and by political office-holders.

To dominate the area economically was likewise to control it politically. Thus the courts and the officers of the law were all too often openly partisan against those opposed to the party in power. Many of the small ranchers and farmers finding practically no protection for their lives and property at the hands of law officers, and with small chance for impartial justice in the courts, turned to direct action and so became branded as outlaws. Even after the killing of McSween, many of his followers, if not actually outlawed, still suffered harassment long after the nominal ending of the Lincoln County War. In the end, however, neither side was a winner. Fortunes had been destroyed and lives lost, but neither faction had achieved and held the economic power for which it had fought.

Robert N. Mullin

PART I

Tinder for the Fire

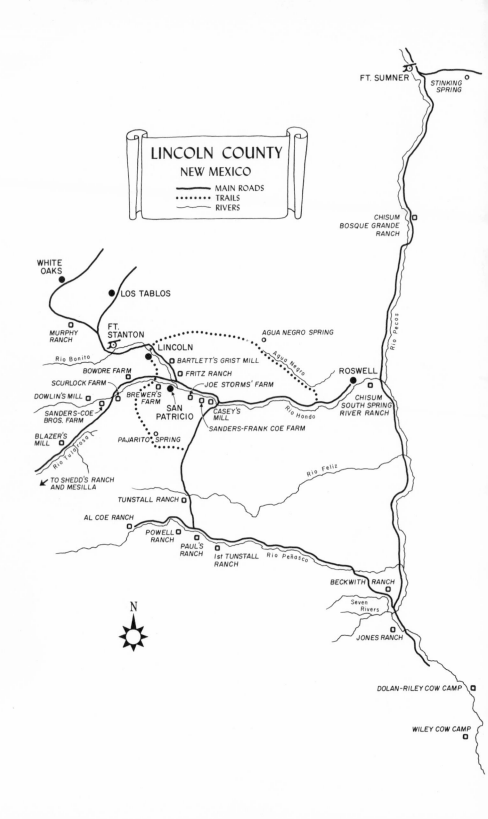

1. A County Born to Disorder

"THE HISTORY of Lincoln County has been one of bloodshed from the days of its organization." Thus tersely did Judge Frank Warner Angel emphasize the outstanding feature of this section of New Mexico in his report to the Department of Justice concerning the troubles he investigated in 1878. He added, "These troubles have existed for years with some occasional outbreaks, each being more severe than the others." Back through nearly ten years ran the stream of turmoil and disorder which had made Lincoln County the synonym for a locality where "men must stand their part, supported by trusty fire-arms."

By 1869 the isolated southeastern corner of New Mexico had achieved enough importance to be elevated into county organization. It was a Gargantuan subdivision that in 1878 included approximately one-fourth of the entire territory of New Mexico. From north to south it measured some 170 miles; from east to west, about 150 miles. The population, meager in the extreme in proportion to the extensive area, was a strange medley even for the frontier. Before the Civil War the section had been largely uninhabited except for roving Indians, winning it the designation on old maps of "Mescalero Apache Country." During the Civil War, or just after it, settlers of Mexican descent had drifted into the fertile valleys of the Rio Bonito, the Ruidoso, and the Rio Hondo. In the western and mountainous section there were several clusters of adobe houses large anough to assume the status of settlements with names, Presidio de la Luz, Tularosa, San Patricio, and La Placita del Rio Bonito, the latter called Placita for short.

[13]

Prior to the Civil War the American infusion became evident mainly through the frontier post, Fort Stanton, established in 1855. The name commemorated a stiff Indian fight in the early part of that year on Rio Peñasco in which Captain Henry W. Stanton of the Dragoons had been killed. During the Civil War, Fort Stanton had been evacuated and the buildings fired in order to deprive the advancing Texas Confederates of any benefit from it. The Confederates, however, fell heir to enough walls of adobe buildings and corrals to justify re-garrisoning; but the single company of soldiers that Colonel John R. Baylor placed there was not impressive enough to keep the Indians in check. The Mescaleros grew bold enough to attack the Fort itself, a circumstance which led the Confederates to abandon it, since their total force in New Mexico was not sufficient to allow a detachment there large enough to keep the Apaches on their good behavior.

With the Confederates checked, Fort Stanton was re-garrisoned with a few companies of New Mexico volunteers under the command of no less a personage than Colonel Kit Carson. The soldiers produced a pacifying effect on the Mescaleros, who promptly sued for peace and were impounded along with the Navajos at Bosque Redondo on the Rio Pecos. The effort to yoke together on one reservation these two tribes, long hereditary enemies, was doomed, however, to failure. In 1866 in general disgust the Mescaleros broke away in spite of the garrison at Fort Sumner and returned to old haunts in the White Mountains and the Sacramentos. Eventually they were induced to try reservation life again but this time on a tract of about five hundred acres of very desirable land located in the White Mountains some thirty miles from Fort Stanton. In this way the old post came back during the 1870's into importance as one of the factors that promoted the development of a section very alluring to settlers if security of life and property was obtainable.

Aside from its value as a defense and protection, Fort Stanton was the mainstay of the section economically. The farmers in the river valley found there a ready market for crops or livestock; prices were always high and vouchers promptly delivered. The Fort also encouraged in a very direct way a stream of settlers that became influential in county affairs. In 1886 the government had embarked upon elaborate repairing and enlarging of the post, creating extensive employment for civilian labor. Those who came for this purpose liked the locality and became settlers. Ex-soldiers, too, formed a noticeable element in the section, especially in the localities close to the Fort. Sometimes from the officer class but more often from the enlisted personnel, they at first tended to form the dominating element but became less influential as the region filled up with other settlers.

While the western section of Lincoln County was being settled under the aegis of Fort Stanton, the eastern section, comprising the Pecos Valley, developed under a different impulse. In 1865 the vanguard of its settlers established themselves at what became known as Missouri Bottom on the Hondo some miles east of its confluence with the Pecos.[1] A few years later came an inthrust of Texans into the Pecos Valley. Most notable of these was John S. Chisum, to whose shrewd eyes the ranges up and down the Pecos River for a hundred miles seemed better than those in Texas. When he and his brother Pitzer established themselves at Bosque Grande in 1868, the eastern or "lower" portion of Lincoln County became dedicated to American influences, both socially and commercially. Naturally this circumstance tended to put the two segments of the county at variance. The western or "upper" portion of the county remained predominately native New Mexican. The long-standing friction between Texan and Mexican cropped up even in this newly settled region.

The American element in the Pecos Valley was strengthened by two other communities. In the extreme southern part and comparatively close to the Texas line was the settlement of Seven Rivers, an important stopping point for the drivers bringing up herds from Texas intended for either Colorado or Arizona. The old Goodnight-Chisum trail went northwards up the Pecos and passed close to another small settlement, some sixty miles above the Seven Rivers area, known as Roswell.[2] The advantageous situation of Roswell about midway between two tributaries of the Pecos, the Hondo and North Spring rivers, gave promise that in the course of time it would grow into something more than the two or three adobe buildings and their corrals which first made up the settlement.

In its formative stages Lincoln County had no town of size or commercial importance. When a county seat was needed, the honor fell upon one of the Mexican settlements which, because of its proximity to Fort Stanton, had begun to receive an influx of American settlers.

---

1. Traditionally, Missouri Plaza or Missouri Bottom was so named because its first settlers were largely ex-Confederates from the state of Missouri. Descendants of early settlers in the section, however, maintain that the new community was established by a group migrating from San Miguel County where some had been engaged in freighting to New Mexico from St. Joseph, Missouri, and thus chose the name Missouri Plaza. The New Mexico Stock and Agricultural Association map of 1876 designates the hamlet as San José.

2. The confluence of the Hondo and the Pecos was known as "Rio Hondo" until the early part of 1872 when Van C. Smith, proprietor of the local mercantile establishment, announced that the place was to be known as Roswell, which was the given name of Mr. Smith's father.

The everyday designation "La Placita" became Americanized into Lincoln, but the change in name did not alter its Mexican complexion. It was a small village boasting perhaps forty or fifty adobe houses in which less than four hundred persons lived. Being the county seat, it displayed sometimes a degree of business and bustle, especially in April and October when court was held. The rivals to Lincoln Plaza were San Patricio, almost directly across the intervening ridge of foothills and in the Ruidoso Valley, and Tularosa farther to the west — in fact on the other side of the White Mountains and at the mouth of the canyon through which flowed Tularosa Creek. Both of these settlements were, even more than Lincoln, predominately Mexican.

From the first, this mingling of diverse frontier elements — Indian, Mexican, American; soldiers, Apache braves, settlers of varied stripes and patterns — gave rise to abundant excitement. Indian troubles were the most conspicuous sources of turmoil and confusion during the first five years of Lincoln County's career. The summer of 1870 especially was a time of terror from Indian incursions, even under the shadow of Fort Stanton. An account of one of these raids, forwarded to the Santa Fe *New Mexican* by someone signing himself "Nimrod," is a good transcript of the times:

Fort Stanton, New Mexico
June 9, 1870

Messrs. Manderfield and Tucker,
    Editors, *New Mexican*

Gents:
    Thinking the following bit of news may be worthy of publication, I take the liberty of sending same. About ten days ago a large party of Indians, supposed to be Navajos, made their appearance in this vicinity and have remained here committing depredations.
    They commenced operations by killing two worthy citizens, who were out hunting, named Luis Penagus and José García. Another of our neighbors, Juan Augustín Torres, is missing. It is not known if he is killed or not. They have also stampeded a sheep herd, belonging, I believe, to one Vigil. Likewise they have killed several head of cattle belonging to Capt. Dowlin and have stolen several horses from Don José Padilla, and also several head of horses from some parties encamped near the Pato Springs. Yesterday three of the "noble braves" rode up within three or four hundred yards of the brewery belonging to Messrs. Murphy & Fritz, but owing to the number of persons there, left without committing any depredations.

Capt. McCleave with "B" troop of the 8th Cavalry is now in the White Mountains engaged in an attempt to overhaul the marauders. He reports that the main party is divided up into many smaller groups, that it is impossible to track them successfully, but that the whole range of mountains in this vicinity seems to be infested with the various members of the "Lo" family, some being mounted and others on foot. He thinks from the tracks of the moccasins that the Indians are Navajos.

There is no further item of news except the continued drought. We have had no rain for nearly three months.

Yours truly,
Nimrod

In September came an even more audacious Indian attack, particularly an affront as two private soldiers were killed in the shadow of the Fort. The pursuit of the Indians by the army was vigorous and active, as this account shows:

Fort Stanton, Sept. 8, 1870

The Fort Stanton wood camp is about 5 miles from the post in the foothills of the Capitán Mountains. On a Saturday two teams went out as usual. About 2 P.M. two mules returned to the post each having arrows sticking in them. A party of troop "B," 8th Cavalry, at once went to the scene. Capts. McKibben, McCleave, Dr. Gibson, also Lieut. Glade. Found bodies both killed with arrows, Pvt. Chas. Hoeffer, Co. "I" 15th Infantry, and Pvt. McGrath, of Co. "B" 8th Cavalry. Bodies were stripped quite naked but not mutilated. The Indians got off with nine of the best mules. Too dark to follow trail that night, but early the next morning, about 3 A.M. Capt. McCleave and 40 men started in pursuit to avenge the murder of these two victims. The trail led into the Guadalupes. The probate judge (Major L. G. Murphy) did not organize a posse of citizens as they were busy cutting grass.

The Rio Pecos section likewise had its share of Indian raids, especially on cattle coming up the trail from Texas. The herds of John

---

*Note that the letter carries the date of 1870 with the word "troop" in matter of fact terms. However, although there was and had been considerable informal use of "troop" instead of "company" for mounted units for a relatively long time, the change was not made official until issuance September 8, 1883, of Army Circular No. 8 over the signature of Adjutant General R. C. Drum stating in part: "TROOP AND COMPANY — The designation 'troop' instead of 'company' should be used for Cavalry organizations (vide sections 1102 & 1103 R. S.) — (Letter to C. G. Div. Pacific, Aug. 7, 1883 — 3202 AGO 1883)."

Chisum were repeatedly "taken in," often when they came into the vicinity of the Guadalupe Mountains, distinguished as a lurking place of the Apaches. Even after Chisum had located in New Mexico and no longer drove up cattle from Texas, the raiding continued. In August, 1873, for example, some Indians rode up to the corral at Bosque Grande with designs on his 125 or so valuable horses. The Chisum men put up a vigorous resistance, shooting from the protection of an adobe building used as a store. The Indians, however, succeeded in stampeding the whole herd.

Most vulnerable to Indian attacks were the isolated camps of Chisum's men. At least twice the Indians killed the employees in charge, Newt Huggins in 1873, in what is now known as Huggins Arroyo, and next year a cowboy named Jack Holt, at Eighteen Mile Bend on the Rio Pecos.

2. Lawlessness of 1873

IN THE LATE SPRING a new disturbance developed in the Tularosa section. What had begun as a race war over ditch rights grew into a contest between the Mexicans living at Tularosa and a detachment of soldiers from Fort Stanton. The following letter written to the Las Cruces *Borderer* by George W. Nesmith, partner of Dr. J. H. Blazer, owner of Blazer's Mill, both early settlers, gave the details of this trouble.

Tularosa Mills, May 31st, 1873

Wm. T. Jones, Esq.:

Dear Sir: — As you have no doubt heard a great many reports ere this concerning our present difficulties in the Tularosa Canyon, and might be somewhat anxious to have a correct statement thereof, I thought I would devote a few moments time in giving you a short sketch of some of the circumstances that have transpired within the past week.

On the 24th inst., an armed mob of Mexicans numbering about thirty-five came up the canyon from the town of Tularosa, Felipe Bernal and José Marcos as leaders, for the purpose of destroying dams and ditches on the ranches of settlers in Tularosa Canyon, which they did as far as the dam of Mr. Andrew J. Wilson, when night coming on they returned to the town, stating to the persons whose property they had destroyed, that if the dams were again put in, they would come and destroy them again, and that from that time forward no man living in the Canyon should be allowed to use another drop of water for irrigating purposes.

[19]

This happened on Saturday and we expected them again on Monday, as the dams were repaired by that time, but they did not make their appearance until Tuesday, when about the same number, under the same leaders, came and cut all the ditches from the town to the dam of Wilson again, and made camp, posted armed men in fortified positions within gunshot of all dams destroyed, told the ranchmen they had come to fight, and to put in the dams again at their own peril. They remained in their positions during Tuesday and Wednesday, threatening and trying to intimidate the settlers several times in two days.

On Thursday morning, the 29th, eight of the neighbors started to the dam of Mr. Wesley Fields for the purpose of repairing it and of helping him irrigate. Before the party arrived at the dam, they were fired upon by the Bernal party, the fire being immediately returned by the others. After a few shots were exchanged, the Mexicans took flight and ran in the direction of the town.

The commanding officer at Stanton, having been informed of anticipated trouble, dispatched Lieutenant Wilkinson with five men, with a letter to the alcalde of precinct No. 10, Doña Ana County, who passed a short time after the shooting took place at Mr. Fields', and when about six miles from the town, met some thirty-five or forty men, who immediately commenced firing upon the Lieutenant and his escort, killing one horse and wounding the Lieutenant's horse in two places. The Lieutenant returned the fire, killing one of the mob and putting the rest to flight, when he, thinking it unsafe to proceed further, with four men (including himself) two men being dismounted, returned to the Tularosa Mill. Men living above the bridge having families deemed it unsafe to stay home, moved them to the mill for safety, expecting it might be possible that the mob would try to carry out some of their threats into execution and attempt the massacre of all the settlers in the valley; and at near five o'clock in the evening a large party of men, mounted and afoot, were seen just below the mill, and approaching it.

Mr. José Lucero of Tularosa, who was at my house, was disarmed and sent ahead to the mill to say that the constable was coming with one hundred and twenty men to arrest Lieutenant Wilkinson and his men for killing one of the party that fired upon him, and also to arrest the eight men that had molested the mob that had destroyed the dams saying that the constable had a warrant for that purpose and that he wished to know whether they would give up or not. The Lieutenant told Mr. Lucero to say to the constable that he had committed no crime, that no warrant had been shown or read to him, and that if the party meant to fight, to come on.

Mr. Lucero met the party about six hundred yards below the mill, and delivered the message, when the party seemed to be forming in two parties, one to approach the mill from the hill behind the house, and the other from the bottom, at which time four men fired at the "flock" from the top of the mill flume, reloaded and fired again, and they (the Mexicans) made some of the tallest running that has been witnessed in the Tularosa Canyon within the recollection of that noted individual, "the oldest inhabitant."

About ten o'clock at night Captains McKibben and Randlett [arrived] at the mill with troop "D," 8th U.S. Cavalry, and a small detachment of infantry with a mountain howitzer. Lieutenant Winkinson had sent a courier at noon to inform the commanding officer of what was transpiring at the Canyon. The troops camped at the mill that night and proceeded to town the next day. The Captain was informed on the road by a citizen that the people were armed and formed to prevent the entrance of the troops into the town; when within a short distance of the town the command halted and sent a man to ask Father Lapaigne and all the prominent citizens of the town to come out and let the Captain know what was the cause of so many armed men guarding the road where it crossed the ditch into town. The padre, José Duran, José Ma. Marcos, Julius Boiseller, and Wm. Ostic came to the command, when the three first acted as spokesmen for the town.

They said that they had orders to let no troops enter the town under any circumstances whatever, but who these orders were issued by, they did not see proper to divulge. The Captain told them he wished to stop at the agency, that he did not, nor would not, hurt a man in town, unless fired upon, and for them to go and inform the people to that effect. They went, and after parleying came to the conclusion to let the troops march in. They stayed all night, left this morning; some have returned to Stanton, and some are camped at Mr. West's ranch four miles from town. So matters stand at the present writing. What the result will be we know not as yet.

More anon.
Yours,
Geo. W. Nesmith

These local troubles in the early part of 1873 were eclipsed toward the end of the year by an outbreak known as the Harrell War. The Harrell clan, consisting of five or six brothers and their families together with some ten or twelve others, kinsmen and hangers-on, had made a hasty exodus from Lampasas County, Texas, where they had become involved with the state police and had, in fact, wiped out a squad of four of the state police. Moving to New Mexico, they settled on the Ruidoso.

On December 1 several of the Harrells went over to Lincoln for a big spree in which they were joined by some of the American residents in the town. A Mexican constable, Juan Martínez, had the hardihood to attempt to restrain three of the troublemakers, Ben Harrell, Dave Warner, and former sheriff Lewis J. (Jack) Gylam, making the customary demand that they turn over their arms to him. This they declined to do and the constable left to get assistance in arresting them. When he returned with several other Mexicans, a shooting scrape quickly developed in which Martínez was killed, as were the three Americans, Harrell, Warner, and Gylam.

Lincoln Plaza was thrown into the greatest ferment so far. Fearing that the whole Harrell clan might descend on the town for vengeance, the citizens invoked the protection of the troops at Fort Stanton. There is no record showing whether the troops came or not. At any rate, there was no overt attempt at retaliation from the Harrells until three weeks later. On December 20 a large group composed of the Harrells and certain other residents of their section of Lincoln County went to Lincoln determined on retaliation. Finding a Mexican *baile* in progress, they proceeded to shoot it up. In the melee four Mexicans, Isidro Patrón, Isidro Padilla, Lario Balazán, and José Candelario were killed. If any efforts were made to arrest the Harrells, they proved unsuccessful for a time. About a month later Alex H. (Ham) Mills, the sheriff, with a posse of perhaps sixty Mexican citizens, attempted to arrest somebody at least. He managed to surround the Harrell crowd in an adobe house on the Ruidoso where they had "forted up." An all day fight occurred without casualties or decisive result. Finally Ham Mills gave over the fight and withdrew to Lincoln.

This outbreak compelled Governor Giddings to forward to President Grant a plea for assistance in keeping peace in Lincoln County. The President requested the Secretary of War to furnish the civil officers with military support from Fort Stanton. This and other developments made the Harrells decide to leave the country. Bag and baggage they pulled up and went down to Roswell. On the way, one of the Harrell contingent called "Little" Hart killed a young settler of good repute, Joe Haskins, for no other reason than that he had a Mexican wife. On this same journey Ben Turner, brother-in-law of the Harrells and very conspicuous in lawlessness, was shot from ambush, presumably by some Mexican glad to inflict at least some degree of vengeance for the ruthlessness of the *Tejanos*.

After the Harrells reached Roswell, the killing of Ben Turner rankled to such an extent that they determined on retaliation. Their program involved nothing less than a wholesale slaughter of Mexicans in Lincoln's vicinity. They made the return trip as far as Casey's Mill and then adjourned to the hills nearby to discuss ways and means. Not coming to any agreement, they decided to return to Roswell and resume their journey back to Texas. On this second journey to Roswell they somewhat satisfied their desire for Mexican blood by killing a party of five Mexican freighters they chanced to meet on the road about fifteen miles from Roswell.

Before departing for Texas, the Harrell band gave another exhibition of lawlessness of a somewhat different quality. Four or five of the Harrell associates — reportedly Zack Crumpton, William Applegate, "Little" Hart, J. D. Scott, and a man named only as Still — stole four mules and two horses from Aaron O. Willburn. Mr. Willburn (whose name sometimes appears as Wellburn) had established in partnership with Van C. Smith the settlement at Roswell, in about 1869. At the same time of the theft from Willburn another group of the Harrells met Robert Beckwith of Seven Rivers on the public road and robbed him of his horse, saddle, and pistol. The two Harrell groups merged at a point down the Pecos and, going to the Beckwith ranch near Seven Rivers, drove off in broad daylight eight head of horses and mules. They made toward the Rio Grande with their booty. Aaron Willburn and his brother Frank promptly gathered a posse and went in pursuit of the thieves. They surrounded the Harrell party at Hueco Tanks early one morning while the stock thieves were asleep and apparently showed no quarter. Some sources report that all the rustlers were killed, but more reliable accounts limit the casualties to only two, Crumpton and Still.

.   Lincoln County indeed breathed more freely when the Harrells returned to their old stamping-ground in Texas. There they became involved in trouble with the Higgins clan — a feud, however, that falls beyond the scope of this account. As conclusion to the offenses perpetrated against the peace and dignity of the Territory of New Mexico, the Harrell muster roll may be given, compiled from the array of indictments which the grand jury, at the spring term of district court, 1874, bestowed upon them, either as principals or as accessories. The list includes Martin Harrell, Sam Harrell, Thomas Harrell, Merritt Harrell, Charles Powell, William Applegate, James Wilson, Thomas Brown, William Lyttle, Robert Honeycutt, C. W. King, James F. Randelett, Frank Reicken, Edward Hart, Zachariah Crumpton, Thomas Keenan, J. D. Scott, David Jacoby, and a few others like

Woods and Jones, "given names not known." Texan Jack Gylam was one of those already in New Mexico who joined the Harrells as soon as they reached Lincoln County.

By the time court convened only one could be brought to trial. Somehow Randelett had been taken into custody and was brought into court as one who had killed four Mexicans. He secured a reprieve by getting a change of venue to Socorro County.

3. Continued Lawlessness – 1875

IF 1873 WAS A TURBULENT TIME in Lincoln County, 1875 was almost as bad. The first month brought to a crisis the long-standing friction between Chisum cowboys and Mescalero Indians over horse-stealing. By this time the Indians, located on a reservation about fifteen miles south of Fort Stanton, were on good behavior except as restless ones occasionally strayed from the reservation. Before returning they usually managed to create trouble for the settlers, especially by stealing horses. At Chisum's South Spring River ranch there was always a large herd most alluring to the Indians. Shortly before 1875 they had stolen so many horses that the Chisum cowboys were practically afoot, and work on the range was at a standstill.

A number of Chisum's men, reinforced by others from the Pecos Valley, undertook to teach the Indians a lesson. They rode up to the reservation and attacked one of the large Indian camps. Badly frightened, the Apaches fled into the mountain canyons where the dreaded *Tejanos* pursued them, killing several. The ruthlessness of the "Big Hats" left an impression which lasted a long time. As they thought the entire crowd of attackers were Chisum employees, the Indians attributed the whole affair to them and for the next few years when a Chisum herd was passing through the reservation on its way to Arizona, extra precautions had to be taken lest the Indian stampede both cattle and horses. As Gus Gildea, who was with one of Chisum's herds in 1876, explains it, "They were mad at Chisum's men who had killed some of them the previous year on the reservation." Chisum, however, with his

[25]

usual shrewdness generally managed to get his herds through in safety by giving presents of several good beeves to the leaders among the Indians.

It is hard to say whether Chisum had ordered punitive measures against the Indians or whether he had simply shut his eyes to what was going on. He was a past master at concealing his hand, not only in a matter like this, but in almost everything. The tradition is that John Chisum, stopping at the Casey ranch, complained about the way the Indians were taking his horses and announced that he proposed to even the score by getting a new supply from the Indians themselves. When Robert Casey opposed the plan on the ground that they should "try to stop stealing in the country, not bring in more," Chisum defended his policy by saying the situation would have to be handled on a tit-for-tat basis.

A few weeks after the attack on the Indians a somewhat different symptom of lawlessness appeared. This time it was maladministration of the county affairs, especially in financial matters. The territorial auditor called to the attention of the legislature the fact that Lincoln County had paid no taxes into the state treasury for the two preceding years. Probate Judge Murphy and others prominent in county politics tried to make light of the charges and to shift the responsibility upon the former sheriff, Jack Gylam, who had been killed in the Harrell troubles and was therefore outside the pale of accountability. Upon his shoulders was laid a defalcation of $20,000. The excuse for failure to turn in the tax money collected after the killing of Gylam was that the disturbed conditions growing out of the Indian rampage in 1873 and '74 had made it hard to collect taxes.

The misuse of funds was not to be thrust into the background so lightly. The Republican newspapers, only too glad of an opportunity to cast stones at a county always Democratic, kept the exposé so prominently before the public that when district court convened in April the grand jury was especially directed to make a complete investigation. The outcome brought indictments against the sheriff, county clerk, treasurer, and even the justice of the peace at Lincoln, accompanied by the following remarks on general laxity in county affairs:

.... We very carefully examined the books and papers of these officers and found it our duty to make presentments holding them responsible for their dereliction of duty. The grand jury can not find any bonds given by county officers as required by law.

We regret to say that owing to the failure of the officers to collect and take care of the county taxes, it has been impossible to take any steps toward the erection of a jail, court house, or

school house, but trust that the action of your grand jury in indicting the officers above named will have a salutary effect in the collection of taxes, and soon enable us to erect the necessary buildings.

The matter did not go beyond indictments, however, for the cases
were never tried; it would hardly have been in keeping with an easy-
going attitude toward public service to have insisted on convictions.
Major Lawrence G. Murphy, who, as probate judge, was supposed to
look after county funds, felt his honor impugned and tendered his
resignation to Governor Giddings. The governor, seriously ill at the
time, failed to act on the resignation, and Murphy continued as probate
judge and political boss of the county.

The political influence of Major Murphy and his mentor, Thomas
B. Catron, did not, however, extend to the Bureau of Indian Affairs at
Washington. Though his store continued to be the almost exclusive
source of supplies sold to the Indians, the Bureau consistently refused
to appoint him as Indian Trader. W. D. Crothers, the Indian agent at
the Mescalero Reservation, insisted on paying only for rations and
supplies actually delivered to the Indians, a policy which incurred the
hostility of post trader Murphy. Furthermore, Crothers loudly protested L. G. Murphy & Co.'s sale of liquor to the Indians and finally
moved his charges from Fort Stanton to South Fork in order to isolate
them from the whiskey-selling at the post trader's store and at the
Murphy brewery at Fort Stanton. On February 2 Murphy commenced
circulating a petition for the removal of Crothers as agent and forwarded it to President Grant. Furthermore, a compliant grand jury
was induced to indict Crothers on the technical charge of running a
hotel without a license. Government investigations, including that of
Congressman John McNulta, quickly exonerated Crothers, and the
district attorney refused to prosecute him on the obviously trumped-up
charges of running a hotel. These setbacks in 1875 did not deter
Murphy, and in the spring of 1876 Crothers finally became disgusted
with harassment and resigned. He was succeeded by Frederick C. Godfroy, an agent much more to Murphy's liking.

The close of 1875 yielded considerable commotion in connection
with the killing of Robert Casey and the trial and execution of his
slayer, William Wilson. Casey was a Texan who had settled in Lincoln
County about 1868 at what was afterward called Casey's Mill. His
killing occurred in the street of Lincoln early in August, just a few
hours after a political convention in which a citizen's victory in nom-
inations for the county ticket seemed likely to break the grip of the
Murphy machine. Almost no one took seriously Wilson's claim that

he killed Casey because the latter owed him eight or nine dollars in wages; Casey had consistently opposed the Murphy machine, and Casey's friends imputed his killing to the antagonism he had aroused by his verbal attack on the Murphy organization at the convention earlier that day. Whatever the cause, this brutal killing in the heart of town outraged the public to such a degree that Wilson would have been lynched had not powerful interests in Lincoln intervened to protect him.

As Casey was an ex-soldier and on friendly terms with the officers at Fort Stanton, the military took an active part in meting out justice to his murderer. They saw to it that Wilson was safely kept in prison at the Fort and were present when court convened in October. Wilson was speedily convicted of murder in the first degree and sentenced. His friends made strenuous efforts to secure a commutation, but Governor Giddings let the law take its course.

The hanging of Wilson — the first legal execution in Lincoln County — turned out to be a ghastly bungle still referred to as "the double hanging."

Lincoln, N. M., Dec. 15, 1875

Editor, *New Mexican*,

On the day appointed, before daybreak, the carpenters were at work erecting the gallows; and even at that early hour strangers, men, women and children, were pouring from the adjacent county.

At eleven o'clock the prisoner in an ambulance accompanied by Captain Stewart, commander of the post, Dr. Corballo, medical director, and Rev. Lamy of Manzano, preceded by Company "G," 8th U.S. Cavalry under command of Lieutenant Gilmore, arrived at the town and proceeded to the residence of the sheriff, Captain Saturnino Baca. The prisoner then arraying himself in his funeral clothes, the procession moved toward the gallows.

Before mounting the platform, Wilson shook hands with several whom he recognized, and mounted the scaffold calm and collected. The escort was drawn in line fronting the gallows, whilst four men dismounted and kept back the crowd, which by this time had increased considerably.

Whilst on the scaffold the death warrant was read first in English and then in Spanish, after which the dying declaration written and signed by Wilson was read and translated. He then received the extreme unction and the *merciful* sheriff declared that the execution would be stayed for half an hour.

However, the leading men of the town, actuated by pity for the poor unfortunate, entered such a vigorous protest against such barbarous proceedings that the sheriff went ahead with the execution. The priest descended from the scaffold, the black cap was adjusted, and the prisoner, with hands tied behind and the noose around his neck, awaited his doom.

The sheriff descended from the scaffold, and in an instant justice, so long outraged, was avenged, and the perpetrator of one of the foulest murders which ever disgraced a civilized community was no more.

After hanging nine and a half minutes, the body was cut down and placed in the coffin, when it was discovered that life was not yet extinct. A rope was fastened around his neck, and the crowd drew the inanimate body from the coffin and suspended it from the gallows where it hanged for twenty minutes longer. It was then cut down and placed in the coffin and buried.

A Rolling Stone

The year 1875 produced another episode of violence which was to have a significant influence in the Lincoln County War which lay ahead. In February, trouble which arose between certain American settlers and native New Mexicans threatened to assume the proportions of a race clash. Two young Mexicans were employed by John Copeland at his ranch seven miles west of Fort Stanton. According to John Riley's version of the matter, the two boys decided to quit and return to their homes near Mesilla in Doña Ana County. One morning Copeland arose to find one of the Mexicans gone and certain belongings missing — rifle, pistol, blankets and household effects—as well as a valuable pair of matched horses. His neighbor, John H. Riley, was missing a new saddle.

Copeland and Riley immediately turned their attention to the remaining Mexican, but the most vigorous cross-questioning elicited only a shake of the head and "*¿Quién sabe?*" When they resorted to other means, and even tied a rope around his neck with threats of hanging, the young man allegedly confessed a plot between his companion and himself. He disclosed also that the other man had taken a certain route to Tularosa where they were to meet.

With this information Copeland promptly started in pursuit and by using a shortcut overtook the man making off with his horses. As soon as the latter saw Copeland he tried to unfasten his rifle but before he could get it into position Copeland was upon him ordering him to dismount and lay down his gun. The Mexican, pretending to be complying, snatched his pistol from his holster. Before he could use it, however, Copeland fired and the Mexican fell dead.

Copeland came back to the ranch with his horses and then turned his attention to the other man, who had been left tied hand and foot.

After consulting Riley he decided to take the prisoner to Fort Stanton where there was a better chance of his being held until he could be tried than in the insecure jail at Lincoln. Copeland and Riley started on foot toward Fort Stanton seven miles away, the prisoner walking in advance. He never reached the post. He was shot and killed "while trying to escape."

The next day Riley and Copeland reported the occurrence to Probate Judge Murphy at Lincoln. Ordinarily the two would have had simply a preliminary hearing and an acquittal, but twenty-odd-year-old Juan B. Patrón, probate clerk as well as a leader among the Mexican-American citizens, instituted an investigation. Patrón's findings differed completely from the story told by Riley and Copeland. Nothing had been stolen from either Copeland or Riley, Patrón was convinced, but the boys had previously complained to friends that they had been continually abused and even threatened with shooting because they had "talked back." Furthermore, according to Patrón's information, the lads had been shot on the premises, not en route to Tularosa.

Patrón demanded that Riley and Copeland be arrested and held pending grand jury investigation. When Probate Judge Murphy refused, Patrón gathered together ten of his neighbors to make the arrest themselves. He had no trouble in enlisting his posse; mistreatment by many Anglos had built up widespread resentment among the native New Mexicans. Ex-Texans in particular displayed an arrogant and overbearing attitude toward those of Mexican ancestry. The latter, even when their irrigation ditches had been cut and their lands appropriated, had found no relief from either law officers or the courts. The killing of the two boys blew the embers into flame.

Making no secret of their determination to arrest Riley and Copeland, Patrón and his party set out for Copeland's ranch the next day. When they arrived there at noon Copeland was not to be found but Riley happened to be in the house. He confronted them coolly and defiantly but deemed it expedient to comply with their order to proceed to his own house nearby. Dr. H. G. Tedeman, post surgeon, happened to be at Copeland's while this was going on and as soon as Riley left for his own ranch the doctor rode posthaste to Fort Stanton to arrange for a detachment of soldiers to come to the rescue.

At Riley's house the Patrón party took possession in high-handed fashion, appropriating corn for their horses and food for themselves. According to one report, they even fired some shots in an effort to intimidate Riley. They kept him under close guard while awaiting the expected arrival of Copeland and when the latter appeared Patrón exhibited a warrant for his arrest. Copeland refused to recognize the warrant, however, pointing out that it was signed by Patrón and questioning the validity of a warrant issued by a clerk of the Probate Court. Nevertheless, Riley and Copeland were, in effect, prisoners and were ordered to guide their captors to the place where lay the body of the last man killed. Here Lucas Gallegos, well known as a hotblood, pointed a cocked pistol at Riley's head and asked, "You shoot that man?" Riley's denial did not relieve the tension. As they watched Patrón and his companions bury the dead boy, Copeland and Riley must have been plagued with uncomfortable thoughts as to what might be next in store for them at the hands of these heavily armed and angry men. Great must have been their relief when it became evident that Patrón was obviously bent on an arrest, not on a killing.

The arrests, however, were not destined to be concluded. When the burial had been completed and the Patrón party were preparing to leave for Lincoln with their prisoners, a large body of horsemen was sighted galloping rapidly from the west. The sight of the approaching United States troops meant but one thing to Juan Patrón; he was only too well aware of the affiliation between Fort Stanton officers and the Murphy-Dolan-Riley contingent. Patrón had no desire to fight American soldiers; no attempt was made to further detain Riley and Copeland when the New Mexicans mounted to commence their return to Lincoln. As they started away, a shot was fired from the Riley house and Patrón pitched from his horse. That Riley shot Patrón in the back was not denied. The *Mesilla News* of September eighteenth and the *Grant County Herald* of the twenty-sixth reported: ". . . the ball entered near the spine and passed into the abdomen, from which place it was removed by the physician, who says Patrón can not live."

Juan Patrón did, nevertheless, survive. Riley was not then or ever arrested for this shooting; on the other hand, Captain McKibben and his detachment took Patrón's companions into custody and locked them up in the Fort Stanton guardhouse; Patrón himself was held as a prisoner in the post hospital. A friendly grand jury promptly acquiesced to Riley's demand that Patrón be indicted. Significantly, however, no attempt was ever made to bring him to trial.

John S. Chisum was an outstanding rancher and personality in the Pecos Valley. Although Chisum himself kept his distance from the actual scenes of battle, his landholding strength, his shrewdness, and his discreet but powerful support of the McSween faction, were significant factors in the Lincoln County War.

4. Troubles Along the Rio Pecos

If ANYONE HAD VENTURED a prophecy in the early part of 1877 as to where peace and tranquility were to be subjected to unbearable stresses in Lincoln County, he would have unquestionably picked the Chisum range along the Rio Pecos, especially the vicinity of Seven Rivers. Matters had become so tense there as to justify John Chisum's expression, "looking pretty bilious." For all his eccentricities Chisum was a shrewd and masterful man, ready to make good, even through rough measures, to protect his interests. The basis of his claim to two hundred miles up and down the Pecos Valley in Lincoln County was what he called, humorously although with a touch of arrogance, "right of discovery." In other words, he was merely a squatter on land as yet not open to settlers and making good that claim purely by his own measures.

His policy was to keep intruders out but by means other than violence if possible. Chisum himself never went armed; one of his reputed sayings was, "a six-shooter will get you into more trouble than it will get you out of." His reliance therefore in enforcing his rights was upon other resources. If the trespasser could not be handled by artful persuasion or appeal to self-interest, Chisum brought into play as a sort of second degree his remarkable powers of sarcasm, beginning with his curious, half-friendly manner but soon changing into derision accompanied by jabs of loud, jeering laughter. Few there were who did not capitulate under such an assault; consequently, seldom did the treatment of an intruder pass to the third degree, which was bestowed by a delegation of Chisum cowboys equipped for a display of force and possibly making use of it.

In spite of all this jealousy for his rights, Chisum had a milder side which he displayed toward those he liked. When R. K. Wiley, likewise a Texan, established himself in the Pecos country and threatened to make an inroad on Chisum's range, he bought Wiley out upon fair terms and even took him into a degree of partnership. The story has it that although Chisum bought the cattle he deemed it best to let them remain in Wiley's name. A reason for this procedure probably existed in certain aspects of Chisum's business affairs. After being in the cattle business in Texas and New Mexico for more than thirty years, Chisum had sold out in 1875 to Hunter & Evans for between $200,000 and $300,000. For the next year or two he was engaged in gathering his cattle and transferring them to Hunter & Evans, either to their ranges in Kansas or to Arizona on government contracts that this large firm had to fulfill.[3]

News of Chisum's selling out provoked certain of his rivals in New Mexico to make renewed efforts to collect on some old notes bearing his name. These had originated from an ill-advised packing house venture at Fort Smith, Arkansas, that Chisum had become involved in in 1867 when still living in Texas. Catron and Thornton of Santa Fe were the attorneys handling these suits and now that he had obtained a handsome sum for his cattle they began to plague him viciously. Chisum had repudiated the notes upon the double ground that use of his name in the firm signature "Wilbur, Chisum & Clark," was entirely unauthorized and that the notes had become barred by the statute of limitation in Texas. As Chisum himself put the matter, "After these old forged notes had been lying around for eight years, William Rosenthal[4] of Santa Fe notoriety sent to New York and other places and

---

3. R. D. Hunter and A. G. Evans of St. Louis, Missouri, were a highly respected firm engaged in large-scale livestock dealings, including government beef contracts.

4. William Rosenthal, friendly with Catron and the "Ring" organization at Santa Fe, raised no cattle himself but as a prime contractor was the largest supplier of beef cattle for the needs of the army and Indian reservations in the Southwest. Unlike L. G. Murphy, Chisum did not act as a subcontractor fulfilling the contracts awarded to Rosenthal; instead, he was Rosenthal's greatest competitor in bidding for government business in southwestern New Mexico. Competition from Chisum inspired Rosenthal to seek out the holders of the discredited notes signed by the one-time Arkansas firm of Wilbur, Chisum & Clark. Securing these for a nominal amount, he succeeded under the guidance of Catron in obtaining a judgment against Chisum in the court at Santa Fe.

gathered up these commercial papers, as he called them, and got the owners to transfer them to him; so he became the owner of these notes and the plaintiff in the case against me." To fight what he thought injustice, Chisum had placed nearly all of his property in the name of his brothers, Pitzer and Jim, his associates in the cattle business, although he had never quite given them the status of partners. Thus, there were reasons why after buying Wiley's cattle Chisum preferred them to remain under the former owner's name.

In regard to cattle-stealing, Chisum had been for a long time reasonable, not to say good-natured. He well knew that under prevailing conditions some stealing must be expected and simply endured. When raided at Bosque Grande by Mexicans from Manzano and other settlements to the north, he had used only mild means to check them. A week before Christmas, 1874, a man named Lucero was found "cutting out" from one of the herds near Bosque Grande. He was severely flogged by some of the Chisum cowboys and warned not to repeat the offense on pain of his life. When cattle-stealing grew to greater proportions and tended to become habitual and professional, Chisum roused himself to more forcible measures. His retinue of nearly a hundred employees contained dozens able to give good accounts of themselves in a fight. What could be simpler than to protect his top interests in approved frontier fashion by these "warriors," as they were generally called?

Soon after Chisum removed to South Spring River, a change almost coincident with selling to Hunter & Evans, he found cattle-stealing taking on larger proportions. The thieves may have reasoned that Chisum would be less severe now that the cattle were not his individual property. If so, they reckoned without their host. In fact, Chisum became more vigorous than formerly about losses among the Hunter & Evans cattle he must gather up and deliver.

The first clash occurred in October, 1876. In charge of the Wiley cattle camp near Seven Rivers was a man named Yopp with two helpers, Buck Powell and Dick Smith. Yopp's protest to his helpers about the disappearance of certain cattle provoked a quarrel out of which came a shooting. The details were sent to one of the New York papers by none other than Ash Upson, then living at Roswell. Succinct though the account is, it gives the incident with a contemporary flavor.

At Wiley's camp, 80 miles below here, about six weeks since, a man named Yopp in charge of the herd became enraged at an employee, Buck Powell. He drew his revolver and fired three shots at him. Buck woke up, seized a Winchester, and shot Yopp in the mouth. Yopp fell and remained for a few minutes insensible. Suddenly recovering, he re-opened fire on Powell. Powell's gun hung fire. He then seized Yopp's own gun and shot him through the heart. Powell did not receive a scratch. He wanted to go some 150 miles and give himself up for trial, but was persuaded not to. So the matter ended.[5]

From this killing of Yopp developed a series of occurrences some-times called the "War on the Rio Pecos" or the "Chisum War." The facts are hard to obtain, for little got into any permanent record, but the sequence of events seems to have been as follows.

Shortly after the killing of Yopp, Chisum learned of suspicious activities around the corrals of the Beckwith ranch at Seven Rivers. The information came from R. M. Gilbert, who had a small farm on the lower Peñasco and who had previously supplied Chisum with reliable information about rustler activities around Seven Rivers. As Chisum was just starting on a trip to Arizona, he could not make an investigation himself but sent his brother Pitzer, accompanied by Jim Highsaw, Chisum's trusted foreman, and several other cowboys. In the vicinity of the corrals they found buried several hundred ears of cattle all bearing the Chisum jingle-bob earmark.[6] The conclusion was ines-capable that many of the Chisum cattle had undergone earmark removal there and had been driven off somewhere.

A few months later, toward the end of February, 1877, the sit-uation again became acute. This time Chisum went down in person, accompanied by several of his cowboys. Learning that some of his cattle had recently been sold in El Paso, Chisum, taking along as usual Jim Highsaw, perhaps the outstanding fighting man among his cow-boys, went to El Paso and not only recovered some of the cattle but, what was perhaps more valuable, secured definite descriptions of the persons who had sold them. After his return Highsaw met Dick Smith,

---

5. Old-time newspaperman Upson habitually bombarded eastern newspapers and some in New Mexico with highly colored items, usually based on second-or-third-hand information and consequently not wholly unbiased. Although Powell was well-known as a Chisum-hater, he had been temporarily employed by Chisum's associate, R. K. Wiley. According to locally accepted legend, Yopp, Wiley's foreman, suspected Powell of surreptitiously making off with some of the Wiley cattle, and when he undertook to question Powell the latter shot and killed him.

6. Since conventional burned brands could be altered or obliterated, Chisum, the victim of wholesale rustling, had adopted an identifying mark which could not be over-burned, a slit along the edge of the ear, the end left dangling. This mark of ownership could be eliminated only by cutting off the animal's ear.

who by this time had set up for himself as one of the smaller cattlemen on the lower Pecos, and directly accused him of stealing the
Chisum cattle. Smith immediately reached for his gun but Highsaw
got his into action first.

The killing heightened the contention between Chisum and the
"little fellows" around Seven Rivers. Highsaw fled to Chisum's South
Spring River ranch for protection. A few days later eighteen or twenty
of Smith's friends rode up determined to get Jim Highsaw. They found
Chisum's men entrenched behind the parapet of the roof with rifles
pointing through portholes and did not venture within range. After a
few threats and curses delivered at the safe distance of several hundred
yards they turned their horses about and rode back to Seven Rivers.

A few weeks later Chisum made a display of force at Seven
Rivers, his intention being to have a clean-up of a situation that had
become intolerable to him. The Beckwith ranch was the stronghold
of the cattle-thieving group whose activities Chisum was determined to
stop. Although the elder Beckwith, Hugh, was reportedly not directly
implicated, his son Bob was said to be involved and his son-in-law,
W. H. Johnson, was considered one of the ringleaders, accounting for
the fact that the others engaged in the activity could come and go freely
at the Beckwith place.

The details of this punitive expedition remain in dispute, but from
the newspapers of the time some idea of it may be gathered. Andy
Boyle, as an adherent of the Catron-Murphy-Dolan interests and thus
no friend of the Chisums, carried a commission as a deputy sheriff. For
District Attorney Catron he prepared a report which Colonel A. J.
Fountain felt justified in publishing in the first issue of the Mesilla
Independent, a newspaper he and certain associates were establishing
for the definite aim of checking lawlessness in southern New Mexico.
This "War on the Pecos" was just the sort of exhibit the new journal
would have liked, for implicated in the cattle-stealing that Chisum was
fighting were certain ones with whom the Rio Grande Valley section
of Doña Ana County was already acquainted. While Andy Boyle's
account might be impugned in some respects as one-sided, it cannot be
ignored:

THE WAR ON THE PECOS

The recent disturbances between the cattle men residing on the
river Pecos in this county, two hundred and fifty miles from this
place, having attracted an unusual amount of public interest, we
deem it to be our duty as public journalists to give publicity to
the following communication which appears to be of an official

character and to come from a reliable source. Having no knowledge of the facts in the case other than that derived from common report, we publish this communication with the hope that it may elicit a response from the other side to the end that the public may be placed in possession of all the facts in the case. The seat of war is so remote that the disturbances reported do not materially affect the people of this valley. Yet the participants are mostly residents of this county, and our peace-loving citizens demand that the majesty of the law shall be asserted in all sections of the county without regard to locality. A full exposition of the doings on the Pecos will result in bringing about this much desired result.

Mesilla, New Mexico
Doña Ana County, June 15, '77

T. B. Catron, U.S. Attorney,

Sir: In accordance with your request I give you the facts of the Chisum war on the Pecos River. John S. Chisum claims to have about 40,000 head of cattle grazing on the Pecos River; also R. K. Wiley has about 3,000 head. These two stock men concluded they wanted all the Pecos River to themselves, a distance of 200 miles.

1st. A man by the name of Richard Smith, Wiley's foreman, was killed by a herder, James M. Highsaw, on March 28, in camp, shot in the back five times with Colt's improved 45 cal. six shooter. Chisum remarking that the war had commenced and he had six more men to kill (the Seven Rivers thieves), viz., Lewis Paxton, Underwood, Charles W. Woltz, R. W. Beckwith, W. H. Johnson, and Buck Powell, these men having each from 200 to 1,000 head of cattle which they were holding in the neighborhood of Seven Rivers. Lewis Paxton happened to go to Lincoln City on business on April 8, when he was informed by Major Brady, sheriff of Lincoln County, that John S. Chisum had been hiring men to kill him and others. Mr. Paxton got on his horse and rode home as fast as possible to let the men know what Chisum intended doing. These men then left their camps and came up to Seven Rivers to the house of H. W. Beckwith for self-defense.

2nd. On April 10, James J. Dolan came down to Seven Rivers after beef cattle, which he wanted for the use of the U.S. troops at Fort Stanton. A party of these men started to go down to Paxton and Underwood's camp to get the cattle when they met six of Chisum and Wiley's men on the public road near Wiley's cow camp, who, seeing this party coming down the road, got off their horses and got down into a water course and prepared to shoot at them, which Mr. Underwood's party seeing, charged down onto them. They fired a few shots on both sides — nobody hurt.

Chisum's men then got on their horses and rode into their camps, remarking that they had got whipped. Chisum then rode off to Fort Stanton to try to get soldiers and arms to assist him in killing these men. The commanding officer told Chisum it was none of his business; he was not there to kill citizens but to protect them. Chisum then tried to get the sheriff of Lincoln County to assist him; he also would not do it.

3rd. On April 20, Chisum and Wiley got all the men that would join them together, some thirty men; went to Seven Rivers, took what horses and mules those other men had grazing, went up above Mr. Beckwith's house about a mile and cut off the water in the ditch that supplied the house, saying he would starve them out, and when they should have to come out to get water, they could waylay them and shoot them down. That night two men, Chas. W. Woltz and Buck Powell, rode past them and went to Mesilla, the county seat, to get warrants to arrest Wiley, Chisum and J. M. Highsaw for the murder of Smith. April 21, Chisum sent a Mr. and Mrs. Gray, who lived at Seven Rivers, to Mr. Beckwith's house to tell the women and children to leave, that he did not want to kill them but that he wanted to kill the thieves that were in there. Mrs. Stafford, Miss Helen Beckwith, and two of Mr. Beckwith's younger children were all the family who were present at Mr. Beckwith's. They refused to leave the house as they would not trust themselves to Chisum's men, Mrs. Stafford replying that she had all the protection she wanted at home. April 22, Chisum advanced to carry his threats into execution telling his men they would try and take the walls on the other party, and kill them all who were in there. They commenced shooting at about 700 or 800 yards distance, the besieged returning the fire. Chisum's men lost courage and would not advance any closer, saying they were not going to get killed for $30 a month, that they had hired to herd cattle and not to fight. Chisum then raised a flag of truce and sent in a man to tell Mr. Johnson to come out, that he wanted to compromise and let everything go on as it was. Johnson told him he could not compromise for any person but himself, as there were men there whom Chisum and Wiley were owing money to and they wanted their money before the business was settled. Chisum then said that he would turn the water on and give them back their horses. He withdrew his men and went down to the river to round up his cattle, along with Wiley. They were going to round up together and separate their cattle when they got above Wiley's ranch. There John Chisum took the smallpox. May 7, Buck Powell having got back from Mesilla with the warrants, I, with a posse of 14 men, rode down to Chisum and Wiley's camp to arrest Chisum, Wiley, and Highsaw. They, having learned that we were coming after them, had gone to South Spring River ranch (Chisum's) which is fortified against Indians, there to resist the law and fight if necessary. We started there in pursuit, after seeing John S. Chisum, who was still too sick with the smallpox and could not be moved. On May 10, got to Chisum's ranch. Wiley, seeing we were there, sent out a man by the name of Charles Moore, whom we had seen at the cow camp, with a note stating there were men in there who did not want to fight and if we attempted to take the place some innocent persons might be killed. I sent him an answer that we did not want to kill any person, that I had warrants to serve and I was going to serve them, that there was no use resisting. Wiley sent word back that he would meet Buck Powell and R. W. Beckwith half way to the house and where we were camped, and he would pay them what he was owing them. They went and met him, and he told them to make out their bills and he would give them checks on the bank for the amount. He then told me that Highsaw was willing to stand his trial but he would not give himself up to my party as he was afraid they would kill him, if I would come up myself or with one man he would become my prisoner. When I got up there he was gone, having gone the back way.

Wiley then told the men he was owing to come down and meet Chisum who was coming up to his ranch, and he would get checks for their money. We all went down and saw Chisum, and Wiley got the checks and paid the men, and I then served the warrant on John S. Chisum and placed him under bond as he was still sick and every man went home about their business.

Andrew Boyle
Deputy Sheriff, Doña Ana County

The trustworthiness of Andy Boyle's account is dubious, and it excited little contemporary protest. What did appear in the newspaper simply touched upon one or two minor issues and left without denial the larger ones. Major Brady, the sheriff, immediately wrote to the Mesilla *Independent* objecting to what had been said of him. It seems clear, however, that Chisum did apply to him for help, although it is strange he should go to the sheriff of Lincoln County against thieves operating in what was then still a part of Doña Ana County. Perhaps Chisum's pretext for doing so was the fact that his South Spring River ranch was in Lincoln County. His failure to get a detachment from Fort Stanton may have come at a time when restrictions on such use of the soldiers was being enforced.

Chisum himself did not reply to Boyle's version but after a lapse of three months the Mesilla *Independent* carried a communication from settlers near Roswell, which tried to show Chisum was not as black as he had been painted. The writers did not deny that Chisum had marched in force against the Seven Rivers crowd; they merely tried to show that Chisum was not hostile to the coming of settlers on his range provided they were the right kind. The signers were members of a Mormon colony Chisum had favored and even encouraged to settle on land he had formerly claimed. They had felt only the milder side of him who had been for nearly ten years overlord of vast stretches of the Pecos Valley.

Rio Pecos, Lincoln Co., N. M.
Sept. 6, 1877

Editors *Independent;*
Sirs:

In your first issue you published a letter signed by one Andrew Boyle, reflecting on the character of John S. Chisum, of which he took no notice, and no one, to our knowledge, has taken pains to contradict or refute the calumnies and falsehoods which it contained, except one item which implicated Major Wm. Brady, our sheriff. The Major promptly and emphatically denied that portion of Boyle's statement, leaving a lie between him and Lewis Paxton to swallow and digest. The whole letter, in spirit and in fact, is as devoid of truth as the lie which has been nailed.

The tone of the letter and the impression which it is intended to convey, is that Chisum wishes to monopolize two or three hundred miles of the Pecos River for his stock range, opposing immigration, persecuting newcomers, and using every endeavor to drive them from the country. This slander, we find, is being industriously circulated by Chisum's enemies, most of whom are indebted to him for their substance, and are using these subtle means to prejudice public sentiment against him for no other reason than that he objects to their longer preying upon him, killing, driving off and selling his stock. We, the undersigned, arrived at Chisum's ranch, South Spring River, about the middle of March last, and camped at its mouth about four miles distant. We had stock, farming implements, seeds, etc. but were out of money and provisions. We were forced to go to work and put in crops to supply ourselves with provisions for the coming year. We found that we were on Chisum's hog ranch and feared that we would interfere with him. We visited the ranch and consulted with Mr. Chisum, who received us cordially, welcomed us cheerfully, and told us to go on with our planting, that his hogs should not interfere with us, and moved them to Bosque Grande. We soon found that we could not take out our acequias in time to get in crops, and again consulted Chisum. He immediately offered us all the land we wanted in his acequia, plenty of water, all the breadstuffs and other provisions we required, in short, free access to his store and supplies, and to build new dwellings, remarking that hard-working, honest men were the class of people he liked to see come to this section and when he saw such people, who were honestly struggling to do for themselves, he considered it his duty to assist them, not with words alone, but with means. And this he has steadily done notwithstanding there were seven families of us, consisting of twenty-four persons, to feed and clothe. There was no inducement held out to him except that we would pay him what we owed him as soon as we could produce it and no security but our word offered or required.

We ask you, Messrs. Editors, what we could do less than defend Mr. Chisum against those foul aspersions upon his character and disposition, when we are twenty-four living witnesses that he is liberal, generous and kind-hearted to all honest men, as we know he is antagonistical and unrelenting towards thieves. We have never heard a single person with a reputation for honesty in our midst speak of Chisum except in terms of praise and gratitude.

Immigration is consistently increasing this vicinity. No less than three farmers from Seven Rivers have taken up ranches here within the past three weeks, and a half dozen others, Americans, are negotiating for lands. Each and every one of them have either come at the solicitation of John Chisum, or have been encouraged by him to settle here, by offers of assistance.

No, Chisum wants to monopolize no more land than the law allows him. He invites honest men to settle about him; but he does strenuously object to living in the neighborhood of thieves.

> Jacob Harris
> George Harris
> Ezra T. Lee

Representing twenty-four persons, living in the immediate vicinity of John S. Chisum's ranch.

To this communication was a postscript, containing a eulogy of Chisum. Rather strangely, the first name signed to it was that of Heiskell Jones, who at the time was in charge of the one and only store at Roswell. Several of his many sons were later to become involved against Chisum in subsequent troubles. The other name signed was that of one of the most respected Mexican citizens in the Pecos Valley.

We, the undersigned, having read the above communication, take pleasure in endorsing its sentiments. We have known John

S. Chisum for 9 years (ever since he has lived in New Mexico) and we know him to be a good neighbor, ever ready to assist those who honestly try to help themselves; and we know of those who came here without a dollar nor a head of stock who are now in good circumstances with houses, lands, cattle and horses, and whom John S. Chisum lifted from the mire, but who are now vilifying him, as a small-minded rascal will ever repay acts of kindness or an ungrateful dog bite the hand which feeds him. More than one that we know have preyed upon John Chisum until they are in easy circumstances, and now uphold and sustain a band of thieves who are robbing him.

Heiskell Jones
Martín Sánchez

The upshot of these claims in the vicinity of Seven Rivers was that a group, mostly very rough characters, became highly inflamed against Chisum. They were eager to even the score with him or any person connected with him.

L. G. Murphy

J. J. Dolan

Emil Fritz

J. H. Riley

Murphy, Dolan, Fritz, and Riley were all at one time or other partners in the mercantile firm founded by L. G. Murphy — long dominant in the struggle for economic and political power in upper Lincoln County, even though faced with the hostility of most of the small farmers and ranchers. Fritz died before the Lincoln County War. Murphy, ill and away from Lincoln during the War, died at Santa Fe three months after its close. Dolan lived to carry on a prosperous political career, and Riley became a successful hog-rancher near Colorado Springs.

5. L. G. Murphy & Co., General Merchants

FROM ALMOST THE BEGINNING Lincoln County had been the plaything, both politically and commercially, of the mercantile firm of L. G. Murphy & Co. At the start it had been Murphy & Fritz, post traders at Fort Stanton, where it did a profitable business selling to the government.[7] Both of the original partners, Emil Fritz and Lawrence G. Murphy, were among the ex-soldiers who settled in Lincoln County after the Civil War, and their titles of Colonel Fritz and Major Murphy were in recognition of their honorable military service, not just mere courtesy.

Murphy was understood to have studied for the priesthood at Meynooth College in his native Ireland, although lack of records implies possible error. Immigrating to the United States as a young man, he had enlisted in the regular army, eventually serving as a sergeant major. When his enlisted term was over, he drifted to Santa Fe and re-enlisted there in 1861 with the First New Mexico Volunteers when the Texas Confederates entered the Mesilla Valley. When the military

---

7. Military records fail to reveal when, if ever, the firm was officially designated as Post Trader, though the Murphy store and the Murphy brewery and saloon were the Post's only civilian-operated establishments. The Bureau of Indian Affairs consistently refused to designate Murphy as Indian Trader even though L. G. Murphy & Co. and its successors continued to enjoy a monopoly in this function on the Mescalero Reservation.

forces of the Territory were reorganized in 1862, he emerged a lieutenant in the First New Mexico Cavalry, commanded by Kit Carson. He was at the battle of Val Verde and later accompanied Colonel Carson to Fort Stanton when it was re-garrisoned. In the summer of 1863 he participated in the Navajo campaign as a secretary to Carson and was promoted first to captain, then to major. In 1866 the regiment was disbanded and Major Murphy was honorably discharged.

Colonel Fritz, the scion of a prominent family in Stuttgart, Germany, had come to the United States as a young man and had been drawn out to California by the gold excitement. When California was sending volunteers to save New Mexico for the Union, Fritz was made captain of Company B, First Cavalry, California Volunteers.[8] The California Column, as it was called, reached New Mexico too late to encounter the Texas Confederates and was forced to content itself with garrison duty interspersed with Indian fighting. Captain Fritz and his company were sent to Fort Sumner to control the Indians impounded at Bosque Redondo, and when Kit Carson organized the expedition in 1864 against the Kiowas and Comanches, Fritz's company went with him. In the battle near the Adobe Walls in the Texas Panhandle in November, 1864, Fritz was responsible for protecting the right flank of Carson's forces and did so well that he received official praise and a promotion. On September 16, 1866, he was mustered out as colonel in the same general disbanding that closed the active military career of his partner, Major Murphy.

In business the two men complemented each other in both temperament and training. Much of the credit for the marked success of the firm must go to Fritz's thoroughness and aggressiveness, while the popular esteem which the firm held in its earlier history can be attributed to the sociability and conviviality that were the essence of Murphy's personality, appreciated by not only the settlers in the area but also the officers at the post and the political nabobs in Santa Fe. If the visions of vast wealth and power which became the firm's goal came from Major Murphy's expansive imagination, the retirement of Fritz removed a counterbalance that might have led the career of the firm in another direction. But Fritz had become more and more inter-

---

8. Emil Fritz was originally appointed 1st. Sgt., Co. K, Regiment of Dragoons, San Francisco, Oct. 1, 1860, according to his grand-daughters, Mrs. Carrie Dolan Vorwark and Mrs. Bessie Dolan Chester. Military records fail to reveal service in the U.S. Army prior to the Civil War, but indicate that at time of discharge his rank was Bvt. Lt. Col.

ested in his Spring ranch, a few miles below Lincoln, one of the most valuably watered pieces of land in the Bonito Valley. He also had tuberculosis and finally in the summer of 1873 he left Lincoln to revisit his old home in Germany, expecting to return in December. His rapidly failing health, however, compelled him to remain in Stuttgart, where he died in the spring of 1874.

Even during the lifetime of Colonel Fritz the firm had felt the need of new blood. When Fritz left Lincoln in the summer of 1873, reorganization of the company had elevated a young clerk, James J. Dolan, into junior partnership. When barely five, Dolan had been brought from Ireland to New York, and at the age of twelve he was clerking in a New York drygoods store. In 1863, when he was fifteen, he enlisted for a two-year-term during the Civil War and was honorably discharged, and in 1866 he re-enlisted for three years. After his second discharge, which seems to have occurred in New Mexico, he was hired as a clerk by Murphy and Fritz. Major Murphy took a great liking to the young Irishman and showed such fatherly interest in him that many believed Dolan to be his secretly adopted son.

Dolan's place with the firm was based, however, on stronger grounds than friendship. He was especially proficient as a negotiator, an ability that counted much in certain aspects of the firm's activities, especially undercover ones. In fact, "Jimmie," as everyone called him, had such a gift of persuasiveness that some suspected him of almost hypnotic powers. His flare for scheming and maneuvering, especially under the cloak of secrecy, was considered even greater than that of Major Murphy himself. Though small of stature, Dolan was self-assertive as well as full of bluster and braggadocio.

It was Dolan, in fact, who caused the Murphy company to be evicted from Fort Stanton in the summer of 1873, when he got into a quarrel with Captain Randlett and threatened his life. Dolan was arrested and the firm was later notified to leave the Fort. Back of the banishment was already a record of shady practices which Captain Randlett described in a letter to the War Department:

This firm I know to have been defrauding the government since my arrival at the Post. Their contract as Indian Agents have been fraudulent to my certain knowledge. So powerful is the ring to which they belong that I am able to prove that this firm has even attempted to force upon an officer of this post contract goods inferior to sample which they were bought at. I consider that L. G. Murphy & Co.'s store is nothing more or less than a den of infamy, and recommend the removal of this firm from this reservation.

A change of base to Lincoln Plaza was easily made at that time, for the firm already had a small branch there called the Placita Store. The little two-room adobe building which had been sufficient for a branch establishment was too small for the combined stock, and work was begun almost immediately on a larger building, situated on forty acres adjoining the western edge of Lincoln Plaza. Murphy sold the building at the Fort for $8,000 and proceeded to build a much larger store that was to be the most pretentious structure in the county outside of Fort Stanton. On the first floor was the store itself, with offices and other adjuncts such as a saloon and gambling hall; the second floor contained living quarters for the members of the firm, all of whom happened to be unmarried. The entire west wing of the second floor was designated as a meeting room, to become known as the "Lodge Room," although no fraternal organization ever used it, and its only access was from the courtyard below, by a ladder which could be pulled up through a window. Across the road from the new building was a boarding house, or "mess" as it was called, which might also serve the general public as a hotel.

The change of base did not involve a change of name; it was still "the Murphy store" or "the House." Even after the L. G. Murphy & Co. was succeeded by J. J. Dolan & Co., in March, 1877, many people continued to call the establishment "the Murphy Store," and to refer to Dolan's followers as "Murphy men," in spite of the fact that Murphy, after a breakdown from heavy and constant drinking, isolated himself at his Fairview ranch home at Carrizo Spring and divorced himself from active participation in Lincoln County affairs.

When Dolan took over the store in 1877, he had two junior partners who had joined the firm earlier. One was John H. Riley, a native of Ireland who had been in New Mexico for several years. "Johnny" Riley had been among the earliest to embark in the cattle business in that section and had found a place to the West of Fort Stanton as early as 1873. His aptitude for that phase of business had led the Murphy store to enlist his services as a partner when it became subcontractors to William Rosenthal of Santa Fe in supplying beef for Fort Stanton and the Indian reservation, as well as subcontractors to Zadoe Staab & Brothers in furnishing flour to the Indians.

Both Dolan and Riley were hotheaded Irishmen of the regular Donnybrook Fair type. In the language of Lincoln County they were "scrappers." Of the shooting scrapes and quarrels on their records, some were generally known, others merely suspected. Riley's affray with the Mexican posse led by Juan B. Patrón has already been mentioned. In the spring of 1877 Dolan killed a young man named Hiraldo Jaramillo. As the affair was delivered to the Santa Fe *New Mexican*, probably by Dolan himself, the Mexican had attacked him with a knife while both were in the corral cleaning up horses. Dolan had shot the Mexican first in the hand, hoping to make him drop the knife he had drawn, then in his arm, and finally, Dolan was compelled to fire a third time, sending a bullet into the young fellow's heart. Dolan gave himself up and was discharged after a preliminary hearing before "Judge" Wilson, Justice of the Peace at Lincoln. The community, however, took this version skeptically, some regarding it as a deliberate killing to help an adherent of the firm, George W. Peppin, out of a tight place. Some features about it seemed to show Dolan's well-known flair for scheming and contriving. In fact, the gashed arm he displayed was thought to have been injured with his own knife.

Another young member of the firm was Jacob B. Mathews, generally known as "Billy." Mathews was a Tennessean and an ex-Confederate soldier. After the war he had gone to Colorado and tried mining and in 1867 had gone into Colfax County, New Mexico, attracted by the mining around Elizabethtown. He remained for about five years, running a claim for an English company. About 1872 he was farming in the Pecos Valley, on a tract of land in the vicinity of Roswell, where he stayed for two years. He then went into the mountains sixty miles southwest of Roswell where he and Frank Freeman planned to get into the cattle business. When the venture was abandoned, he secured a clerkship in the Murphy store at Lincoln, and in 1877, when the reorganization made it J. J. Dolan & Co., he was admitted to the firm as a silent partner. As his partnership was not generally known, he appeared in the role of the disinterested party and under such a cloak could accomplish the ends that were outlined for him.

There is no gainsaying the fact that L. G. Murphy & Co. was in bad repute because of its unwholesome business methods. As has been indicated already, it was constantly involved in frauds in its dealings with the government. In 1873 L. Edwin Dudley, the superintendent of the New Mexico Indians, wrote as follows about the firm:

> Murphy and his partner Fritz have a great influence over the Indians. While officers of the volunteer army, they came into contact with them and have since managed Indian affairs and been the actual agents. They have made larger claims against the government, some of them of doubtful character. They could easily induce the Indians to become troublesome.

This influence with the Apaches the firm did not hesitate to brandish over the heads of the different Indian agents in order to get them to fulfill the wishes of the firm. S. B. Bushnell, one of the agents who would not bow to L. G. Murphy & Co., described in a report to the Bureau of Indian Affairs their tactics:

> L. G. Murphy is the Indian trader; J. J. Dolan his confidential clerk. They control issues and the agent. "It don't make any difference who the government sends here as agent. We control these Indians," Major Murphy says. The Indians very likely would protect his life and property if occasion rose. The agent is dependent upon this firm for supplies; all they expect is that he will sign vouchers at the end of the month. L. G. Murphy claim that $60,000 is owing them. In 1871, the Indians numbered 400; in 1872, over 1,800; in 1873, over 2,200. Dolan's latest list calls for 2,679. Here is a rapidity of increase which leaves rabbits, rats, and mice in the shade. How this is done is very plain to one with his eyes open.

W. D. Crothers recorded the same methods:

> L. G. Murphy & Company is the chief troublemaker. The firm now supplies the Agency with beef on the Rosenthal contract. Once Murphy presented a bill for salt for $400., which amounted to only $40. John Riley said to me, "We have always made some money out of this agency until you came here, but we can't make money out of you. The department at Washington expects us to make money and it is expected the agent will aid us. We all make money, including the agent."

In their relations to the settlers of Lincoln County, to use the local expression, they had "peoned" the whole section. L. G. Murphy & Co., were despotic and oppressive to an extreme. A general recital of the grievances laid at their door was prepared by Alexander A. McSween for Judge Angel in 1878:

> Lawrence G. Murphy and Emil Fritz, doing business under the style of L. G. Murphy & Co., had the monopoly of the sale of merchandise in this county and used their power to oppress and grind out all they could from the farmers, and to force those who were opposed to them to leave the country. For instance, the farmers would buy merchandise from them at exorbitant prices and were compelled to turn in their produce in payment thereof at prices that suited L. G. Murphy & Co., and if a farmer refused to do so, he was subjected to litigation and the whole judicial machinery

was used unwittingly to accomplish that object. The result was that L. G. Murphy & Co. were absolute monarchs of Lincoln County and ruled their subjects with an oppressive iron heel.

This state of affairs had existed from some time — at least ten years — and was carried out either by L. G. Murphy & Co. or their successors. To effect their schemes, L. G. Murphy & Co. would drive out a settler who had opposed them or would not follow their beck and call, and without a particle of right, title or claim, take possession of such person's real estate and claim that it belonged to them. They would then rent it to some person who was led to believe that it belonged to them; and, if such a person should afterwards find out that they had no right, title or interest in the property and refuse to pay the rental thereof, a system of persecution would be instituted, which would result in either the opposing party giving in or leaving the country.

By 1876 or 1877 current accusation went farther, from extortion and intimidation into thievery. The firm, it was generally believed, was filling its beef contract as subcontractors for Rosenthal by buying stolen cattle. The firm maintained a cow camp in the Pecos country near Seven Rivers and carried on dealings with the cattle-rustling contingent. It was understood that Jesse Evans and his associates, the most formidable and consistent band of cattle thieves then operating in Lincoln County, were on a secret payroll of the Murphy firm and were to earn their income by steadily stealing from the Chisum herds.

By 1877 the Murphy group had become exceedingly arrogant and boastful. They felt that they dominated politically as well as commercially and that such joint control made them impregnable in the county. They could install their henchmen in the county offices as easily as dealing a deck of cards and also see that they obeyed orders afterwards. They plumed themselves on the fact that they even controlled the territorial court, especially the district attorney, William L. Rynerson. They went so far as to claim they also had the backing of federal officialdom at Santa Fe, represented particularly by Thomas B. Catron, United States district attorney, and Samuel B. Axtell, governor of the territory. In other words, they looked upon themselves as the local understudies of the powerful "Santa Fe ring" which, comprising half a dozen or so prominent businessmen and politicians, was supposed to be enslaving and exploiting New Mexico. Naturally the existence of the "ring" was hard to prove. Those supposed to be of the circle pooh-poohed the idea and denied loudly. Others, especially the opposite political persuasion, persistently shouted, in the language of a newspaper editorial, "The Santa Fe ring has the territory by the throat and is throttling its development by and for the interest of the people."[9]

Astute ones like John Chisum who said little, but kept his eyes open, definitely believed that there was a Santa Fe ring. In 1878, when he thought that certain members of the ring were trying to wreck him financially by pressing the collection of the old packing-house notes, he wrote an opinion of the ring tinged with the humor characteristic of him:

> I know it is said by many of the citizens that there is a ring in Santa Fe; but the governor said in his last message that there was no ring. I am of this opinion. If there was a ring, there would be some show to get through it or to get on the outside or the inside of it. But the thing they have got up there is perfectly hard and solid; it cannot be penetrated from either side or end and it is perfectly solid. When this substance strikes a citizen, it goes right through him and leaves him in such a condition that he never recovers from it, it is so powerful that it not only ruins citizens but sometimes it ruins whole counties.

The last sentence hinted that Governor Axtell had helped the Santa Fe ring extend its tentacles into Colfax County, one of the most flourishing counties in the northern section of the territory.

In all this pother about a ring, the odor of politics was strong. The question of its existence always was debated most sturdily when

---

9. In Twitchell's *Old Santa Fe* there appears this admission of the existence of a Santa Fe ring: "The close of the Civil War brought to Santa Fe an increase in its population in the learned professions particularly, consisting of men of talent and spirit who became leaders in the political parties of the territory. These men in most instances had played a prominent part, on one side or the other, in the great conflict. Within a brief period this group found themselves the leaders in all public affairs, and were, indeed, in control of thought and sentiment throughout the entire territory. Among those equally ambitious, who had taken up their residences in other communities and smaller towns, the dominating spirits at New Mexico's capital were popularly known and designated as 'the Santa Fe ring,' a combination and organization which was apparently successful in dictating or influencing all political appointments locally and at Washington. The professional connection made by them with the representative families of the *río abajo* and the *río arriba* in guarding their interests in the matter of titles to Spanish and Mexican land grants enabled them to maintain what seemed to be an invincible position in the control of all matters of a business or political character." Although no names are given, Twitchell undoubtedly had in mind the law firm of Catron & Elkins, both members of which were influential in business and politics. In 1872 Catron had been appointed United States District Attorney for New Mexico, his law partner, Stephen B. Elkins, being at the time delegate to Congress from the territory.

the political pot was boiling vigorously, as at the convention to select candidates for office. Those in the ring were almost to a man the outstanding Republicans of New Mexico. Those who protested against it were generally Democrats who coveted those offices. In Lincoln County, however, the situation was rather in reverse from that in the territory as a whole. Under the political leadership of Major Murphy, it was always "the banner Democratic county." Those loudest in outcry against the Lincoln County ring were in the Republican party. All this, however, did not shake L. G. Murphy & Co.'s affiliations with the Santa Fe ring. Political garb was lightly worn in New Mexico and could be easily forgotten except when it was advantageous to wear it. Republican and Democrat might become bedfellows when the sleep of both was visited with dreams of money to be gathered under coalitions that ignored party lines. There was no great anomaly in Major Murphy and his associates currying favor with influential businessmen and political officials in Santa Fe, even when the former were Republicans.

So far as Lincoln County was concerned, the situation was that if the territory as a whole had its large ring, then Lincoln County had its small ring in the Murphy firm. Certainly a relation between the groups was discernible; the members of the Murphy firm were hand-in-glove socially, and financially, with those in the Santa Fe ring. They worked together as friends, as politicians, and as businessmen. Some of those thought to be in the Santa Fe ring had financial interests in Lincoln County. Thomas B. Catron, for instance, seemed to have such close connection with L. G. Murphy & Co. and its successor, J. J. Dolan & Co., that some believed he was virtually a partner. Even Governor Axtell himself was gossiped about having placed himself under financial obligation to the firm, having accepted a loan of $1800.

6. J. H. Tunstall & Co., Merchants Likewise

"THEY'LL NEVER DO MUCH business in that store." This sinister remark was ascribed to J. J. Dolan as he walked past the building being erected for the store of J. H. Tunstall & Co. Up until 1877 L. G. Murphy & Co. had encountered no business competition worth mentioning. The few other stores in Lincoln, those of Juan Patrón, Isaac Ellis & Sons, and José Montaño, were virtually negligible. In the spring of 1877 a rival was making a formidable debut. The personnel of the new store was sufficient to show that its business ethics would offer a marked contrast to the practices by which the older, established firm had lost popular favor.

The "Co." of the new firm included Alexander A. McSween, who never had a financial interest in the business although he had arranged with John Tunstall to sell him an interest when and if he had the necessary funds to invest — an arrangement which had not been ful-filled at the time of Tunstall's death. McSween was a prospering lawyer in Lincoln although a newcomer, having arrived in the spring of 1875 from Kansas. Born of Scottish parents on Prince Edward Island, he was well educated, the family having followed the custom of dedicating the brightest boy to the ministry. But McSween, though a man of deep religious principles, was too ambitious for fame and fortune to be a Presbyterian dominie, and he had adopted the law for his profession. In August, 1873, shortly after gaining license to practice, he had married Miss Susan Hummer at Atchison, Kansas. As his health was not good in that state — he was a chronic sufferer from asthma — the

young couple decided upon a change to the Southwest. With no location definitely in mind they approached New Mexico and heard of
Lincoln County as a coming section of the territory. Learning that
there were few if any resident lawyers within its limits, not even at the
county seat, the McSweens bent their course and arrived in March,
1875.

The location was indeed well chosen. He hung out his shingle as
a lawyer promptly. When the district court convened in April, he went
through the formality of being admitted to practice and scored a first
success in defending W. W. Paul for larceny, a term in those times
equivalent to cattle-stealing. From then on McSween's name was often
in the docket book; he handled many matters for John Chisum, who
took a great liking to both the shrewd lawyer and his vivacious wife.
Clients so multiplied that in the summer of 1877 McSween induced
a brother-in-law, David P. Shield, to move his family to Lincoln
and become his partner.

McSween, aggressive and frankly ambitious, sought to reap a
fortune from his adopted section. Known as a high-priced lawyer who
usually gave value received by winning his cases, he had the knack of
finding some strategy or technicality that would enable him to turn
the tables on the opposing side. He had high professional ideals and
did not hesitate to decline cases he felt were not just. And a sincere
interest in bringing law and order into his section made him observant
of the corruption overspreading the area. One day as some freighting
wagons were stopped in the road near his house, he walked out and
took samples of the flour intended for the Indian reservation. Judging it
as "worthless stuff, ground in some Mexican mill, that the Murphy
store is palming off as first quality," he placed it in an envelope which
he handed to Mrs. McSween, saying, "Take good care of this. Some-
day there will be an investigation to how the big store is handling its
flour contract with the government, and then this sample will come
in handy."

Not content with merely destroying what was harmful, McSween
also heartily encouraged moves for bettering the community. Feeling
that schools and churches were essential — certainly one of the crying
needs of Lincoln, which then had no church whatsoever and only a
poor excuse for a school — he influenced the Presbyterian church to
promise to send out "home missionaries." He expected to aid these
workers himself by giving a valuable lot for the church and by con-
tributing liberally toward the cost of church and school.

McSween's ambition, naturally, led him into active participation
in politics. At the Republican gatherings in Santa Fe he was much

Alexander McSween, lawyer, became allied with John H. Tunstall, youthful British investor, whose mercantile and banking firm posed the first real economic threat to Murphy and Dolan. With the killing of Tunstall, McSween embarked on a troubled sea of revenge in which he was eventually to die by violence.

John H. Tunstall came to the New Mexico Territory armed with the ambition to succeed and a Victorian British sense of fair play in business dealings. Both these qualities antagonized the faction in power and helped to bring about the killing of Tunstall as the first act in the stark drama of the Lincoln County War.

in evidence as representative of the slender Republicanism of Lincoln County. His oratorical ability made his speeches conspicuous; indeed, it was beginning to be said of him that he would be a good man for Congress before long — a suggestion that displeased T. B. Catron, the political dictator of the territory, who was thinking of exchanging before long the United States district attorneyship he had held since 1872 for a seat at Washington as territorial delegate. In politics as in other fields McSween seemed to have a great talent for making enemies who awaited a chance to undo him. Perhaps it was a hostility arising from essentially differing temperaments and viewpoints. Possibly McSween was so overbearing and sharp-tongued as often to irritate and even anger, such as when he had presented a bill for $100 to the Murphy store for attorney's services, a bill which Riley haggled over. "All right," said McSween acidly, "I'll cut the bill in half, as you wish. I consider it worth $50 to find out the sort of man you are."

Early in November, 1876, John H. Tunstall came to Lincoln. He was a young Englishman who had chosen the Southwest not because he wished to spend money wildly or lavishly but because he sought opportunities for long-range investments. He was the only son of John Partridge Tunstall of J. P. Tunstall & Co., a well-established mercantile firm at 8 Bow Church Yard, Cheapside, London. Tunstall senior also had an interest in Turner, Beeton & Tunstall, a trading firm that for twelve years had conducted both a wholesale and a retail business in Victoria, British Columbia. The son, John H., had gone from London to far-off Victoria in order to represent his father in Turner, Beeton & Tunstall. Behind the scenes was a good deal of wire-pulling by the first two partners in this firm in an effort to eliminate the third, Tunstall's father. In consequence, young Tunstall found his connection so uncomfortable that he relinquished it and went elsewhere.

He had acquired such liking for the frontier parts of North America that he had no inclination to go back to England. In the spring of 1876 he went to California in search of a suitable opportunity for investing the five or six thousand pounds his father proposed to place at his disposal, expecting to try the sheep business for which California was famed. Hearing on his arrival that New Mexico was a much better possibility, he proceeded thither after a brief stop at Denver. His entry into the territory was under good auspices; he carried letters of introduction to several prominent men, among them Governor Axtell, who formerly had lived in California. At Santa Fe he sought information as to the most promising locations and after considering various areas, finally decided to make a first-hand study of Lincoln County. The result was that the young Englishman arranged for the filing upon public land first on the Peñasco and shortly later on the Rio Feliz. Here a small house was built and a small herd of cattle purchased.

Tunstall's decision that cattle offered greater opportunities than sheep had been approved thoroughly by his father, who promised capital as soon as actually needed. The family fortune had become diminished and young Tunstall viewed it as his duty to try to recoup it. The Tunstalls were a small and closely knit family consisting of the parents, both elderly, and four children separated into two groups widely apart in years. John H. and a sister, Minnie, were fifteen or twenty years older than the two younger sisters. As the only son, John H. regarded himself as the mainstay of the family and was determined to build up a comfortable fortune, not for the benefit of himself but for the sake of his sisters, especially the two younger.

His enthusiasm for making money was so great that sometimes the members of the family wrote him precautionary counsel. His sister Minnie wrote, for instance, in November, 1876, when she learned of his decision to go to Lincoln County:

> The only thing you must bear in mind all the time you are making money is not to allow yourself to be spoilt mentally or morally or physically for enjoying it and being a first-rate member of society in every sense. I believe you are quite alive to it, too, but I cannot help saying it though I do not fear it — it so often comes to my thoughts and we have often spoken of it together when we have heard of millionaires quite powerless of enjoying, or even to be aware of the power they have gained.

As Tunstall became familiar with conditions at Lincoln, he was impressed with the opportunities for a new store, one well-financed, completely stocked, and above all known for fair dealing. With the experience gained in Victoria he felt himself competent to pilot such a venture to success. In consequence, the ranch project for a time received only secondary attention. As the store venture took shape Tunstall frequently turned to McSween for advice and left all legal matters and many business details in McSween's hands. Tunstall and McSween had been drawn together by mutual liking, possibly aided by the fact that both had been born under the British flag. The lawyer was anxious to own at least a small interest in the new mercantile business, but since he had no ready money to invest, Tunstall generously agreed to an informal arrangement for a few months, setting May, 1878, as a date when a joint ownership might be concluded. In the meantime, McSween was to move his office from the community hall, which also served as a part-time courtroom, and establish himself in a room to be partitioned off at the west end of the Tunstall store. He was to act as Tunstall's attorney and agent in return for which he would receive one-half of the profits up to May, after a deduction of eight percent on Tunstall's invested capital. When the articles of partnership were eventually signed, McSween was to be allowed eight percent on what was then on the books as McSween's accumulated share. In other words, even though McSween should invest no actual cash, he would acquire an interest in the business.

Mrs. McSween's womanly intuition made her dubious about the store venture, feeling strongly that "Mac" and "John," as she called them, had better let well enough alone and stick to other livelihoods. Plainly the new store would be a thorn in the side of the Murphy-Dolan-Riley organization, and very likely they would resort sooner or later to means fair or foul to oust the competition. Tunstall's father likewise held up a warning finger. The son had written home glowingly not only about taking the lead in mercantile matters at Lincoln but even of reaching out and obtaining the post trader's business at Fort Stanton. In the father's reply, although he renewed the offer of four thousand pounds, with willingness to leave the use of it entirely to the son's judgment, the elder Tunstall wrote an item of advice which in the light of subsequent events was strongly prophetic:

> As regards the banking and storekeeping and the intricate way of making money of course it is quite impossible for me to see that as you see it, my not being on the spot; but I have no doubt you may be right, and were we to meet you would make me see it the same as yourself. But in a poverty-stricken, cut-throat country like New Mexico, you would always be liable to be broken into and liable to be shot by some of your drunken customers; and that occupation would not be so good for your health. And now the importation of meat has so set in from the States to this country, I should think that the raising of cattle would be wonderful, providing you have the means of sending your cattle to market.

In spite of all resistance, friendly or hostile, Tunstall went ahead, one venture begetting another. Hardly was building for the new store underway when Tunstall conceived the idea of a bank and dedicated to that use one end of the adobe building being erected. In southern New Mexico there was no bank; in fact, there were only one or two elsewhere in the entire territory. Santa Fe boasted the famous First National, started by Lucian B. Maxwell, but by this time fallen into the hands of those supposed to be ringleaders in the Santa Fe ring — notably Stephen B. Elkins and T. B. Catron. Tunstall succeeded in getting John Chisum to be an auxiliary in the Lincoln County Bank, as it was called. Its letterhead displayed its officers as John S. Chisum, president; Alexander A. McSween, vice-president; and John H. Tunstall, cashier.

Tunstall was a frank, friendly person who fitted in well with the community. While his ways and ideals were different, he nevertheless won confidence pretty generally. Some smiled at his English mannerisms and peculiarities, but his genuine friendliness and democratic attitude kept him from becoming the butt of ridicule, as an Englishman so frequently was on the frontier. His sense of honesty and fair play was ingrained and inflexible, best described as characteristically English or even sturdily mid-Victorian. He had inherited business ideals in the best tradition which he did not intend to desert even in New Mexico, where business seemed to have lost all ethics in the mad scramble after wealth and power and where opportunities were so limited that men adopted the most cut-throat methods.

Tunstall was also endowed with the Englishman's passion for legality. Hardly could he conceive any other way of settling disputes and difficulties, personal or other, than by due course of law. The prevalent lawlessness of a locality which lived under the code that every man should protect his rights by himself, for himself, and of himself, was to him almost incomprehensible. He was frankly puzzled and even taken aback by what he found in Lincoln County, a section that had practically agreed to ignore even what legal machinery there was and use instead the rifle or revolver to protect life and property. A companion characteristic of Tunstall's was a tendency to think independently and to be outspoken with his views. This was counter to that section of the frontier code which read, "Always mind your own business." A man managed to keep the breath in his body during such trying times by disregarding all idea of becoming his brother's keeper. Men kept their mouths shut no matter how strongly they might dislike certain conditions. Tunstall, however, was one of those who believed in open criticism and active attempts at reform if reform seemed called for.

So auspiciously did the new firm start its career that it disarmed those who had been doubting Thomases. An elaborate stock of goods was procured from wholesalers at St. Louis and freighted in by wagons from the nearest railroad point, Trinidad, Colorado. The people flocked to the new firm, seemingly glad to escape the rapacity and ruthlessness of L. G. Murphy & Co. and its recent successor, J. J. Dolan & Co. The two stores, only a quarter of a mile apart, were poles asunder in methods and ideals. In anticipation of opposition and hostility Tunstall made the new building convertible into a near citadel if emergency should arise. The thick adobe walls were in themselves bullet-proof, and the vulnerable parts — doorways and windows — were "armored." In particular, windows were provided with heavy wooden shutters of double thickness, between the inner and outer layers of which were placed steel plates.

Sam Corbet was placed in charge of the store as clerk, book-keeper, and general factotum. Another person connected with the operation was Robert A. Widenmann, a native of Ann Arbor, Michigan, who had drifted to the West after completing his education in Germany. Tunstall had found him in Santa Fe, leading a precarious hand-to-mouth existence.[10] Out of sheer kindness Tunstall invited Widenmann to come to Lincoln and make his home with the young Englishman until Widenmann could get on his feet. The arrangement was not one of hire and salary; Tunstall simply "put him up" for a time, giving board and lodging and perhaps a few presents of clothing and such things. There was no understanding that Widenmann was to give explicit services in return; he was allowed, however, to putter around the establishment and help in one way or another with the different irons Tunstall had in the fire.

Widenmann, however, did not impress other persons in Lincoln at all favorably. McSween in particular disliked him and in a letter to Tunstall's father mentions him as one of the only two matters of disagreement between himself and Tunstall. One was Tunstall's mania for owning fine horses; the other was this inordinate friendship for Widenmann. What caused McSween to frown on Widenmann was chiefly bumptiousness, a word that covered both his self-conceit and his officiousness. He was also too much of a hanger-on, with the implication

----

10. One of the most illusive and controversial figures in the Lincoln County War, Robert Adolph Widenmann, was born January 24th, 1852, at Ann Arbor, Michigan, son of Karl August Widenmann, Consul in that area for the German Kingdom of Wurttemburg. After attending the Lutheran parochial school at Ann Arbor, he went to Germany to complete his education. Returning home, he left Ann Arbor for the southern United States, spending some time in Atlanta, Georgia, Canton, Mississippi, and other points before reaching New Mexico. He went back to Michigan after leaving New Mexico and following his visit with the Tunstalls in England he again returned to Ann Arbor. When away from home for some strange reason of his own he attempted to conceal his family connections and sometimes claimed Atlanta as his home. He took full advantage of his Ann Arbor connections, nevertheless, when he wrote about the Lincoln County troubles to Carl Schurz, Secretary of the Interior. His letters to Schurz carried considerable weight because of the friendship of Schurz and Widenmann, Sr., who had been fellow passengers on the ship which had brought both to America.

The Tunstall store in Lincoln as it appeared shortly after the Lincoln County War, before a room was added at the west and the original flat roof covered by a gabled roof. The store provided fuel for the fires of vengeance kept burning by the Murphy-Dolan faction. Later the store played a part in the financial and political recovery of James J. Dolan.

of servile flattery and other earmarks of the parasite. In spite of all protests and warnings, Tunstall, however, remained loyal to Widenmann, although he might have fared much better without him. Because Widenmann was the kind hard to shake off, Tunstall may not be blamed altogether for the connection.

Inevitably the new store brought to a head the steadily increasing animosity of J. J. Dolan & Co. toward Tunstall. When he had first come to Lincoln they had received him cordially. They viewed him not merely as one bringing capital into the section but as a prospective purchaser for one of the ranches to which by hook or crook they had claimed title. If the Britisher was looking for a good investment in cattle ranches, none was better than Fairview at Carrizo Spring, thirty miles northwest of Lincoln. Major Murphy, nominally the owner, would sell willingly now that his health was poor. McSween stepped in and by friendly caution about the generally unsettled state of titles held by this firm put Tunstall on his guard. When he and Major Murphy next discussed the matter of purchasing, the Englishman by pointed and embarrassing questions about the validity of the deed showed that he was not to become the dupe of this shrewd and masterful man.

By the time of Widenmann's arrival, that is, about the middle of February, 1877, the attitude of the Murphy-Dolan group toward Tunstall had become so openly antagonistic that they were casting slurs upon him at every opportunity. When Widenmann one day explained to Major Murphy that he had come to Lincoln to join Tunstall, who happened then to be away on a business trip to St. Louis, the major had shaken his head disparagingly and said, "Mr. Widenmann, I am afraid your friendship for that Englishman will not advantage you here in Lincoln. He is not in very good standing with the people."

When Widenmann told Tunstall about the remark, he dismissed the matter with a laugh, saying, "I'll tell you why they disapprove of me. They found I was not the sucker they thought I was when they tried to get me to buy one of their ranches. I told them I must have a title strong enough for my attorney, McSween, to approve. Since then they have had little use for me, and now that I am going to start my store, they would like to get rid of me. But I'm in Lincoln to stay. You've heard about our English tenacity? Well, I have my share of it. I am going ahead with my store. If they make trouble, I'll not hesitate to show up their crookedness and general rottenness. They have oppressed this section long enough. I shall do all I can to lift their yoke from it."

The handwriting on the wall was clearly visible to the Murphy-

Dolan group. Their establishment was perceptibly on an uneven keel financially, and its reorganization in April, 1877, as J. J. Dolan & Co. had so far not bettered the situation. They felt keenly the loss of customers now dealing at the new store.

The case of Dick Brewer was typical. That young farmer, living on Ruidoso at the place where four years before the Harrells had settled, began to take his crop to John H. Tunstall & Co. When he first came into the country from Wisconsin he had secured his ranch from L .G. Murphy & Co., agreeing to pay the price asked within a stipulated period of years. The firm had accommodated him with credit for all the supplies he needed to get started at farming. As the returns from the sale of his produce to L. G. Murphy & Co. at their low rates was never sufficient to release him from debt, he had found himself getting steadily into a worse and worse financial state with no prospect of improvement. In his discouragement he had talked over the situation with McSween, who opened his eyes to the fact that L. G. Murphy & Co. had really no title to the land. Then he recommended the Tunstall store, where Brewer could obtain a fair price for what he had to sell from his farm.

When Brewer's defection was noticed by the Dolan people, they determined to put the screws to him in their Lincoln County style. Dolan, Billy Mathews, and Billy Morton, impressively armed with rifles and pistols, rode over to Brewer's ranch to demand that he either leave the ranch or pay for it as agreed. Brewer, acting under McSween's instructions, told them they had no title to the land but they could have it if they would pay for the improvements he had put on it. Dolan angrily declined the proposal and told Brewer that if the ranch was not turned over he would make it "a personal matter with him," an expression in those times with unequivocal meaning. Brewer replied, "I know my rights, and if necessary will defend them. I am not hunting a fuss, but I won't run from one." Dolan's departing bluster was, "If you don't turn the ranch over, you will damn soon find your fuss."

As the three rode back toward Lincoln, Dolan delivered his opinion of lawyers in general and of McSween in particular. He remarked that there had been entirely too much "lawing" since McSween had hung out his shingle at Lincoln, and he made the grim prediction that "The House" would find ways to be rid of such bothersome people as McSween, Tunstall, and Brewer.

7. Some Lawbreakers and Hard Cases

FROM THE START Lincoln County was a catch basin, not to say asylum, for more than the usual share of frontier flotsam and jetsam. Judge Angel mentioned an important factor in the lawlessness when he wrote in his report to the Department of Justice: "Lincoln County is unfortunate in adjoining the arid belt of western Texas from which cowboys and desperadoes periodically swarm. These Texans in travelling around nearly always bring trouble in their track. Murder is no new thing in Lincoln County." The troublemakers did not always come from the eastward; frequently they were a sort of backwash from the mining sections of New Mexico and Arizona. When these localities grew too law-abiding for the comfort of this class of men, they hastened to a new refuge in Lincoln County.

One curse of the section was organized outlawry. The first appearances of this came from groups engaged mainly in horse-stealing. For two years prior to 1876 the four Mes brothers — Juan, Paz, Jesús, and Juanito — and their confederates made up perhaps the most threatening band. In December, 1875, they brought matters to a climax by killing Oliver Thomas in Lincoln, and as a result a detachment of 9th Cavalry from Fort Stanton descended upon their hide-out at La Boquilla on the Rio Hondo. The place was fortified like a citadel with scouts on the watch and underground tunnels connecting the houses, but the soldiers succeeded in capturing or killing six or seven members of the band, including two of the Mes brothers themselves. The rest of the band shifted its headquarters to Puerto de Luna on the Pecos, taking along a number of horses stolen from the Mescalero reservation.

In July the Indian agent, Major Godfroy, determined to recover these horses but knowing the reputation of Puerto de Luna as a thieves' nest, applied to Captain Purington, then in command at Fort Stanton, for a detachment of soldiers. This request met with refusal but Godfroy went ahead, placing his agency clerk, Morris J. Bernstein, at the head of a party of Indians. Bernstein met with unexpected success, for with the aid of the civil authorities of San Miguel County and several of its influential citizens, he recovered seven horses. On his return he diverged to Fort Sumner as he had received a report that a civilian living there had a horse belonging to one of the Mescaleros. He found this to be the case and thus brought his talley up to eight. The excursion to Fort Sumner turned out fortunate in another way. As the route taken from Fort Sumner to the reservation on the return was different from what he would have used had he gone directly back from Puerto de Luna, he escaped being waylaid. A number of this band of horse thieves had congregated on the road ordinarily used, giving grounds for the supposition they were waiting to waylay Bernstein's party.

Another band of horse thieves in Lincoln County had a triumvirate leadership composed of Juan Gonzales, Nica Meras, and Jesús Largo. Unlike the Mes brothers, who usually sold their stolen horses in Chihuahua, Mexico, this band made southern Colorado their market place. In the summer of 1876 two of this band, one being Nica Meras himself, were captured and killed after stealing five horses including a valuable stallion from two settlers, Frank Coe and Ab Sanders, on the upper Ruidoso. Frank Coe, Josiah (Doc) Scurlock, Charlie Bowdre, and other neighboring farmers took part in the capture of the culprits and their summary punishment. A few weeks later another of the three leaders, Jesús Largo, was captured by a party of Mexicans and taken to Lincoln for safekeeping. When the news reached the Ruidoso section, Frank Coe, and several associates, among them Sanders, Scurlock and Bowdre, started for Lincoln. As their intentions were clearly to take matters into their own hands, the sheriff, Captain Saturnino Baca, proceeded to take measures to protect his prisoner. With a posse of Mexicans as guard he started with him for Fort Stanton. Frank Coe and his companions intercepted them and without difficulty got Jesús Largo into their hands and lynched him. A short time afterwards the third and last of the leaders, Juan Gonzales, was killed in the vicinity of his hide-out by Sanders and another man.

THE JESSE EVANS GANG

Organized outlawry, however, raised its head most conspicuously in 1876 and 1877 through a band chiefly composed of Americans.

Most of them had drifted into Lincoln County from the Rio Grande Valley, where they had created such disturbances they could no longer remain. This band bore a variety of names: in the newspapers they were the "banditti," but the people called them "the boys" or "the Jesse Evans gang." Little is known about the early life of the leader, Jesse Evans, except that he was from Missouri and while still very young had drifted into the Southwest; he was, in fact, merely nineteen years of age when he first saw New Mexico in 1872.[11] He had first worked as a cowboy in the Pecos country, but by 1875 he was seen most frequently in the vicinity of the Mesilla Valley, where he was known as a cattle and horse thief. Early in 1876 he became involved in a more serious crime, the killing of Quinino Fletcher, a young man of a well-known family, who was shot on his way home from a saloon. The reason for the killing was that Fletcher was suspected of having killed two of the Jesse Evans crowd when all were in Old Mexico on a cattle-stealing expedition.

This trouble made it expedient for young Evans to change his base of operations from the Mesilla Valley. In Doña Ana County he had met Jim McDaniels, William Morton, and Frank Baker, all of whom had first-hand acquaintance with current conditions in Lincoln County. McDaniels knew the ropes pretty well; he had left the employ of John Chisum because of a dispute over an alleged indebtedness, and he liked to parade his grievance as a ground for getting even with old John. Already McDaniels had come to be considered a desperate character fit not only for rustling but for murder. The leadership of the lawless element which McDaniels had seemed about to win, however, passed to Jesse Evans, who soon after his arrival in Lincoln County was dubbed "Captain," a title he wore during the next four or five years. His position was strengthened by a close association with James J. Dolan, who was fast becoming in many ways one of the most influential men in the county. A legend, one of questionable credibility, has it that Jesse Evans' influence was responsible for the arrival in Lincoln County toward the close of 1877 of a lad whose dramatic career so intrigued the public fancy that his name lives on even today,

11. According to the records of Rusk Prison in Texas, where he was admitted December 1st, 1880, Evans was born in Missouri in 1853, was 5'5 ¾" in height, weighed 150 pounds, with limited education and of intemperate habits. The official report to the Attorney General at Washington, covering Special Agent Frank Warner Angel's investigation of the Lincoln County troubles, includes an affidavit signed by Jessie (sic) Evans stating that he, Evans, had first come to New Mexico in 1872, working for Borrowson & Grier and later for others, including John Chisum.

long after most of his contemporaries in derring-do have been forgotten.

The newcomer came to be known by a variety of names. His mother had been known as Mrs. Catherine McCarty during her periods of residence in Indiana, Kansas, and Colorado before her marriage to William H. Antrim at Santa Fe, New Mexico, on March 1, 1873.[12] Her son, as a witness to his mother's marriage, was recorded as Henry McCarty, and it was by this name he was first known at Silver City, where the family moved immediately after the marriage. Later he was frequently called by the name of his stepfather, Billy Antrim. He did not assume the name Bonney, presumably a parental family name, until he reached the Pecos Valley. It was in Graham County, Arizona, in 1875 that his boyish appearance won him the appellation "Billy the Kid," or merely "Kid," a name which followed him to Lincoln County.

Residents of Silver City have been unanimous in saying that Henry McCarty — or Billy Antrim — did not kill anyone during his stay in that place. What caused him to flee the town slightly less than a year after his mother's death, September 16, 1874, was a more commonplace incident. An older man, George Shaffer, had purloined a bundle of washing from a Chinese laundry and had persuaded Henry and another boy to hide it. The sheriff, Harvey Whitehill, locked up Henry in the town jail, probably intending nothing more than to give the lad a good scare. Henry, however, fearing his stepfather's reaction to the arrest, made his escape through the fireplace chimney and struck out for Arizona.

THE KID'S FIRST KILLING

For two years the young fellow called Kid Antrim worked as a teamster and at various other occupations in the Graham County area of eastern Arizona. Then in August, 1877, he became involved in his first killing. The victim, Frank Cahill, was an army blacksmith whose frequently overbearing manner had earned him the nickname "Windy." He seems to have taken a delight in tormenting the Kid and on this occasion paid for it dearly. By one account the boy snatched the blacksmith's pistol from its holster; in any event he shot Cahill and was jailed the following day when the blacksmith died. Quickly escaping custody, the Kid fled back to New Mexico.

---

12. Colonel Fulton's notes are obscure as to the sources of his information concerning Catherine McCarthy's residence in Indiana and Kansas, but his conclusions are largely confirmed by the later findings of Mr. Waldo Koop as detailed in his article "Billy the Kid, the Trail of a Kansas Legend," *The Trail Guide*, Kansas City, Mo., September, 1964.

At the Knight ranch some miles south of Silver City he was accorded a friendly reception. He remained there some weeks but the place was too near Arizona to afford permanent sanctuary. The first community of any importance east of Silver City was Mesilla and early October found him in the Mesilla Valley. Here he met a young man named Tom O'Keefe and accepted the latter's invitation to join him in journeying to the Pecos Valley. Crossing the Guadalupe Mountains the two had an encounter with Indians, lost their horses, became separated, and escaped on foot. O'Keefe made his way back to Mesilla, but Billy continued the journey eastward. In escaping the Indian country he concealed himself by day and proceeded only under cover of darkness. He had been without food or water for two days before he came upon the Heiskell Jones ranch north of the community of Seven Rivers.

Under the Jones' hospitality William Bonney, as he now called himself, soon recovered from the rigors of his flight from the misadventure in the Guadalupes. During the time he spent at the ranch he became strongly attached to the Jones family, particularly Heiskell Jones' son John, a friendship which was to endure even after Billy and the Jones boys were enlisted in opposing forces in the Lincoln County War. Riding a pony supplied by the Jones family, he rode up the Pecos to John Chisum's South Spring River ranch where like all the visitors he was made welcome. Although he remained here for a time he never became a Chisum employee. It may be as some writers have claimed that about this time he encountered the Jesse Evans gang but it is certain that he never joined in their depredations. Leaving Chisum's, Billy rode up the Rio Hondo to the Ruidoso valley, stopping at farms or ranches along the way until he reached the Coe farm a short distance below Dowlin's mill. During his relatively long stay with George Coe, he made among the neighboring settlers some friendships which lasted throughout the remainder of his short life.

8. Ineffectual Civil Authorities

JESSE EVANS AND HIS RUSTLERS did not exhaust the tally of "lawless resolutes" in Lincoln County in 1876-77. The Evans gang was well organized and was somewhat conspicuous due to its reputed affiliation with the powerful Murphy-Dolan party, but there were others who contributed to turbulence and disorderliness, men nominally living on their own small farms or ranches but always ready for marauding, a shooting affray, or some other form of frontier adventure. Andy Boyle, for example, a former British soldier living in his *chosa* below Seven Rivers, was as ruthless a fellow as could be found in the county and seems to have become involved in any mischief that might be afoot. Another troublemaking group was the vagrant class — those who would have one job today and another tomorrow. Many "punched" cattle, first for one large owner, then for another. Some became helpers, occasionally renters, on the larger farms, though seldom for more than a single season. A few became clerks in stores or in commissaries at some of the larger ranches. A good representative of these might be John Long, who hung around ready for whatever might present itself; George Hindman, too, belongs in this category. There were many others.

Lincoln County had, on the surface, adequate means for law enforcement. Administration of the law, however, was too frequently in the hands of men influenced by greed and by factional antagonisms. Furthermore, many held offices for which they were not particularly qualified, a situation not infrequently encountered on the frontier where the legal structure, like the rest of the civilization, had to be built from the ground up using materials at hand, even when of makeshift quality. Much of the responsibility for law enforcement fell on the local justices of the peace, successors of the *alcaldes* of the Mexican regime. These justiceships were as a rule filled by men of but mediocre caliber.

J. B. Wilson, for instance, who was appointed magistrate of Precinct One of Lincoln County in 1876, was known to be an honest man, but his lack of legal or other particular qualifications for the job resulted in some remarkable methods of dispensing justice. One incident which the community long remembered occurred in December, 1876, after W. W. Campbell had shot and killed Thomas King in a quarrel over King's impoliteness to a certain young woman whom Campbell had gallanted to a dance. Campbell surrendered and was taken before Justice Wilson for a preliminary examination. After five hours deliberation Campbell was acquitted under the plea of self-defense. The next day, however, Campbell was rearrested, along with L. S. Tesson, the former as principal and the latter as an accomplice. A second examination of Campbell was about to start when Wilson's attention was called to the fact that he could not try a man twice for the same offense. Thereupon the Justice, accepting the correction in his procedure, discharged Campbell but went ahead with his examination of Tesson and bound him over to the district court under a $300 bond, charging him with abetting Campbell in a crime of which Campbell had been declared innocent.

The sheriff was, of course, the most important figure in the enforcement of law. At the organization of the county in 1869 Major William Brady had been chosen sheriff (although he had had to take out his naturalization papers before he could qualify. Then in succession the incumbents had been Lewis J. ("Jack") Gylam, A. H. Mills, and Saturnino Baca. In January, 1876, Brady took office for the second time. Like his sponsors, Major Murphy and Colonel Fritz, he had served in the army and settled in Lincoln County when discharged from military service. It was commonly recognized that Brady was a Murphy henchman and took his orders from the man who had been responsible for placing him in office.

As local matters were largely in the province of the probate court, the judgeship was an important plum that at first had always gone to Major Murphy. But the exposure of corruption in county financial affairs in 1875 forced Murphy to relinquish the post. In 1876 Florencio González, a substantial farmer and a leader of the Mexican-American element in the community, took over as probate judge. The probate clerkship was capably filled by Juan Patrón for several successive terms until the accession of Florencio González, when Patrón moved a rung or two up the ladder of local politics. The killing of Paul Dowlin by Jerry Dillon in the spring of 1877 made vacant a seat in the territorial legislature and at a special election Patrón was named to fill the vacancy. Although barely twenty-one years of age he had become a dominating figure among the native New Mexicans and as their representative had sometimes clashed with the political powers controlling the county. He had taken over the management of his father's small store when the elder Patrón was killed in the Harrell troubles of 1873. Along with his work at the store he had found time to serve without pay as Lincoln's only schoolmaster. This and his reputation for complete integrity had won him the respect of the newcomers as well as of the native elements in the community.

The rest of Lincoln County's judicial machinery was nonresident. The county was part of the third judicial district, the general headquarters of which were at Mesilla. There resided the judge, Warren Bristol, while the district attorney, Wm. L. Rynerson, lived in the neighboring town of Las Cruces. Judge Bristol had come to New Mexico in April, 1872, under an appointment from President Grant. He was a native of New York State but had lived for a number of years in Minnesota where he served in several judicial and legislative capacities. His official acts involving Lincoln County inspired, not without some foundation, the opinion that he was strongly partisan in favor of the Dolan interests and openly antagonistic to McSween and his supporters. Partisanship was also charged in Grant County, which was within his jurisdiction; in 1876 a petition for his removal was signed by 280 Grant County citizens, but Bristol managed to retain office.

In its district attorney, Colonel Rynerson, the third judicial district had a character strikingly typical of the frontier. Born in Kentucky, he had gone west in his young manhood, lured to California by the gold excitement. The story was that he had walked the greater part of the way over the old Oregon Trail. When the California Column was recruited in 1861, he had been active enough in the formation of Company "C," 1st California Infantry, to be selected second lieutenant. Promotion came rapidly, until at the end of his military service he was quartermaster of the District of Arizona and had been brevetted major and lieutenant colonel. Upon being mustered out he had secured the post trader's store at Ft. Bayard, N. M., but by 1869 he had become a lawyer as well as a politician. He served several terms in the legislature, during one of which he attained regrettable notoriety by killing Judge John P. Slough, territorial chief justice, in the Exchange Hotel at Santa Fe. Rynerson had introduced a resolution charging the Judge with unfitness for office. The evening of the day the resolution was adopted the Chief Justice made a bitter verbal attack on Rynerson. The latter restrained himself at the time but the next day sought out Judge Slough and demanded a retraction. The Chief Justice refused and allegedly made a move toward drawing a derringer. Rynerson whipped out his pistol and inflicted a wound from which Slough shortly died. Although a coroner's jury exonerated Rynerson on the ground of self-defense, he preferred to clear his record still more completely by standing trial, the result, of course, being acquittal. The affair, however, was an indication of the spirit and temper of the man.

The judicial set-up for the territory included also the United States district attorney, at that time Thomas B. Catron. No very sharp distinction then existed between the federal and the territorial courts, especially in the matter of judgeship. Judge Bristol, for example, would try both territorial and federal cases at the regular terms of court in his district. However, the United States district attorneyship was an office altogether separate from the territorial district attorneyships and much more important. The incumbent since 1872 had been Catron, who had forged ahead rapidly since coming to New Mexico from Missouri in 1867. Catron had been through the Civil War as a Confederate but in New Mexico had found it expedient to align with the dominant Republican party. From the start he had a way of getting what he wanted. For example, even before he was admitted to the practice of law in New Mexico he had obtained appointment as district attorney for the third judicial district and had moved from Santa Fe to Mesilla to qualify. While at Mesilla he formed an association with Stephen B. Elkins, decidedly a kindred type. When Elkins became delegate to Congress, he obtained the United States district attorneyship from President Grant for Catron.

Catron was indeed the foremost lawyer in New Mexico and the firm of Catron & Thornton at Santa Fe had a practice coextensive with the territory. As Catron had lived in the southern part of New Mexico at Mesilla, virtually the capital of that section, he knew the commercial importance of that district and made substantial investments there, particularly in Lincoln County. His method, however, was not to make these investments outright and directly but rather to work through agents and understudies, even though some time might elapse before title to properties could appear in his name. He had a dominating personality, not to say ruthless, and during the eighteen seventies as well as a decade and a half longer he was virtually dictator of New Mexico, politically, commercially, and professionally. He thus played a dominant role in the troubles besetting Lincoln, though he remained, as it were, off-stage.

Despite the proper machinery for law enforcement, New Mexico had suffered for years from the lax execution of the criminal statutes. There existed a general feeling that any law might be violated except that of the federal government or one in which certain public officials had a personal interest. To some extent the people of New Mexico contributed to the situation by their acquiescent attitude. The territory had a large proportion of peaceable, law-abiding citizenry, but they submitted too tamely to a few who made a practice of flaunting the laws. The lawless element were emboldened by the general aversion to drastic measures and by the fact that money or influence could save anyone who might fall into the clutches of the law.

Another factor promoting lawlessness was the prostitution of the law by the corrupt practices and partisan activities of so many of the very men entrusted with the duty of maintaining law and justice. As one of the newspapers put it editorially: "From the highest positions in the territory down to that of constable, most of the offices have, for years, been filled by men whose only object has been self-aggrandizement or the persecution of personal or political enemies.... New Mexico can trace much of her lawlessness to the demagogism and avarice of many of her political leaders."

9. Frank Freeman's Final Rampage

In early August, 1877, certain explosions, so to speak, showed that Lincoln and vicinity were destined to new tumults. Echoes of what was taking place reached the small settlement of Roswell and furnished Ash Upson material for the following excited paragraph in a letter to relatives in Connecticut, August, 1877.

> We have been having a regular war between cattle thieves — American and Mexican — and proprietors. A crowd of the robbers attacked a house where John S. Chisum was stopping in the plaza of Lincoln, about a week ago, firing more than a hundred shots through the doors and windows, riddling furniture, etc., but hitting no one. One of the thieves was killed outright, and two others were severely wounded. There are now a posse of fifteen soldiers and a sergeant led by the sheriff and a posse of some 20 deputies after them in the Guadalupe Mountains. They have a residence on the Rio Peñasco, where they expect to capture them.

The "lawless resolute" mainly responsible for the disturbances was Frank Freeman, who had come originally from Alabama and liked to parade the fact that he was highly tinctured with the Southerner's antipathy for Negroes. He boasted of having been a "nigger-killer" and in Lincoln found occasion to make proof of the claim owing to the occasional presence in that town of Negro cavalrymen from Fort Stanton. Sometime in December, 1876, he had shot a soldier who had attempted to eat at the same table at Wortley's Hotel in Lincoln. The man was merely wounded and shortly recovered but Freeman fled to

Texas, believing he had killed the soldier. In partnership with Jacob B. ("Billy") Mathews, Freeman had "squatted" on public land on the Upper Peñasco, which was included in the tract which Tunstall later obtained by filing under the Desert Land Act. Though not legally obligated to do so, Tunstall insisted on paying Mathews one or two hundred dollars for the living shack and the corral which Freeman and Mathews had erected before they abandoned the place. Mathews had spent the money, possibly as part of the payment he had made in acquiring his small and secret interest in the J. J. Dolan & Co. store.

In the summer of 1877 Freeman again made his appearance in Lincoln County and Mathews had occasion to tremble in his boots lest Freeman forcefully demand his share. He need not have worried; Freeman busied himself with the activities of the Jesse Evans gang and did not seek out Mathews when that contingent rode up to Lincoln on Sunday, August 5. The performance they put on made the whole town panic-stricken, particularly those unfriendly with the Dolan faction. A letter published by Colonel Fountain in the Mesilla *Independent*, September 8, 1877, probably based on information from McSween, tells the story; because it also offers a sensitive picture of the growing alarm of the townspeople, the entire letter is reprinted herewith.

Editors, *Independent:*

Gentlemen: Your favor requesting particulars of the late troubles in this county, for publication in your very valuable paper, is received, and it affords us pleasure to give you the facts in the case, extenuating nothing, and nothing setting down in malice. The whole truth should be known and the reputation of every community should be able to stand such a draft; but we question the propriety of recording against Lincoln County all the crimes committed within our borders, for the simple reason that the depredations for which we have such unenviable reputation have invariably been committed by migrating vagabonds from Texas, Doña Ana County and elsewhere, who have no real interest in the prosperity of this county. If there be one fact more patent than another, it is that the permanent residents of Lincoln County in their love of law and order are foremost among the people of the Territory. Especially is this true of the Mexican portion of them. When, however, any depredation is committed, the odium does not attach solely to the guilty party but our general reputation for peace and quietness suffers; this distorted view turns the peace-loving immigrant to other less favored localities, and our county suffers in reputation and prosperity. The evil has become so burdensome that our citizens who subsist by labor have determined that they will no longer submit to the injury that is daily being inflicted upon us by vagabonds who live by stealing. It is unfortunately true that we have been cursed to a great extent by the presence of many of this class; they roam in bands of five or six through-out the county, and whenever the amount of plunder is sufficient to attract them, they concentrate like vultures around a carcass.

The *Independent* has taken such a bold and commendable stand, and has shown the lawless element that the identification of members is no longer a matter of doubt, that we cheerfully comply with your request. For a long time our county has been infested with a band of thieves, desperadoes, and outlaws, who have openly defied the laws and who have been a terror to our best citizens. Their enmity appears to have been directed against one of our largest tax-payers, evidently for the purpose of alarming them into buying their safety. In this respect our outlaws bear a strik-ing resemblance to the Italian brigands; when some uncommon atrocity would arouse public sentiment against them, they would flee to Doña Ana County to rusticate, generally taking with them a drove of horses or cattle stolen from our citizens. When our present efficient sheriff, Major William Brady, was elected, he determined to suppress this brigandage at all hazards; he advised all suspected characters to act peaceably, and several against whom indictments had been found by our grand jury, he noti-fied to come in peaceably and enter into bonds for their appearance in court. Some of them replied that they would not come in and that there was not law enough in Lincoln County to reach them. Dreading a recurrence of the dreadful scenes of four years ago when this or a similar band overran and terrorized the county, Sheriff Brady endeavored to persuade them to yield peaceably, but they evidently became convinced that he was afraid of the gang.

While matters were in this shape, Frank Freeman, a desperado who had been compelled to leave the county for the cowardly shooting of a soldier about a year ago, arrived from Texas, accompanied by others like himself, amongst them a man named Armstrong. Freeman, accompanied by a would-be desperado, Charles Bowdre, came to the town of Lincoln on Sunday evening (Aug. 6th) and compelled Don José Montaño to open his store and forced him to give them liquor; they then commenced smash-ing things generally, breaking lamps, bottles, glasses, etc. Meet-ing with an innocent sergeant from Fort Stanton and there being no other victim at hand, Freeman, who had one of his murder fits on, took the sergeant by the hand in a friendly manner, and with his other hand reached around and placed the muzzle of his pistol at the back of the sergeant's head and fired. Fortunately the wound was not mortal; Freeman, supposing that he had killed the sergeant, accompanied by Bowdre, rushed through the streets of the town shooting at every object that met their view, Freeman shouting that his "name was Frank Freeman and no twenty men could arrest him," that "he had had his man for all meals in the day and that he intended to kill every man in town that he didn't like." Thus they paraded the streets, shooting and yelling like demons. After awhile another idea seemed to strike them. Coolly reloading their weapons, they proceeded to the residence of A. A. McSween, attorney at law, a prominent and good citizen, where John S. Chisum was stopping as a guest. Two ladies and five children were also in the house. They fired a number of shots promiscuously in the house, broke a window open, and forced an entrance. The inmates fled for shelter. The ruffians then riddled a sewing machine with bullets, and shouted that "if John S. Chisum or his corpse was not turned over to them, they would burn the d---d house down." About this time a Mexican servant in the employ of Mr. McSween obtained a firearm and discharged it at the ruffians, slightly grazing Freeman in the arm, whereupon they ingloriously fled, and made their way to the store of J. J. Dolan & Co. where they had intruded and left their horses on their arrival in town.

In the meantime, Sheriff Brady, who lives below town, had been notified of what was going on, and obtaining a warrant, he proceeded to arrest the ruffians, taking the precaution to summons a posse (and every citizen responded with alacrity). The sheriff entered the house of J. J. Dolan & Co. and there found Freeman and Bowdre. About this time Freeman leaped into his saddle and declared his intention of shooting every man he met. Brady arrested Bowdre, and Freeman interfered and pulled his six-shooter. Brady done the same, and would have shot Freeman then but for the interference of Bowdre. Messrs. J. J. Dolan and J. B. Mathews then came to the assistance of Brady and probably saved his life. A scuffle ensued, resulting in the sheriff mastering the situation. Freeman and Bowdre were turned over to the posse. The citizens being greatly enraged and highly excited, Sheriff Brady deemed it prudent to apply to Col. George E. Purington, commanding officer at Fort Stanton, for an escort to take the prisoners to the post for safe keeping, which request was complied with. The desperadoes were taken before Justice Wilson and examined. Freeman's bond was fixed at $1,000 and Bowdre's at $500, which the latter succeeded in obtaining. Freeman could give no bond, but succeeded in escaping from the escort while en route to Fort Stanton.

About a week afterwards we had reliable information that Freeman had joined a band of men like himself on the Ruidoso and that they were threatening to come over and burn the town. Among the lawless characters acting with Freeman and his party were Nicholas Provencio and several other equally bad men from your county, also a desperate character from Grant County. In the meantime Armstrong came to town and boasted that he was en route to meet Freeman and aid him in carrying into execution the above-mentioned threats. He got some whiskey and then commenced shooting promiscuously. A warrant was obtained for his arrest and placed in the hands of deputy sheriff Francisco Romero y Valencia for service. The deputy sheriff with posse attempted to make the arrest, when Armstrong fired at the deputy and fled toward the Ruidoso shooting at the posse as he ran. The posse returned the fire and Armstrong was killed. Fearing that the band on the Ruidoso would now carry their threats into execution, the sheriff took ten of the best citizens of the county as a posse and determined to endeavor to arrest the outlaws at their rendezvous. Having obtained reliable information that they had a comparatively large and well-armed force, Sheriff Brady deemed it prudent to apply to Col. Purington for a military force, and that officer kindly responded by sending Lieutenant G. W. Smith and fifteen cavalrymen to assist the sheriff. The party proceeded to the ranch of Charles Bowdre on the Ruidoso, which was known to be the rendezvous of the outlaws.

Upon arriving at this place the sheriff deployed his men on each side of the creek. His presence was soon discovered by Freeman, who rushed out and fired at Brady — and missed. He then sprang on his horse which stood ready saddled. In an instant the horse fell, riddled with bullets. Freeman, still unhurt, endeavored to make his escape through a corn field, firing as he retreated. He was pursued and killed. Bowdre escaped by wading down the bed of the stream; others of the party were captured and taken to Lincoln where they were examined and committed for trial.

The above is a correct statement of the late troubles, and we regret to add that there are still a large number of unarrested brigands evading the law who have been committing thefts in both Lincoln and Doña Ana counties; our sheriff will do all in his power to cooperate with Sheriff Barela of your county in bringing these men to justice.

We avail ourselves of this opportunity to state that the good citizens of Lincoln County and especially the sheriff, feel grateful to Captain George E. Purington, commanding officer at Fort Stanton, for the aid so promptly given by him to law-abiding citizens in their efforts to bring to justice a noted band of desperadoes and outlaws. We return our heartfelt thanks. We also return thanks to Lieutenant Smith and his detachment of "boys in blue" for the valuable service rendered.

Everything is at present quiet, the air is purer, and everybody breathes easier. Major Brady has done good service *and he expects to do more of the same kind.* His course has given all law-abiding men entire satisfaction.

The course of the *Independent* has also given us satisfaction. We rejoice that there is at least one newspaper in your county that has had the courage to speak of things as they are. You may rest assured that the good citizens of Lincoln County will sustain you.

10. Raids by the Jesse Evans Gang

IN THE WAKE of the killing of Frank Freeman there came additional harassment from the outlaw element, beginning with a raid on the Indian agency August 11. The few details obtainable beyond the fact that several horses were stolen are embodied in the report sent by the Indian agent, Major Godfroy, to Washington under date of September 1.

> On the evening of August 11, it being yet daylight, some of these men [i.e. desperate characters infesting the country] made a descent on the agency herd under our very noses. Having no arms to furnish my employees, it was impossible to pursue the thieves until assistance had been obtained; so I dispatched my clerk [Bernstein] to Fort Stanton that night with a requisition on Captain Purington, the post commander, for troops to pursue the robbers. The next morning a detachment of fifteen men under command of Lieutenant Davenport started from the post. The pursuit by the military was unsuccessful, in spite of their promptitude, on account of severe rainstorms having obliterated the trail.

About the situation in Lincoln County generally, Godfroy went on to say:

> The civil authorities are almost powerless to protect life and property. Within the last three weeks two men [Armstrong and Freeman] have been killed openly resisting the sheriff's authority. In both instances they fired several shots at the sheriff before

being killed. My own life and that of my clerk have repeatedly been threatened on account of the active steps taken to stop this stealing from the Indians. . . . In consequence of these threats I have almost decided upon removing my family, who have been with me since last December, and who have by their presence done much towards assisting me in my labors. My daughter is engaged in teaching school, and my wife has, during her leisure moments, cut out and made garments for the Indians, besides teaching them how to do such work alone. The moral effect of their presence is making itself gradually felt, and I shall retain them here as long as I can do so with safety but in justice to them and to myself, I cannot keep them here at the peril of their lives.

The raid on the agency attracted a good deal of attention from the Mesilla *Independent*, but the news was so conflicting that it is hard to determine what the sequel was. Rumors piled up with incredible rapidity under the general excitement. The *Independent* even ran a circumstantial account of an attack upon the Jesse Evans band in a hide-out in the Guadalupe Mountains, stating that Jesse Evans, Nicolas Provincio, George Davis, and another member of the crowd had been killed by the pursuing posse. The item seems to have been made up out of the whole cloth, the wish being father to the thought. What is rather probable is that Brady, the sheriff, got together a posse and possibly had an encounter with the band. At any rate, someone at Lincoln signing himself "Eyewitness" wrote to the *Independent* on August 16:

> Sheriff Brady deserves great credit for the prompt action in this matter. He is now on the tracks of the gang of outlaws and you may look out for them your way soon, as it is getting too sickly for them here.
> Information has just been received here of a fight between the outlaws and the troops. We do not know of the result except that the thieves got whipped. Nelson [a desperate character from the Gila] was at the head of the band who no doubt will be run down into your country. We are organizing a militia company here for the protection of our lives and property.

Whatever may have happened to the banditti in August, they were up to their old tricks again by the middle of September. This time they made an onslaught upon Dick Brewer's ranch on the Ruidoso and carried off some horses and mules belonging to Brewer, Tunstall, and McSween. The following letter from McSween which appeared in the Mesilla *Independent* indicates briefly what took place:

Lincoln, N. Mex.
September 18, 1877

Editor, *Independent*,

This forenoon my horses and those of Mr. Tunstall were stolen from a ranch on the Rio Ruidoso. I valued my horses at seven hundred dollars. Tunstall's cost over a thousand dollars. Two of mine were fine American horses. Among Tunstall's were one of the handsomest team of mules in this section of the country.

Good citizens are in pursuit of the thieves and I hope they will overtake them and plunder.

For the recovery of these animals we will pay a liberal reward. The thieves were seen driving off the animals. "The boys" are known.

Yours,
A. A. McSween

These horses, at least Tunstall's, were part of the equipment for his cattle ranch placed for the time being with Dick Brewer, who was foreman of the Tunstall ranch. For several months Tunstall had been so completely absorbed in starting the store that the development of the ranch had temporarily fallen into abeyance. He had picked a good property in the former Mathews and Freeman place on the Peñasco, for it included valuable springs of a larger and much more desirable tract on the headwaters of the Rio Feliz. At once he had made provisional filings on it under the Desert Land Act and looked forward to developing his ranch energetically, using some 400 head of cattle he had bought for the nucleus of his herd.

Luck had played into his hands in getting these cattle. At a public sale of some of the Casey cattle he had bought the lot at bargain price, which represented about half their value. Not being inclined to profit by another's financial adversity, Tunstall had informed Mrs. Robert Casey, the former owner of the cattle, that if the judgment necessitating the sale could be satisfied in some other way within a reasonable time, the cattle might be had back for the price paid plus moderate interest. In this transaction as indeed in all others Tunstall tried to be entirely fair while still being sure of his ground. His father, writing from England, had repeatedly urged that he be careful about titles first and always, and Tunstall had found the advice congenial.

In selecting men for the ranch he had tried to employ only those who were both honest and competent. The selection of Dick Brewer as foreman was in every way commendable. For helpers he had to choose among the flotsam and jetsam in Lincoln County and had picked John Middleton, Fred Waite, William Bonney, and possibly one or two others as among the most promising. In all matters relating to the ranch, Tunstall was acting for himself exclusively, although McSween was advisor and occasionally agent. That their interests, however, were considerably intertwined, the note to the *Independent* indicates.

As soon as the theft was discovered, Brewer enlisted the aid of two neighbors, Charlie Bowdre and Doc Scurlock, who were at the moment leading quiet lives on their farm after the fight that ended Frank Freeman's career. They started in pursuit of the thieves, who had gone westward toward Doña Ana County, probably intending to reach some hide-out on the east side of the Organ Mountains. At San Nicholas spring they divided, Brewer going alone to Mesilla to try to get warrants from a justice of the peace, while Bowdre and Scurlock went to Shedd's ranch near the San Augustin Pass to see if they could learn news about "the boys." If anywhere in that vicinity they would turn up at Shedd's ranch, notorious as a clearing house for stolen stock.

Their expectations were completely fulfilled. They found the four stolen horses at Shedd's in possession of Jesse Evans, Nicolas Provencia, Frank Baker, Tom Hill, and three others of the band. When Scurlock and Bowdre demanded the animals, the band refused to give them up, saying sneeringly that they had gone to too much trouble to get them. All that was left for Scurlock and Bowdre to do was to continue on to Mesilla and report to Dick Brewer.

The Doña Ana County officials flatly refused to lend Brewer any support or cooperation against their friends at Shedd's; and since he was unwilling to use any but lawful means to recover the stolen animals, there was nothing for Brewer to do except return to Lincoln and report to McSween and Tunstall. The horse thieves seemingly went on over to Grant County, an old stamping ground for several of them, but after a few weeks they rode back toward Lincoln County. At least that was the editorial view of the *Mesilla Valley Independent* for October 13, 1877, which contained the following account of the movements of Jesse Evans and his band together with glimpses of their treatment of the populace along their route.

THE BANDITTI

After having supplied themselves with a fresh outfit of horses in Grant County and elsewhere, "Captain" Evans and his party crossed the Rio Grande moving eastward. They stopped awhile at San Augustin where they supplied the inner man with the choicest viands to be found on Mr. Shedd's table, and then took the main road to Tulerosa. Near Whitewater they left a fine bay horse dead on the road, probably one of the animals recently "appropriated" in Grant County. On arriving at Tulerosa, the "Captain" and his party extended to themselves the hospitality of that quiet village and manifested a creditable degree of modesty in their demands. After indulging in a big drunk, and having fired a hundred or more shots promiscuously about the town as a parting salute, they moved on up the Tulerosa.

At the house of one Sylvestre ————— (who on a former occasion had appeared as a witness against one of "the boys"), they made another familiar call and treated the humble and defenceless occupants to a specimen of their marksmanship by shooting a dog and riddling the entire house with bullets. The frantic appeals of the helpless man to spare the lives of his sick children only excited these "gentlemen" to shouts of derisive laughter. Late in the afternoon they halted at a store of the Trader near the Indian Agency; here they interviewed our old friend John Ryan who was in charge of the store, and demanded provisions and other supplies, which were, of course, furnished. A portion of the proceeds of the former raid made by these gentlemen upon the Indian Agency was the mare belonging to Miss Lou Godfroy, daughter of Major Godfroy, the Indian Agent. Miss Godfroy prized the animal highly and was deeply grieved at her loss. The bold raiders had this animal with them, and "Captain" Evans upon his arrival at the store, informed Mr. Ryan that he had heard the mare belonged to a young lady and that his gallantry forbade his retaining her property without her consent — in fact he would scorn to retain the animal under such circumstances (especially as the mare had been badly used and was no longer serviceable) and requested Mr. Ryan to deliver the animal to its owner with his ("Captain" Evans) affectionate kiss. Here they made inquiries as to when the members of the court from Lincoln County would be along, asked as to the whereabouts of other obnoxious parties, and moved on.

Near the summit of the Sacramento Mountains they went into camp for the night, placing sentinels out to guard against surprise. About 8 o'clock p.m. Messrs. Riley and Longwell came along in a buggy; the sentinel, on hearing their approach, gave an "owl hoot" as a warning to his comrades, which was responded to at once by those in camp. Riley and Longwell passed within a few feet of the guard, an American, who responded to their greeting in Spanish, and on passing, the entire party, numbering seventeen well armed and mounted men, paraded on the roadside. Near the Agency they separated, one party going up the Tulerosa; the other went toward the Ruidoso.

The same issue of the *Independent* contained a contribution from Lincoln by someone signing himself "Fence Rail," burlesquing the cool way the Jesse Evans contingent thumbed their noses at officers of the law or anyone else who tried to thwart their activities.

GRAND REUNION OF "THE BOYS"

Lincoln, N. M. Oct. 9th, 1877

Editors *Independent:*

I am requested to furnish you with a copy of the proceedings of a reunion held "at rendezvous in the Sacramento Mountains" on this day, which are as follows:

"At a reunion of 'prominent citizens' of Southern New Mexico held at one of their numerous rendezvous on this 9th day of October A.D. 1877, Captain Jesse Evans took the stump (which served as a chair) and after having congratulated the gentlemen of the road present on the brilliant record they had recently made in the line of their profession, announced that the object of the present reunion was to compare notes, perfect their organization, and prepare a plan for the coming campaign. Nor was this all; they had received valuable assistance in their labors from citizens who were not so prominent as they, and it was but *justice* (here a murmur was heard, Captain Evans begged pardon for having made use of the unpalatable word, and proceeded) it was but right that they should award honor where honor was due. The first thing to be done was to perfect their organization.

This business was concluded with the following result. Captain Jesse Evans was promoted to the colonel. Nick Provencio and Frank Baker, on account of their proficiency in horse stealing, etc. were elected captains, and all the balance of the band were made captain by brevet. The following resolutions were then adopted:

'Resolved: That we return our warmest thanks to our friends and sympathizers who have so disinterestedly harbored and sheltered us, who have furnished us with provisions and ammunition, who have assisted us to dispose of the proceeds of our labors, retaining not more than 50 per cent of the gross profits.

'Resolved: That those who have so generously and continuously warned us of every effort being made by the despotic, tyrannical and arbitrary authorities of Southern New Mexico to deprive us of our liberties and incarcerate us in their vile dungeons, we return thanks, and add that in the opinion of this band, an occasional beef steer is inadequate compensation for the valuable information furnished us by these faithful friends.

'Resolved: That that portion of the press of New Mexico which notwithstanding our many open and notorious robbers and murders has persistently denied that organized lawlessness exists in Southern New Mexico and which has held us to the public as paragons of virtue and honesty, is entitled to favorable mention. Having no further use for the services of such champions, however, (we having reached the conclusion that even murder and horse stealing cannot be made respectable by our friendly newspaper correspondents and editors) we hereby reconsider our intention to present each one of our said champion editors and correspondents with one of the next bunch of horses that we shall appropriate.

'Resolved: That we shall take the first opportunity of getting even with the "*Independent* clan" and regret that an unwillingness to experience the disagreeable sensation of "pulling hemp" has operated as an obstruction to carrying into execution heretofore our intentions in this regard. In the meantime we applaud those newspapers who abuse the *Independent* in our interest.

'Resolved: That the public is our oyster, and that having the power, we claim the right to appropriate any property we may take a fancy to, and that we shall exercise that right regardless of consequences.'

These resolutions having been adopted Captain Nicholas Provencio produced a copy of the *Independent*, a huge fire was built, and the obnoxious paper was thrown into the flames. The gang, headed by Colonel Evans, now marched around the pyre to the inspiring strains of the "Rogues' March" performed by Captain Baker on a fine tooth comb."

Fence Rail

Early in October it became common knowledge that Jesse Evans and his followers were again at Beckwith's ranch at Seven Rivers. Promptly Tunstall and McSween determined upon another attempt to capture them, this time making use of the sheriff. After much prodding, Brady bestirred himself enough to accompany a posse to Seven Rivers. Court had been in session; doubtless this had something to do with Brady's effort. Tunstall bore all the expense even to furnishing arms and equipment; Brewer, the real leader, saw to it that the personnel included men he could count on. The expedition was successful; four outstanding members of the banditti were brought back to Lincoln and deposited in the jail.

The occurrence inspired two letters to the *Independent* dated at Lincoln, October 20, neither signed with the true name of the writer. Considering the well-known reluctance of Brady to accompany the posse, the correspondent signing himself "Ewing" achieved a rare note of irony, if not sarcasm:

Editors Independent:

About 2 o'clock this afternoon, Sheriff Brady and posse came into town having in their possession Jesse Evans, Frank Baker, Tom Hill and George Davis. They were followed and arrested after a feeble resistance early on the 17th day of October at Beckwith's ranch, Seven Rivers, New Mexico.

Regretting that there should be an occasion for such a display of civil authority, one can but rejoice that its execution fell into hands so efficient, and its termination was so peaceful and life saving. Although force had to be resorted to before final acquiescence to constituted authority, still there are no "life wounds" or corpses to add "regrets" to expended powder and ball.

To Sheriff Brady is owing *entirely* the projection and skillful consummation of the order of arrest from the last district court. Too frequent sins against our worthy and vigilant sheriff have been bandied about in reference to his ability to carry out justice in opposition to certain friends of his. To all such "croakers" I can now safely say: *forever afterwards hold your peace.*

In the face of a sudden and terrible storm of snow and rain, insufficiently appointed in food and clothing, facing *expected death* in case of collision, our sheriff boldly pushed on and crowned his arduous pursuit with complete success.

As chief, all hail to our noble and deserving Sheriff Brady. We are proud of that noble and self-sacrificing posse (all residents of our renowned county) who so cheerfully followed and ventured with the determined leader.

The *chiefs of that band* are now lodged securely in the new jail at this place. And, we trust, being now cared for by the law's course will be permitted to go to its finality

D. H. Ewing

The second letter might be construed as an invitation for the outlaw friends to help them:

Dear Editors:

Let it be told in Doña Ana and published in Grant that Jesse Evans, Tom Hill, George Davis, and Frank Baker are this evening in the Lincoln County Jail. Our Sheriff and posse have rounded them up.

They had one of Mr. Tunstall's horses in their possession, as also Mr. P. M. Chisum's riding horses. These have been delivered to their owners.

"The Boys" at this writing are playing cards in the dungeon. They are outspoken and brave. They speak of their friends succoring them; we want to see their *friends*.

They were shown their resolutions as published in the last *Independent*, and they expressed a desire to promote Mr. Fountain. They said they will beat that in a future issue of their News; they said the dying "Echo" would be heard like the roar of a cannonade.

Mesilla *News* and Las Cruces *Eco* please copy.

Yours,
Order

Exactly a month later a correspondent of the *Independent* signing himself "Lincoln," probably McSween, wrote in a different tenor entirely. The rescue for which the captured leaders of the "banditti" had hoped was carried out. Once more they were at large and "Lincoln's" letter gave the details, although somewhat meagerly.

Lincoln, N. Mex.
Dec. 3rd, 1877

Messrs. Editors:

In detailing the escape of "the boys" from our three thousand dollar jail, I stated they stole five horses from Brewer's ranch. I should have said eight. They done a vast amount of promiscuous shooting at Brewer's — excessive joy frequently causes wanton acts. Hours before they left Brewer's, every man, woman, and child, justice, constable, and sheriff knew that they were there, but none of us could be induced to make any effort to re-arrest them.

Since that Saturday morning that shrouded us in disgrace we have maintained the silence of the dead in these matters. Among the rescuers of "the boys" was their ally and champion, the famous Pasha Boyle, the distinguished historian of the "Pecos War," having by that history gained by clear right to be called the champion falsifier of 1877.

On their way to the Feliz, they met Juan Trujillo and borrowed his saddle, gun, and pistol, for Don Lucas Gallegos. They refreshed the inner man and cleaned the outer at the Feliz. From there they went to R. M. Beckwith's. Here they related their hairbreadth escape, left their jaded horses, and started to hunt for others.

We have recently heard from them. They were between Fort Stanton and Major Murphy's cow camp, and were there seen and interviewed. Lucas Gallegos was the spokesman. He told our informant that McSween's, Patrón's and Montaño's death warrants had been signed.

The last *Eco* comments on my last to you. This was "the unkindest cut of all." Every word of my statement is true. The *Eco's* supposition is reasonable but the facts are against him. They are as stated by me. The escape of these men is a disgrace to our officers charged with their keeping and an irreparable injury to our county and territory.

Lincoln

P.S. After the escape the cells were found to be liberally supplied with files, knives, and augers, as also cotton sacks with rocks weighing from ten to twenty pounds. How's that for vigilance?

The jail delivery at once produced a sharp cleavage of opinion at Lincoln and added abundantly to the crop of grudges and jealousies in the town. A few days later came a personal clash between Brady and Tunstall. Brady, half intoxicated, went into the Tunstall store and indirectly accused him of giving credit for the arrest of the Jesse Evans contingent to Brewer. As the conversation grew heated, Brady launched the charge that Tunstall had aided the prisoners in preparing for their escape. Tunstall riddled such accusation by saying, "You know their shackles are filed and they have holes cut in the logs. Yet you take no pains to secure them; and now you dare to accuse me, who aided in their arrest, with assisting them to escape — those persons who have threatened my life. Nothing could be more absurd."

This reply angered Brady and his hand moved toward his revolver. McSween, standing near, promptly stepped between the two and placing his hand on Brady's shoulder said, "Major, remember you are a peace officer. It ill becomes you to violate the law yourself by shooting some one." Brady's hand moved back from his pistol, but he blustered at Tunstall as he turned to leave. "I won't shoot you now, but you haven't long to run. I ain't always going to be sheriff."

A few days later the four important prisoners had escaped, along with Lucas Gallegos, in custody for killing Sostero García in January, 1877, at San Patricio. The guarding of the jail had not intensified; if anything, it had been relaxed. When a party of some twenty-five or thirty associates and sympathizers, mainly from the lower part of the county, came on the night of November 17 or 18, there was little need of their aid. The prisoners and the party of rescuers hurried away from Lincoln without opposition and proceeded to Brewer's ranch on the Ruidoso, bent on a festival of plunder and revenge.

The escape from the Lincoln jail brought conditions in Lincoln County more generally into the limelight. In Governor Axtell's message to the territorial legislature, which convened a few months later, there was a section of comment under the heading "Bad White Men:"

Besides mad Indians we have bad white men who need the strong hand of government to restrain them from preying on their fellow men. I will cite a recent instance from Lincoln County for the purpose of stimulating you to memorialize Congress to permit the regular army to aid civil authorities of New Mexico to preserve the public peace.

Four desperate men, outlaws and robbers, were roaming over Lincoln County; the sheriff raised a posse of some 30 men, surrounded their camp and made them prisoners. He brought them to Lincoln, within 9 miles of Fort Stanton, and confined them in such a jail as a new county and a poor county is able to furnish. The confederates of the prisoners collected in the vicinity to the number, it is said, of some 30 men, and gave out publicly that they intended to rescue them. The sheriff applied to the commander of Fort Stanton for troops to protect his jail; the troops could not be furnished. Capain Purington, the commander of Fort Stanton, is as good a man as there is in the army, but he had no authority to grant this request. The rescue was made, and these desperadoes were set at liberty. These men had among other crimes stolen horses from the Mescalero Indian Agency belonging to the United States; they had been indicted in United States district court; yet United States troops within 9 miles of the place could not be employed to guard them. These four men and the 20 or 30 who rescued them are still at large, fired by revenge and bent on raping and murder. Yet four companies of United States troops are standing idly by, fettered and entangled by somebody's theories.

Governor Axtell, it seems, was inclined to attribute the disturbing conditions to the fact that Captain Purington was so fettered by the orders from the War Department that he could not help Brady when the sheriff needed him. The Governor raised the question whether an exception ought not to be made in the case of a territory like New Mexico and the troops used in the "service of criminal process, . . . keep the prisoners at the guardhouses of the post." Thus at this early stage arose the problem of how far the soldiers could support the civil authorities. As time went on it grew in importance and became the very pragmatic question of which faction could secure the support of the "military," as it was generally termed.

For the next few weeks after their escape Jesse Evans and his companions were conspicuous by their absence from Lincoln County. They and some of the others of the same inclination, including Andy Boyle, responded to the call of Sheriff Kerber to come into the El Paso section and help put down the outbreak known as the San Elizario Salt War.

The Mexicans, indignant at being deprived of an ancient privilege of helping themselves to these salt beds now under the ownership of an American, were rioting in a way that threatened to grow into a general massacre of Americans. Sheriff Kerber, unable to raise the hundred special rangers he was authorized to enlist, telegraphed to New Mexico for recruits. The Rio Pecos county sent its quota along with Silver City and Mesilla.

In the meantime Widenmann, who had secured an appointment as a deputy United States marshal, was on the lookout for the Jesse Evans gang with some United States warrants charging them with stealing horses from the Indians. Learning that they had returned to Lincoln County and were staying with L. G. Murphy at his ranch, he made an attempt to arrest them but failed to find them. The interesting point of the attempt, however, was that he found convincing evidence of their having been at the ranch, although Major Murphy vigorously denied it. Widenmann's effort served to confirm the report that, although long divorced from "The House" and its activities at Lincoln, L. G. Murphy was sometimes still able to protect his friends from the law.

PART II

The Flame Is Kindled

11. Wrangle Over the Fritz Insurance

WITH THE JESSE EVANS CONTINGENT off stage for awhile, Lincoln developed a stir-up from another angle. Scratch beneath the surface and you will find one thing as the prime mover in most of the Lincoln County troubles — money. In this case it was proceeds from a $10,000 life insurance policy taken out by Emil Fritz in favor of the beneficiaries of his estate. At Colonel Fritz's death in June, 1874, the insurance company failed to make payment, and the following May, Fritz's surviving partner, L. G. Murphy, placed the estate's accounts receivable in the hands of attorney McSween for collection. In accordance with the instructions of Mrs. Emilie Fritz Scholand and Charles Fritz, administrators of the Emil Fritz estate, McSween at his own expense went to St. Louis and on to New York in October, 1876, spending two months trying to effect collection. Although the insurance company was said to be insolvent and in the hands of receivers, McSween was finally successful in obtaining settlement. On August 1, 1877, Donnell, Lawson & Co., the New York financial firm which had assisted in the settlement, notified McSween that his account had been credited with $7,148.94, the net proceeds of the policy after deducting the firm's fees and expenses. No sooner had McSween notified Mrs. Scholand and Mr. Fritz that the supposedly uncollectable claim had been settled, than J. J. Dolan, successor to L. G. Murphy & Co., set up claim for the whole amount, basing it on an alleged indebtedness of Fritz to the firm. The Dolan store was in financial distress and the insurance company money would have been a veritable bonanza. McSween, however,

[95]

resisted stubbornly all importunities and maneuvers, not only because he believed the claim invalid but also because he wished to safeguard the interests of all heirs to the estate. He felt that besides the brother, Charles Fritz, who lived on the Fritz ranch near Lincoln, and the sister, Mrs. Scholand, who was at the time living in Las Cruces, there were probably other heirs living in Germany. He was determined to have the matter closed equitably and legally, and for a few months was able to check the various efforts of the Dolan firm to get their hands on the money.

In December, however, the firm sprang a coup obviously designed and largely executed by Dolan. On the eighteenth McSween started for St. Louis accompanied by Mrs. McSween and his client and friend, John Chisum. No secrecy surrounded the trip. All had been planned weeks in advance and announcement made generally that it was in the interest of Chisum business. Very openly McSween had busied himself in putting his business affairs in shape for an absence of several weeks. The trip was also for the benefit of Mrs. McSween, whose nerves were proving unequal to the strain of life in Lincoln County.

As soon as the party started on its overland journey via Las Vegas to Trinidad, Colorado, the nearest railroad point, Dolan left Lincoln for Mesilla. At Las Cruces he called on Mrs. Scholand, who wrote and read the English language imperfectly, if at all, and easily induced her to sign an affidavit to the effect that she believed McSween was leaving the country for good and intended to convert the insurance money to his own use. Dolan took the affidavit, dated December 21 to District Attorney W. L. Rynerson to bring about the arrest of McSween on a charge of embezzlement. Rynerson wasted no time in informing his ally T. B. Catron, of Mrs. Scholand's affidavit.

Arriving at Las Vegas on Christmas Eve, both Chisum and McSween were detained by the San Miguel County sheriff, pending the receipt of a warrant charging McSween with embezzlement and a court order prohibiting Chisum from leaving the jurisdiction of the court, which papers were forthcoming according to a telegram received by the sheriff from Catron at Santa Fe. Catron and his law partner, W. T. Thornton, had as clients not only J. J. Dolan but certain other persons who were enemies of Chisum and who claimed to hold court judgments against him, including William Rosenthal, who had managed to secure the old notes on Wilbur, Chisum & Clark, the meat-packing project in Arkansas. The fact that the proposed partnership had never been consummated by Chisum and that his name on the notes was without his knowledge or consent did not deter his foes from using the unpaid notes as a weapon against him.

On a mere telegraphic request Chisum and McSween were held in Las Vegas forty-eight hours by the sheriff of San Miguel County. When no warrants came, they were able to convince the sheriff that they were entitled to freedom. Acting upon the advice of several Las Vegas attorneys, McSween and Chisum started on their way toward Trinidad. Hardly were they half a mile outside the town when they were overtaken by the sheriff accompanied by a large posse, some armed with pistols, some with rocks, and some with clubs, all united in stopping the vehicle in which the McSweens and Chisum were riding. With more force than was needed, McSween and Chisum were pulled from their carriage and Mrs. McSween treated with great rudeness. It was hardly needful for the sheriff to drag away the two men and leave Mrs. McSween sitting alone in the vehicle on the roadside without driver or protector. Chisum, who seems to have taken the whole experience with *sang-froid*, had to allay Mrs. McSween's fright by prevailing upon a responsible young Mexican to drive her back to the Wagoner Hotel.

In the ensuing legal moves, McSween's case was soon settled. The whole affair seemed so much of a frame-up that he scorned all proposals of compromise and insisted on going back and facing the charges. By making light of the affair he prevailed on Mrs. McSween to continue the journey to St. Louis, feeling that her highly nervous condition could not fail to be helped by an absence from Lincoln. Chisum, however, was less tractable to the schemes of his enemies. That streak of stubbornness which had appeared in all the controversy connected with the packinghouse transaction came to the front and he set himself doggedly to countercheck his enemies. Catron and Thornton had invoked an old statute which imposed imprisonment when a person against whom a judgment had been procured refused to list his assets. Chisum had presented what seemed to be a very modest list, especially as he was known to be selling out to Hunter and Evans, and so his enemies proceeded to apply the whip. In a spirit of spite he let them exert the extreme measure and endured about eight weeks of confinement at Las Vegas without succumbing to their demand for a new and complete rendering of his assets. To while away the tedium he wrote out an account of the whole matter, trying to show that he was the butt of hostility for the Santa Fe ring.

On January 4, 1878, McSween left Las Vegas in charge of two San Miguel deputy sheriffs, A. P. Barrier and Antonio Campos. When the party reached Lincoln, they learned that Judge Bristol was not at Mesilla. Barrier, a sympathetic and accommodating custodian, allowed McSween to remain at Lincoln for two or three weeks in order to look after business matters. During this period McSween prepared a review of his actions as attorney for the Fritz estate and made it public through the *Eco del Rio Grande*, a Las Cruces newspaper.

Lincoln, N. M.
January 10, 1878

Mr. Lapoint:

Dear sir: — An editorial paragraph in the *Eco* of the 3rd inst. does me great injustice. By written contract and general power of attorney with and from Mrs. Emilie Scholand and Mr. Charles Fritz, administratrix and administrator of the estate of Emil Fritz, deceased, I became attorney of said estate during the month of October, 1876. Agreeably to an understanding previously had with them, I went to New York to ascertain the real condition of the policy on Col. Fritz' life. Whilst there, as Messrs. Donnell, Lawson & Co., 92 Broadway, will bear testimony, efforts were made by certain parties to compel me to accept fifty cents on the dollar in full for the policy. When it was found I would not compromise, it was said that the whole claim was lost through my obstinacy. In order to get the policy out of the hands of the party having it, seven to eight hundred dollars had to be paid. Upon payment of this sum the policy was reluctantly surrendered. The matter was then put in the hands of Donnell, Lawson & Co., aforesaid. I was absent on this business two months. I paid all the expenses of the trip out of my own pocket. Immediately on my return I informed Mrs. Scholand and Mr. Fritz of what I had done. I filed with the clerk of probate an account of every cent necessarily expended by me during the trip — where and to whom I paid.

In May, 1875, Maj. Murphy, the surviving partner of Col. Fritz, placed the estate's accounts in my hands for collection. Upon all payments, as reported by him, I charged ten per cent.

In December, 1876, I notified the administrator and administratrix that during the January 1877 term of our probate court I would present my account against the estate of Colonel Fritz for allowance. Mrs. Scholand acknowledged service of said notice, but was not present during said term. Mr. Fritz, however, was present and approved my account, as did also the probate judge. The amount of the account was $3,815.15.

August 1st, 1877, I was informed by Donnell, Lawson & Co. that they had credited my account $7,148.94, that sum being the proceeds of the policy after the deduction of their fees. Under that date I wrote to Mrs. Scholand and Mr. Fritz that the policy was paid and that I was ready to settle with them.

J. B. Patron and J. B. Wilson held approved claims against the estate to the amount of $280; these I paid by order of Mr. Fritz.

I told Mr. Fritz repeatedly that I was ready, anxious and willing to pay the balance in my hands over to him and Mrs. Scholand; that if Mrs. Scholand could not come in person she could authorize him or some other person to receive the money for her.

I was never asked to settle, nor did I promise or agree "to surrender the amount at the next session of probate court."

I was requested to go to St. Louis on business for Col. Hunter. Every man, woman, and child in the town knew I was going three weeks before I left. Before leaving I wrote Captain Crouch, Judge Bristol, Judge Newcomb, and Mrs. Fountain of my contemplated trip, how long I expected to be absent, &c. Two or three days before leaving Mr. Fritz called at my office and asked if I would pay him a specific sum of money; I replied in the affirmative. I told him I was going; how long I expected to be absent; that Mrs. Shield of this place would have charge of my business during my absence; that when Mrs. Scholand came over or sent her order, the balance in my hands would be paid. I left in my own private conveyance for the railroad. After reaching Las Vegas I was informed that certain parties had telegraphed to know if I were there. I told my informant to telegraph that I was. I waited 24 hours to know what was wanted. The sheriff of San Miguel was ordered by telegraph to arrest me; he did so. I offered to waive all formalities and give bonds in $20,000 that I would appear before Judge Bristol within ten days and answer; this was refused.

I remitted Mrs. Scholand some money at the suggestion of a member of the Doña Ana bar. L. G. Murphy, surviving partner &c, recently filed claims against the estate to the amount of $76,000 (seventy-six thousand dollars!). The whole of this claim was this day disallowed by Judge Gonzales, for want of evidence. On the other hand, taking Maj. Murphy's own statement, the surviving partner owes the estate over thirty thousand dollars, so that his claim to the insurance money has "faded."

It has been said that every man has his price, but ten thousand dollars and interest is not my price; for whilst I continue acting honestly and uprightly, I can easily command double that sum if necessary. In addition to all this my personal and real interests in this town of Lincoln far exceed the amount of money in my hands belonging to the Fritz estate. The sheriff of San Miguel County offered to compromise the matter and allow me to go east; I declined to do so even though he would accept one dollar in full discharge.

Hoping that a sense of fairness will secure the foregoing a prominent place in your next issue,

I am your obedient servant,
Alex A. McSween,
Attorney for the Estate of
E. Fritz, Deceased.

The Dolan interests published no reply to McSween's letter. The nearest to an official statement from them came six months later when the government agent, Judge Frank W. Angel, elicited an affidavit from Dolan. McSween also submitted his account, virtually the same as that in the *Eco del Rio Grande*, although less succinct. The Dolan affidavit set forth the other side of the wrangle as follows:

The cause of the present troubles is that Alexander A. McSween tried to defraud the Fritz estate of $10,000 insurance, or rather the proceeds of a policy for that sum. There were no troubles before this. I know of no other cause for these later troubles. . . .

In relation to the Fritz estate, the papers are in the exclusive charge of Judge Newcomb at Mesilla and W. T. Thornton at Santa Fe. I can give no detailed statement for this reason. My partner and I have paid about $30,000 of the indebtedness of the old firm of L. G. Murphy & Co., which was composed of L. G. Murphy and Emil Fritz, deceased. I was bookkeeper for the firm at the time of Fritz's death, and at that time the firm was insolvent.

As to the $23,000 found by the commissioners, McSween, Patron, and Christie, this amount was found by taking the good and bad debts into account, no deduction being made for bad debts and no allowance being made for $57,000 which Murphy had paid individually on account of said estate.

About December 1st, I had a conversation with McSween as to the Fritz estate and the money collected on the insurance policy. I told him I was desirous of having the estate matter settled up and requested him to call a special session of the probate court, if it was possible. He said it was and that he would have it done. But he kept putting it off from time to time, until I saw Judge Gonzales and had him call a special session for December 10th, I think. On that day I attended, as did also Fritz, administrator, Sheriff Brady, D. P. Shield, F. G. Christie, and Rafael Gutierrez.

McSween was sent for and came, saying that he was ready to pay over the money if Mrs. Scholand, the co-administrator, was present. I and the others informed him that the parties were very much troubled about the matter, and wanted the money. We requested him in order to quiet every one to deposit the money

with the court subject to the order of the court. This he refused
to do. The result was court adjournment to the first Monday in
January, 1878, at which time Mrs. Scholand was to be present,
she to be notified by the clerk of the court. The understanding was
that the money was then to be paid over. McSween made no objection and said nothing about his going away and consequently
being unable to be present.

Before the meeting of the court, McSween left for St. Louis,
as every one believed, never to come back. I went down to Mesilla
and communicated the facts to Mrs. Scholand. Thereupon
McSween was arrested and brought back to Mesilla on the charge
of embezzlement.

The only interest I had in the money was to have the court
decide to whom it belonged — whether it belonged to us or
whether the estate should keep it. My interest in the money arose
out of the fact that L. G. Murphy & Co. had a claim against the
estate. There had never been a suit or any other legal proceedings
held on this claim, and I have been informed Charles Fritz refused
to recognize it. This was the only claim I had against the estate.
The amount of the claim was about $57,000.

I went to Mesilla directly after meeting McSween in court
December 10th because I became suspicious of McSween and
believed he never intended to pay the insurance money over. My
only object in going to Mesilla was to obtain legal advice and
secure counsel to represent me before the probate judge at Lincoln on the third Monday in January. While I was at Mesilla,
word was brought by James Longwell that McSween had left
for St. Louis. I did not go to Mesilla expressly to see Mrs. Scholand. I do not remember whether I called upon her before I
received the information or whether I called on her afterwards.

When Judge Bristol returned to Mesilla, McSween, escorted by
Deputy Sheriff Barrier, and Tunstall, eager to help his friend and business advisor in all possible ways, left Lincoln for Mesilla. Included
in the party were McSween's brother-in-law, attorney David P. Shield,
as well as Squire Wilson and others of McSween's friends. The party
reached Mesilla on January 28th but Judge Bristol postponed the
examination until Saturday, February 2. As Sunday intervened, it was
a rather long, drawn-out proceeding, lasting until Monday, February
4. District Attorney Rynerson, openly antagonistic, was reported as
being harsh, in fact almost insulting, in his questioning of McSween.
Even Judge Bristol seemed to display considerable prejudice. One of
McSween's most important winesses, Juan P. Patrón, was not present
because he could not get excused from the legislature then in session.

Another, Florencio Gonzales, the probate judge of Lincoln County, was absent also. Judge Bristol acquiesced to a continuance until the meeting of the grand jury at Lincoln in early April.

The inconclusive outcome of the hearing at Mesilla brought about the question of bail. Judge Bristol agreed to allow it, fixing the amount at $8,000 and leaving the approval to the district attorney, Rynerson. Barrier was ordered to take McSween back to Lincoln and turn him over to the sheriff of Lincoln County who would hold him in custody until bond was made.

12. Dolan Tries to Badger Tunstall

ON FEBRUARY 5 McSWEEN started back to Lincoln in the custody of Barrier. On the return trip he was accompanied by several of those who had come over with him to Mesilla, either as friends or as witnesses. By sundown of the first day out the party had reached Shedd's ranch on the eastern slope of the Organ Mountains, not far from San Augustin Pass, and proceeded as was customary to make camp there for the night. Shortly after establishing themselves Jesse Evans put in an appearance, accompanied by two of his associates, Frank Baker (alias Hart) and John Long (alias John Longmont, alias Frank Rivers, alias Jack Long). The pretext for the visit was that they wanted to know if the McSween party had passed Dolan on the road. Shield, brother-in-law of McSween, acting as spokesman, replied that they had not seen anything of Dolan. He also added that he had understood that Dolan did not plan to leave before the morning of the sixth. Frank Baker, who was inclined to "shoot off his mouth," said with great assurance that they had always found Jimmie very punctual with his engagement and felt sure he would come that night.

All this was not very reassuring to the McSween group. They one and all recalled the threats Jesse Evans and his followers had made a few months before against the lives of both Tunstall and McSween for having them arrested for stealing horses from Dick Brewer's place. They realized that such desperate fellows were capable of carrying out their threats. Particularly ominous was it to encounter them at a lonely and remote spot like Shedd's ranch with its sinister reputation as one of the hangouts of the banditti. Neither was it reassuring that the next day's journey had to be across the desolate valley between the Organ Mountains and the Sacramento Mountains, in which lay the vast dunes of the white sands.

About one or two o'clock in the night Dolan arrived with some of his companions and went into camp some little distance from that of the McSween party. Nothing untoward developed between the two bivouacs until the next morning about eight or nine o'clock. While the McSween party was having breakfast, McSween caught sight of two men apparently trying to slip up close to their camp under cover of a corral wall. These two men, whom he took to be Dolan and Jesse Evans, had emerged furtively from the ranch house some distance away and rounded the corner of the corral. Dolan threw down his Winchester carbine on Tunstall, at the same time demanding whether he was ready to fight and settle their difficulties. In some confusion as to what Dolan meant, Tunstall countered with the question, "Do you want me to fight a duel?" Dolan replied, "You damn coward, I want you to fight and settle our difficulties." His words were accompanied by moving his rifle, which he was holding in his hands at full cock, toward his shoulder as if about to aim.

Barrier quickly stepped between Dolan and Tunstall and brought the quarrel to a less desperate stage. As Dolan turned away he muttered at Tunstall, "You won't fight this morning, you damn coward, but I'll get you soon." When he had gone away some twenty yards he turned around and hurled as a parting jeer, "When you write to the *Independent* again, say I'm with 'the boys!"

Dolan's words disclosed what had set his teeth on edge as far as Tunstall was concerned. There had been cause for friction and ill-feeling in the past, ever since the Tunstall store had made inroads on the patronage of the Dolan store. This had reached an acute stage when Dolan came to believe, as he stated in his affidavit to Judge Angel, that Tunstall was spreading hurtful gossip about the Dolan store.

> They, that is McSween, John H. Tunstall, and John S. Chisum, and their employees, afterwards formed a combination to ruin me and my partner. They spread reports that our checks had been protested and sent untrue reports to commercial agencies at Denver and St. Louis as to our commercial standing stating that we were not worthy of credit. In order to contradict such reports, I went to Santa Fe and obtained a sworn statement from the acting cashier of the First National Bank of Santa Fe, with which we had always deposited our money, to the effect that our checks had never up to that time been protested.

I brought this back to Lincoln and showed it to McSween, who read it. I desire to add the name of Ellis Sons to the combination against us. Will Dowlin informed Mr. Howison, traveling agent of Dodd, Brown & Co. with whom we were dealing that we were broken up and he had better be careful of us. Howison afterwards informed my partner, John H. Riley, that he had applied to T. B. Catron of Santa Fe, who informed him that we were perfectly good and he would endorse our note for $10,000. This occurred last June, and before we had given a chattel mortgage on our property in Lincoln to Catron. Since then Catron has endorsed and advanced us more than $20,000. We gave the chattel mortgage voluntarily without his asking for it.

Dolan's words to Tunstall, however, related to a more recent occurrence. The message of Governor Axtell to the legislature which convened in the early part of January had contained a reference to the fact that Lincoln County was in arrears in its payment of tax funds into the territorial treasury. The stigma on the county had aroused Tunstall, who had ingrained repugnance for mishandling of public money, and who was just then boiling over in wrath because of what McSween was undergoing. He was entirely willing to strike back at those responsible for all the annoyance and damage McSween was being made to suffer. He therefore had sent the following letter to the *Independent*, published shortly before McSween's hearing at Mesilla:

OFFICE OF JOHN H. TUNSTALL

Lincoln, Lincoln County, N. M.
January 18, 1878

"The present sheriff of Lincoln County has paid nothing during his present term of office." — Governor's Message for 1878.
Editor of the *Independent:*
The above extract is a sad and unanswerable comment on the efficiency of Sheriff Brady and cannot be charged upon "croakers." Major Brady, as the records of this county show, collected over Twenty-five Hundred Dollars, Territorial funds. Of this sum Alexander A. McSween, Esq. of this place paid him over Fifteen Hundred Dollars by cheque on the First National Bank of Santa Fe, August 23, 1877. Said cheque was presented for payment by John H. Riley, Esq. of the firm of J. J. Dolan & Co. This last amount was paid by the last named gentleman to Underwood & Nash for cattle. Thus passed away over Fifteen Hundred Dollars belonging to the Territory of New Mexico. With the exception of Thirty-nine Dollars, all the taxes of Lincoln County for 1877 were promptly paid when due.

Let not Lincoln County suffer the delinquency of one, two or three men.

By the exercise of proper vigilance, the taxpayer can readily ascertain what has become of what he has paid for the implied protection of the commonwealth. It is not only his privilege but his duty. A delinquent taxpayer is bad: a delinquent tax collector is worse.

J. H. T.

Tunstall's letter added fuel to the fire. Dolan, who had journeyed over to Las Cruces in order to be on hand for the preliminary hearing, promptly offered the *Independent* the following letter, which was published.

Las Cruces, N. M., Jan. 29, 1878

To the Editor of the Independent,
Dear Sir:

In answer to a communication in reference to taxpayers of Lincoln County published in your issue of the 26th and signed J.H.T., I wish to state that everything contained therein is false.

In reference to Sheriff Brady, I will state that he deposited with our house Territorial funds amounting to nearly $2,000, subject to his order and payable on demand. Owing to sickness in the family of Sheriff Brady he was unable to be in Santa Fe in time to settle his account with the Territory. This I hope will explain satisfactorily how the Governor in his message had our county delinquent.

If Mr. J.H.T. was recognized as a gentleman and could be admitted into respectable circles in our community, he might be better posted on public affairs. For my part I can't see the object of Mr. J.H.T.'s letter, unless it is to have the public believe that Alexander A. McSween is one of the largest taxpayers in our county, when in fact he is one of the smallest.

Sheriff Brady is ready at any time to show uneasy taxpayers what disposition he has made of the money paid by them; he can also show clean receipts for the Territorial treasure for his account.

Respectfully,
J. J. Dolan

Dolan's letter betrayed the weakness of his firm's position in the matter. Having gotten wind of possible trouble when the arrearage was mentioned in the governor's message, Dolan had hastened to adjust the matter. The territorial treasurer's office might, as Dolan boasted in the last sentence of his letter, show that the money had been paid;

but it would not disclose that Catron had paid the money, January 9, out of the proceeds of some Indian vouchers made out to Riley and forwarded by him to the bank for deposit. Besides, there was a telltale cancelled check that ultimately came back to McSween and was submitted as an exhibit to his statement filed with Judge Angel. This check, dated August 23, 1877, was drawn to the order of Sheriff Brady and was for $1,543.03 in territorial script. The endorsements were "Wm. Brady, sheriff and ex-officio collector," and "Jno H. Riley."

Dolan's version of the clash between him and Tunstall at Shedd's ranch, submitted to Judge Angel, may be set beside that of McSween which has been followed in the main in the preceding account. It consisted of mere categorical denials, but such as it is, it is given:

> I left Mesilla on February 5th. At San Augustin I heard that Tunstall, McSween, Barrier, Shields, and Squire Wilson were there. The next morning I went to their camp to see Tunstall about the letter he had written the *Independent*, which was untruthful, and about his attempt to injure us. These facts made me angry; I was armed; I talked to Tunstall in a very severe manner. He acted in a very childish manner. I tried in every way to see if he was a man. He made no resistance although he was armed. I did not drop my carbine on him; I only threw it over my shoulder with the butt towards him.
>
> I told him I was ready to give him any satisfaction he wanted. I made no threats against him. I never said, "When you write the *Independent*, say I am with the 'boys,'" or any words to that effect. Any assertion to the contrary by any one is absolutely false. I went there to take no advantage of him. My gun was neither loaded nor cocked, nor did I sneak up to where he was. I wanted him to stop his lying statements about me or stand accountable for his assertions to me personally. That was the only object I had in going to see him.
>
> Jesse Evans was standing in the corner of the stable near McSween's party's camp. He evidently saw I was excited and followed after me. He did not follow me by request, either directly or indirectly. I had no appointment or engagement with either Baker, Evans or Rivers to meet me at San Augustin or anywhere on the road, and any assertions to the contrary are absolutely false. The way Evans came to be riding with me in the ambulance from San Augustin was as follows: on account of his being wounded, Evans could not ride in a saddle. I am not positive whether he asked me or I asked him; at any rate I allowed him out of charity to ride with me in the ambulance. Baker and Rivers followed behind us on horseback. I must confess I was afraid I would be killed on the road, and I did not object to their following

after us. At Whitewater, I left Fritz, Longwell, Rivers and Evans, and went on to Tularosa on horseback, insisting on going alone. But nothwithstanding my request, Baker rode with me as far as Tularosa. Then he left me, and I went on alone to the Indian Agency, where I obtained conveyance and reached Lincoln.

The latter part of Dolan's statement was intended as a defense against another rather incriminating incident. When the McSween group had gone about twenty miles beyond Shedd's ranch, they had been passed by Dolan, Jesse Evans, and the trio that had awaited Dolan's arrival at Shedd's place. Riding with Dolan in his ambulance were Evans and Baker, while the other two were on horseback. Immediately panic spread throughout the McSween party. What could it mean but that they were hurrying on ahead in order to set an ambush somewhere, especially when the route wound up the Tularosa Canyon and then through the White Mountains?

The peace of mind of the McSween party was further disturbed when they reached the threshold of the ominous part of the journey. At the Mescalero Reservation they found Baker, Hill, and Long of the banditti hanging around and basking in the favor of the Indian agent, Godfroy, in spite of the fact that they had previously made raids on the horses of the Indians. Godfroy used the occasion to get Tunstall to straighten out a tangle in regard to one of the horses that had been among those stolen from Brewer's ranch the summer before by the Jesse Evans crowd. Godfroy had purchased the horse from Hill, but when the horses had been recovered this particular one had been taken along with the rest and placed on Tunstall's Feliz ranch. It had once been McSween's but McSween had disclaimed ownership, admitting that he had sold the animal. What Godfroy had wanted was an order from Tunstall for those in charge of the ranch to relinquish the animal. Tunstall did not hesitate about giving Godfroy a note of the desired tenor, although it was not an opportune time to be reminded of the old grudges the Jesse Evans men were nursing.

After settling the matter of the horse, McSween and his companions proceeded on to Lincoln. Nothing further that savored of danger happened, although high nervous tension continued all the time they were riding the thirty or forty miles of mountain road that lay between them and Fort Stanton, which was close enough to Lincoln to be called home.

13. The Killing of Tunstall

WHEN MCSWEEN ARRIVED back in Lincoln Sunday, February 10 he found his enemies already making sport over his plight. News of the outcome of the preliminary hearing at Mesilla had actually reached Lincoln sooner than the prisoner himself. Sheriff Brady was exulting over the situation, saying to cronies that although Tunstall and McSween had accused him of being a defaulter he would now show them he would make no "default" when it came to keeping McSween in jail and taking the spirit out of him. Brady also averred that even if Evans, Baker, Hill, and Davis had managed to give the slip to the Lincoln jail, Lawyer McSween would never get a chance to get out. He even joked about contracts with Mexican mills to grind corn for McSween's gruel, the point of the jocularity being its allusion to McSween's threatened exposé. One of the well-known fraudulent methods of the Dolan store in filling their government contracts was to have the meal cheaply and poorly ground in Mexican mills. Riley, too, rejoiced greatly and in great hilarity cleaned up the jail himself in order to be able to say in the future that he had swept out the room in which McSween was imprisoned. The matter did not go to the extreme expected because Barrier, the San Miguel deputy sheriff, did not turn McSween over to the Lincoln County sheriff but continued in charge of him. McSween was allowed to go to his house, with Barrier as custodian.

About the Tunstall store there was great commotion. Under a writ of attachment that had arrived from Mesilla by courier in a remarkably short time, Brady had started to levy on all of McSween's property in sight. First he had levied on the home and its furnishings and now he was levying on the store. Widenmann, in charge during Tunstall's absence, had protested when Brady appeared at the store accompanied by four deputies, George W. Peppin, James Longwell, John Long, and F. G. Christie. He declared that the store was Tunstall's individual property but Brady brushed aside the protest with the remark, "I guess we all know that McSween's got a part interest in the store." Widenmann then warned Brady that he and his bondsmen would be held responsible for any loss or damage to the property, but Brady's reply was a peremptory demand for the keys. When Widenmann refused point-blank, Brady searched him and took the keys from his pocket. The writ required only that the sheriff attach enough property to secure the sum of $8,000, but he attached property that was easily worth $30,000 to $40,000.

When Tunstall arrived at Brewer's ranch and learned what was going on, he grew indignant. On Monday, February 11, he and Widenmann went to the Tunstall store, which was then in charge of guards placed there by Brady. They found F. G. Christie engaged in making an inventory and the others lounging around. Without hesitation Tunstall spoke his mind in unequivocal fashion about his property being taken, as he put it, "for a debt of McSween's." Finding his protest of no avail, he uttered a warning — possibly it might be termed a threat — to the effect that he would eventually make all suffer who were taking part in what he termed "that damned high-handed business."

Longwell, as spokesman for the guards, reminded Tunstall that he could take the matter into court. "Do you think," answered Tunstall with fresh recollections of the bias Judge Bristol had shown toward McSween, "that I can get any justice in the district court? Haven't I just seen how prejudiced are both Judge Bristol and Colonel Rynerson?" "Well," continued Longwell, "if you can't get justice in the district court, you can carry your case before the United States court." "God, man," exclaimed Tunstall more hotly than before, "you can't get justice there either. It's the worst outfit of all and is completely in the hands of that damn Santa Fe ring."

Both Widenmann and Tunstall were armed when they went to the store. They also had an armed escort consisting of Fred Waite and Billy the Kid, who remained outside fully equipped with Winchesters and pistols while Tunstall and Widenmann went inside to talk. The situation was so tense that an incautious gesture or word from anyone on either side might have started a shooting.

TUNSTALL WINS A POINT

On a minor issue Tunstall's effort to protect his property was successful. He was able to convince Brady that six horses and two mules in the corral to the store were indisputably his private property and Brady at once exempted them from the attachment. In order to be on the safe side Tunstall at once dispatched these animals to his Feliz ranch in charge of two of his employees, cowboy John Middleton and ranch cook Godfrey Gauss, along with William McCloskey, a cowboy who was available whenever temporary help was needed at one ranch or another. When Widenmann asked to be allowed to go along with them, Tunstall gave his consent, perhaps reluctantly, as there is evidence that Tunstall lacked complete confidence in the good judgment of his friend Widenmann.

While all this was going on McSween spent this eventful Monday trying to make bond. This proved to be no easy matter, for Dolan used all his influence to keep those in Lincoln whose financial standing qualified them as bondsmen from going on the bond. Merchant José Montaño received intimations that his business would be ruined if he went on the bond. When Dr. A. M. Blazer, of Blazer's Mill near the Indian agency, showed a willingness to become a bondsman he received an intimation that, if he did so, an old charge of cutting timber on public lands for his sawmill woud be revived. He was also reminded that Rynerson, the United States district attorney, would likely prosecute the matter vigorously since he was the personal friend of those in the Dolan store and was zealous for its welfare. At last on Tuesday, February 12, McSween was able to submit to Rynerson a bond, the sureties of which represented an aggregate of $35,000. Rynerson promptly rejected it on the pretext that the sureties were not really worth what the bond indicated. The names of the sureties attached to this rejected bond were: John H. Tunstall, $20,000; James West, $4,000; John Copeland, $3,000; Isaac Ellis, $4,000; Refugio Valencia, $2,000; and José Montaño, $1,500.

On Wednesday, February 13, Widenmann returned to Lincoln from the Feliz ranch bringing word that the expected had happened. On Tuesday a posse sent by Brady had visited it and attempted to make the writ of attachment apply to the cattle. If Tunstall's blood had reached the boiling point at the way his store had been treated it rose higher still at this news. Some confusion might exist in the minds of the Lincolnites as to whether McSween had an interest in the store, since he maintained his office in one room of the building. In testifying before

Judge Bristol, Tunstall had made it clear that no such partnership existed, although such an arrangement was contemplated for some time in the future. Nevertheless, such a delicate difference could not count for much with the faction that was making the trouble for the new store. In the case of the cattle, however, there was no foundation for the view that McSween had an interest in them. Both ranch and cattle were known to be Tunstall's independent and private venture. That was what he had really come to Lincoln County for, and the store was the side issue. Nevertheless, the Dolan party, thinking that now they had their rivals on the hip, expected to close them out completely. McSween they had brought into discredit. Now Tunstall was to be harassed in order that he might grow sick of Lincoln County and quit. In reality he was the more important of the two for he represented capital. He must be eliminated first.

In obedience to orders Brady had got together a posse of supporters of the Dolan faction. Brady did not himself take the field but deputized Jacob B. ("Billy") Mathews, a silent partner in the Dolan firm, to lead the force, which included George Hindman, Johnny Hurley, Andrew L. ("Buckshot") Roberts, Manuel Segovia ("The Indian"), Jesse Evans (alias Graham, alias Davis), Frank Baker (alias Hart), and Tom Hill (alias Chelson). The last three of this formidable force of fighting men were notoriously associated with lawless activities and were known to be "wanted" by the law. This posse was later strongly reinforced by a party of Dolan's men from the Río Pecos, led by William ("Buck") Morton, which joined them at the Río Peñasco.

At the Tunstall ranch were Dick Brewer, Fred Waite, John Middleton, and Billy the Kid, or Billy Bonney as he was best known to his friends. Also there were Robert Widenmann, Godfrey Gauss, and William McCloskey, who had just arrived from Brewer's ranch with horses which the sheriff had released when he seized the Tunstall store.

When those at the ranch house saw the Mathews party approaching, they deemed it highly ominous. Widenmann in particular had reason to fear the worst when he recognized the three members of the Jesse Evans gang; he had heard of their threats to kill him because of his efforts as a deputy U.S. Marshal to effect their arrest. Dick Brewer went out alone to require Mathews and his party to stop about fifty yards from the house, allowing Mathews to come forward alone and state his business. When Mathews announced that he had come to attach the cattle in the case against McSween, Brewer informed him positively that he would only be allowed to round up the cattle and see if any belonged to McSween. Brewer said also that Mathews would not be allowed to take any cattle away but must leave them on the ranch with a suitable man in charge until the courts could settle the matter.

THE TENSION INCREASES

These terms were so reasonable that Mathews was on the point of acquiescing when Widenmann stepped out to complicate the situation. Irritated by the sight of the Jesse Evans contingent, Widenmann asked Mathews to be allowed to arrest these three. Mathews, however, refused, giving as his reason that if his ranchers, as he called them — meaning Hindman, Roberts and Hurley — should countenance such a proceeding, Dolan would make them suffer for it. Though Widenmann did not press the matter further, he had brought upon himself a renewal of the ire of the Jesse Evans delegation.

As things seemed likely to be settled amicably, Brewer invited Mathews and his companions into the house for food. While they were eating, Jesse Evans insolently turned to Widenmann and asked, "Do you want to arrest me?" Widenmann curtly replied, "You will find it out quickly enough when I want to arrest you." Evans then inquired, "Have you a warrant for me?" Widenmann gave a short answer, "It's none of your business." Evans then became the blusterer, saying, "If ever you come after me, you are the first man I am going to shoot at." Widenmann closed the conversation with, "All right; I can play a hand at that game as well as you." Then turning to Mathews, Widenmann said, "Billy, why did you allow those fellows to come along with you?" "I did not summon them," Mathews answered. "They came along of their own accord. Jess told me he wanted to find out if you had a warrant for him." At this point in the discussion Baker turned to Roberts and said in an undertone, "What the hell's use of talking? Let's pitch in a fight, and kill all the damn sons of bitches."

Mathews found himself in a quandary about the cattle. Brewer's refusal to let them be taken from the ranch put a crimp in his orders from Brady. Since the best course seemed to be to defer action, he announced that he would go back to Lincoln and get further instruction. Then Brewer made a proposal; "Billy, you see we want to do the right thing. What's the use of bringing so many along when you come back? Just yourself and another man will be enough, don't you think?" Mathews agreed and left, accompanied by all his posse. When Mathews departed to get further instructions from Dolan, Widenmann felt that Tunstall, too, should be informed of developments. Brewer agreed, but insisted that Widenmann should not undertake the shortcut by way of Pajarito Mountain alone and that Bonney and Waite should go along as bodyguards. The three rode for a short distance with Mathews and two or three of his companions, and before the two groups separated Mathews asked Widenmann what he thought would happen if the posse went ahead and seized the cattle. Widenmann replied, "We will not forcibly resist your doing so, provided you leave the cattle on the ranch. But if you drive them away to the Indian Agency or any other place, as we heard you intend doing, then you may be sure we will put up a fight." He added that the only way to conserve Tunstall's interests was to insist that the cattle remain on the place, since not a cent was likely to be recoverable from Sheriff Brady's bondsmen, who were generally understood to be insolvent.

Riding at a brisk pace, Widenmann and his companions reached Lincoln the same evening, Wednesday, February 13. Early the following morning they left again for the ranch. Tunstall was much wrought up over the attempt to take his cattle but remained firm in his determination to protect himself by legal means only. Later, however, from a Negro ex-cavalryman, George Washington, Lincoln's great newsmonger, he learned that the Dolan men were boasting that they now had a posse of forty-three and proposed to "settle the difficulties with Tunstall and McSween once and forever." They were also crowing over the fact that they had behind them the district attorney, the judge of the district court, and all the influence of the Santa Fe ring. Then came the even more disquieting news that Dolan himself had slipped away from Lincoln, presumably to Paul's ranch where his forces were said to be assembling.

Tunstall had grounds to feel that all circumstances were working against him. His English attitude toward extra-legal measures began to totter. Why not try fighting fire with fire? It must have been with a feeling of this sort that he started from Lincoln in order to be at the crisis in person. First, however, he rode to the Pecos to see if help could be had from the Chisum place. The visit brought no results. John Chisum himself was still under confinement in Las Vegas, and his brothers, Pitzer and Jim, were not willing to allow any of their cowboys to become involved. Tunstall rode on to his ranch, his loyalty renewed to the principle he had given McSween before he left Lincoln: "I will not sacrifice the life of a single man for all the cattle. I am going to the ranch to do all I can to prevent trouble. If needful, I will have all my men leave and come to Lincoln. Mathews and his crowd can take my property, and I will seek remedy in the courts."

The distance from Chisum's to his Feliz ranch being some sixty miles, Tunstall did not reach the ranch until Sunday night, February 17 about ten o'clock. He found his men fully informed of the activities at Paul's ranch, seven or eight miles away, where a large force of Anglos and native New Mexicans had gathered; the latter, it was reported, were to round up and drive away the cattle and the rest of the force was to take care of the Tunstall men at the ranch.

When Tunstall called his little group into consultation, he found them almost unanimous in their desire to resist any attempt to take the cattle. They showed him their readiness by displaying the portholes cut in the adobe walls of the house and the sand bags placed before the door. Tunstall, however, vetoed the plan, saying that they would withdraw to Lincoln the next morning. He directed McCloskey, who was known to be friendly with some of the Brady party, to start about three a.m. for Paul's ranch with a message to Mathews to the effect that he could take the cattle under the terms Brewer had proposed, namely, that he would leave a representative in charge and that Mathews would also leave someone. McCloskey was also instructed to go to the place of Martin Martz, known as "Dutch" Martin, who was considered a nonpartisan, to ask him to come to the ranch and remain as Tunstall's representative. Martz was not only to be on hand when the cattle were counted but, along with Gauss the cook, was to remain at the ranch to look after the cattle until the matter was settled in the courts. The rest of his men Tunstall ordered to be ready for the start to Lincoln early the next morning. The question was raised as to what should be done with the horses sent over to the ranch from Brewer's a few days before, after they had been exempted from the attachment. Tunstall settled the matter by saying, "We'll take them to Lincoln with us. That will be proper enough, since Brady himself released them."

CAVALCADE TO LINCOLN

About 8:30 the following morning, Monday, February 18, the cavalcade started out on the road which wound in a northerly direction toward the Rio Hondo, where it joined the main road from Roswell to Lincoln, near the site of the later-day hamlet of Tinnie. After riding together for about ten miles, Waite continued on the road with the wagon while the others, driving the small herd of horses, took a short-cut, ascending the trail which ran along the west side of Pajarito Mountain. They made slow progress on account of the herd and it was after five o'clock in the afternoon when they reached the canyon through which ran the trail leading to the Ruidoso, some four miles to the north.

It was here they startled a flock of wild turkeys which scurried away through the undergrowth. Tunstall, Brewer, and Widenmann happened to be riding in front somewhat ahead of the horses, which followed in single file. Middleton and Billy the Kid were some five hundred yards in the rear, riding leisurely and unsuspectingly. The sight of the turkeys naturally aroused a desire to bag some of them, and Widenmann, as he told the story later, offered his gun to Tunstall. The later, however, declined it, saying, "I'll stay with the horses. You and Dick go after the fowls."

Brewer and Widenmann rode after the turkeys, over a hill to the left and up a second hillside. They were out of sight of the trail where Tunstall was riding when, still following the turkeys, Widenmann's ear caught the sound of hoofbeats below the top of the ridge they had crossed. Turning to see what was taking place, he saw a group of horsemen coming over the hill at a gallop. Another and much larger body of men was some distance behind but approaching rapidly. He had hardly shouted a warning to Brewer when a bullet whizzed past. A whole fusillade quickly followed though there had been no shouted command to halt. Recognizing the hopelessness of their exposed position, Widenmann called to Brewer, "We can't hold this place. Let's make for the hill over there and make a stand behind the boulders." They reached protection safely but the shooting had suddenly stopped.

In the meantime Middleton and Billy the Kid had also spotted the attackers. Before he and his companion sought the protection of the trees and rocks on the hillside, Middleton spurred forward with a shouted warning to Tunstall to seek cover. Moments later some of the attacking party caught sight of Tunstall, the man they were chiefly after, and turning their attention from Widenmann and Brewer, they rode quickly back down the hill to the trail at the bottom of the canyon. A few moments later Tunstall's companions in their places of concealment heard two or three shots. Middleton gave voice to the dreadful surmise they each must have felt, "They have killed Tunstall!"

John Middleton's words were indeed true. Tunstall had been shot down almost immediately after Widenmann and Brewer had been fired on. The whole affair was over within a matter of minutes.

From their places among the trees and boulders of the hillside, Widenmann, Brewer, Middleton, and Billy the Kid could not see the trail. All four were caught off-balance by the sudden attack, and they chose a route over the hills to the Ruidoso as they returned to Lincoln with their melancholy news. Widenmann in particular had had good cause to feel the cold sweat of panic when the first bullets came from the attacking party and he turned to recognize Jesse Evans, a known killer who had vowed to end Widenmann's life. Middleton and Billy the Kid were accounted exceptionally good shots as well as cool and self-possessed whatever the emergency. Brewer, while not considered a fighting man in the same class as Middleton and Bonney, was esteemed as highly courageous. It may be asked why they did not pursue and attack the men who had killed Tunstall. The answer is plain. These men were realists; seeing themselves outnumbered by at least four or five to one they well knew that an attack then would be not only foolhardy but hopeless.

Morton's posse made a brief gesture toward rounding up Tunstall's companions, but some of its members, perhaps shocked by the initial tragedy, declined to be parties to any more bloodshed and threatened to quit the posse then and there. In consequence the whole party turned back toward Tunstall's ranch where Dolan, Mathews, and some others were waiting for them. They reached the ranch about two a.m. and Morton made the report that Tunstall had resisted the attachment, had fired on the posse, and had been killed in the return fire. Thenceforward this was the stock version of the Dolan faction. It was incorporated in Brady's report to Rynerson, dated March 5:

> I then increased his (Mathews') posse to about twenty four of the best citizens procurable, and again sent him to enforce the attachment, which he did, except as to the horse herd, which they attempted to run off; and while a portion of the posse were in pursuit of the party, J. H. Tunstall fired on the posse and in the return fire he was shot and killed.

None of Tunstall's companions was a witness to what occurred when the attackers came face to face with their victim. Had they been able to say unequivocally "I saw" and "I heard," the details of the murder would have been less confused. As it was, there were from the start conflicting accounts.

When Judge Angel made an investigation five months later in connection with a possible indemnity claim against the United States, he established several of the circumstances through affidavits from the members of both parties. One of the indubitable facts was that the killing was done by a small group in the van of the attacking party. The rest came on the scene a few moments later and, not being eye-witnesses, had to swallow the version of those directly responsible. When Sam Perry, for example, who was rather toward the rear of the posse, reached the scene of the killing, he was told by Morton that Tunstall had been shot because he had resisted the serving of the attachment. To make the story circumstantial, Morton even described how, as the writ was being read, Tunstall had drawn his pistol and fired at Morton, leaving Morton no other recourse than to return the fire. Such an account never carried the slightest degree of conviction to any of those who knew Tunstall. It was altogether improbable that a man as quiet and inoffensive as he could lose his accustomed self-control and his inherent respect for law and its processes.

A more credible account was embodied in the affidavit of George Kitt. He too, was riding too far in the rear to see the shooting, but he stated that when he came to where Tunstall's body lay on the ground he was told that Tunstall had been killed by "the boys." He learned that Tunstall had made no attempt to join his companions in seeking the protection of the hillside but had turned his horse and ridden toward Morton, Evans, and Hill, the foremost ones in the attacking party. One of these three called to Tunstall to come on up to them and assured him that he would not be hurt. Nevertheless, all three threw up their guns so that the stocks rested upon their knees. As Tunstall approached one of them said in an undertone to the others, "Not now; let's wait until he gets nearer." When Tunstall had come still closer, Morton brought his rifle to his shoulder and fired, the bullet striking Tunstall in the chest and causing his body to pitch off the horse. Jesse Evans then snatched Tunstall's revolver and fired a shot into the back of his head. It was Evans who turned the revolver toward Tunstall's horse and sent a bullet into the animal's head.

Almose instinctively those in the group responsible for the shooting resorted to that favorite way of the old West for disguising cold-blooded murder. The two empty chambers in Tunstall's pistol were distorted into evidence that Tunstall had resisted. It might have served the purpose just as well for Evans to have fired into the air, but then he would not have vented his hostility toward Tunstall. He went the length of barbarity in sating his desire for revenge on account of Tunstall's vigorous efforts to recover the stolen horses the September before.

From this point in the story George Kitt was able to relate a more personal activity in the affair. When he came on the scene he saw Tunstall's revolver in Tom Hill's hand. Hill passed it to Montoya, who in turn handed it to Sam Perry. The latter placed it by Tunstall's side and then assisted by Tom Green, Wallace Olinger, Charlie Kruling, and George Hindman, laid the body out, placing it beside the horse. Tunstall's head was laid on his folded overcoat. The crude sense of humor prevalent on the frontier led someone to pillow his horse's head on Tunstall's hat. Enough decency, however, was shown the body of the murdered man to place it on a blanket and cover it with another. Thus horse and rider were left surrounded by somber pines in the early darkness that closed a tragic February day.

The man whom Dolan had tried to bait into a gunfight a few days before was now dead. Of the three leading enemies of "The House," the first one had now been eliminated. The identity of the man who actually pulled the trigger is perhaps of secondary importance. Jesse Evans, Tom Hill, and Buck Morton have all been named as the killer in one account or another, though the best evidence points to the latter. There is, for instance, Mathews' affidavit of June 26, 1878, which states that following the killing Morton reported to Mathews that "Tunstall fired at him, that he (Morton) fired back, killing Tunstall." Regardless of which individual fired the fatal shot, the responsibility must lie with the Dolan foreman, Morton, leader of the posse which pursued and overtook the young Englishman.

This same affidavit lists the names of those in the posse on the day of the killing: R. W. Beckwith, Thomas Cochran, J. J. Dolan, Pantaleón Gallegos, Thomas Green, George Hindman, John Hurley, George Kitt, Charles Kruling, Charles Marshall, J. B. Mathews, Felipe Mes, A. H. Mills, Ramón Montoya, Thomas Moore, William Morton, J. W. Olinger, Pablo Pino y Pino, Samuel Perry, Andrew Roberts, Manuel Segovia, E. H. Wakefield, and Charles Wolz. No mention is made of the group of Mexican-Americans ostensibly brought along to gather the Tunstall cattle. Most significantly, this official list fails to mention at least four others who were known to be in the posse, two of whom were among those with Morton when Tunstall was shot: Jesse Evans, Tom Hill (Chelson), John Long (Rivers), and Frank Baker.

When the scheme for molesting Tunstall fell into delicate balance through the inclination of Mathews to accept Brewer's obviously fair offer, Dolan had appeared in person and taken command. The posse surrounded the Tunstall ranch house Sunday morning, approaching it cautiously, for they were expecting a fight. To their surprise they found no one there except Martin Martz and the cook, Gauss. When it was learned from them that Tunstall had left instructions to permit Mathews to attach the cattle provided they would be left on the ranch, some one in the posse raised a question about the horses. Gauss and Martin answered that Tunstall had taken them with him when he and his employees had started to Lincoln earlier that morning. While Mathews was trying to make up his mind whether to follow after them and take the horses, Dolan came up and cast the deciding vote. "Let's start some of the men after them," he said. "If they are overtaken before they reach the plaza you men can bring them back here." Dolan at once began to designate certain ones to go on the pursuit. The foreman of Dolan's Pecos cow camp, Buck Morton, was placed in charge, a position he accepted readily, and he was heard to say as he called the crowd together, "Hurry up, boys. My knife is sharp and I feel like scalping some one."

While the sub-posse was being organized, the Jesse Evans group came forward with evident intention of going along. As Pantaleon Gallegos started to write their names in the list he was compiling for the official records, someone — either Dolan or Mathews — said, "Don't include them." Evans, overhearing this and taking it to mean that they were not allowed to go, began to complain vigorously. "You bet your damn life we are going," he said, "for we want our horses we loaned to Billy the Kid. They tell me they have been taken away with the other horses." No further protest was made against their going. Probably there never was any intention of hindering it. All that Dolan or Mathews was concerned about was their appearance in the official records. That could be incriminating, for Jesse Evans and his three associates were generally regarded as mainstays of the Dolan organization. Brady must have anticipated the criticism which was sure to follow his use of notorious outlaws in his posse. In his report to District Attorney Rynerson he wrote:

> It has been falsely averred that attached to the deputy's posse were men against whom U.S. warrants had been issued. To disprove this, I present you a letter which reached him before he attached and in addition to my minute verbal instructions.

Lincoln, N. M., Feb. 15, 1878

J. B. Mathews,
  Dept. Sheriff,
Dear Sir:

> You must not by any means call on or allow to travel with your posse any person or persons who are known to be outlaws. Let your Mexicans round up the cattle and protect them with the balance. Be *firm* and do your duty according to *law* and I will be responsible for your acts.

I am, Sir,
  Respectfully yours,
  Wm. Brady, Sheriff
  Lincoln County

Note or no note, however, Jesse Evans and his followers had been taken along. Though their names were not on the official list of the posse, they played a most conspicuous role in the removal of Tunstall, the capitalist, from participation in the business affairs of Lincoln County.

14. Open War

THOUGH TUNSTALL WAS killed in a remote locality entirely off the main traveled roads and almost at nightfall, the sensational news of the murder spread through the country like wildfire. About ten or eleven o'clock that night Widenmann and Billy the Kid reached Lincoln and reported what had happened. The plaza was aghast at the news, calloused though the little settlement had become in regard to the taking of life. Everyone became intensely nervous over what might ensue. The jealousies and hatreds, smoldering these many months, would doubtless burst into flame, and who could foretell how far its devouring force might go? The general expectation was that McSween would be the next target. After him would come Widenmann, Brewer, and possibly Billy the Kid and Middleton, as they constituted important witnesses to the circumstances of Tunstall's murder. Since little reliance was to be placed on the sheriff and his deputies in efforts to apprehend the persons responsible in this murder, McSween sought aid at once from the authorities at Fort Stanton. Widenmann was off for the fort soon after he had told McSween the circumstances of the killing. The officers at Fort Stanton, aside from their Dolan partisanship, were not inclined to interest themselves in this killing of a civilian by other civilians. Within an hour or two that same night some sixty men had congregated at McSween's house for the double purpose of hearing the details of the killing and of assuring McSween that they would give him full support in his efforts to bring to justice those directly or indirectly responsible. Public opinion so generally condemned the killing of Tunstall that the Dolan element grew alarmed. As Dolan was still with the posse at Tunstall's ranch, it fell to Riley to drop in at McSween's late that night to see which way the wind was really blowing. He was so drunk that he hardly seemed to know what he was doing or saying, but he somehow realized he was *persona non grata*. On first coming into the house, he took off his revolver and laid it on the table. Then in order to show that he carried no other weapons, he proceeded to turn his pockets inside out, all the time in maudlin fashion declaring his friendly intentions.

Riley's visit played into the hands of the McSween faction most opportunely. From one of Riley's pockets dropped a memorandum book which someone in the room retrieved and handed to McSween. It contained conclusive evidence of the shady transactions of the Murphy (now the Dolan) store. Some entries substantiated the general belief that there was collusion between the Dolan store and the Indian agency. One recorded the times Steve Stanley had hauled sugar and coffee from the agency to the store. Other entries were still more interesting, for they showed the occasions when Riley had bought cattle for the store from certain of the notorious cattle thieves of the section, especially the Jesse Evans gang. In the book also was a list of persons classified according to their friendliness or hostility to the Dolan store. Opposite each was a pseudonym suggestive of a secret code. United States District Attorney Catron was designated as grapes; the Indian agent Godfroy was Hampton; the agency clerk, Morris J. Bernstein, as soapweed; the acting quartermaster at the fort, Lieutenant C. M. Delany, as Warwick; Major Murphy as box; the territorial district attorney Rynerson as oyster; the Indians as trees. The climax, however, to the whole list was McSween's name, opposite which was the significant designation *diablo*. Elsewhere in the book were notes concerning McSween, made while the squabble over the Fritz insurance was in the acute stage.

In addition to the memorandum book Riley left a letter from the district attorney, Rynerson, which verified the boast that the Dolan party had been making. Four days before Rynerson had replied to their inquiry as to whether they might have not gone too far in the attachment of the Tunstall store:

Las Cruces, Feb. 14, 1878

Friends Riley and Dolan,

I have just received letters from you mailed the 11th inst. Glad to know that you (Dolan) got home o.k. and that business was going o.k. If Mr. Widenmann interferes with or resists the sheriff in the discharge of his duties, Brady did right in arresting. Any one else who does so must receive the same attention. Brady goes into the store in McSween's place and takes his interest. Tunstall will have the same right there he had before, but he must not obstruct the sheriff or resist him in the discharge of his duties. If he tries to make trouble, the sheriff must meet the occasion firmly and loyally. I believe Tunstall is in with the swindlers — with the rogue McSween. They have the money belonging to the Fritz estate and they know it. It must be made hot for them, all the hotter the better — especially is this necessary now that it has been discovered there is no hell.

It may be that the villain "Green Baptista" Wilson will play into their hands as alcalde. If so, he should be moved around a little. Shake that McSween outfit up until it shells out and squares up, and then shake it out of Lincoln. I will aid to punish the scoundrels all I can. Get the people with control — Juan Patrón, if possible. You know how to do it, and be assured, I shall help you all I can, for I believe there was never found a more scoundrelly set than that outfit.

Yours &c,

W. L. Rynerson

Later during the night McSween sent a messenger over to John Newcomb, whose place on the Ruidoso was only five or six miles from where Tunstall had been killed, with a request that he go to the scene of the murder and bring the body to Lincoln. Newcomb sent word to some of his neighbors along the river asking them to go with him as soon as it was daylight. Those accompanying Newcomb included Florencio González, Patricio Trujillo, Lázaro Gallegos, and Ramón Baragón. It was Baragón, an experienced tracker, who located the body. It had been concealed in the trees on the hillside some hundred yards from the place on the trail where bloodstains indicated the killing. Since the body of the horse was nearby, it was deduced that apparently Tunstall's body had been placed across his horse and taken to the place of concealment, after which the horse had been shot; no cartridge shells were found nearby. Hoofprints in the bed of the canyon revealed another significant fact: the tracks showed plainly that the horse herd the posse was ostensibly seeking had stopped quite a distance behind the place where the killing had occurred and must have been passed by the posse before they overtook Tunstall. They had to strap the body on the back of a horse and lead the animal slowly down the hillside and along the rough trail to the road which led to Newcomb's place. Here they transferred it to a wagon and made the journey to Lincoln over the road leading down the Ruidoso valley to the junction with the Bonito, and thence up that valley to Lincoln. As all this took practically the entire day, it was after nightfall that the body finally reached Lincoln.

Fate made a strange juxtaposition on that Tuesday, February 19, when it brought into Lincoln about midday the party of Presbyterian home missionaries McSween had been instrumental in securing. The group — Dr. Taylor F. Ealy, who was a physician as well as a minister, Mrs. Ealy, and their two children, together with Miss Susan Gates, who was a teacher — were to establish church and school in Lincoln. They had made the journey from Pennsylvania by rail as far as El Moro, Colorado, and then had travelled the rest of the way by wagon. The night before, they had stopped at Fort Stanton, where Dr. Ealy had heard about the killing of Tunstall. He had also received strong advice that he ought to turn back. Dr. Ealy, however, decided to attempt to carry out the mission assigned to him, the establishment of a church and school at Lincoln.

As he drove toward Lincoln the next morning, he had a foretaste of the times. At a point on the Bonito known as the Double Crossing, about three miles from Lincoln, he was stopped by some of the Dolan faction, who searched his wagon thoroughly for arms. As nothing contraband was found, Ealy was allowed to proceed into the town. On reaching the plaza he stopped at the Dolan store at the western edge of the village to ask directions for finding McSween. His inquiry provoked frosty looks from the group of men congregated around the doorway of the store. When informed of Dr. Ealy's purpose in Lincoln, someone in the crowd jeeringly remarked, "We don't take much stock in your school and church talk; but if you're a sawbones, you'll get plenty to do. Hell's breaking loose in Lincoln, and some folks are surely going to get hurt. Know anything about gunshot wounds, Doc?" The crowd laughed and Dr. Ealy drove on down the street toward McSween's house, about two hundred yards farther to the eastward.

Here also he found excitement prevailing. In and about the house were a number of men, and from rifles and revolvers in evidence it might have been taken for an armed band. McSween welcomed the Ealy party to Lincoln and gave him a summary of the situation, ending with the comment, "You are likely, Doctor, to find this what the Bible calls stony ground. What we are drifting into is really a struggle of the people to throw off a galling yoke of corruption, robbery and persecution. We have locally the Dolan store, which holds several government contracts; it accumulates money by purchasing cattle from irresponsible parties for a small part of their actual value and by getting part of its stock of goods from government supplies, through collusion with government agents. They have been carrying on their business in this way, arrogantly and oppressively because they render themselves useful to the closed corporation dominating New Mexico, the Santa Fe ring. They that sow with wind, shall reap the whirlwind."

Dr. Ealy replied he was ready to try to serve the community no matter how great the obstacle might be. "We need you, Doctor," continued McSween, "and I admire your determination. My wife is away just now — in St. Louis, and I fear I cannot make you as comfortable as I would wish." Then indicating Waite, Billy the Kid, Middleton, and others in the house he added, "You see I have a number of vistors at this time. But I can arrange for your party to stay with my law partner, Shield, and his wife, who live in the east wing of this house. In a few days I will find you quarters elsewhere. I think I will then turn over to you the suite of rooms in the store over yonder, which my dead friend Tunstall built for his own use. Poor fellow, he has no more use for them."

McSWEEN'S FIRST MOVES

In doing something about arrests in connection with the killing of Tunstall, McSween had already made his first moves. Realizing that those implicated would have the powerful protection of the Dolan organization, he knew it was useless to attempt to have them arrested by the ordinary process of warrants placed in the hands of the sheriff. All that would be done would be to pocket the papers and ignore the matter. McSween resorted to technicality. Selecting Brewer and Billy the Kid, he had them go before the justice of the peace, Squire Wilson, and make affidavits against several in the posse they had recognized. Squire Wilson promptly issued the warrants and placed them in the hands of Atanacio Martínez, one of the constables. As the day was over and as Tunstall's body was expected almost any hour, McSween did not seek to have the arrests made just then.

Darkness was coming on when John Newcomb drove into Lincoln with the body of Tunstall in his wagon. It was taken to McSween's house and immediately Squire Wilson empanelled a coroner's jury composed of George B. Barber, R. M. Gilbert, John Newcomb, Samuel Smith, Frank Coe, and Ben Ellis. The outcome of the formal inquest was a report that Tunstall had been killed by Jesse Evans, Frank Baker, Thomas Hill, George Hindman, James J. Dolan, William Morton, and others not identified by witnesses that testified before the coroner's jury. The next day, February 20, Dr. D. M. Appel, the post surgeon, went to Lincoln and assisted with the embalming of Tunstall's body. Sheriff Brady arranged for Dr. Appel to perform a post-mortem for which he was to be paid $100, an amount almost unheard of in those days, which raised the eyebrows of the citizens of Lincoln. Widenmann's written account related that "Morton . . . shot Tunstall through the head, smashed Tunstall's skull with the butt of his gun." Dr. Ealy, who examined the body before he assisted in the embalming, went on record to the effect that in addition to the bullet holes Tunstall's head was badly mutilated. Little wonder then that many people imputed some connection between the high fee paid Appel and his official report which emphasized the fact that except for the two bullet wounds there were "no other bruises on head or body."

The same day brought another element of excitement. McSween resumed the effort to have arrests made of some of those responsible for the killing. The constable, Atanacio Martínez, accompanied by Bonney and Waite, went to the Dolan store after some ten or twelve of the wanted men. Brady, however, backed by an impressive show of arms, refused to permit the constable to serve the warrants. He took the position that inasmuch as the men wanted had been members of a legally constituted posse they were immune from arrest. Then, as if to show in whose hands resided power, he placed Martínez and his two companions under arrest. Martínez he did not dare hold longer than nightfall; Waite and Billy the Kid remainded in custody. Such high-handed proceedings made Billy the Kid implacably hostile toward Brady. It seemed that because he was a principal witness in the Tunstall killing, Brady was deliberately persecuting him. To his youthful ideas of right and wrong there could be no middle ground; he or Brady would have to settle the matter sooner or later.

One reason that Brady felt so all-powerful was that a detachment of soldiers from the fort had come down to guard the Dolan store. The large gathering at McSween's house had so alarmed the leaders of the Dolan faction that they had appealed to their friends at the fort for a guard of soldiers. The commanding officer, Captain G. A. Purington (brevet lieutenant colonel), was befriending the members of the firm of J. J. Dolan and Co., who were always so accommodating to the officers, against any reprisals from the friends of Tunstall. This was in considerable contrast to the cold shoulder that Widenmann had received at the fort when he sought the support of authorities there.

The following day, Thursday, February 21, not so eventful as the two or three preceding ones, McSween was ready to cross swords with his enemies at every point. Even in the midst of preparations for Tunstall's funeral, which had been set for Friday, he felt compelled to resist further arrogance on the part of Brady. When he learned that Brady was allowing the soldiers to feed their horses hay belonging to the Tunstall store, he promptly went before Squire Wilson and made an affidavit charging Brady, together with Charlie Martin, John Long, and James Longwell, guards in the store, with the unlawful appropriation of Tunstall's property. All those named in the warrant, including

Brady, submitted to arrest and were given an immediate hearing before Squire Wilson. That magistrate sustained the charges against Brady and bound him over to the grand jury at the approaching term of court. The others were discharged.

THE TUNSTALL FUNERAL

On Friday, February 22, Tunstall was buried a short distance from the store he had been so much interested in developing. To the east of the store was a lot McSween had intended to give for the church Dr. Ealy was to build, and behind this was a level stretch which, extending to the banks of the Bonito, was to become the burying lot. Already two of the Shield children had been buried there. Beside their small graves another had been prepared for Tunstall. Dr. Ealy conducted a simple service using as text the Scripture, "If a man die, shall he live again." There was a large attendance of the friends and sympathizers of both Tunstall and McSween. It was significant that every man was heavily armed. Not even at a funeral could anyone risk laying aside his weapons. There was, however, no discord in town that day. The presence of the soldiers was unquestionably a factor in keeping the situation in hand. Anticipating that the day of the funeral might bring on some kind of clash between the factions, Brady had sent an official request to Captain Purington for soldiers to help in keeping order. Lieutenant Delany with a detachment of Company "H," 15th Infantry, was on hand and as the soldiers always created a wholesome sense of awe and respect there were no untoward developments. Captain Purington, somewhat doubtful whether the use of soldiers in this way was sanctioned by his orders or not, qualified his directions to Lieutenant Delany in this fashion: "Until instructions are received from Judge Bristol, judge of the United States court, no interference will be made with the civil authorities in the excution of their duties further than the protection of life and property." This effort to juggle with army orders about using soldiers in civil disturbances was the beginning of a vacillating attitude that characterized Fort Stanton officers in their relation to the Lincoln County troubles. The war department was rather inclined to restrict the use of the military forces. The officers at Fort Stanton seemed eager to project themselves and their men into the row.

Immediately after the Tunstall funeral a mass meeting was held at McSween's house to discuss the situation. There was considerable indignation over Brady's refusal to make any arrest himself or to allow any to be made by others. After considerable heated discussion a committee was appointed to interview the sheriff and learn just what he meant by the course he was taking. At the head of the committee was Florencio González, the probate judge, and his fellow-members were three citizens of repute — Isaac Ellis, José Montaño, and John Newcomb. The committee saw Brady and shortly returned to the meeting, to report that when the committee inquired why he had arrested Martínez, Waite, and Bonney, and why the two latter were still detained, all the answer he would vouchsafe was the blunt, "Because I had the power." They had found him entirely noncommittal on the question of what he would do about the arrest of those implicated in the killing of Tunstall. The committee had also sought to learn what he intended to do about McSween's bond in the embezzlement case. On this matter they were able to elicit very definite information, for Brady said emphatically, "I will not take a bond from McSween of any kind or amount."

All this seemed evidence enough that the sheriff was in league with the Dolan faction and would not make any serious effort to arrest anybody connected with the killing. The attitude that this faction was taking was to wait until the grand jury convened in six weeks or so and could investigate the whole matter. McSween and his sympathizers knew that this delay would enable the men most wanted to make their exodus from the country and get across the line into Texas, Arizona, or even Mexico. McSween had all along counselled that all measures must be strictly legal. He had explained that the killing of a British subject was a serious matter and would unquestionably bring some demand from the British government for redress. This would mean that the United States government would conduct an investigation through its legal machinery. All this would take time. The imperative need was to get into the hands of the law the ones implicated and keep them there until the matter could be aired by the courts.

Others present at the meeting were for simpler methods. They advocated the old frontier code of retaliation and summary dealing, but McSween's advice carried and the meeting adjourned, leaving it to McSween as a lawyer to make whatever next move he considered legal and proper. As everyone felt that he would carry on the matter with determination, the large group of his friends felt there was no need for them to stay in Lincoln longer and dispersed themselves to their homes in various parts of the county.

This strenuous day had another development which was highly disquieting. Dolan left town on another of his trips to Mesilla, one which forecast some further plot to bring about the downfall of McSween. What needed to be done right away was to stop McSween's activities about the arrest of Tunstall's murderers. He was still in the custody of Deputy Sheriff Barrier, although the instructions from Judge Bristol had been to turn him over to Sheriff Brady. Barrier nevertheless had been prevailed upon to keep McSween in his custody and so thwart those who very much wanted to get their hands on him. Barrier justified his disregard of orders by saying that he believed McSween's life would be unsafe in Brady's hands. Naturally this did not suit McSween's enemies and Dolan had started to Mesilla with the avowed intention of having Judge Bristol issue an alias warrant in order to bring about the re-arrest of McSween on the embezzlement charge. Of course the arrest would be accomplished by none other than Brady.

There was a strong impression that Dolan expected to accomplish another thing on this trip. Now that the lines between the two factions had been sharply drawn, he realized that his side was weak in fighting men in comparison with those who now supported McSween. Doña Ana County was prolific in outlaws and desperadoes, among whom the most redoubtable was John Kinney, a brutal and reckless ruffian who usually had at his beck and call a band of fellows as desperate as himself. It was rumored that Dolan intended to negotiate with this crowd and to import them for service in Lincoln County. This resort to the use of hired bravos was a distinct contrast to the spontaneous impulse of indignation and self-protection that had brought McSween his adherents.

15. Widenmann's Coup

THE DAY AFTER Tunstall's funeral, that is, on Saturday, February 23, Bonney and Waite had been released by Brady and the situation became more acute in regard to the Tunstall store. In the week before, possession of it by Brady's deputies had threatened to create a clash. When Billy the Kid and Fred Waite came to Lincoln on February 15, they had brought on trouble. First they had stopped Sam Wortley, the keeper of the hotel frequented by the Dolan following, as he was carrying a meal to the guards at the store, and at the point of their rifles had ordered him to take the food back. Sam Wortley had obeyed without protest or delay. Later that day there had occurred something without a tinge of jocularity. Billy the Kid, passing the store, happened to see James Longwell, one of the guards, standing in the doorway and thereupon got his rifle into position and shouted defiance to those in the store, "Turn loose now you sons of bitches! I'll give you a game!" Just then Steve Stanley, a noncombatant, happened to pass in front of Longwell and Billy held his fire. The danger passed; none in the store responded to the Kid's invitation. Either they did not relish an encounter with one who, though barely eighteen, was accounted a deadly shot, or they realized that if a fight started the Kid would receive reinforcements in such numbers as to make the odds hopeless.

Widenmann realized the difficulty of dislodging the guards by forcible means and resorted to strategy. Through his deputy United States marshalship he had the right to ask the Fort Stanton authorities for soldiers to assist him in executing warrants. He applied to

Captain Purington for a detachment of soldiers to help him serve warrants against Evans, Baker, Hill, and Davis for stealing government mules, and his request was promptly honored. Lieutenant M. F. Goodwin arrived with a detachment of soldiers secretly in the night, and Widenmann's first step was to go to the Dolan store. Then, having posted the soldiers in a cordon around the building, he went inside, taking with him Martínez, Waite, Billy the Kid, and several others of the group who were becoming prominent in the moves of the McSween faction. He made a thorough search without finding any of the four men. The search seems to have been conducted in an orderly manner although the other side promptly hurled the accusation that both the store and the living quarters of the proprietors had been ransacked. They charged also that the Rynerson letter, the loss of which nettled them, was acquired by McSween at the time this search was made.

After the visit to the Dolan building, Widenmann proceeded down the street to the Tunstall store still endeavoring, so he said, to locate Evans and his companions. At this store he used the same tactics as at the other, the soldiers keeping guard while he and the others entered. The five men on guard — George Peppin, Jim Longwell, John Long, Charley Martin, and a Negro ex-trooper named Clark, who was a Dolan employee — offered no resistance and were disarmed and marched over to the jail. They were kept for the rest of the night and the next day were given a hearing before Squire Wilson. They were released but did not go back into the Tunstall store. The store was again in the hands of the McSween crowd, where it remained for the succeeding months.

Brady made but a feeble attempt at retaliation. He succeeded in having the civilian group in Widenmann's posse arrested on a charge of rioting. Those put under arrest were: Atanacio Martínez, Samuel Corbet, J. G. (Doc) Scurlock, John Middleton, William Bonney, Samuel Smith, Frank Coe, George Coe, Ignacio González, Jesús Rodríguez, Esequio Sánchez, Ramón Baragón, Frank Macnab (often misspelled as McNab), Fred Waite, Robert Edwards, George Washington, and George Robinson. A hearing before Squire Wilson resulted in his binding the crowd over to the grand jury at the next term of court. Incidentally, only four — Martínez, Corbet, Washington, and Robinson — were ever hauled into court. In April, 1878, they pleaded not guilty and were allowed a change of venue to Doña Ana County. The cases against the others were continued — indication that they were then inaccessible in Lincoln County.

Widenmann's activities indicated that he was ambitious to place himself in charge of Tunstall's property. On February 23, the same date he repossessed the store, he wrote a long, high-wrought letter to Tunstall's father relating the particulars of Tunstall's death and offering advice about the handling of Tunstall's estate.

> You will see by the enclosed paper [a copy] that dear Harry [Widenmann's pet way of referring to Tunstall, although others called him John] left a will. Mr. McSween thought prudent that another person, a Mr. Ellis, a good and honest man, should be appointed administrator for the present under $10,000 bond, but after the appraisal the bond will, according to law, have to be twice the amount of the appraisement, or about $50,000. Now there is not a man in the country who could give this bond, and according to law, if the bond can not be furnished, the sheriff takes the property into custody. But the sheriff is indirectly the cause of poor Harry's death, and the property would go to ruin or be stolen. To avoid this I would advise you to send me or some other honest and reliable person a full and complete power of attorney so that everything can be properly managed and every cent saved.

McSween also wrote to Tunstall's father on the same date. After recounting the circumstances of the killing, McSween likewise passed into the question of looking after the property.

> In the event of anything happening to us, it was understood that the one who survived would close up the estate of the other without charge. The evening he left he took me into his room and said, "Mac, I want you to promise me that if I'm killed, you'll wind up my estate and give every cent in it to my two little sisters — for God's sake, remember my two little sisters. If you die, I'll wind up your estate and give every cent in it to Mrs. McSween; this we'll do without charge." Of course, I promised.
>
> After his death, Mr. R. A. Widenmann showed me what he called a will, dated May 23, '77, signed by John — it's his handwriting without doubt. But the paper is simply a power of attorney. At the time it was given, your son had no property to amount to anything, and I think the power of attorney was only intended to cover what he had then. He never mentioned the fact to me, and it's the only thing I have known him to withold from me. I think the matter escaped his mind. He met Mr. Widenmann in Santa Fe and took a strong liking to him. Mr. Widenmann being "hard up" as they say here, John invited him down to share his hospitalities until something turned up. Mr. Widenmann accepted the invitation and came here in March last. John frequently told me that the fellow had many good points he

admired, but he was paying him no wages — only giving him his board and clothing. Now, so far as my knowledge goes, Widenmann was a strong friend of your son's and your son was a very strong friend of Widenmann's.

Mr. Widenmann informs me that he too promised your son to wind up his estate, as I did, and that was his only reason for wanting to be administrator. I told him that for my part I would accept no trust of that character as long as there were other good, honest, and competent men to fill the position who could give good bonds; that I would much sooner write you as John's friend than as his administrator; that I could not consent to have the court issue him letters without bonds, for however faithfully he might discharge his duties, I considered it would be unjust to his representatives and against my promise. That it was immaterial who was appointed; it was my intention to watch their administration and report their irregularities, if any occurred, to the court. I recommended the court to appoint Isaac Ellis, a good, honest, substantial property holder as administrator. He done so. Bonds, until the inventory is taken, we put at $20,000. After inventory is made, it will be put at double the amount. I have promised the administrator to do all the legal portion of the administration free of charge.

He had between 3,000 and 4,000 acres of land, the title to which has not yet been perfected — he had three years in which to do that, though it was his intention to perfect the title the following summer. Though the title is in this condition, the interest he had is safe and will so remain for three years. But should his heirs desire to withdraw the money invested, I think they can easily do so with interest. His other property consists of merchandise, horses, and cattle — he had about 4,000 head of cattle.

Behind the lines of the two letters can be read an incipient contest over the management of Tunstalls' estate. Widenmann evidently was itching to be placed in charge; he was the assertive type and even in Tunstall's lifetime he had over and over pushed himself into positions of management. In the letter to Tunstall's father dated February 23, speaking of Tunstall's absence from Lincoln at Mesilla at the time of the McSween hearing before Judge Bristol, "During the time Harry and the others were away, I took charge of the business, as in fact I always did when here." McSween, on the contrary, evidently was seeking the good of the estate. He had declined to become administrator himself and had picked out Isaac Ellis, an eminently respectable person, for the task, which was likely to be not only arduous but dangerous as well. Without doubt the estate would become a bone of contention, more or less, as time went on. The three or four thousand acres of desirable range on the Feliz, the title to which was incomplete under the Desert Land Act provisions, would excite the cupidity of some of the elements struggling for power in Lincoln County. The four thousand head of cattle were already under the thumb of the Dolan faction, since Brady had them under attachment.

Another source of danger might be found in the temperament of Widenmann. In the past he had shown himself excitable and imprudent. In regaining the Tunstall store he had displayed the same tendencies. He had gone so far as to propose to Lieutenant Goodwin that he withdraw the soldiers and let the two sides engage in a death-grapple fight. Such a proposal was rejected by Lieutenant Goodwin on the self-evident ground that the soldiers had been sent to protect life and property and he even went so far as to say to Widenmann, "If a fight starts, I will at once place my troops between the two factions. That will force them into a dilemma; either they must stop shooting or run the risk of the serious consequences of wounding or killing some of the soldiers."

Widenmann had further probed Lieutenant Goodwin about undertaking the arrest of Brady. To this idea the Lieutenant gave a noncommittal answer — noncommittal but sufficiently disapproving to cause Widenmann to drop the idea. The question was fraught with decided significance, for it betrayed a developing animus against Brady for his inertia about arresting Tunstall's murderers. The McSween side was beginning to charge openly that he was shielding them at the behest of the Dolan side. His inactivity had grown noticeable and the indignation stirred up about it tended to focus upon Brady personally. The situation boded ill for the future.

With matters tending to look rather "bilious," as John Chisum used to express it, McSween grew more determined than ever about apprehending the persons implicated in the killing. On Sunday, February 24, he wrote a short letter to Tunstall's father, the chief purport of which was to ask authorization for the offer of a reward "for the apprehension and conviction of the murderers of your son." Then he added, "This would be well, tho' I feel satisfied that some of them shall have been sent to their 'long homes' before this reaches you."

On the same Sunday the friends of McSween held a mass meeting in Lincoln and canvassed the situation. The majority felt that the best course was to leave the town, at least for the time being, and go to some place of safety until things had quieted down. He was now the outstanding figure in the faction that was becoming known by his name. He was pushed into the position by force of circumstances and not because he desired leadership. It was well known that he did not believe in the settlement of differences by six-shooter or rifle. As he put in one of the letters to the Tunstall family, "I have never carried a fire-arm in my life — don't now — don't expect to. I have lived 35 years without them and without drinking whiskey, and I can, I hope, get along the balance of my days without."

REVENGE AND SELF-DEFENSE

Two impulses urged him to assume the leadership of his faction. One was to see that the death of his friend and business associate was fully avenged by legal means; the other was to protect his life. Among the other side there was a war cry, "Tunstall is gone. We must get McSween next."

When his friends came to him late at night with the advice that he leave Lincoln, McSween at first flatly refused, but finally he agreed to accede to their wishes. He firmly declared, however, that he would not go a mile farther from Lincoln than was absolutely necessary. He also assured them that, though he might be absent, he would continue his activity regarding the apprehension of the murderers of Tunstall. He gave them to understand that he intended not only to use the funds he expected the Tunstall family to put at his disposal but also every dollar of his own money, if necessary.

In regard to himself he felt that lease of life would not be long. On Monday, February 25, he put his affairs in order by making a will. This gave all his property to Mrs. McSween and stipulated that John S. Chisum was to become executor without bond. If he should not serve, then Mrs. McSween was to become executrix. She was not to be required to give bond, for McSween felt that "as a matter of security they (bonds) are unnecessary, as nothing that will come into her hands or under her control will be wilfully wasted or destroyed." He also paid a tribute to John S. Chisum as a friend, saying, "I know him to be a friend to my wife and myself, and I know that he would give her the last cent in my estate, and I firmly believe that were she left without means of support, he would furnish her all that would be necessary to make her comfortable during her life, if in his power to do so." The witnesses signing the document were D. P. Shield, S. R. Corbet, and T. F. Ealy.

What made the friends of McSween so insistent about his going away from Lincoln was persistent alarms from Mesilla as to what Dolan contemplated. One which received a good deal of credence had it that Dolan had written Riley directions to have the military on hand in Lincoln, ready to assist in making arrests, by the time he returned with the alias warrant for McSween and also a warrant for Barrier.

Mingled with this rumor was another that Dolan had written that he would have Jesse Evans and his crowd ready to do their part as soon as the military had left town. So fevered with excitement and alarm were the minds of almost everyone in Lincoln that all this seemed a matter of likelihood; it all looked like another plot. At any rate, after this budget of rumors became current in the town, that is, on Wednesday, February 27, Barrier departed with McSween. It was generally assumed that they would make the Chisum ranch their refuge; but, as McSween did not care to go so far from Lincoln, most of the time they were in camp in secluded places in the hills within a radius of thirty or forty miles from Lincoln.

16. Crusade of the Regulators

A FEW DAYS BEFORE McSween's departure from Lincoln what was virtually a vigilante organization sprang up, calling itself "Regulators." As Brady seemed disinclined to arrest any of those implicated in the murder, Brewer and eight or ten others banded themselves together for that undertaking. Some were actuated by genuine friendship for Tunstall, this being the case with his employees such as Brewer, Waite, Billy the Kid, and Middleton. Frank Macnab, employed as a "cattle detective" by such large stock owners as the firm of Hunter & Evans, was quick to join forces with anyone declaring war on the cattle rustlers. Others like "Doc" Scurlock, Charley Bowdre, Henry Brown, Sam Smith, and Jim French were moved by grudges against the Dolan firm. Justice of the Peace Wilson appointed Dick Brewer as constable and the others were duly deputized. Brewer was given warrants for the arrest of those believed guilty of the Tunstall murder. Thus they fell into a different category from the frontier vigilante of law and order. All ten were alike in determination to see that some arrests were made in what the majority of the people considered a cold-blooded and flagrant murder.

They unified their organization by an oath requiring each to stick to the other no matter what might happen. To offset any untoward effect on public opinion, they announced that they would not execute summary justice on those they might arrest but would merely take them into custody and deliver them at Lincoln to be held for trial at the next term of court, then only four or five weeks off. As a further precaution against being misunderstood they disavowed strongly any connection with the wrangle over the Fritz money. That, they said, was McSween's private affair, not theirs. They were, so they averred, the champions of justice, so openly and flagrantly being flaunted by county officials sworn to uphold it, and did not intend to be drawn into any collateral commotions. Such at least was the spirit in which the organization was conceived.

The Regulators became active immediately. News came to Lincoln that several involved in the killing of Tunstall were down on the Pecos at Dolan and Riley's cow camp. Dick Brewer mustered his Regulators and soon the grimly determined men were riding thither. Reaching the Pecos about March 4, they scouted around and were rewarded on the sixth by the discovery of some of the men they were after. Just a little below the "crossing on the Peñasco" Brewer and his companions "jumped" five, who dashed away in two groups. Morton, Baker, and Sam Lloyd made off in one direction, and the other two went in another. Brewer recognized Morton and Baker and decided to let the others, whoever they were, escape while he undertook to capture two of the more conspicuous ones in the Tunstall killing. The pursuit was desperate; it became a "running fight," extending five or six miles. Sam Lloyd's horse became exhausted and fell, but since Lloyd had not been involved in the Tunstall killing, Brewer did not stop the chase of the other two in order to capture him. Finally the horses of Morton and Baker gave out, and the two men took refuge in a depression in the ground covered heavily with *tule*. Even this protection did not enable them to elude their pursuers. Realizing that the odds were hopeless, they surrendered. Morton had been leader of the sub-posse that overtook Tunstall and faced their victim in his final moments. Baker had been another of the group directly responsible for the shooting. Understandably they feared the worst from their captors.

Brewer gave them, however, a pledge that their lives would be protected. Some in his party objected strongly, Billy the Kid being especially outspoken. "Dick," he said, "we've got two of them and they are the worst of the lot. Let's avenge John Tunstall by killing them right now." Brewer refused to entertain the proposal and started at once toward Lincoln with the prisoners. As the capture had been made rather late in the afternoon, the party had to spend the night at one of the Chisum cow camps in the vicinity. The next day they completed a longer stage of the journey, getting as far as the Chisum headquarters ranch at South Spring River. There they remained Thursday night, March 8, and on Friday morning took up the journey to Lincoln, expecting to arrive there late Sunday. Brewer's men had begun to grow uncertain what reception would await them at the plaza, especially when they returned with two prisoners so vitally connected with the Dolan faction. If they turned Morton and Baker over to Brady, would they not be at large again shortly? To add to the quandary, they encountered at Chisum's ranch a new crop of disquieting reports from Lincoln. Dolan had collected a body of men — twenty or more — and was sending them to intercept the constable's party and effect the release of Morton and Baker.

Another perplexity came about from the presence of McCloskey. While not one of the Regulators, McCloskey presented himself as a sympathizer if not an active partisan of the McSween faction. He had on occasion been temporarily in the employ of Tunstall and was on friendly terms with some of the men with Brewer. Somehow he had attached himself to the expedition after the capture of Baker and Morton and was with the Brewer party at Chisum's ranch. On the other hand, he had been with the second and larger Mathews posse and had seemingly attached himself to that side, although he had not been in the sub-posse that actually shot Tunstall. This fact put a stain on his credentials and made all the Brewer party look on him with suspicion. He was generally regarded as a troublemaker, so his attaching himself to the Brewer party gave rise to anxiety. What if he was a spy? Brewer treated his two prisoners with consideration during the stay at Chisum's ranch, but at the same time he made sure they were guarded vigilantly.

An opportunity was given Morton to write to a kinsman in Virginia. This letter reveals his forebodings:

South Spring River, N. M.
March 8, 1878

H. H. Marshall,
    Richmond, Va.
Dear Sir:

Some time since I was called upon to assist in serving a writ of attachment on some property wherein resistance had been made against the law.

The parties had started off with some horses which should be attached, and I as deputy sheriff with a posse of twelve men was sent in pursuit of same. We overtook them, and while attempting to serve the writ our party was fired on by one J. H. Tunstall, the balance of the party having ran off. The fire was returned and Tunstall was killed. This happened on the 18th of February.

The 6th of March I was arrested by a constable's party, accused of the murder of Tunstall. Nearly all of the sheriff's party fired at him, and it is impossible for any one to say who killed him. When the party which came to arrest me, and one man who was with me, first saw us about one hundred yards distant, we started in another direction when they (eleven in number) fired nearly one hundred shots at us. We ran about five miles, when both of our horses fell and we made a stand. When they came up, they told us if we would give up, they would not harm us.

After talking awhile, we gave up our arms and were made prisoners. There was one man in the party who wanted to kill me after I had surrendered, and was restrained with the greatest difficulty by others of the party. The constable himself said he was sorry we gave up as he had not wished to take us alive. We arrived here last night enroute to Lincoln. I have heard that we were not to be taken alive to that place. I am not at all afraid of their killing me, but if they should do so, I wish that the matter should be investigated and the parties dealt with according to law. If you do not hear from me in four days after receipt of this, I would like you to make inquiries about the affair.

The names of the parties who have me arrested are: R. M. Brewer, J. G. Skurlock, Chas. Bowdre, Wm. Bonney, Henry Brown, Frank McNab, "Wayt," Sam Smith, Jim French (and two others named McCloskey and Middleton who are friends). There are two parties in arms, and violence is expected. The military are at the scene of disorder and trying to keep peace. I will arrive at Lincoln the night of the 10th and will write you immediately if I get through safe. Have been in the employ of Jas. J. Dolan & Co. of Lincoln for eighteen months since the 9th of March '77 and have been getting $60.00 per month. Have about six hundred dollars due me from them and some horses, etc., at their cattle camps.

I hope if it becomes necessary that you will look into this affair, if anything should happen, I refer you to T. B. Catron, U.S. Attorney of Santa Fe, N. M. and Col. Rynerson, District Attorney, La Mesilla, N. M. They both know all about the affair as the writ of attachment was issued by Judge Warren Bristol, La Mesilla, N. M. and everything was legal. If I am taken safely to Lincoln, I will have no trouble, but will let you know.

If it should be as I suspect, please communciate with my brother, Quin Morton, Lewisburg, W. Va. Hoping that you will attend to this affair if it becomes necessary and excuse me for troubling you if it does not,

I remain
Yours respectfully,
W. S. Morton

Lincoln,
   Lincoln Co. N. M.

About ten o'clock in the morning of the ninth, the Brewer party left the Chisum ranch and started their journey toward Lincoln. They travelled some ten miles or more on the road usually taken but then abruptly changed their course northward, following a more circuitous road to Lincoln, seldom used since it swung out almost to the foot of Captain Mountain before turning toward Lincoln. The most plausible explanation of this change of route is that it was a precautionary measure. If the report was true that the Dolan faction contemplated ambushing the posse on the road to Lincoln and rescuing the prisoners, this change of route should defeat that purpose. It might also have the advantage of lengthening the journey so as to reach Lincoln under cover of darkness.

By late afternoon the riders, strung out along the winding road through Blackwater Canyon, had reached a place about five miles below Agua Negro spring. Suddenly Brewer, riding at the rear of the line, heard a fusillade of shots around the bend just ahead. Spurring forward, too late, he found Morton, Baker, and McCloskey shot to death.

To this day the affair remains controversial. The account given circulation by the Dolan partisans was that McCloskey had been killed because he openly declared himself the protector of the prisoners and that the others were shot while on their knees begging for their lives. As a matter of fact, by best reports Morton's body contained nine bullet holes, all in the back. The version which McSween sympathizers accepted — or tried to accept — was that Morton, riding in front with McCloskey, snatched the latter's pistol and shot him with it and that Morton and Baker were killed as they made a dash for liberty, hardly more believable than the story that Tunstall singlehandedly had attacked the Morton posse. It is certain that some members of the party were too embittered to accept Dick Brewer's contention that two wrongs don't make a right but angrily demanded an eye-for-an-eye.

Whatever the circumstances, the fact remains that two of the men directly involved in the murder of Tunstall were now dead and the body of the third man, doubtless a "fifth-columnist" in the posse, lay in what was thereafter to be known as Dead Man's Draw. Brewer rode to a cow camp near the spring and arranged with some native New Mexicans to bury the bodies. The other members of the posse, faced with Brewer's wrath, did not continue on to Lincoln but instead cut across country toward San Patricio and the safety of its surrounding hills. A grim-faced Dick Brewer rode on to Lincoln.

It was late in the evening, Sunday, March 10, when Brewer reached the plaza and sought out McSween for advice as to the proper way for him, as constable, to make his return about the killing of Morton, Baker, and McCloskey. McSween had returned to Lincoln only the day before. He had come to the conclusion that the course adopted at the request of his friends — that of hiding himself away from Lincoln — was ill-advised. He had come back with the determination of remaining in town and submitting to whatever order Dolan might bring Brady from Judge Bristol at Mesilla, even if by doing so he lost his life. This was an act of some courage, coming as he did from one who never "packed a gun." It was a re-affirmation of his determination to be law abiding, to seek his ends through legal means rather than the six-shooter.

17. The Governor Visits the Front

McSWEEN'S RETURN COINCIDED with the visit of Governor Axtell. News of what was happening in Lincoln County had reached Santa Fe. In fact the Dolan side, who counted the Governor as their friend, had seen to it that he was invited to come down to Lincoln and view the troubles from close at hand. On March 8 late in the day he reached Fort Stanton and spent the night there. The next morning he came to Lincoln but spent barely three hours investigating the trouble, all in the company of J. J. Dolan. In fact, the Governor scornfully and superciliously declined to avail himself of any opportunity open to him for getting an impartial view of the situation. He might have interviewed Isaac Ellis, or Shield, or Widenmann, all of whom had been in Lincoln during the recent five or six troubled weeks. Even McSween was not so far away but that he could have appeared in Lincoln had the Governor evinced the slightest desire to talk with him. When someone tried to give him the full history, he said, "I know all about the matter and its cause, and I have already taken such action as I deem necessary."

If the Governor's failure to investigate with impartiality aroused indignation, it became even greater when it transpired what was behind his cryptic remark. The main outcome of the trip to Lincoln County was a proclamation which must rank as one of the most extraordinary official acts ever performed by governor of state or territory. The proclamation itself, together with appropriate editorial comments, is here given in an extract from the Cimarron *News and Press* for March 21, 1878:

LINCOLN COUNTY TROUBLES
Proclamation by the Governor

To the citizens of Lincoln county:

The disturbed condition of affairs at the county seat brings me to Lincoln county at this time. My only object is to assist good citizens to uphold the laws and keep the peace. To enable all to act intelligently it is important that the following facts should be clearly understood.

First — John B. Wilson's appointment by the county commissioners as a justice of the peace was illegal and void, and all processes issued by him were void, and said Wilson has no authority whatever to act as justice of the peace.

Second — The appointment of Robert Widenmann as U. S. Marshal has been revoked, and said Widenmann is not now a peace officer, nor has he any power or authority whatever to act as such.

Third — The President of the United States, upon an application made by me as Governor of New Mexico, has directed the post commander, Col. Geo. A. Purington, to assist territorial civil officers in maintaining order and enforcing legal process. It follows from the above statements of facts that there is no legal process in this case to be enforced, except the writs and processes issued out of the third judicial district court by Judge Bristol, and there are no territorial civil officers here to enforce these except sheriff Brady and his deputies.

Now, therefore, in consideration of the premises, I do hereby command all persons to immediately disarm and return to their homes and usual occupations, under penalty of being arrested and confined in jail as disturbers of the public peace.

(Signed) S. B. Axtell
Governor

Lincoln, N. M., March 9, 1878
A true copy.

Geo. A. Purington,
Capt. 9th Cav'y
Cmd'g Post of Fort Stanton

To understand the true inwardness of the above proclamation it must be known that Mr. Wilson, the justice of the peace, had issued warrants for the apprehension of the outlaws Baker, Evans, et al., and that Robert Widenmann, the Dept. U.S. Marshal, had openly expressed his indignation at the conduct of Sheriff Brady and the killing of Mr. Tunstall.

The governor says there is no writ to be enforced except that issued out of the district court, and no officer must be recognized but Sheriff Brady and his deputies — the outlaws Evans, Baker and others who were the murderers of Tunstall.

It seems as if Lincoln County was going through an experience similar, in many respects, to that of Colfax a few years ago. The more the facts are made public the more outrageous do some recent events appear.

The murder of Mr. Tunstall seems to have been a most damnable and dastardly crime. He was a merchant and broker, and was a bold outspoken man, as the lamented Tolby was. He exposed some of the acts of the sheriff in misappropriating public moneys, and using the taxes to speculate in cattle instead of paying his collections into the treasury. Thereupon he is pursued by a sheriff's posse composed partly of notorious outlaws who had broken jail while in custody of this sheriff, and murdered in the most brutal and revolting manner.

The indignation of the people at such an infernal deed was naturally intense, and it began to look as though the locality would be made too hot for this sheriff and those in whose interest he seemed to be running his office, and thereupon his Eminence, Gov. Axtell, went to the rescue and secured an order from the President of the United States to have the military suppress the indignation and assist this sheriff and his OUTLAW deputies to administer the law.

We are in daily receipt of letters from responsible men of Lincoln County, who charge that the whole of the governor's efforts were directed to protect the members of the sheriff's posse that killed Tunstall, and that he pays about the same regard to the representation of the people of that section that he did to the repeated requests of the citizens of Colfax County to visit us and investigate affairs for himself.

It would be interesting to know just what these troops are called in for. Is it to assist in bringing to justice the murderers, or is it to protect the members of a ring who fear that the forbearance of an outraged people has reached its limit?

It is about time that this thing of employing the military to assist partisan tyranny was brought to the attention of Congress.

The first section of this proclamation seemed to be an attempt to throw dust in the eyes of the people and make them believe that the only officials having legal authority were those known to have friendliness for the Dolan faction.

The proclamation jolted the citizens of Lincoln County. It was generally conceded that the Dolan element had scored heavily, but it was felt also that even though the position assumed by the Governor might be to some degree right and proper, it was decidedly of doubtful expediency. With the citizenry already wrought up to a lawless and semi-rebellious mood, legal hair-splitting was untimely to say the least. Almost immediately the harmful effect of the proclamation became evident. In the next three or four weeks matters went rapidly from bad to worse. As the inflammation grew more acute, more and more thoughtful persons throughout New Mexico laid the responsibility upon Governor Axtell.

No sooner did McSween learn of the Governor's proclamation than he foresaw what the results would be. The Governor was clearly aligned with the Dolan faction. More dismaying still was the possibility that the military at Fort Stanton would be drawn into the affair. Prior to the visit to Lincoln, Governor Axtell had asked President Hayes for authorization to use soldiers in civil disturbances. This request had borne fruit when from Santa Fe on March 5 the district commander, Colonel Hatch, had telegraphed explicit instruction to Captain Purington at Fort Stanton. What made the position taken by Governor Axtell in this proclamation the more astonishing was that he nullified a law passed only two years before by the territorial assembly and signed by himself. This law distinctly empowered the county commissioners to appoint justices of the peace. Under it Squire Wilson had been appointed by the county commissioners in 1876 and had functioned for two years undisturbed by any question of the legality of his appointment. His removal from office put a new aspect on the activities of the Regulators. Now that the appointment was revoked, possibly the warrants held by Dick Brewer as special constable were not worth the paper they were written on. In the whole proceeding the tricky hand of partisanship was discernable.

Much of the same attitude could be perceived in the references to Widenmann. The statement that his appointment as deputy United States marshal had been revoked was designed to put a quietus on his activities. True it was that in the first excitement following the killing of Tunstall the United States marshal at Santa Fe, John Sherman, had revoked Widenmann's appointment, but a few days later, upon finding some of the stories that reached Santa Fe about Widenmann's conduct were misrepresentations, he had promptly reinstated him.

The real object of the proclamation became evident in the third section. In drawing attention to the fact that the district court and the sheriff were alone empowered to issue and execute warrants the Governor became so misleading as to ignore the fact that Lincoln County had four other justices of the peace besides the deposed Squire Wilson. Unquestionably these were still empowered.

When Brewer brought in the report of what had happened to Morton and Baker, McSween had to tell him that Governor Axtell's proclamation and the new orders about the use of soldiers put him and his companions in a parlous state. His actions as constable could be construed as extra-legal. In fact, Brady was supposed to be already taking steps to arrest Brewer and his associates for their recent activities. The news of the killing of Morton and Baker, as soon as it leaked out, would most assuredly add fuel to the fire. The best advice McSween could give was for Brewer and all others to give Lincoln a wide berth until court convened, when there might be some chance to get the tangled situation straightened out. Seeing that this was the only course, Brewer left Lincoln the same night for his farm on the Ruidoso. To his companions in the vicinity of San Patricio he carried the news that they were virtually outlaws.

The possible repercussions from the killing of McCloskey, Morton, and Baker caused McSween to leave Lincoln the second time. Once the community got into a ferment over these killings, clearly he would be in danger — so his friends argued — and he finally was brought to acquiesce to their advice. On Monday the eleventh, McSween, accompanied by Barrier, in whose custody he was, fled Lincoln. This time he decided to go down to the Pecos and seek sanctuary in the vicinity of Chisum's ranch. He proposed to stay there until court convened, when he expected to return to Lincoln and be on hand for his trial on the embezzlement charge. The selection of the place of refuge was in some degree influenced by the fact that John Chisum had just returned to Lincoln County after release from the confinement at Las Vegas that had been his lot since January. Now that Lincoln County affairs were growing more critical — one faction had its one notable killing, that of Tunstall, as its score; the other, three, those of Morton, Baker, and McCloskey — the active support of John Chisum would mean much. The hospitality of the Chisum ranch would also make it possible for Mrs. McSween, who was expecting to return from St. Louis where she had been since January, to be in the vicinity of her husband. Her aggressive disposition was certain to give her a part in subsequent events; her vivid personality was certain to be focused on the shrewd old cattle king of the Pecos Valley in an attempt to draw him into active partisanship on behalf of the McSween side.

On the thirteenth of March, just two days after McSween's flight from Lincoln, the Jesse Evans contingent came into notice again. While Brewer and the Regulators were in the Pecos country, Jesse Evans and Tom Hill had sneaked down into the vicinity of Tularosa from their main hiding place in the Sacramento Mountains. They descended upon the camp of John Wagner, an old German who was

The South Spring River Ranch of John Chisum was a place of refuge for McSween and others when the Murphy-Dolan faction was in pursuit. After the Lincoln County War was over, the cattle king of the Pecos country turned his attention to agriculture — orchards and field crops — and built the adobe "long house" pictured here to replace the original flat-roofed ranch dwelling.

taking a flock of some 4,000 sheep from California over to the Concho country in Texas. When the raid was made, the camp happened to be in charge of only one man, the driver of the wagon; the others were with the sheep at a watering place some distance away, so Evans and Hill encountered no resistance. While they were looting the camp they were so intently engaged that they failed to notice the approach of Wagner returning alone from the place where the sheep were being watered.

Seeing what was going on, the old man snatched up the rifle belonging to Hill, which had been left leaning against a tree, and blazed away at the intruders. Hill was killed and Jesse Evans wounded. One of the wounds was in the wrist, the other in the lungs. In spite of his condition, Evans made his escape with a remarkable display of stamina. He rode all night and reached Shedd's ranch in the Organ Mountains, where he was certain of a friendly reception. After remaining there for a few days in concealment, he decided that the wise thing was to go to Fort Stanton and give himself up to the commanding officer. This step would enable him to get proper attention to his wounds and would afford him protection from the Regulators. The Fort accepted him as a prisoner to be held until court convened, when he was certain to be tried either under some of the old warrants or under some new ones that were certain to be forthcoming. He made a good recovery from his wounds although the one in the wrist might develop a permanent lameness. The raid on the sheep camp had cost the life of one of his associates, but even that loss might have its compensation. Might it not afford a scapegoat upon whom might be placed the responsibility of the actual killing of Tunstall? Now that Tom Hill had been wiped off the slate, what could be handier than to claim that he had fired the shot that killed Tunstall?

18. Widenmann Versus the New Mexican

DURING MARCH, WIDENMANN'S zealous and indefatigable pen earned for him a vicious attack from the Santa Fe *New Mexican*, the recognized organ of the Santa Fe ring. Shortly after the killing of Tunstall, Widenmann had written briefly of the murder to R. Guy McClellan, a prominent lawyer of San Francisco. Widenmann had turned to him as an influential friend of Tunstall, knowing that from McClellan had come some letters of introduction to Governor Axtell and others which Tunstall had brought to New Mexico. Widenmann's letter happened to become part of the communication from McClellan to Governor Axtell and the Governor in turn handed it to the *New Mexican*. That journal took the opportunity to riddle Widenmann to its heart's content. The reason for the attack was obvious; Widenmann's frank and succinct statements had galled and pinched certain ones at Santa Fe. The letter that stirred up the journalistic furor was as follows:

> 330 Pine Street
> San Francisco, Cal.,
> March 9, 1878

Hon. S. B. Axtell,
    Governor of New Mexico:
My Dear Sir:

At this moment I write you respecting a painful matter. I here insert a copy of a letter just received by me from your territory.

Office of John H. Tunstall
Lincoln, Lincoln County, N. M.,
Feb. 26, 1878

To R. Guy McClellan,
    San Fancisco, Cal.
Dear Sir:

I am under the painful necessity of informing you that my dear friend, Mr. John H. Tunstall, was murdered about 11 miles from here by a party of 18 outlaws and murderers on the 18th inst. about 5½ o'clock, p.m. Three others and I, who were with Mr. Tunstall at the time, only escaped by taking a determined stand. It was a cold-blooded and premeditated murder, committed in the interest of the New Mexico ring, and as the ring controls the courts of the territory, it is difficult to bring the murderers to justice. Even our sheriff here is in the ring and refuses to allow the murderers to be arrested.

I have laid the case before the British minister at Washington, and would politely request you to bring all your influence to bear with the British Minister and the authorities at Washington to have the murder thoroughly investigated.

Yours truly,
Robert A. Widenmann.

The above is the letter and all I that know of the affair. That such a state of affairs can exist, as here stated, I can not believe, and therefore refer the matter to you, both as a friend, and in your high official capacity, so that no such disgrace, if true, may rest upon any section of our country.

Yours respectfully,
R. Guy McClellan.

The *New Mexican* rushed to the fray. The opening paragraph of comment as follows:

The above correspondence was handed to us for publication by Governor Axtell. It will be noticed that Widenmann wrote within a few days after the death of Tunstall and before it was possible for the district court to take any action. Its regular meeting is on the second day of April, where there will be a grand jury called and the whole affair fully investigated. Since Widenmann's letter was written, arrests were made under color of the law by some of the party who were with Tunstall, of two of the men accused of assisting to kill him; these two men were killed by the party who had them in charge. One of the arresting party was also killed. The facts in the case have not been fully ascertained.

The next section of the article praised Governor Axtell for his activity in the matter, mentioning that he had telegraphed a request to President Hayes for authorization to use the soldiers at Fort Stanton to help the civil authorities in Lincoln County maintain order. It also brought out the fact that the Governor had personally visited Lincoln County. This led next into a general account of Lincoln County as understood by other sections of New Mexico.

> Lincoln is the southeast corner county of New Mexico. It is partly inhabited by Indians, the Mescalero Apache, who blows where he listeth; by Texas cattle men, a few traders and business men, and a few skeleton companies of United States troops. In the late El Paso and San Elizeario troubles, quite a number of the outlaw class rode down to the scene of the disturbance, for where the carcasses are, there jayhawkers gather. There they were Texas Rangers and fought for God and liberty. After signalizing themselves by deeds which will be recorded when the commission makes its report, they rode back to Lincoln.

At this point in the article the guns were turned upon Widenmann personally:

> This man Widenmann was appointed a deputy United States marshal by Marshal Sherman to take a company of United States troops from Fort Stanton and arrest the worst of the band, dead or alive; unfortunately he failed to do so, and the life of Tunstall, a worthy and valuable citizen, has been lost. All the facts in this case are yet to be investigated by a grand jury, and we do not think it proper to speak about them further at present. The slanders upon the courts by Widenmann are without any foundation in fact. He has forfeited the confidence of Marshal Sherman and all good men here, and has been removed from office. Col. George A. Purington, 9th Cavalry, Sheriff Brady of Lincoln County, Col. W. L. Rynerson, of Las Cruces, district attorney for the third district, and Hon. Warren Bristol, United States judge presiding over the district — each and every one of them enjoy and deserve the confidence and esteem of the best men in New Mexico.

This letter provoked Widenmann to a sharp reply, which was published in the Cimarron *News and Press* early in April.

Lincoln, N.M., March 30, 1878

News and Press — The *New Mexican* of 23rd inst. contains a copy of my letter to a gentleman in San Francisco and the editorial comments thereon.

The comments, like all others made by the gentlemanly (?) editors, are full of Billingsgate and blatherskite. Mud and dirt are, as usual, freely thrown, and I with others am of the opinion that the editors unfortunately mistake their calling. They would have made excellent adobe layers for they could then have indulged in their favorite pastime to their heart's content. Now for a glance at the comments.

The *New Mexican* says: "Arrests were made under color of law." The facts are that warrants were sworn out for the arrest of Mr. Tunstall's murderers before Justice of the Peace J. B. Wilson, and Morton and Baker were arrested on these before his Excellency the Governor arrived here and arbitrarily withdrew Mr. Wilson's commission. Morton killed McCloskey while riding by the side of the latter with Mc's own pistol, and he and Baker started to run, firing back at the posse at the same time. Sheriff Brady refused to allow the other murderers, who at the time were at the house of J. J. Dolan & Co., to be arrested, but on the other hand arrested and disarmed the constables' posse when they came to serve the papers and held two of the posse prisoners for 24 hours.

The question is often asked: What did the Governor do here? Did he call a meeting of citizens to ascertain from them the cause of the trouble? Did he take the opinions of good and respectable citizens, weight them as to their merits, and then form his course of action? No! When one of our most esteemed and respected citizens attempted to give him a history of the trouble and its causes, he quietly remarked: "I know all about this matter and its cause, and I have already taken such action as I deem necessary." The question is, where did he learn the facts, and what were they? Powers behind the throne are generally well posted as to the facts on their side of the case. The Governor also said: "God deliver us from such citizens as there are in Lincoln county," to which I answered that the citizens were all right, but "God deliver me from such executive officers." I do not think it is hard to see how at least one officer of the territory could have "done more," as the *New Mexican* says. The editors of the *New Mexican* would do well to study the map of the territory more closely. All the maps I have seen show Doña Ana to be the southeast county of New Mexico, not Lincoln.

No doubt during the El Paso troubles many of the outlaw class (the *New Mexican* will please bear in mind that last fall it denied the existence of any such class or clan, and threw mud at the Mesilla *Independent* for saying that there was such a band in existence) were there, but they left those fertile regions in time to meet J. J. Dolan at San Augustin, there with Dolan to threaten

Mr. Tunstall's life, to drive from San Augustin to the Indian agency in the same ambulance with Dolan, and arrive here in time to form part of Sheriff Brady's posse, notwithstanding this same man Brady had warrants for their arrest, and had once had them in jail, from which place of confinement they escaped (?).

I tried my utmost to arrest Evans, Baker and others, but with such powerful friends ready to aid them, to harbor and conceal them, to furnish them horses and supplies as J. J. Dolan, J. H. Riley and others, no one who knows this country will doubt that their arrest was a matter of the utmost difficulty. One of the parties who escaped from jail, and for whose arrest Brady had a warrant, only the other day was one of his posse, and was at the house of J. J. Dolan with him.

Morton is said to have been a good man; so says the *New Mexican*. Are the editors aware of his having murdered a man, in cold-blood, on the Pecos; of his killing two men in this county, and of his killing his partner in the mines in Arizona? Truly, a good man!

As regards the complimentary names given me by the editors of the *New Mexican* and their story of my actions at the time of the murder of Mr. Tunstall — which story is simply a base lie — I pass them over as nothing, considering the source they come from. The editors have long since shown their faculty of judging others by themselves. Only an idiot could conceive the idea that a Deputy U.S. Marshal had the right to run off a band of horses. Mr. Tunstall himself came to the ranch and decided to bring the horses with him, all but three or four of them having been declared free from the attachment by the sheriff two or three days before.

I still desire a thorough investigation of the murder of Mr. Tunstall, and feel certain that an honest enquiry will show facts which will open the eyes of many a person.

The Governor's action has made it almost impossible, so far, to bring the murderers to justice.

Every line of the *New Mexican's* lengthy tirade, shows, that the shoe pinches not only one but several corns.

The viper is again aroused; may it be its death struggle.

Very truly yours,
Robert A. Widenmann

This letter from Widenmann gave the *News and Press*, always on the opposite side of the fence from the *New Mexican*, an excellent opening to indulge in baiting the *New Mexican*. The following appeared in the issue for April 4:

THE *NEW MEXICAN* ON ITS EAR

Robert A. Widenmann, Esq., deputy U.S. Marshal in Lincoln County wrote a letter to R. Guy McClellan of San Francisco, giving an account of the murder of Mr. J. H. Tunstall, and asking him to "use all his influence with the British minister and the authorities at Washington to have the assassination thoroughly investigated." The *New Mexican* published this letter — which had been sent to Gov. Axtell — last week, and vented its feeble rage on Widenmann, noting with especial satisfaction that he had been removed from his position by Marshal Sherman. It seems that the Governor felt a similar satisfaction, so great, indeed, that he could not refrain from making it the subject of an executive proclamation.

In the meantime, however, Mr. Sherman, learning the facts, reappointed Widenmann, and thereupon, in this week's issue, the *New Mexican* starts off in a flight so hyperbolic that we tremble lest it may not get back into its wonted tranquil orbit. It says that the U.S. Marshal Sherman has reappointed Widenmann and thus endorsed his utterances. This is certainly a very substantial kind of endorsement, and one that will add great weight to Mr. Widenmann's statements, and we are happy to find that the marshal's views coincide so nearly with ours.

In frothy rage the *New Mexican* observes that Widenmann, a U.S. officer and so forth, etc., goes to the British Minister "with his complaint that a murder has been committed." Truly, he must be an over-particular sort of an official if he complains of so trivial an occurrence. If he had only lodged a complaint against some of those who have been slandering the banditti — who endorsed the *New Mexican* by resolution in their meeting in the mountains, a few months since, as published in the *Independent* — there would have been some sense in it.

"What has Attorney General Devens done that he should be ignored?" it cries. We are sure we don't know, but we expect he is getting used to it, as the *New Mexican* took especial pleasure in announcing that he had been snubbed by Attorney General Breeden.

"Where is the President of the United States?" Well, we cannot be certain, but as likely as not he is taking a cold water cocktail with Stanley Matthews over the lucky stroke by which the Louisiana Supreme Court helped him and the returning board out of a bad scrape. It wants to know "if the United States marshal in this territory is disgusted with the territorial government." To be frank, we must say we think it extremely probable that he is, and also that a very large number of the people of New Mexico are of the same feeling, and join the *News and Press* in the opinion that in this respect Marshal Sherman exhibits remarkably good taste and good judgment.

"Has a British subject, resident in New Mexico, any other or different rights from any other resident?"

His rights in New Mexico depend very largely upon his position, relative to a well-known circle, whose center is not very far from the palace in Santa Fe.

"Does this renegade American; this traitor to the honor of his flag; ask that British tribunals shall try the murderers of Tunstall? Would he have them transported beyond seas for that purpose?"

If he did, it would be no worse than what those, whose organ the *New Mexican* is, did to the whole county of Colfax for two years.

"If Judge Bristol does not lay him by the heels in jail till he is purged of this infamous contempt, we are mistaken in our judge."

We don't know whether Judge Bristol — "our judge" — will be guided in his judicial action by the dictation of the *New Mexican*, but we are happy to say that he is the only judge in New Mexico who is likely to be thus influenced.

A week later the *News and Press* came forward with another article which showed how fallacious was the charge made by the *New Mexican* that Widenmann was responsible for the death of Tunstall because he had not succeeded, as deputy United States marshal, in arresting the Jesse Evans contingent.

A LOGICAL CONCLUSION!

The *New Mexican* says Mr. Widenmann, the deputy U.S. Marshal, is responsible for the murder of his friend Mr. Tunstall, and all the troubles in Lincoln County, because he did not arrest the outlaws, who murdered Tunstall, long ago, and then proceeds to empty its sewers of filth on him in its usual style.

This is strange logic. Mr. Widenmann wrote a private note to a gentleman in San Francisco, in which he expressed his opinions pretty freely. This letter coming into the hands of Governor Axtell for information on the subject, he chose to have it published.

The papers in the southern part of the territory have been filled continually with complaints because the outlaws were allowed to frequent all the large towns, right under the nose of the authorities, and make boast of their robberies and immunity from arrest.

In an article in the Mesilla Valley *Independent* of Feb'y 2nd, '78, which article we would like to republish in full, would our space permit, the writer expresses intense indignation at the indifference of the authorities in the matter, and in a warning voice declares, that the public feeling has already reached a point where the people, for self-preservation, will soon take the law in their own hands.

Now taking into consideration that, in addition to this fact, Sheriff Brady found it necessary to write his deputy special instructions not to employ notorious outlaws in his posse, and that he, Sheriff Brady, was often in their company, indeed had one in his company at the time of his death; and taking, also, into consideration that the Governor, when it became necessary, called in the military to protect these men, is it to be wondered that Mr. Widenmann found their arrest a difficult matter to accomplish?

Language is strained by the *New Mexican* to find epithets bad enough to fling at Widenmann because he could not arrest somebody for stealing U.S. property, but we have failed to find in its columns any word of denunciation for the officials who employed bandits and escaped jail birds in their service, or for those who planned and executed the assassination of J. H. Tunstall. That paper, which so long denied the existence of outlaws and bandits in that region, may dodge the real issue, but the people will not forget it.

19. The Killing of Brady and Hindman

IRONICALLY ENOUGH, APRIL 1 had witnessed one of the grimmest incidents of the Lincoln County conflict. On that day the feud reached a point where some of the Regulators acting independently of both McSween and Brewer, the recognized leaders of their faction, deliberately ambushed Sheriff Brady and George Hindman, one of his deputies.

A session of the district court was scheduled for April 8, but due to some misunderstanding had been announced for April 1. Some members of the Regulators, expected in court either as witnesses or as the accused, had gathered at Lincoln during the evening of March 31 to be on hand for the court sessions. These, reportedly Macnab, French, Waite, Middleton, Billy the Kid, and Henry Brown, spent the night on the premises of the Tunstall store. They discussed what they considered the wrongs they and their friends had suffered at the hands of the Dolan party, particularly from its instrument, Brady. They must have worked themselves up into a fever of hatred; some, at least, proposed to put a summary end to this injustice and persecution. The attempt was not long in coming.

It was about nine o'clock on Monday morning when Brady, Hindman, Mathews, Long, and Peppin walked from the Dolan store at the west end of the hamlet to the building which served as a courthouse, an adobe building located back from the road near the Montaño store. Their walk took them directly past the Tunstall store, which they passed without incident. Near the courthouse they stopped to notify some prospective jurors of the error in announcement of date. Then they started back to the Dolan headquarters.

The corral at the rear (north) of the Tunstall store was surrounded by a high adobe wall and had a narrow extension along the east side of the building to form a driveway to the road. The driveway led to a wooden gate located about two-thirds of the distance between the rear and the front of the store, thus being set back several feet from the front of the building and from the road. From this point there was a clear view of anyone approaching from the east, while the store building cut off the view of anyone approaching from the west until the area immediately in front of the gate had been reached. It was from this gate that the Regulator group watched as the Brady party, scattered rather than in a single group, were leaving the court building.

Suddenly rifle shots rang out. Brady fell in his tracks mortally wounded, his body pierced by several bullets. Hindman, wounded by a single shot, managed to stagger back a few steps toward the courthouse before he, too, fell. Before he died he moaned a plea for water. His plea was answered by Ike Stockton, who was at his saloon in the corner room of Montaño's store, just east of the courthouse. Jack Long, who was in the road almost directly in front of the court building, according to the map drawn at the time by Dr. Ealy, was also hit.

Gregorio Wilson, who as a boy of eight had witnessed the affair, described to this writer how he and his sister had been playing in front of their home opposite the Tunstall store when his father, Green Wilson, was the victim of a stray bullet. Mr. Wilson, quietly hoeing the onion patch beside his house, received flesh wounds in both legs between the hips and knees. Billy the Kid received a wound on the inside of his left thigh, according to Gregorio, when he stooped to pick up his rifle which Brady had confiscated from him in February and which had now fallen from the sheriff's hands. This shot, from the Cisneros house, has been generally attributed to Billy Mathews, though Jack Long was later quoted as claiming the credit.

When the town quieted down after the fight and none of their enemies appeared in sight, Macnab and the others, except Billy the Kid, rode out of town. When they had passed the outskirts of the village four shots from John Long's rifle followed them, one shot seriously wounding Jim French; Long's fire was returned and they withdrew. Billy was forced to remain at Lincoln for a day or so since his wound, though not serious, made horseback riding uncomfortable, if not impossible.

Summoned by Peppin, Captain Purington and twenty-five soldiers from Fort Stanton arrived in town shortly after noon. Lincoln

Lincoln, New Mexico, became the county seat but retained the closely knit appearance of a small Mexican village, as seen here from the mountains. Note the proximity of the houses to one another. Few changes had occurred when this photograph was taken, presumably about five years after the Lincoln County War. Strategic locations in the Five-Day Battle are identified on endsheet maps.

cherishes many legends about the unsuccessful search through the houses and the country surrounding Lincoln that afternoon. One, told in dramatic detail, relates that the wounded Billy was harbored in the small home of a Mexican-American family and that when Peppin and a party of soldiers were seen approaching, the housewife hastily concealed the young man in an empty barrel, over the top of which she placed a board on which she continued to mix dough for *tortillas* as she invited the visitors to search the place.

There are other stories, at least one of which bears the stamp of authenticity. Miss Ruth Ealy, an infant at the time of the Brady killing, in later years wrote out her father's account:

> Father stated that someone ran out to pick up either Brady's or Hindman's gun and was shot as he stooped over, not through the bowels as reported, but through the left thigh. Father said that the man came walking through the door and he treated him by drawing a silk handkerchief through the wound and binding it up. Soon the Murphy-Dolan crowd, who had tracked the man by his blood, came to search the house. It seems that Sam Corbett had taken the wounded man in charge and they disappeared. Afterwards, father learned that Sam Corbett had sawed a hole under a bed and laid the man there with a gun in his hand.

Expecting that court was to start on the first, McSween had come up from the Pecos country and reached Lincoln about noon. With him were a number from the eastern part of the county — Mrs. McSween, John Chisum, C. Simpson, a man named Howes, and Dr. Montague R. Leverson. The latter was a visitor who had been staying at Chisum's; he had come from Colorado into the Pecos Valley looking for a suitable place to establish a colony of settlers he expected to get together. Few at the time suspected he was the holder of a trump card to be played in the Lincoln County troubles, but such was the case. He had unusual influence with the Hayes administration and was able to bring discomfiture upon some of the prominent politicians of New Mexico.

So fearful was McSween of an attempt on his life while in Lincoln that he and his companions had made a circuit which took them by Fort Stanton so that McSween could endeavor to get a guard of soldiers to insure his safety. His request had been refused by Captain Purington, and the McSween party had come on to Lincoln without having any inkling of the developments of the morning. Only when they came to the outskirts of the town did they first hear that Brady and Hindman had been killed.

In the early afternoon the arrival of Captain Purington with a detachment of cavalry added fuel to the commotion. Brady's adherents immediately became galvanized into action and started a round of arrests. Peppin, solely on the strength of having been one of Brady's deputies, and entirely ignoring the fact that his office had expired with the death of his chief, started right and left among the McSween faction. Unable to get his hands on any of the actual six, one or more of whom had done the shooting, he turned to others like Widenmann, who admitted that he had been in the corral early that morning but claimed he had no part in the later shooting. He also took into custody George Washington and George Robinson, who had also been inside the corral walls. He arrested McSween's brother-in-law, Shield, who had been in his living quarters and knew nothing about the matter until he heard the shots. McSween was arrested as soon as he came back to town, though his absence obviously exonerated him from any degree of complicity. Although some of those in the corral were prominent members of the Regulators, this bushwhacking could hardly be considered an officially planned act of the McSween faction; since the killing of Morton, Baker, and McCloskey, Brewer had confined himself to long-neglected work at his farm on the Ruidoso, and McSween had been absent from that part of the country, in hiding in the Pecos Valley. The men in the Tunstall corral, mulling over an accumulation of grievances at the hands of Brady, suddenly saw a way of evening the score and doing away with their oppressor. It is doubtful whether they contemplated such an overt act when they came to Lincoln; probably the whole affair was a matter of impulse. The realization that out in the street were five of the other faction, all of whom had taken some part in the killing of Tunstall, proved too much of a temptation for their trigger fingers.

Peppin, however, did not have things exactly his own way in making these arrests even though he was reinforced by Captain Purington. When he went to the Tunstall store to get Widenmann, the latter naturally asked in his usual grandiose manner, "By what authority do you arrest me?" Purington replied brusquely, "Don't put on any frills," and Widenmann submitted without more ado. The arrest of McSween was less easy. Accompanied by Lieutenant C. W. Smith and two soldiers, Peppin went down to the Ellis place where McSween was and sent in word to McSween by Isaac Ellis that he was there to arrest him. McSween replied that he would not recognize Peppin's authority. Lieutenant Smith then sent in an inquiry whether McSween would see him. McSween answered affirmatively and as the outcome of the interview agreed to surrender to Lieutenant Smith. He made it clear, however, that he regarded it as a step to place himself under the protection of military authorities. Lieutenant Smith accepted that as the understanding and promised McSween entire safety.

As the three were coming away from the Ellis place they chanced to meet Captain Purington. When he learned of the arrangement entered into by Lieutenant Smith and McSween, he flatly refused to hold McSween under military protection unless Peppin, whom he spoke of as the "acting sheriff," gave permission. This displeased McSween and he started to argue the matter. Peppin then brought up the question of searching the McSween residence to see if some of the murderers of Brady might not be using it as a hiding place, or at least concealing guns and ammunition. To this McSween objected vigorously, asserting that Peppin had no legal authority to enter his house and make a search. Peppin appealed to Purington to empower him to go ahead. Although the Captain would not go to the length of sending soldiers with Peppin, he did not seek to interfere when Peppin went ahead and made an entry into the McSween home.

At this point Dr. Leverson became highly excited over the high-handed proceedings. He had no connection with either side; he was a mere stranger who had come along with the party from Chisum's ranch mainly in order to see more of the country. He arrived just in the nick of time to see how the law had become a beggary in Lincoln. Unable to hold his peace at such doings, he began protests against flouting American constitutional provisions regarding security of person and property from seizure or search without due warrant. His intrusion got decidedly on Captain Purington's nerves and brought from him an unguarded expression of contempt for the constitution. Such a remark from an army officer shocked Leverson, not beyond expression, but rather to inspire expression. Turning to the soldiers present, he began a harangue to them. He even advised them in a matter of this sort to disobey their officers. This was going entirely too far, Purington thought; he said to Leverson sharply, "Shut up! You are making a damn fool of yourself!" This broke up the address to the soldiers but it did not keep Leverson from firing the parting shot, "God knows, I would not live in a country where such outrages as these I have witnessed this afternoon are countenanced." All this drew from Purington was a curt, "Sir, you have my permission to suit yourself."

The row between Leverson and Purington afforded McSween a cue for a final protest against the searching of his home. To Purington he said, "If your soldiers were not here, Peppin would never dare to enter and search my house." The only reply vouchsafed to this from Purington was an order to his men to prepare to return to Fort

Stanton. It seemed to McSween and the others placed under arrest highly important to remain under the aegis of the military and thereby escape being left in the hands of Peppin, which was virtually to hand them over to the Dolan faction. They climbed into the wagon which was ready to take them to the Fort and followed the cavalcade of soldiers.

At the Fort, McSween and his four companions, Widenmann, Shield, George Washington, and George Robinson, had anything but a cordial reception. Captain Purington grudgingly allowed them quarters but troubled not a whit about their comfort. McSween managed to get two rooms at the post trader's, one for his wife and himself and the other for Widenmann and Shield. The two Negroes had to accept the guardhouse. All were technically under close confinement except Mrs. McSween, who had come along simply to be with her husband. Evidently Purington did not like to harbor the group, but he was afraid that if he did not he might be called a partisan of the other side.

That night McSween penned a long account of the day's momentous events and sent it to the Cimarron *News and Press*, which published it in the issue for Thursday, April 11. The extract gives such a full review that even at the risk of some repetition of details it should be inserted:

Thursday, April 11, 1878

LATEST FROM LINCOLN COUNTY
Killing of Sheriff Brady
and One of the Murderers of Tunstall

Fort Stanton, N. M., April 1, 1878

News and Press. — William Brady, sheriff of Lincoln County, and George Hindman were killed today in the town of Lincoln. The former gave the murder of Mr. Tunstall a legal color, whilst the latter was one of the perpetrators of that foul deed. For this deplorable state of affairs Gov. Axtell, in the opinion of our people, is, to a great extent, responsible. In his famous proclamation of the 9th ult., he states: "The disturbed condition of affairs at the county seat brings me to Lincoln County at this time. My only object is to assist good citizens to uphold the law and keep the peace." So far so good. How did he proceed to ascertain the position of affairs? He came here on Friday evening, on Saturday morning he went to Lincoln and conversed with L. G. Murphy — "the big dog of the political tanyard" as the N.M. style him. After having the Murphy story, the good Governor was satisfied, and had neither time nor patience to hear the people's version of the difficulties. Messrs. Ellis, Shield, and Widenmann offered to give him their version and implored him to visit the people and learn from himself; this his Excellency indignantly refused to do. His stay at Lincoln did not exceed three hours, so that he could not have spent much time seeking information from which to deduce a correct and impartial conclusion. Having fully informed himself, on all the points he wanted, he devoted his time to the issuing of the proclamation referred to, and which will make his Excellency forever famous in the annals of New Mexico.

In this proclamation he starts out by stating that John B. Wilson, J.P. for Precinct No. 1, is not a justice of the peace, that his appointment by the county commissioners as such was illegal and void, "and all processes issued by him were void." To understand this remarkable executive document intelligently, let it be borne in mind, that Mr. Wilson had in good faith issued warrants for the arrest of the alleged murderers of Mr. Tunstall, and placed them in the hands of a special constable. At the time the Governor was writing his proclamation, that constable was endeavoring to apprehend the murders of Tunstall by virtue of a process that his Excellency characterized as void. Strange that Governor Axtell, well learned in the law as he is, should at this late day discover that the county commissioners had no power to appoint Mr. Wilson as J.P., when the act empowering county commissioners to fill designated vacancies was approved by him two years ago! Stranger still, the Governor usurps the province of the courts. If Mr. Wilson were not a justice, as the Governor proclaims, then a proceeding should have been instituted in our courts to test that fact. But this would have been too tedious, and numerous arrests of murderers, etc. would have been made that he evidently desired to avoid. (On what other hypothesis can this strange action of the Governor's be explained? — Ed. N. & P.) He goes on to state that the appointment of R. A. Widenmann as U.S. marshal was revoked — which was none of his business; that Col. Purington had been directed to assist civil officers in maintaining order, etc.; that it followed from what he had said of Wilson that there was no legal process in this cause (what case? that against the murderers of Mr. Tunstall?) and no civil officer to enforce them except Sheriff Brady and his deputies; that there were no legal processes except those issued by the Third Judicial District Court. He overlooked the fact that Mr. Wilson was not the only J.P. in the county, there being four other J.P.s duly elected by the people at the last election, and commissioned by Governor Axtell; there is also a corresponding number of constables duly elected, etc. Cannot the former issue processes and the latter serve them? The venerable governor's "thirdly" is entirely too sweeping, and shows the cloven foot.

The special constable referred to arrested Morton and Baker, two of Tunstall's murderers, by virtue of a warrant issued by Mr. Wilson as above stated. He came to Lincoln to report their arrest and death, when and where he was informed of the governor's conduct. He left town for a while. The next thing we knew "The House" obtained warrants for his arrest and for those who were with him. These warrants were issued by a J.P. at Blazer's mill, though the governor proclaimed that there could be no legal warrants except those issued by the Third Judicial District Court. These men having committed no other crime than serving warrants duly issued, and knowing that "The House" thirsted for their blood, took to the mountains rather than be arrested by Brady, for that meant their death. The governor had actually made their efforts to apprehend Tunstall's murderers a crime. Had he pursued a course worthy of his office, he could have calmed the troubled waters and put an end to lawlessness. Instead of issuing such a proclamation as he did, how much more honorable it would have been for him to offer a reward for the apprehension of Mr. Tunstall's murderers, and thus show his disapproval of that brutal deed. Instead of that his language was that he thought it better to leave Tunstall's murder, if such it was, without further investigation until court met; but he thought vigorous measures should be taken to arrest the special constable and posse who arrested Messrs. Morton and Baker by warrants issued by Wilson! The sheriff's posse who killed Tunstall was composed of thieves, murderers, and escaped prisoners; not one of whom ever paid five dollars taxes in this county, except J. J. Dolan. Couple with this the fact that the governor secured the sheriff and that posse military aid to arrest the men who undertook to arrest those murderers, and you have the reason why the whole people of this county censure the governor, and have given vent to their wraths in such violent deeds as is my painful duty to record at this time.

Col. Purington, previous to Gov. Axtell's visit, expressed himself in the strongest terms against L. G. Murphy, J. J. Dolan and J. Riley, jointly styled "The House;" said they harbored thieves, outlaws, and murderers, and kept such characters in the company by buying stolen cattle from them at five dollars per head, when the stockmen could not afford the same class of cattle for less than fifteen dollars per head, thus driving honest industry out of the country. The people thought he sympathized with them in their efforts to rid themselves of these murderers until they saw a copy of his report of the troubles to General Hatch. In that he states that Robt. A. Widenmann, deputy U.S. marshal, when searching "The House," for Evans, Baker, Hill and Davis, broke and ransacked trunks, etc., and abstracted therefrom jewelry, a book, letters, etc., using the detachment of soldiers with him indirectly to steal. This is a lie. When Widenmann searched "The House" there were two citizens of Lincoln with him, from the time he entered until he came out; and for truth the character of these men has nothing to lose by a comparison with that of the gallant colonel. The fact is that no bureau, trunk, or box was opened or searched.

On the night of the 18th of February, after news of Tunstall's death was received, about 12 o'clock, J. H. Riley came to the house of Mr. McSween in a drunken condition. There he found the men who were with Tunstall when he was killed. He was bareheaded and without a shirt. He wanted to assure the men that he had no concealed weapons, and as a guarantee of that he threw the contents of his pockets on the table. That valuable cargo consisted of a book, letters, etc., referred to by the Napoleon of Fort Stanton in his wilfully false report. Mr. Riley was not very formal in his departure. After he left, the men in the room discovered that he had left that book, letters, etc., where he had thrown them. The book is valuable, chiefly because in it is faithfully enough recorded the important and widespread business of "The House;" the letters have their value; the etc. is worthless. The book shows the number of cattle sold "the house" by Baker, Evans & Co. at $5 per head; shows the amount of coffee, sugar, etc., hauled from the Indian Agency, and the men who freighted these staples from the Agency to Lincoln; shows that Indians are known in the ring by the very suggestive name of "trees," and their agent as "Hampton." I understand, too, that the book about which such a fuss is made shows the delivery to L. G. Murphy, by said Baker, Evans and Co., familiarly known as the "Boys," of thirty-five head of half breeds from Hunter's range; these are now on Murphy's ranch. This book, I am assured, shows the men who are "spotted" by "the house," and the way they are to be disposed of.

A year ago Col. Hunter tried to stop cattle stealing from his range. The thieves were well known. He procured warrants for their arrest and put them in the hands of the misguided Sheriff Brady for execution; he replied that the force of the county was insufficient for the purpose. But whilst declining to serve the warrants he certified the fact to Col. Purington, but the Col. declined to give any assistance.

Today when news of the killing of Brady and Hindman was received here Col. Purington and Lieutenant Smith, with a detachment of twenty-five soldiers, went to Lincoln, and arrested

Messrs. Widenmann, Shield, Washington and Robinson at their respective homes. Upon reflection, if he had room for such, he concluded it was jeopardizing his commission, and credited G. W. Peppin, one of the employees of "the house" with the arrests. He then shamefully abused Rev. T. F. Ealy, lately from Pa., and Mr. Leverson, from Douglass county, Col., the guests of Mr. McSween, using language towards them too indecent for print or repetition. He then told Mr. Peppin to search Mrs. McSween's house for arms, though he afterwards tried to disown the order by saying that everyone might do as they pleased.

Col. Purington maliciously allowed this so-called deputy sheriff, and a few of the Tunstall murderers, to over-awe citizens and arrest them without any authority of law, and for such purpose used U.S. troops. He directed this man Peppin to arrest Mr. Ellis, a merchant lately from Colfax County, but Peppin thought he had done enough for one day. Mr. Ellis is conceded to be one of the best, most honorable and solid citizens in the county; a man who would be foremost in any community.

I am informed that the only arms Peppin and posse found in McSween's house was a double-barreled shotgun.

Where will all these troubles end? The people have waited patiently for legal redress, but this failing, our horses and cattle being stolen so that we can make no crops, the people's patience has given way in violence and the end cannot be predicted.

Stanton

20. Dr. Leverson Writes Two Letters

DR. LEVERSON HAD REMAINED at Lincoln and that night after the hurly-burly of the day he sat in his room and wrote two letters. He had talked over the situation with John Chisum and, acting somewhat as understudy for the old cattleman, he composed these significant letters. One was to Carl Schurz, the Secretary of the Interior; the other, to President Hayes. The events he had been eyewitness to that day had reinforced all that he had heard from Chisum and McSween before coming to Lincoln; hence, a large amount of pent-up indignation vented itself in these letters.

In the one addressed to Carl Schurz he presented grave charges against the governor of the territory, the United States district attorney, and others of prominence, whose names were commonly associated with the Santa Fe ring. In regard to Governor Axtell the comments were particularly severe. Dr. Leverson even went so far as to make the assertion that the governor was the mainstay of thieves and murderers. Then he went into particulars, going back to the Pecos war the summer before for the commencement of the present lawlessness. "Only last year," he wrote, "John Chisum was refused all aid by the sheriff, by the military, and by the governor, to protect him from the bandits, who in bands of twenty and thirty were stealing the cattle of his employer (R. D. Hunter of St. Louis)." Leverson also hinted at further rottenness in Santa Fe, saying he was informed that Mr. Elkins (delegate to Congress from New Mexico) offered Hunter $5,000 if he would give up to him a certain beef contract and coupled with that amount of money a guarantee of protection from further stealing of his cattle.

OFFICERS DECLARED THIEVES

Dr. Leverson went on to declare that all the United States officers except the marshal and his deputies were at the head of "a gang of veritable thieves." He asserted that it was not the Mexican element of the territory that was responsible for the trouble but rather the American, and especially the Irish. He also exposed the trickery in Governor Axtell's proclamation of the tenth of March and reiterated that in 1876 the governor had approved the bill directing county commissioners to appoint justices of the peace and other county officials in an emergency. It was under that law that Squire Wilson had been made justice of the peace and "had so acted from February 1877."

He then related how Squire Wilson had issued warrants upon sworn statements laid before him for the murderers of Tunstall and placed them in the hands of a special constable appointed by him. He also referred to Governor Axtell's revoking Squire Wilson's appointment by his proclamation and thereby making null and void all his official acts. In the close, Leverson gave it as his unequivocal opinion that the horrendous crime committed that day in Lincoln was directly traceable to the attitude of W. L. Rynerson, the district attorney, protected and reinforced by both governor and the district judge.

The letter to President Hayes was even stronger than that to Secretary Schurz. In it Leverson complained about the partisanship of the army and flatly demanded a court-martial for both Captain Purington and Lieutenant Smith. He explained that he had come into southern New Mexico in hope of finding location for a large colony of settlers from England and New England. He had first gone to Chisum's ranch, hoping to find suitable land in the vicinity of the Pecos. Though he had found the land, he had been unable to find that security of life and property needful to his venture and now felt that he must look elsewhere.

In regard to the recent occurrences he gave some details which did not appear in the letter to Secretary Schurz. On March 29, he went on to say, Brady had come to Chisum's ranch with a detachment of soldiers commanded by Lieutenant Smith intending to make certain arrests, McSween among others, and to summon jurors, both grand and petit. Just at that time affairs at the Chisum place were in bad shape. Nearly all the horses and mules had been stolen, presumably by some of the lawless element supposed to be protected by Governor Axtell. Chisum had just returned from an unjust imprisonment at Las

Vegas which had lasted for nearly two months. When someone inquired of Brady why he came with soldiers, he answered that he could not get any of the citizens to accompany him. They had paid no attention even when he threatened them with a $50 fine and had said to his face that if they were summoned to go in pursuit of the murderers of Tunstall they would gladly go along.

Dr. Leverson brought out the fact that since Lieutenant Smith could not remain at Chisum's ranch until Mrs. McSween could make the trip to the place where her husband was in hiding and get him to return to Chisum's with her, an arrangement was made by which, if McSween agreed, John Chisum would drive him as rapidly as possible and overtake the detachment of soldiers on the road to Lincoln. McSween could place himself in their charge and so pass through Lincoln in safety. Heavy rains, however, had made it impossible for the McSween party to make the journey rapidly enough to overtake the soldiers. They had to spend Sunday, March 31, at a ranch some miles below Lincoln, having been able to make only a bare twenty-five miles that day. The next morning they had reached the Fort by making a detour that avoided Lincoln. After finding that Captain Purington would not accord McSween any protection, they had continued on to Lincoln. When they reached the town, they learned for the first time of the killing of Brady and Hindman.

To add weight to his letter Leverson pointed out that back in 1868 he had done the nation some service by uncovering certain widespread naturalization frauds. Over his own signature he had exposed them in the *New York Tribune*, his action being the more resounding because he had refused a $3,000 bribe to suppress the report. He begged President Hayes to give immediate attention to the situation in Lincoln County.

The request proved effective. From this time forward the government at Washington began to show more interest than previously in the Lincoln County disturbances. The killing of Tunstall was already in process of becoming a matter of governmental investigation at the request of the British embassy, acting for the Tunstall family. Letters from McSween and others were directing the attention of the Department of the Interior to another focus of fraud, that is, in the management of the Indian reservation. Such an accumulation of irregularities, overt and rumored, pointed to an unwholesome condition that called for immediate investigation.

21. The Fight at Blazer's Mill

APRIL 4 BROUGHT the Blazer's Mill fight, an episode now classic among the gun battles of the old West.

The six men involved in the assassination of Brady and Hindman had gotten out of town quickly and retired to the Ruidoso country. Brewer and others in his group condemned the killing of Brady and Hindman as a betrayal of the true purpose of the Regulator organization, but now the die was cast. A common cause and a sense of loyalty to one another kept the group together.

Just why a party of the Regulators and some of their friends went to Blazer's Mill on that particular day has been a matter for debate. One widely accepted explanation is that the Regulators, returning to their original purpose, went looking for other members of the crowd that had killed Tunstall. News had reached them that Andrew L. Roberts and George Kitt could be located in the vicinity of Tularosa and on the principle that one might as well be hanged for a cow as for a calf they determined to renew their efforts to capture — or kill if necessary — others of those implicated in the murder of Tunstall. Their friends, however, were more apt to accept the Regulators' own version. This was to the effect that they had received information from a reliable source that a considerable number of Tunstall's cattle had been driven to San Nicolas spring a few miles north of the notorious Shedd ranch in the Organ Mountains. When they reached Blazer's Mill they were en route to San Nicolas to look into the matter, ready, of course, to take drastic action if necessary to recover the cattle. But the most unlikely — and certainly the most lurid — was the theory that they were headed toward Mesilla, intent on assassinating District Attorney Rynerson and possibly Judge Bristol; someone from "The House" went so far as to suggest that a detachment of soldiers be sent to Tularosa to protect the judge and the district attorney from attack on their journey to Lincoln for the opening of court on April 8.

On their journey through the Ruidoso Valley the Brewer party had picked up five new recruits, the most important of whom were Frank Coe and his cousin, George Coe. Although from the start sympathizers with the McSween cause, these two men had remained on their farms; now, however, the situation had become so threatening that they felt the time had come for active participation.

It was about eleven o'clock Thursday morning when Brewer's party rode up to the building owned by Dr. Joseph Blazer and leased to the U.S. government as a headquarters for the Mescalero Indian agency. Here they ordered dinner from Mrs. Frederick Godfroy, wife of the Indian agent, who operated an eating place for the convenience of travelers. While they were in the dining room, Andrew Roberts rode up on his mule. As he could not see the horses of the Brewer party within the walls of the corral, he did not suspect its presence. Divesting himself of his pistols and cartridge belts and leaving his rifle in the boot of the saddle, he approached the building. Then, through the front door he caught sight of a number of rifles stacked against the wall and quickly went back and secured his own rifle and pistols. The room in the northwest corner of the building had been reserved by Dr. Blazer as an office for the operation of his sawmill, which was located something over a hundred yards away across the road; in this room, too, he attended to his duties as postmaster. It was toward the door of this room that Roberts walked; he was preparing to leave the country but was first awaiting the arrival of certain important letters.

In the meantime someone in Brewer's party caught sight of him and called out, "Here's Buckshot Roberts!" The name stirred them to action. Here was another of those for whom Brewer was still carrying warrants. Here was another of those who had been in the posse which had killed Tunstall. It would have been easy for any of the men in the room to have picked off the approaching man, but Brewer restrained himself and the others long enough to try, through peaceable measures, to get Roberts to surrender. He detailed Frank Coe, who knew Roberts very well, to go out and talk the situation over with him.

The two walked along the west side of the building and Roberts suggested that they enter Dr. Blazer's office to have their talk. This Coe declined to do, fearing that Roberts might try to make a hostage of

— R. N. Mullin Collection

At Blazer's Mill in a classic gun battle of the old west, Andrew Roberts, member of the posse that shot Tunstall, and Dick Brewer, leader of the Regulators, were both killed. Roberts was mortally wounded on the doorstep of Dr. Blazer's home — the foursquare building with small tower. Managing to push his way into the house, he fired out the door from a prone position, wounding several of the Regulators and instantly killing Brewer who was behind the logs by the sawmill, the long, low building in the foreground.

him, and they sat down on the doorstep of the room, a wide one characteristic of adobe structures of this sort. Coe told Roberts frankly that
Brewer had a warrant for him and felt compelled to arrest him. He
assured Roberts that he would be protected and would be delivered
safely to the proper authorities. "Give me your rifle," he said "and we
will walk around to the crowd. I will stand by you whatever happens."
Roberts was not to be persuaded. "Surrender? Never, while I'm alive.
Kid Antrim is with you and he would kill me on sight. Don't I know
what happened to Morton and Baker?"

For some time Coe continued to argue the matter, trying to convince Roberts that to give himself up would be the sensible course —
that failing to do so would mean a fight — that he, single-handed,
stood no chance against more than a dozen antagonists. But the salty
old fellow stood firm. He was an ex-soldier with so many wounds
received in fights with Indians, Texas Rangers and others that he had
earned the name "Buckshot." He was a small man with one arm so
crippled that he could not raise a rifle to his shoulder. Yet he was pure
grit and ready to take his chances in a fight of one against fifteen.

THE CROWD IS RESTLESS

While this was going on, Brewer's crowd became impatient. They
were concerned as to what might have happened to Coe. Lest some
hothead precipitate an unnecessary fight, Brewer detained most of his
party but sent George Coe, Middleton, and Bowdre to attempt to make
the arrest. When they came around the corner, Roberts and Frank
Coe were still talking. Bowdre called out, "Roberts, throw up your
hands." Roberts shouted back at once a defiant "No," and sprang to
his feet. Bowdre, however, "got his shot in first," inflicting that terrible
wound spoken of as a "gut shot." Roberts groaned from the intense
agony but retained presence of mind enough to push open the door and
step inside the room. He dragged a mattress from the bed and tossed
it across the doorway, whence he could fire from a prone position with
a minimum of exposure. Within a matter of seconds he went into
action. One of his first shots cut off Bowdre's belt; another struck
George Coe's trigger finger and took it off at the first joint; a third
bullet went into Middleton's chest, inflicting a serious wound in the
lung; still another grazed the arm of Billy the Kid, who had run out
and was near a wagon standing beside the building.

By this time the rest of the party were outside the house but kept
themselves out of range of the hornet's nest that was apparent at the
side doorway. They had learned that Roberts' activity was not limited
to the number of bullets in his pistols and the cartridges in the magazine

of his Winchester; in the room was Dr. Blazer's Springfield and 1000 rounds of ammunition. Brewer told the others to remain out of the line of fire and he himself crossed the road and took a position where he could see the doorway from behind the protection of some large logs near the sawmill.

The end came quickly. As Brewer raised his head to make a survey, Roberts saw the hat rising above the log 140 paces away. He aimed for what he knew must be below it, a thin strip of forehead. The bullet struck almost between Brewer's eyes.

The loss of their leader threw the others into confusion. They deserted the field without even stopping to take up the body of their dead leader and retired to George Coe's place on the Ruidoso. The whole affair was over less than two hours after their arrival at Blazer's Mill; the time spent in shooting was actually only a few minutes. In the beginning the firing had been lively. Then it had ceased until the single shot which killed Brewer. In spite of his wounds, Roberts lived until the next day. As quickly as possible Major Godfroy and Dr. Blazer sent over to Fort Stanton for a doctor and Dr. Appel, the post surgeon, came over. It was impossible, however, to save Roberts' life. He was buried the next day, his grave beside that of Brewer. The body of the latter had been buried promptly because the day was unusually warm, making it necessary to dispose of the body almost immediately.

When the news of the Blazer's Mill fight reached McSween, then at Fort Stanton, he penned the following account and forwarded it to the Cimarron *News and Press*, which published it in the issue for April 18.

FROM LINCOLN COUNTY

Fort Stanton, N. M., Apr. 5, '78

News and Press. — Yesterday, Richard M. Brewer and some other citizens were at Blazer's Mill. There they met one of the famous Jesse Evans' gang now known as A. L. Roberts, one of the sheriff's posse who so foully and brutally murdered Tunstall. Since the perpetration of that inhuman deed, he has been in the employ of Murphy, Dolan & Riley. It appears that Roberts expressed himself as sorry for what had happened; that having found out the composition of the outfit he intended to abandon it. He had his six-shooter and carbine. Some one asked him to give up his arms, that they had a warrant for him, whereupon he drew his revolver; but before he could use it, the man who demanded the surrender shot him in the stomach. He then pulled down a mattress on the floor, dragged it to the door, and laid upon it. He now began to shoot indiscriminately. Mr. Coe was the first to receive a shot, being badly shot in the hand; the next, John Middleton, being shot in the chest. Brewer was about 100 yards from the room occupied by Roberts when the shooting commenced. He fired only once. When raising up the second time Roberts shot him in the head, killing him instantly. The wounds of Coe and Middleton are not considered dangerous. At last accounts Roberts was dying.

The above account may not be correct, but I give it as I received it from an eye witness. Whether correct or not, I want to say a few words concerning Mr. Brewer.

Richard M. Brewer was one of nature's noblemen. Physically faultless; generous to a fault; a giant in friendship; possessing an irreproachable character and unsullied honor; kind, amiable, and gentle in disposition, he has fallen early into the "three by six" promised him eighteen months ago.

Outside "the House" no one knew Mr. Brewer but to respect him. He was a young man without vices of any kind. Had he been content to enslave himself, he would, no doubt, be living now, but to a man of kingly nature, existence would be intolerable under the conditions sought to be imposed.

Murderers and horse thieves hated him; their friends hated him. But the people, Mexican and American, held him in the highest possible esteem. He had a fine ranch on the Rio Ruidoso, which he had been cultivating the past four years. It was his intention to make Lincoln County his permanent home.

Peace to your ashes, Dick! as you were familiarly called. Sweet and pleasant be your slumbers! Ever green and fresh be your memory. Some will malign you, but that will not disturb you, for when the mist has cleared away and the horizon of truth is clearly seen, even they will be shamed to silence. Death has deprived your father and mother of an obedient and loving son; your sister and brother of the prince of brothers; the county of Lincoln of one of her best, most industrious, sober, upright, and honest citizens. He died young — 27 years of age.

His father and family live in Wisconsin.

Stanton

The killing of Brewer was a serious, not to say disastrous, loss to the McSween side. The tribute paid to him in McSween's newspaper account was well-deserved. Although there might have been some riffraff among the group over which he stood, he himself was of a different stripe. He never drank and he never quarrelled except upon extreme provocation; he was esteemed by everyone as an honest, hardworking farmer. In buying from Murphy the farm which the latter

Dick Brewer, young rancher on the Rio Ruidoso, had been Tunstall's foreman, loyal to the interests of his employer and later to McSween as the avenger of Tunstall. He became leader of the Regulators and was killed at Blazer's Mill.

did not own, he had gotten into debt to "The House," and when through the advice of McSween he had escaped the trap they had set for him and his property, their hostility had descended upon him. As Tunstall's foreman, he had been loyal to the interests of his employer, ready instantly to do anything. If Tunstall's horses were stolen, it was Brewer who went after them when Brady would make no move. If Tunstall's cattle were to undergo attachment, it was Brewer who withstood the posse that Brady dispatched. If Tunstall's murderers were to be brought to justice, it was again Brewer who shouldered the responsibility of leadership. Facing, as the McSween faction did now, the certain loss of a great deal of public sympathy on account of the killing of Brady and Hindman, they had great need for men of recognized standing in the county, such as Brewer. In this respect he had been a tower of strength.

22. Newspaper Skirmishes

THE KILLING OF BRADY brought to both sides sharp realization of the need for appealing their cases to the public. McSween, as already shown, prepared even under the great excitement of fateful April 1, the day Brady was killed, a review of the entire situation which the Cimarron *News and Press* carried in the issue of April 11, 1878. This stimulated Riley to attempt a reply, which the Santa Fe *New Mexican* published in the issue for April 20. Riley's retort was as follows:

Editors, *New Mexican,*

I have noticed a scurrilous article in the Cimarron *News and Press*, reflecting on the honor of Major Murphy, Mr. Dolan and myself, evidently written by A. A. McSween and based on a tissue of falsehoods.

The commencement and cause of the present troubles in our county was the serving, or trying to serve, a legal writ of attachment on property of this McSween, who, after a careful investigation before Judge Bristol (lasting two days) was bound over for the criminal offense of embezzlement of the money for which the attachment was issued — McSween, besides this amount, owes our house the sum of seventeen hundred dollars which we have been trying to legally recover. Every fair-minded and unprejudiced mind conversant with the facts knows, as I do, that McSween is an unprincipled, scheming villain who, when he thought justice would overtake him, through the instrumentality of men opposed to us in business, aided by some who are owing our house, threw Lincoln County into a state of anarchy, plotting and nearly destroying the lives of ourselves and friends. That this was not accomplished is owing to the humane and determined action of Col. Purington and officers under his command at Fort Stanton.

The unfortunate killing of Tunstall and the sympathy created thereby, aided by lying representations of McSween and Widenmann as to the manner of Tunstall's death, gave these cowardly assassins capital which they were not loath to take advantage of by stirring up the blood of bad men to anticipated deeds which, when the truth comes out and the matter is decided before a legal tribunal, would shame and be a blot on the history of Apaches. In carrying out these plans, McSween, being a fugitive from justice, had a willing tool in Widenmann, a worthless scoundrel and respectable loafer devoid of honor, who left Santa Fe without paying his board bill, and having nothing to lose either morally or financially, in a cowardly manner and carrying out the instructions of his superior, assassinated one of the United States' best citizens, the sheriff of our county, a thorough gentleman and a noble man. Poor Brady! After an honorable record of twenty years as a soldier and an officer, a greater portion of which was served in the war of the rebellion, to be so assassinated by a cowardly sneaking tool of an unprincipled and ambitious man — and yet the article referred to in the *News and Press* seems to justify this foul murder. Who in New Mexico can say aught against Sheriff Brady? As an officer he was respected and feared by citizens in our county, and as such was in the way of the man McSween. He leaves a wife and nine young children to mourn his untimely death — and while Widenmann is trying, through his usual hypocritical lying and the medium of far-off newspapers, to hurt his fair name, the best men in New Mexico are determined to see this man and his co-murderers legally brought to justice — and these men cry in hypocritical innocence, "How long will this thing last?" I think not long. We have been waiting and are still with confidence that law, though slow, will reach the guilty parties in Lincoln County, and whoever they are, let them be punished!

There certainly are good men executing the judiciary power of the Territory. Does McSween and mob want matters decided by the courts? If so, and history teaches us that this is the only proper method of adjusting matters, why did Widenmann with thirteen men lie in wait in McSween's house on the anticipated day of court and murder Sheriff Brady and one of his men while going towards the court house — and it is believed by every disinterested person in Lincoln County that they intended treating

Judge Bristol and Col. Rynerson in the same way — why are they now rushing to far-away newspapers to misrepresent us by cowardly lies, such as are contained in the Cimarron *News and Press*, and the lame statement contained in the last issue of the Trinidad *Enterprise and Chronicle?*

They openly stated at the Indian Agency, when fifteen of them murdered Roberts (their last brave act as far as heard from) that they intended killing my partner (Mr. Dolan) and myself as soon as any opportunity offers, and may do so, and still there are newspapers who knowing their acts against law, publish their lies and thereby countenance and encourage them. The press is an instrument of great benefit to a community, but does it not also have a counter-effect when encouraging men like McSween and Widenmann mob of Lincoln County?

The facts in the Lincoln County troubles when investigated thoroughly and before proper tribunals, will bring forward proof of a systematic plot to murder and assassinate every man who could not be intimidated and was connected with our house. Although grossly misrepresented, we have not desired to enter into a newspaper discussion in reference to these matters, as it is not the proper place to decide them, and now we only desire to state to the public that it is now, as it always has been, our desire to live as good citizens, amenable to the laws of the country, and not to the assassinating mob.

Major Murphy's reputation for honor and everything that constitutes a gentleman is so well established in the Territory that it cannot be hurt by any anonymous newspaper correspondent.

Jno. H. Riley

The article in the Trinidad *Enterprise and Chronicle* to which Riley referred was by Isaac Ellis, who usually signed himself "Thine in the Right." Probably he wrote very much what McSween had sent to the Cimarron *News and Press*. To this article Major Murphy made a reply, writing it a few days prior to the adjournment of court, when he realized that the status of the firm with which he was connected was parlous. Even in so desperate a situation, the best he could offer was merely the *argumentum ad hominem*, as the letter written at his "Fairview" ranch but dated at Lincoln, reveals:

Lincoln, N.M., April 18, 1878

To the Editor of the
Trinidad *Enterprise and Chronicle*,

Sir: In your issue of the 11th inst. is contained what is supposed to be a truthful history of the deplorable events which have taken place within this unfortunate county, and given, as stated, at your request. In so far as myself and friends are concerned, I only hold you accountable for the selection you made of your correspondent. You could not have made a worse one, and it is to be hoped, for your sake, that when you knew him he bore a better character than he shows in his "history." It is greatly to be regretted that a public journal will lend itself to the publication of such a series of falsehoods as is contained in that "history." And I repeat that no matter what his previous character may have been, he has now shown himself alike destitute of common honesty, decency, and truth. Without intending advice, it is permitted me to suggest that it would have shown more wisdom on your part and his to have awaited the action of the court now investigating the very matter therein treated of. It is not a little strange that your "historian" had to leave the territory, where the facts are known and understood, to enlighten the outside world with his falsehoods.

I have studiously refrained from noticing the slanders previously published since the lawlessness of which "Thine in the Right" is the apologist and defender commenced; nor do I propose to do more now than enter the general denial herein made, leaving to a more appropriate occasion to show the correctness of my position.

Very Resp'y &c,

Lawrence G. Murphy

A month after Murphy's letter, Dolan's pen became active. He was prompted by what had appeared in the Mesilla *Independent* in the issue for April 27. Colonel A. J. Fountain, who had been at Lincoln during the term of court that was about to end, sent to his paper the result of his firsthand acquaintance with the disorders in Lincoln County, which was published under the heading "Editorial Correspondence." This review of the situation was not only full but, more to the point, it was sane and judicial. Colonel Fountain did not mince words in regard to either of the factions. The McSween party he condemned roundly for the killing of Brady and Hindman. The Murphy crowd came in for an even larger share of condemnation, as the following extracts will show:

> The causes which have brought about the present conditions of anarchy in this county are as follows: For the past two years a gang of outlaws, consisting of Jesse Evans, Tom Hill, Frank Baker, and ten or twelve others, have systematically plundered the citizens of Lincoln County. Their thefts were committed openly and without any attempt at disguise. It is alleged that during all this period the outlaws were in the employ of certain

persons who had contracts to supply the government with beef
cattle, and that the cattle stolen from the citizens by the outlaws
were turned into the government on these contracts. All efforts to
break up this systematic stealing and to punish the perpetrators
by process of law, failed for the reason, it is asserted, that the
influence of the employers was successfully exerted to protect
their outlaw servants from arrest. On one occasion they were
arrested; and the good people of the county began to hope that a
better era was dawning. But they were doomed to disappointment;
the outlaws walked out of jail and immediately re-entered upon
their vile occupation. All these things surely tested the patience
of the suffering citizens, who still, perhaps, would not have
resorted to extreme measures, had they not been roused to frenzy
by an act of unparallelled atrocity [the killing of Tunstall]. From
what had previously transpired, the people were justified in believing, as they do believe, that Tunstall's death was the culminating
act of a series of outrages that had long tried the patience of the
people. Wrought to frenzy, they poured into the town of Lincoln
and at once inaugurated measures to bring the murderers to
justice . . . .

Everyone reading the Fountain article would at once recognize
that the beef contractors referred to were none other than "The House."
No sooner did it reach Dolan, who was by then in Santa Fe following
the discomfiture his faction had received at the session of district court,
than he prepared a lengthy rejoinder which appeared in due course
in the columns of the *New Mexican*. A reading of Dolan's letter shows
its weakness; all that he seemed able to do was to make countercharges,
the effect of which was much reduced by their querulous tone.

Santa Fe, New Mexico, May 16, 1878

Editors, New Mexican,

Gentlemen: — I see by the last issue of the *Independent* that its
editors still continue to publish their malicious lies in regard
to the Lincoln County troubles, and it surprises me very much,
they just returning from there and knowing the true cause of the
difficulty; and one of the editors stating to me before leaving Stanton that as soon as he returned home he would be in charge of the
paper and that there would be a different statement of the trouble
from that heretofore published. Mr. Editor got home, but only
makes a halfway apology, says a lot without a meaning.

Now the only excuse I can make for the editors of the *Independent* is that they, like the last grand jury of Lincoln County,

were told that Mr. Chisum and Mr. McSween had one hundred armed men on the hills surrounding Mesilla ready to pounce on them and take their lives, unless they continued their previous course of evading the truth and kept before the public their lying statements, so as to better enable them (McSween and Chisum) to crush Murphy, Riley and myself. Either that, or they might have received "hush money," one hundred dollars each, the same as Mr. Fritz and his sister did before Mr. McSween started for St. Louis to be absent for two years for the purpose of completing his education as a lawyer, after which he was to return to New Mexico. Oh God! what a good thing it was for the community he was deprived of those two years; with what little brains he now has, aided with the embezzled ten thousand dollars and a few willing tools, he has defied the law and ruined one of the best counties in the Territory; he has managed it by misrepresentation and for no other purpose than to enable him to cover his robbery and other foul acts.

They say "outraged prominent citizens," "regulators." Who are these prominent citizens and regulators? I will here state William H. Antrim, alias "the Kid," a renegade from Arizona, where he killed a man in cold blood; Fred Waite, from the Indian Territory — I know nothing about his character previous to his coming to Lincoln but while there I know him to be one of the murderers of Mr. Morton, Sheriff Brady, George Hindman, Mr. Roberts, and others; he has no interests in the county. R. M. Brewer I always considered an honest man and treated him as such until he became contaminated with Mr. McSween, his "legal advisor." It didn't take Mr. McSween long to initiate him into the way he should go, as it was only a short time after they became acquainted that Mr. Brewer came to me and offered to sell me about twenty head of beef steers, he knowing them to be the property of Mr. Chisum and that they were taken out of a herd of Mr. Chisum's which passed his ranch on the Ruidoso a few days before. I was much surprised at Brewer, as I always thought him honest. I told him I would not buy or have anything to do with the cattle, and advised him to turn them over to the owner.

He (Brewer) next tried to defraud us, on advice received from Mr. McSween, out of two of our ranches situated on the Ruidoso, which we had rented to him on leaving our employ, by entering them under the Desert Land Act, but failed to prove up on his right. The circumstances are well known to Mr. Bowman of the Land Office and another gentleman living in the Mesilla valley and in Lincoln County. Mr. Brewer is owing our firm over two thousand dollars. This is Mr. McSween's respected citizen; blessed be his memory!

Bowdre and Scurlock came to us about three years ago for assistance; they had nothing. We, being anxious to help them, sold them a ranch on the Rio Ruidoso for $1,500, which cost the firm of Fritz and Murphy about two thousand dollars, and gave them three years to pay it in. We also furnished them farming implements, provisions, and paid their employees — this we done up to a short time before the trouble commenced and only stopped their credit after learning that they had disposed of their crops to McSween & Tunstall for the purpose of defrauding us. They are now owing us for the ranch and over three thousand dollars book account.

The Coes complain of our taking contracts too cheap to suit them. McSween wants to keep the ten thousand dollars collected for the Fritz estate, and he knows he can't do it as long as Mr. Riley and myself live; therefore he desires to have us assassinated. We are in Chisum's war because our business conflicts. He wants to control contracts in New Mexico as well as in Arizona. In this we have bothered him.

Mr. "L. S. or Thine in the Right" is a merchant who lately came to our county, and from what I can learn, hasn't left a very clean record behind him. When the trouble commenced he thought he saw a good chance to get rid of a competitor in business. So he linked arms with the so-called Regulators — assassins would be more appropriate — and has played a very conspicuous part in their foul work from the beginning. The balance of the so-called Regulators are *tramps* without name or character.

Now, Mr. Editor, what I here state is subject to proof, and can you or any honest man wonder why they seek our blood? When the *Independent* says that the cause of the Lincoln troubles originated from the fact that certain parties (nameless) had hired outlaws to steal cattle, etc., for them, it states that which they know to be a malicious and bare falsehood. Its editors know the cause of the troubles as well as Judge Bristol to whom I refer all inquirers who are desirous of knowing the truth.

I will further state about Mr. Chisum a little circumstance which happened between him and Mr. Riley. About a year and a half ago, Bowdre and Scurlock came to Mr. Riley and offered to furnish him cattle at very low figures from Mr. Chisum's cattle range. Mr. Riley answered stating he was not doing that kind of business, and a short time afterwards notified Mr. Chisum in writing of the fact. I believe the letter was confidential. Mr. Chisum, instead of acting as a gentleman should, sent Mr. Riley's letter to Bowdre and Scurlock, knowing them to be unscrupulous villains. The result was Bowdre and Scurlock denied the charge and swore vengeance against Riley. After such treatment as this,

I don't think a man would be warranted in breaking his neck to look out for property of such an ungrateful wretch.

A short time ago you may have noticed an article published in your paper signed "Cow-Boy." Everything contained therein is the truth with the exception of the time Mr. McSween was in possession of the embezzled money. It was a few months less than the time stated. Mr. McSween can have all the proof he requires in regard to the truth of "Cow-Boy's" statement, and I will here state that he must have the cheek and horns of an enraged Texas cow to ask for proof, he being the one of the principals in the release of the prisoners mentioned in "Cow-Boy's" letter — was to recover their saddles, etc., from Sheriff Brady by power of attorney.

"Cow-Boy's" letter was answered by McSween in that filthy sheet called the Cimarron *News and Press*, in which Mr. McSween tries to make it appear that "Cow-Boy" lies; that Evans, Baker and Co. received in merchandise sent them from our store files, saws, etc. by which they cut their shackles and sawed the logs in the jail. Such is not the case, and his statement is without any respect to truth. We are charged with being kind to some prisoners who were confined in the Lincoln County jail, and, if this were so, it was a grievous fault, and we are so constituted that we will repeat the fault and submit our act to the judgment of God and our fellow men.

It is now subject to proof that Juan B. Patrón and other villains like him had entered into a conspiracy for the purpose of assassinating men under the charge of Sheriff Brady and a few other citizens who desired the law to be enforced. The night they intended to carry out this brutal act, I was in Mr. Patrón's house, the headquarters of the would-be assassins; and I will here ask Mr. Patrón if he remembers asking Sheriff Brady if "the prisoners had any sympathizers present," and Sheriff Brady's answer, "No, only in so far as seeing them done justice."

It would appear from the action taken that the citizens of Lincoln County endorse the violence and lawlessness which predominates, by which children have lost their parents and wives their husbands, but such is not the fact. There are just as good citizens in Lincoln County as there are in other portions of the Territory. Nor can they, or ought they, to be confounded with the lawless element that has wrought so much evil in our midst.

My character is so well known in New Mexico that I neither require nor seek endorsement for my veracity.

In answer to Messrs. *Independent*, why don't those that started the fight, stay at home, fight it out, and not have others do it for them? I beg to state that we did not start a fight of violence. We started it in one of the district courts of the Territory, leaving it entirely to said court to decide whether we were right or wrong, and we were willing to abide by its decision. Should any one feel aggrieved at this statement, which I claim to be the truth, I intend to remain in the Territory and will always be pleased to meet the aggrieved, and if possible ease his mind. Mr. Tunstall's father offers a reward of five thousand dollars for the arrest, etc. of the murderers. Arrest Mr. McSween and Widerman, and you will have them. The winding up of Tunstall's estate, no doubt, will satisfy those concerned of the character of Mr. Tunstall's "bosom friends."

James J. Dolan

Dolan's references to "Cow-Boy's" letter and McSween's answer carry the story back a few weeks. In the same issue of the *New Mexican* in which Riley's reply to McSween had appeared was another discussion of Lincoln County affairs. "Cow-Boy," as the writer called himself, went back to the preceding summer and discussed the escape of the Jesse Evans gang from jail. He elaborated the old charge that this escape had been through the connivance of Tunstall and McSween under an agreement that if the rescue was successful the stolen horses and mules should be returned. "Cow-Boy" also discussed the wrangle over the Fritz insurance money, making it appear that McSween was trying to appropriate the money. "Cow-Boy" also had indulged in his version of the killing of Tunstall, which was that Tunstall had been killed while resisting the service of attachment papers. The account of this killing was as follows:

When Deputy Sheriff Matthews and posse arrived at the Felix ranch, Tunstall and party had been gone about two hours and a half. Some of the McSween party had sent a runner to Tunstall with word that the sheriff was coming and had the Pecos cowboys with him. Brewer remarked, "If the Pecos cowboys are with the sheriff, I am not going to fight."

J. J. Dolan and others of the sheriff's party stopped at the Felix with the cattle; the rest went in pursuit of Tunstall and party to attach the horses. It was thirty miles from the Felix ranch to where the sheriff's party caught up with Tunstall's crowd. A running fight took place. How and by whom Tunstall was killed, the courts can only decide. If he was killed by thieves, murderers, and escaped prisoners, as Brewer and party say, these thieves, murderers, and escaped prisoners were turned loose upon the country by Brewer with the knowledge and consent of Tunstall and McSween.

This communication from "Cow-Boy" aroused McSween, who sent to the *New Mexican* the following letter, intended as a reply jointly to the two communications, the *ex parte* statements of Riley and the immoderate charges of "Cow-Boy."

Lincoln, N.M., April 27, 1878

Editors, *New Mexican.* — Yours of the 20th inst., freighted with the letters of J. H. Riley and "Cow-Boy," is before me. As these gentlemen evidently dig in the same pit, as the operator and fool always do, I will answer both letters in this, so far as they relate to me, taking Mr. Riley's first.

Never have I written anything *unjustifiably* "reflecting on the honor (!) of Maj. Murphy, Mr. Dolan and myself" — Mr. Riley.

As in "the commencement and cause of the present troubles," there appears to be a difference of opinion between Mr. Riley and the people. He, with a modesty (!) peculiar to a Riley, charges all the blame upon me. The people, if I mistake not, lay the responsibility upon the trio I have named. The report of the grand jury shows that the present troubles are only a revival and continuance of troubles dating back five or six years. Immediately after the adjournment of the District Court, the people from every section of the country held a meeting for the purpose of considering these troubles, and they, by their resolutions, say of the troubles, that they are not of this year, but a revival and continuance of feuds dating back five or six years. Hundreds of the residents of Lincoln County, including the officers of the county, have signed a *petition* asking Messrs. Murphy, Dolan and Riley to leave the county as there never could be peace while they remained in it. That petition charged them with being the cause of all the troubles that proved so disastrous to the prosperity and growth of the county during the past six years. Do you not think, Mr. Riley, the people have a more correct and impartial view of "the commencement and cause" than you have? Really, the fact of your departure from the county, reveals the fact that even you, gentlemen, are forced to acknowledge the force of public opinion.

In regard to the charge of embezzlement, Mr. Riley, I would simply call your attention to the report of the grand jury. As in all your other undertakings against me, you have failed. Like the balance of your persecuting adventures, the honey-combed skeleton of this one crumbled and fell, burying you, instead of me, in its ruins. Your mountainous effort has cost you thousands of dollars, but yet you have failed entirely.

Mr. Riley says that I owe them, ("our house") "seventeen hundred dollars, which we are trying to recover legally;" let me state the facts as they can be proven by Messrs. Thornton and

Conway, our respective attorneys. You brought suit against me for six thousand dollars. You were careful not to make any effort to obtain service, as you were not positive that I would be killed before court convened. I asked you for my account before starting for the East last fall. I wrote you for it. I could not obtain it. Your clerk, F. G. Christies, in presence of E. W. Dow, informed me that he had positive orders from you not to let me have it, nor even to let me know the amount of it. I waived service during the present term of court and, in this way, secured by order of the court my account. I furnished you mine last fall. I consented to most of the changes you suggested in my account against you, and yet I only owed you one hundred and six dollars after purchasing over four hundred dollars scrip of you. What became of your seventeen hundred dollars? Add to this the fact that you still owe me over eleven hundred dollars, which, owing to circumstances over which you have no control, was not included in the above settlement. Fiction is good in its place, but your style of it is too extravagant. You, to be sure, used to be the *un*accountable public administrator, but your sun has set forever; the shades of night have enveloped you. I regret that you have obliged me to bring to light private personal transactions in which the public can take but small interest, if any.

I went to the Pecos to save my life from the bloodthirsty *posse* who murdered Mr. Tunstall. This I did at the earnest solicitation of such citizens as Hon. Florencio González, Isaac Ellis, José Montaño, Frank Coe, and John Newcomb. Enjoying the good opinion and confidence of such men, I am not particular as to what Mr. Riley may say. In this way I would rather be a "fugitive from justice" than submit to the order of any court, to be murdered. All you regret, Mr. Riley, is that you were not able to oblige me to become a permanent "fugitive." Had you heeded the advice and example of such gentlemen as I have named, you would today be spared the humiliation of being invited by them to leave Lincoln County. Yes, you would have been spared the ignominy heaped upon you by the last grand jury. "Poor Brady!" So say I. Let the mantle of charity cover his connection with our late troubles as effectively as the clods of the valley do his coffin. You abused his confidence! What did you do with the territorial funds deposited with "our house" by him? Look in your memorandum book! Why did you not make the amount good when he went to Santa Fe to settle with the auditor? Why did you not save him some of the mental anguish he suffered? Names and particulars can be given you if you desire.

Mr. Widenmann has never been in my employ nor in that of Mr. Tunstall. While he is in difficulties, and I am satisfied of his

innocence, I will continue to befriend him on account of his friendship for Mr. Tunstall. He has never served me in any capacity
whatever, nor is he likely to do so.

The last *Independent*, the editors of which were here at court,
gives a correct statement of the killing of Brady so far as I am
concerned.

The whole county was opposed to you in business. You
acknowledged that by selling out. Your yoke, as a matter of business, was intolerable, but it is now in fragments.

Now for Mr. "Cow-Boy." Horses belonging to me were stolen
by Jesse Evans and Tom Hill last summer, but were never
returned. Baker, Evans and Co. were arrested by Brady and
posse.

If Brady and Brewer were living, I would state, as our people
know, to whom the credit of these arrests belonged. Baker, Evans
& Co. were shackled about a month after their arrest. Files and
augers were packed in goods bought on their account in the store
of J. J. Dolan & Co. In this way they were enabled to file their
shackles and cut out the logs in their cells. Brady knew this. He
was informed of it by Hon. J. B. Patrón. Brewer and Tunstall
never conversed with Baker, Evans & Co. except in the presence
and hearing of Maximiliano de Guevarra, the jailor, private audi-
ence with the imprisoned "cattle kings" being only allowed to
members of the "White House."

There was no sub-jailor the night of the escape. Brady knew
this. How did the rescuers find it out? We can only conjecture.
The fact that Baker, Evans, Hill and Davis after the escape or
rescue, wined, dined, and roomed with Brady, and that they several times served as his *posse* afterward, make the conjecture
almost a certainty. Mr. Brewer had no knowledge of the escape.
I ask "Cow-Boy" for his proof. Brewer wrote me a note stating
that the agents of "the House" had been to his ranch and helped
themselves. He implored me to try and get Brady to pursue them:
that he would raise men again as he had before, and rearrest
them. Brady's reply was: "I arrested them once and I'll be damned
if I'll do it any more; I am going to look out for Brady hereafter."
Brewer and Tunstall are dead, but that is no reason why "Cow-
Boy" should be allowed to blacken their memories. I call upon him
to prove any one of his assertions against them. Brewer went as
far as Seven Rivers, after the horses were stolen by Baker, Evans
& Co., from Brewer's ranch, and found them at the cow camp of
J. J. Dolan & Co. Some of them have not yet been found. "Cow-
Boy" says that he can prove that Mr. Tunstall tried to hire Baker
as foreman of his horse and cattle herd; I call upon him for the
proof. Mr. Tunstall was above that as a man, and too much of a

business man to hire a man who, like Baker, had once been in the employ of Murphy, Dolan and Riley.

Mr. Brewer sold me his property to pay a *just* debt he owed me, and not to avoid payment of what he may have been owing L. G. Murphy & Co. In doing this he did no more than J. J. Dolan & Co. have lately done for Mr. Catron. I challenge "Cow-Boy" to prove that Brewer ever said that he would not pay L. G. Murphy & Co.

Charles Fritz is not "deceased." I was advised August 1, 1877, by Donnell, Lawson & Co., 72 Broadway, N.Y., that they had realized $10,000 from the policy on life of Emil Fritz, deceased, that costs of collection were $2,851.51 leaving the estate $7,148.49. Immediately upon receipt of that letter I advised Mrs. Scholand, and Mr. Fritz, of the fact. Now, "Cow-Boy," if you are a truth lover, you can ascertain the above facts. You can easily see that I could not have "used it twelve months."

To set your mind at rest, "Cow-Boy," let me assure you that no portion of the money belonging to the estate has as yet been used. Would that I could with equal ease satisfy the vulture-like impecuniosity of your masters. I did not dispose of my property as you charge. Please examine the records of the county and satisfy yourself.

Neither Mr. Tunstall or myself armed anyone. John Middleton comes from Hunter's employ in Kansas with a *clear record*.

Mr. Waite is part Indian, but not a "refugee from justice." He is from Paul's Valley Indian Territory, and makes no secret of his descent, nor need he do so. He is a young man of means and respectable connections who proposes to make Lincoln County his home. I do not know whom you mean by "the kid;" Tunstall was not at the ranch when the infamous Matthews went there with his *posse*. The murder of Tunstall by the *posse* is too well known now to need repetition so I will leave the last two paragraphs of your letter a monument to your falsity. The last grand jury have settled the matter by indicting those of the murderers who are living.

And so it went. Few opinions were changed by these charges and counter-charges. It was the kind of a contest where nobody could win. About all that was accomplished was to keep alive old hatreds and add fuel to the flame.

PART III

Conflagration

23. Spring Term of Court, 1878

On April 8 district court began its regular session in Lincoln. Judge Bristol's arrival a few days late added to a general impression that he would not try to hold court, but he had never wavered in his determination to hold the session as usual. As a matter of prudence, he and the other court officials established themselves at Fort Stanton and came down each day under an escort of soldiers as a protection from any outbreaks of disorder. The town, however, was singularly free from disturbance of any sort.

At the outset Judge Bristol was confronted by a formidable obstacle in the killing of Brady, the sheriff. Peppin and others of Brady's deputies were complicating matters by trying to act in their old capacity, when they had no legal grounds for doing so. Steps had to be taken immediately to provide a duly authorized sheriff. The recently enacted New Mexico laws provided that in an emergency the county commissioners should choose a sheriff for the unexpired term, but no move in that direction had been taken in the intervening week or ten days. Judge Bristol cut the Gordian knot by appointing John Copeland sheriff for the time being.[1] The first service required of him was to make more regular the arrest of Widenmann, Shield, George Washington, and George Robinson in connection with the killing of Brady. On this mission he carried warrants from Judge Bristol bearing the unusual notation:

---

1. Bristol's appointment extended only to the serving of warrants on those accused in the killing of Brady. The County Commissioners apparently recognized Copeland as Acting Sheriff, though it was not until at a special meeting, April 27, that they took action in appointing him to that office.

It appearing that the sheriff of Lincoln County in the territory of New Mexico is dead and that there is no officer at present authorized to serve the within warrant, I hereby appoint and authorize John Copeland to serve such warrant.

Warren Bristol
District Judge

April 8th, 1878

Judge Bristol also secured a detachment of soldiers to aid Copeland both in serving these warrants and in keeping the prisoners at Fort Stanton until they had hearings.

By the thirteenth, Judge Bristol had the grand jury organized and functioning. On it were: Joseph H. Blazer, foreman; Juan B. Patrón; Crescencio Sánchez; Vicente Romero; Camilo Núñez; Wesley Fields; Robert M. Gilbert; Francisco Romero y Valencia; Desiderio Zamora; Jerry Hockradle; Andrew Wilson; A. M. Clenny; Juan José López; Ignacio de Govera (sometimes Gobaro) and Francisco Pacheco. With the grand jury organized, Judge Bristol delivered a comprehensive charge, reviewing the recent lawlessness. He expatiated on the McSween embezzlement case, betraying a decidedly hostile attitude toward McSween, and seemed almost desirous of convicting him before trial. Beginning his address, he acknowledged the existence of two factions: "There seem to be two principal parties, standing somewhat in the background and under cover, who are the real authors and instigators of these troubles. Mr. McSween and his adherents on one side, and Messrs. Murphy, Dolan, and Riley with their adherents on the other."

Judge Bristol next went into the McSween case at length, stating that it was "the immediate starting-point and occupied a conspicuous place in all the violence and bloodshed" that Lincoln County had endured lately. He complained that McSween and his friends had endeavored to manufacture public opinion favorable to themselves but prejudicial not only to the court but also to him personally. "Why has this been done?" he queried, and he answered by saying:

> The circumstances of the case point to but one conclusion as to the motive, and that was to induce desperate men to come to the aid of McSween, armed with deadly weapons, for the purpose, among other things, of offering open and violent intimidation or resistance to this court. They have so far succeeded as to resist successfully by force the processes of the court under circumstances which I shall hereafter relate to you.

Among the falsehoods put in circulation for the purpose, is one that the courts of New Mexico are controlled by a corrupt "ring." Another is that the court, with the officers, are arraigned [sic] on the side of Murphy, Dolan and Riley, for the purpose of crushing McSween.

After this preamble, Judge Bristol reviewed the embezzlement case, growing blunt and even harsh in his criticism of McSween's handling of the matter. He attacked McSween's explanation of his refusal to make a settlement with Charles Fritz and Mrs. Scholand, the administrators of the estate. Since this part of the charge presents the other side of the story, it is given below:

He has been frequently urged to settle the matter but has never done it. The only satisfaction the administrators have obtained has been promises and pledges that he was ready and willing to pay over the money, but he has never paid it. Whenever it has come to the point of paying, one pretence and another has been interposed for not turning over the money. He has had it now for about eight months. In the meantime what has happened? Let us see.

In December last McSween started for a distant state with his family to reside for some time, without any settlement with the administrators as to this money. He was arrested at Las Vegas and brought back. He admits that he was going to St. Louis in the state of Missouri. He says that he had deposited this money in a bank in the town of East St. Louis in the state of Illinois.

It seems to me from the evidence that it was so deposited in the name of McSween, not as a fund by itself, but with other money belonging to him and all subject to his order and control, and that from time to time, as he needed money for his immediate use, he has been in the habit of drawing from all money so deposited indiscriminately. If these facts are true, it is pretty strong evidence tending to prove embezzlement.

About this time another very singular transaction took place which will perhaps throw some light on the motives of McSween in retaining this money under his control. It took place in the probate court. It is a record of that court in the handwriting of McSween, purporting to be an allowance of a claim of his against the estate in the sum of $3,815.50. The record specified among other things that Mrs. Scholand was not present, but she was represented by McSween in the capacity of attorney in agreeing to the allowance of the claim against the estate so far as she was concerned and in favor of himself. Now as a matter of law, McSween had no authority from his general power of attorney to act for Mrs. Scholand in that capacity for the purpose of putting this money into his own pocket. The whole transaction, so far as Mrs. Scholand was concerned, was a fraud upon her rights as administratrix.

The record also specified in effect that Charles Fritz was present and consented to the allowance of this claim. Mr. Fritz denied under oath that he ever agreed to the allowance of $3,815.50 as specified in this record, but admitted that he did agree to the allowance of 380 odd dollars and some cents (the exact amount I do not remember) for McSween's expenses in going to New York on this business and nothing else. Others who appear to be active partizans of McSween stated that Mr. Fritz knew well the amount of the claim as it appears on record and assented to it. The amount is not written out in words, but put down in figures.

Now when we consider all the circumstances relating to the record, they are sufficiently suggestive of fraud to justify an investigation to ascertain whether some deception was not practiced upon Mr. Fritz whereby his apparent consent was obtained to something he had never in reality agreed to.

Now even if it should be considered right and proper for McSween to retain this $3,815.50 out of this insurance money there still remained $2,000 about which there was no dispute. There has been no payment or tender of payment of even this amount. This is the case as presented to me on which Mr. McSween was held in bail for the crime of embezzlement. These facts, if proven, tend strongly to show an intention never to pay the money now in his possession.

Judge Bristol next discussed the attachment proceedings.

The administrators commenced a civil suit against McSween to recover the amount of this insurance money, and sued out a writ of attachment against McSween's property. The sheriff, as I am informed, levied the attachment upon the McSween interest in the stock of goods in the Tunstall store, as he was perfectly justified in doing under the circumstances. Subsequently, as I am informed, a body of men armed with deadly weapons entered the store and forcibly dispossesed the sheriff, and he has been kept out of possession ever since. Here the process of the court was openly defied and resisted successfully by force. This, gentlemen of the jury, was a crime of a serious character that calls for your prompt investigation.

Subsequently another attempt was made to serve the attachment on the property which was likewise successfully resisted. In another attempt, Mr. Tunstall was killed. There are conflicting rumors as to the manner of his being killed — one tending to justification, the other not. It is your province to get at the truth of the matter if you can; and if it shall be proven to your satisfaction that he was killed without justification and murdered, you should find an indictment against the guilty.

Subsequently the sheriff of the county and his companion, Mr. Hindman, were shot down and killed, while quietly walking along a public street in this town by a body of armed men concealed upon Mr. McSween's premises. Others have been killed in various parts of the county under various circumstances growing out of this McSween case.

In closing this charge Judge Bristol turned his attention to the Murphy-Dolan faction, although he devoted much less space to them than to the McSween side. He spoke of McSween's claim that the firm sought to get hold of the insurance money, but declared that such a belief was no justification for McSween's conduct. "As a lawyer, he knows perfectly well that there are several speedy and effective remedies in law for preventing any misappropriation of this money." He presented as a more serious matter the reiterated charge that the Murphy-Dolan firm employed a gang of outlaws and professional horse and cattle thieves and accepted stock from them knowing that it was stolen property. "I know nothing of the truth or falsity of this charge," said the Judge, "but if it is true, it is one of the most damnable and disgraceful crimes that can be committed in any community. If it is true, I do not blame the victims who are being plundered for becoming indignant and enraged."

On April 18 the grand jury completed its investigations and reported as follows:

To the Hon. Warren Bristol, Associate Justice of the Supreme Court of the Territory of New Mexico, and presiding Judge of the 3rd. Judicial District thereof:

The grand jury for the April, 1878, term of the district court for the county of Lincoln, deeply deplore the present insecurity of Life and property, though but the revival and continuance of the troubles of past years.

The murder of John H. Tunstall, for brutality and malice, is without a parallel and without a shadow of justification. By this inhuman act our county has lost one of our best and most useful men; one who brought intelligence, industry, and capital to the development of Lincoln county. We equally condemn the most brutal murder of our late sheriff, William Brady, and George Hindman. In each of the cases, where the evidence would warrant it, we have made presentments.

Had his excellency, S. B. Axtell, when here, ascertained from the people the cause of our troubles, as he was requested, valuable lives would have been spared our community; especially do we condemn that portion of his proclamation relating to J. B. Wilson as J. P. Mr. Wilson acted in good faith as such J. P. for over a year. Mr. Brewer, deceased, arrested, as we are informed, some of the alleged murderers of Mr. Tunstall by virtue of warrants issued by Mr. Wilson. The part of the proclamation referred to virtually outlawed Mr. Brewer and posse. In fact, they were hunted to the mountains by our late sheriff with U.S. soldiers. We believe that had the governor done his duty whilst here, these unfortunate occurrences would have been spared us.

Under the impression that stealing the property of the United States was a crime against our territory, we heard evidence in regard to the administration of affairs at the Mescalero Apache Indian agency in this county; but we are now informed by the district attorney that crimes of the character thus investigated by us, are not indictable in this court. We have, however, ascertained by evidence that the Indians are systematically robbed by their agent of a large and varied assortment of supplies. We mention this here for the reason that it will explain why the Indians are migrating marauders and steal from and murder our citizens. The witnesses by whom these facts can be proven are residents of this town and neighborhood, and a list of them has been furnished by us to the United States District Court clerk.

On examination of the affairs of the county, we find that the county has outstanding warrants amounting to $3,314.48½. Due from Sheriff Brady and Constable Griego, $366.04.

The above shows the present financial condition of the county, excepting such warrants as are not as yet audited by the board of county commissioners and due for salaries of officers for the present year. Most of the county indebtedness is due to the erection of jail and jailor's house, which, upon examination, we find in its present condition entirely insecure, and call the attention of the board of county commissioners to this fact.

Your Honor charged us to investigate the case of Alex A. McSween, Esq., charged with the embezzlement of $10,000 belonging to the estate of Emil Fritz, deceased; this we did, but were unable to find any evidence that would justify that accusation. We fully exonerate him of the charge, and regret that a spirit of persecution has been shown in this matter.

Your Honor, too, charged us to investigate the charge of cattle stealing, &c., against Messrs. Dolan and Riley. This we did and the result is a matter of record.

We acknowledge the punctuality and earnestness of Dist. Attorney Col. W. L. Rynerson in attending the grand jury during its arduous and responsible labors; and most respectfully request from your Honor to be discharged from further duty as grand jurors.

J. H. Blazer,
Foreman

The results of the grand jury sessions, translated into terms of indictments and arrests, were as follows:

In connection with the killing of Tunstall, indictments were brought against Jesse Evans, George Davis, Miguel Seguro and Frank Rivers (an alias sometimes used by John Long) as principals, together with James J. Dolan and J. B. Mathews as accessories. Of those classed as principals, Jesse Evans was the only one who could be found and arrested. This was done, and he was placed under a $5,000 bond. Both of those designated accessories were arrested and placed under bonds of $2,000 each. All these several cases were continued.

In connection with the killing of Brady and Hindman, indictments were found against four, Wm. H. Bonney (Billy the Kid), John Middleton, Fred Waite, and Henry Brown. In connection with the killing of Roberts, an indictment was found against Charlie Bowdre. As none of these could be located, no arrests were possible just then, and the warrants were left in the hands of the new sheriff, Copeland.

The refusal to make any indictment freed McSween from the criminal charge of embezzlement, but left him still under the civil suit that had provoked the attachment proceedings. The grand jury did not return indictments against Widenmann, Shield, George Washington, and George Robinson; consequently they were released.

Concerning the Dolan store's encouraging cattle stealing, which Judge Bristol had brought to the attention of the grand jury, the report contained the following brief statement: "Your Honor, too, charged us to investigate the charges of cattle stealing, etc., against Messrs. Dolan and Riley. This we did and result is a matter of record." In other words, indictments had been found against them for cattle stealing.

The accomplishments of this term of court were given wide publicity in the New Mexico newspapers. Within a few weeks after the adjournment of court on April 24, the Cimarron *News and Press*, in its issue for May 2nd, editorialized upon the situation as follows:

LINCOLN COUNTY

The information which we lay before our readers this week from Lincoln County, is of the utmost importance and interest. The district court has closed its labors, and to the result of them every one has looked for a solution of various disputed questions. We have heretofore given very full reports, and have, in the light of abundant private information which we believed to be worthy of credit, commented freely upon the affairs of that troubled section. We were led from a sense of right to espouse the cause of the people, and we have been convinced that official authority and power, from the governor down, was employed to bolster up the fortunes of a small combination of government contractors who were speculating at the expense of the people, and wished to crush out every sort of rivalry or competition in business by fair means or foul. It is therefore with no little satisfaction that the *News and Press* points to the report of the Lincoln County grand jury as a full confirmation of its views.

Editor Crouch of the Mesilla *Independent* — himself clerk of the district court — says the grand jury was a good one. They were charged by Judge Bristol in a lengthy effusion, which after being carefully read, we are bound to say is one of the most partisan charges we ever heard from the bench, and which sounds much more like the argument of an attorney seeking to convict McSween of a crime than the address of a judge before whom the facts are likely to come to trial, and who, from his high office, is presumed to be impartial and disinterested. Three-fourths of the charge, occupying three columns of the *Independent*, is devoted to an argument seeking to prove A. A. McSween guilty of embezzlement, while a paragraph, less than an inch and a half in length, is all the space which Judge Bristol can afford to devote to the murder of J. H. Tunstall.

The grand jury, with this one-sided charge as a starting point and under the supervision of District Attorney Rynerson, whose relations to the parties are shown in the letter published elsewhere and who was present and examined the witnesses, &c., have made a thorough investigation of the late troubles in the light of the sworn testimony of witnesses produced before them. The result is McSween is exonerated of the charges made against him by Dolan, Riley and Rynerson and solemnly promulgated from the bench by Judge Bristol, and it is shown that the proceedings against him have been a persecution of his enemies.

It is found that Tunstall's killing was a brutal murder, and a number of parties were indicted therefore.

Indictments were also found against the murderers of Sheriff Brady, but in regard to this McSween, Shield, and Widenmann were entirely exonerated.

Indictments have been found against a number of parties for cattle stealing and receiving stolen cattle, which, it is thought will break up the arrangements heretofore existing and entirely destroy the usefulness of Capt. Jesse Evans and his band in that section.

The defeat of the Dolan group had been so much a foregone conclusion, even while court was in session, that Dolan had published in the Santa Fe *New Mexican* and other papers favorable to him, a card which was virtually a valedictory. It was as follows:

A CARD TO THE PUBLIC

The condition of affairs now existing in the county is such as to make it unsafe for the undersigned to further continue business as they have heretofore done. They take this occasion to assure their friends and the public that the suspension will be only temporary, and that they will resume when peace and quiet shall take the place of lawlessness, and order be restored in the county. Asking for continued confidence, and hoping for a renewal of business relations, we remain,

Very respectfully,
Jas. J. Dolan & Co.

Lincoln, N. M., April 17, 1878

Behind this statement was the desire of T. B. Catron to protect himself in connection with notes of the firm in the hands of the First National Bank at Santa Fe with his endorsement. In return for the endorsement, Dolan and Riley had mortgaged to him virtually all the property — the forty acres upon which the store and other buildings stood, the store with its merchandise and accounts receivable, and 1,500 head of "Arrow" brand cattle ranging on the Pecos near Black River.

The members of the firm, reading the handwriting on the wall so far as their business future was concerned, took their departures from Lincoln. Things had gone against them so decidedly that their leaving was virtually an expulsion. Major Murphy, broken in health, left Lincoln County for Santa Fe, where he remained until his death on October 19. Dolan accompanied Murphy to Santa Fe, but after a brief stay he returned to Lincoln determined to recover the field if possible. Riley emigrated to Las Cruces but reappeared for a while in Lincoln to join Dolan in the effort to re-establish their hold on the business, or at least to help Edgar Walz wind up their affairs. Young Walz, Catron's brother-in-law, who had left Minnesota in 1877, had come to Lincoln as Catron's agent in winding up the affairs of the Dolan firm.

Both Dolan and Riley felt that their backs were to the wall, and the time had come for roughest measures. What these were to be may be gathered from a conversation between Dolan and Rynerson, which Atanacio Martínez, the constable, overheard. At the close of court, Rynerson had said to Dolan, "Don't give up. Stick to that McSween crowd. I will aid you all I can, and will send you twenty men. Stick to the fight, and give it to those rascals. That is the only way to win." Whether such a conversation took place or not, the fact remains that shortly afterwards, a "Rio Grande posse" appeared in Lincoln County, composed of John Kinney, a very hard character from Doña Ana County, and several companions of like complexion. The arrival of the Kinney crowd augured the use of more ruthless measures than heretofore.

Indications were strong that the McSween side would press home its advantage. On the same day that Dolan published his card to the public, McSween composed for the newspapers an announcement of a different tenor. He had secured authorization from the Tunstall family to offer a reward for the murderers:

$5,000 REWARD

I am authorized by J. P. Tunstall of London, England, to offer the above reward for the apprehension and conviction of the murderers of his son, John H. Tunstall, at Lincoln county, New Mexico, on the 18th day of February, 1878. The actual murderers are about twenty in number, and I will pay a proportionate sum for the apprehension and conviction of any of them.

A. A. McSween

Lincoln, N.M., April 17, 1878

McSween wrote long letters to Tunstall's father and his sister Minnie, who had become Mrs. Behrens. The letter to the father began in a lyrical strain, an outcropping of an oratorical side of the man. The letter also revealed a premonition of what the future held in store for the surviving member of the pair whose association had been so close.

Widenmann informs me that you do not purpose removing the remains; of this I am glad as this will enable us to sleep by him and Brewer when we shall have "been gathered to our fathers." With tears in my eyes I say to you that I think I shall sleep that long sleep easier by their side!

Since these troubles commenced, I often feel that I would like to share their sleep. Dear boys, are you not witnessing my struggles and triumphs? Do you not, whilst anchored in the tranquil harbor, feel interested in that little barque you left on the tumultuous seas? Or are you so wrapt up in the felicities of your celestial home as to be unmindful of the ones on this side? Peace be to your ashes. Green be your memory. As long as we live flowers will bloom on your graves, and at your head we'll place marble stones with suitable inscriptions. When the grave shall unclasp its frigid arms, our corruptible bodies shall put on incorruption then we'll see each other. I miss you, the best friends I have ever had outside my own family.

This world is a furnace. Happy we, if we can come out like the refiner's gold or purer.

After this outpouring, the mood of the letter descends to commonplace. In a few paragraphs, the property interests of Tunstall and their management. The closing paragraph must have been written with the reward notice in mind. McSween wrote: "The murderers are energetically pursued. They all will be brought to accounts for the fearful crime." Behind the brevity resided a grim determination — a dedication in fact.

To Tunstall's sister he wrote some of the details of the pursuit of the murderers:

> Seven of his murderers are now dead; two are wounded. There will be no peace here until his murderers shall have paid the debt. The whole country is in arms. But this news is marred by the fact that your brother's best friend, R. M. Brewer was killed; John Middleton, James French, W. Bony (sic), Charles Bowdre, and George Coe wounded. They are recovering rapidly. I have had all that human skill could do for them done. Some of them are farmers, and you may imagine what actual state of things existed when they took up their guns. They knew, and so did the whole community, that your brother's murderers would never get their due in our courts.
>
> He always said that the man who killed Mac would be before the throne a short time after committing the deed if he could see him — that he would devote his life and means to the avenging of my death. I would gladly do the same for him. To know that *all* who planned and executed the inhuman deed had each received their due, I would part with every dollar I have. Never while I have life, shall I turn aside from the accomplishment of that mission.
>
> But it will only endear his memory more to state to you that I am not alone in these feelings and designs. Even women such as Mrs. Isaac Ellis and Mrs. McSween and Mexican women want to hear of the murderers having paid the debt. John S. Chisum, a

man worth half a million dollars, is doing all he can in the same direction — he's been over three weeks working for that purpose. He is a bosom friend of ours, and John took him as such. He always calls himself, my wife, and myself, "the family." Your brother asked Chisum to include him in the term, which was done. Chisum is an old single man, John was single, we had no children; I tell you that we were happy. Your brother thought a good deal of Chisum, and Chisum did of him. I can say that I have never known Mr. Chisum to think so much of a young stranger as he did of John H. Tunstall at the time of his death.

The tears shed when the funeral services were performed at our house are a sure indication of the general esteem in which he was held and the abhorrence cherished for the terrible deed. I can only give you a few names of those who are willingly trying to avenge his death; such as John N. Copeland, Isaac Ellis, and sons, George Barber, Sam Corbet, Frank and George Coe, A. Sanders, McNab (a brother Scot), D. P. Shield, John Newcomb, and a hundred others.

Slim enough were prospects for the return of peace and good order in Lincoln County, even after the voice of the court had been heard. McSween, with his zeal for social improvements heated by the sordid murder of his associate and friend and by instinctive protection of his own life, and Dolan with his flair for schemes and strategems became two "mighty opposites," each girding himself for a continuance of the grudges and maneuvers that were keeping the section in a ferment.

In Lincoln there was a great celebrating of what seemed a decided McSween victory. No sooner had court adjourned on the twenty-fourth than the town became ebullient. Within an hour after the close of court, the room used by Judge Bristol was the scene of a mass meeting of representative citizens. Juan B. Patrón called the meeting to order, and guided it through the selection of a set of officers. The probate judge, Florencio González, was chosen as chairman, Captain Saturnino Baca and José Montaño, then the county treasurer, were selected as vice-chairmen. Alexander A. McSween and Ben Ellis were elected secretaries. Judge González stated that the object of the meeting was the consideration of the present troubles convulsing the county. His speech was followed by those of Juan Patrón and José Montaño who set forth what they considered the causes and what remedies were expedient.

After the speeches came suitable resolutions. A committee composed of Patrón, Chisum, and Clenny presented the following, which were adopted:

BE IT RESOLVED:

1. That it is the sense of this meeting that our present troubles are only a continuance of old feuds, dating back five or six years, that will now cease as the cause has been removed.

2. That the thanks of the people of Lincoln County are due and are hereby thanked to Lieutenant Colonel Dudley, U.S.A., commanding Fort Stanton, N. M., for his conduct as an officer and a gentleman. That we do and will consider the day he took command at Fort Stanton an important era in the history of our county. That we assure him of our appreciation of the intelligent, cautious, and earnest manner in which he has applied himself in ferreting out the cause of our troubles, this — his non-partisan conduct and frankness toward the people on one hand and these men on the other — is a guarantee that he *alone* is the commanding officer at Fort Stanton. Therefore we thank him our heartful thanks in recognition of our appreciation of a man who discharges his duty fully.

3. That we condemn without qualification the conduct of our governor, S. B. Axtell, while here in March last. Both his conduct and proclamation of March 9th, 1878, are unworthy of an officer filling his exalted station. His refusal to investigate our troubles stamps him as a little, one-sided partisan. As a result of that proclamation, he is responsible for the loss of life that has occurred in this county since his visit.

4. That we recognize with expressible pleasure the good and united feeling that binds all our people, Mexican and Americans, together. We recognize our mutual dependence upon each other, and we pledge our lives and our property to the protection of each other and the maintenance of the laws.

5. That a vote of thanks be tendered to the United States Soldiers, non-commissioned officers and privates, for their commendable conduct while here during court.

6. That we tender our thanks to John H. Copeland for having accepted the office of sheriff and for his important and efficient discharge as such, since he took charge.

7. That the secretaries of this meeting furnish copies of the proceedings thereof to the President of the United States, to the Honorable Secretary of War, to his Excellency, S. B. Axtell, and that copies thereof be furnished to the *Mesilla Independent* and the *Cimarron News and Press* for publication; and also that they furnish copies for Hon. Florencio González, Hon. Juan B. Patrón, and Isaac Ellis, Esq., who are hereby constituted a committee to wait upon Lieutenant Colonel Dudley, U.S.A., commanding Fort Stanton, N.M., to deliver to him the proceeding in English and Spanish as a token of respect.

The lavish attention given Colonel Dudley betokened the cordiality with which he was welcomed as the new commander at Fort Stanton. He had assumed charge the day after the killing of Brady and Hindman, and had shown himself a prompt, decisive officer. Captain Purington, who had been in command, had seemingly ceased to be neutral in the troubles, and Colonel Hatch, commanding the entire district of New Mexico, had decided upon a change. Colonel Dudley, who had been stationed at Fort Union for a year and a half, was elected. His military record was impressive. He had been appointed to the army in 1855 from Massachusetts, and prior to the Civil War, had served on various Indian campaigns in the Northwest. During the Civil War he had become a colonel in the 30th Massachusetts Volunteer Infantry and had participated in important campaigns in the far South. After the Civil War, he had been stationed at several points where reconstruction difficulties seemed to require military surveillance. Later he had been transferred again to the Northwest, whence he had come down to Fort Union.

He was considered an efficient officer, although he secured his results largely by fear and coercion. His manner was stern and arrogant to the nth degree. He was also highly irascible and impulsive. At Fort Union about a year before his coming to Fort Stanton, he had led an attempt to force a marriage between a young man living in the vicinity of the Fort and a young woman, a relative of the post chaplain. Colonel Dudley organized a party of brother officers, which proceeded to the home of the young man, and threatened him with severe punishment if he did not marry the girl at once. Those who knew Dudley could see that his motives were right, but they could also see his inveterate tendency to act hastily and beyond bounds, especially when his emotions became highly wrought up. Moreover, Dudley was notorious for his heavy drinking and when under the influence of whiskey he was a very different man from the Dudley when sober. But, with all allowances made, Dudley's participation in this attempt to force a marriage was both officious and rough. Such, at least, was the court-martial decision in November, 1877, which found Colonel Dudley guilty and imposed a loss of several grades in the promotion list. His defense had been conducted by the Santa Fe law firm of Catron and Thornton, thereby establishing a connection with the powerful firm which further extended its influence in Lincoln County.

The advent of Colonel Dudley at Fort Stanton started a struggle between the two elements in Lincoln County to see which could curry his favor. So far he had been circumspect. The war department required weekly reports from Fort Stanton, so that Colonel Hatch at

Santa Fe might be cognizant of the military activities. Colonel Dudley, however, went beyond this formality. He had a mania for making records and keeping documents; when he took over the reins at Fort Stanton he inaugurated a policy of having down in black and white everything, even to a degree exceeding the army's ordinary procedure. At first he was hopeful of keeping the balance even between the two factions, and that he was succeeding, the applause at the mass meeting was ample testimony. Some two hundred of the more substantial people were willing to applaud the record of his first two weeks of command at the post.

24. The Seven Rivers Gang
Takes a Hand

WITH THE LAST OF APRIL a new angle had unmistakably developed
to the Lincoln County War. The Pecos region, particularly Seven
Rivers, became zealous for a part in the feud. Up to this time, the disturbances had been confined to the "upper" part of the county, but now
the "lower" part was itching to take a hand. One of the first indications
of such an inclination came from Roswell, then a small two- or three-
house settlement six miles north of Chisum's South Spring River ranch.
In the *Las Vegas Gazette* appeared a letter undertaking an analysis
of the situation in Lincoln County, especially with respect to the outcome of the recent session of court. The letter bore the signature of
Marion Turner, a member of the firm Turner & Jones, the only store
in Roswell; the authorship, however, presumably belongs to Ash
Upson, the postmaster, who was the only person in the place literate
enough to produce it. Although he never participated actively in the
fighting, Ash Upson was a Murphy-Dolan sympathizer. He would
find it congenial to write a version of the recent developments and to
guard his reputation for neutrality by publishing it as Marion Turner's.
The letter was as follows:

Rio Pecos, N. M.
April 28, 1878

Editor, *Las Vegas Gazette:*

As far as legal proceedings are concerned, the difficulties in
Lincoln County were settled on the 15th of this month.

The charge to the grand jury by Judge Bristol was denuncia-
tory to the action of McSween, and laudatory to the opposite

party, the head of which is supposed to be Major Murphy and the firm of J. J. Dolan and Company.

The majority report of the grand jury sustains McSween whilst a minority report modifies, in some degrees, the majority report as affecting the rights of the contestants for supremacy as rulers of the interest, pecuniary and political, of this county are concerned.

Let me give you, as I understand it a brief summary of the condition of affairs, not for today, but for seven years past, with the money magnates of the county.

The firm of Fritz & Murphy, afterwards Lawrence G. Murphy & Co., were sutlers at Fort Stanton from 1870. They controlled the business of this country, as no farmer, stock raiser, artisan, or mechanic within a radius of 100 miles could secure employment, except through this firm, directly or indirectly.

They accumulated wealth. They were the mercantile aristocrats of the country.

In 1875 Alex. A. McSween arrived at Lincoln. He came here with his wife penniless, hauled here in a farmer's wagon by Martín Sánchez, a rancher now living at El Bordo. He expressed his intention of making his El Dorado at Lincoln and he has accomplished his design.

It is not for me to say by what means, whether by the honest prosecution of his profession (the law) or by "ways that were dark and tricks that were vain," as he is charged, he has accomplished his object; but it *is* true that he has so pursued his avocation that at the last session for the Lincoln County court (3rd judicial district) he has defeated the firm of Murphy, Dolan, and Riley, as by the decision of the grand jury but under the protest of Judge Warren Bristol and Prosecuting Attorney Wm. L. Rynerson.

This is the action of the court and jury which adjourned and was dismissed on the 24th of April, 1878. This county and the county of Doña Ana have been in a state of anarchy for the past two and a half years, the cause of which I understand as well as any man perhaps in the territory. I have been since 1872 a citizen of the county. My impression is that as there was a power (pecuniary) on the Rio Pecos, the perquisites of which both parties sought to procure, a struggle ensued in which bad blood was engendered. I also believe that both parties were unscrupulous, and used such means to accomplish each their object that they employed unlawful instruments, and that the result has been bloodshed and disaster — that it has cost the lives of good citizens against whose characters no breath of scandal has reached — against the lives of citizens who leave behind them friends who before this feud they would have sacrificed their lives to save.

There are two parties, designated as the "Murphy Party" and the "McSween Party." Both are charged with murder; the Murphy party with murdering Tunstall, Brewer, and others; the McSween party with murdering Major Brady, Morton, Baker, and others.

My firm belief is that although the adherents of these parties have been guilty of "killing their enemies," there was no murder in the matter, but a contest for "the best of the fight," which any good man will try to get. Let any man stand in the shoes of any one of these men and try to restrain his propensities. "Let him who is without sin cast the first stone."

M. Turner[2]
Roswell, N. M.

The contention in the closing paragraph is significant in view of Marion Turner's subsequent activities. By taking the fighting out of the category of mere personal feud and giving it the quality of outright war, he betrayed how he and others, apparently foreign to the original trouble, were able to find an excuse for participating. The veiled references in the letter are easily interpreted. What is called the "power (pecuniary) on the Pecos" could be none other than John Chisum. This indicates a desire to wrench the real cause of the trouble from business rivalry and personal animosity at Lincoln. The Pecos men were ready to inject into the tangled situation their load of grievances against Chisum. As the cattle king of the Pecos and McSween were linked in business and friendship, the Pecos men were refusing to regard them as two separate and distinct factors in the situation.

But the Pecos men had a more particular cause for their intrusion. Frank Macnab, who had succeeded to the leadership of the Regulators when Brewer was killed, had in the flush of the McSween victory in the district court, made the unqualified and open threat that the Regulators intended to "close out" everyone connected with cattle stealing in Lincoln County. This was the challenge to Seven Rivers, a place of which it was sometimes said that no man would be tolerated there unless he stole from the Chisum herds. Macnab had even made his threat specific and sent a warning directly to several Seven Rivers people that the Regulators were coming down shortly to "clean them up." The response of the Seven Rivers contingent was what might have been

---

2.   Letter attributed to Ash Upson, whose zeal as an anti-McSween propagandist obviously sometimes led him far afield from known facts. Too, it is interesting to note that although L. G. Murphy had divested himself of his Lincoln interests and isolated himself at his distant Carrizo Spring ranch more than a year before his letter was written, Upson nevertheless includes Murphy in his defense of the Dolan party's position.

expected. The voices of all might be heard in Jim Ramer's remark about the Macnab threat. "What do they think they are — a pack of mice?" Jim Ramer's excitement was a symptom that local patriotism was coagulating both the cattle thieves and the worthy and law-abiding citizens of the Seven Rivers section into one mass, both elements being friendly toward Dolan and Riley while more or less antagonistic to Chisum.

The Pecos men, however, cloaked their actual entry into the fighting under the guise of crusading in behalf of law and order. They avowed themselves greatly distressed because Copeland, the new sheriff, had made no arrests of those implicated in the deaths of Brady, of Hindman, or of Baker, Morton, or McCloskey. They assembled themselves to the number of about thirty and affected an organization, the leadership going to W. H. Johnson, formerly a deputy under Brady. Buck Powell and Marion Turner were his chief lieutenants. Then the Pecos crowd declared that they were going up to Lincoln, some 125 miles distant, and offer themselves to Copeland as a posse to help on the arrests of those responsible for the five killings. In this way they would test the sincerity of Copeland, of whom it was already being said that he would not arrest any McSween adherents, since he owed his appointment to McSween's influence.

A complete roll of this band from the Rio Pecos is unobtainable, but most of them were named in the *Cimarron News and Press* for May 9. In addition to the three leaders, there were the two Beckwith brothers, Bob and John, Lewis Paxton, Joe Nash, John Long, Thomas Cochran, Tom Green, Dick Lloyd, Charley Martin, Sam Perry, Milo Pierce, Jim Ramer, the two Olingers, Wallace and Bob, Sam Cochran, "Dutch Charlie" (Charles Kruling), and John Galvin. Besides these residents of the Rio Pecos section, there were several from Lincoln who happened to be sojourning in the vicinity of Seven Rivers. Among these were G. W. Peppin, J. B. Mathews, and Johnny Hurley, all loyal supporters of the Dolan side. In all there were thirty-five men, ten of whom had been in the posse that had murdered and killed Tunstall.

The men gathered together for the expedition to Lincoln so secretly that no inkling had reached the upper section of the county. Otherwise, Macnab, Frank Coe, and Ab Sanders would never have ridden right into their midst and precipitated an important skirmish on the evening of the thirtieth of April. On the twenty-ninth, the Pecos men had come up as far as the Fritz ranch on the Bonito, about eight miles below Lincoln, and were giving themselves and their horses an afternoon's rest before going the rest of the way. For safety's sake, too, they had thought to approach the town after dark.

After their evening meal at Lincoln, Coe and Sanders started for their farm on the Hondo, along with Macnab who was returning to the Hunter and Evans range on the Rio Pecos. Down the road they jogged until, rounding a sharp curve, they were spied by some of the Pecos men. Instantly the Pecos men recognized three McSween adherents, one of whom, Macnab, was a veritable king pin, "captain" of the Regulators, and hated by the Seven Rivers gang as a scourge to rustlers in his work as a cattle detective for the firm of Hunter and Evans. Frank Coe had not been so outstanding a figure in the disturbances, although he had been in the fight at Blazer's Mill. Sanders had played an almost inconspicuous part in the fighting, but he was Frank Coe's partner in the farm on the Hondo, a circumstance in itself sufficient to implicate him.

Before the eyes of the Seven Rivers men was a trio of enemies, and this was war. At the first volley Macnab fell from his horse, his body riddled with bullets. Sanders also fell, not killed but severely wounded. Frank Coe dropped from his horse unscathed and at once crawled into a depression on the hillside deep enough to afford concealment, and kept up firing at the attacking party as long as his ammunition lasted. However, as he was on friendly terms with several in the crowd, especially Wallace Olinger, and as the lust for killing had diminished among the Pecos men with the death of Macnab, Coe surrendered under promise that his life would be protected. The wounded man, Sanders, being considered almost a noncombatant, was cared for as well as possible and ultimately taken to Fort Stanton, where he was admitted to the post hospital.

When darkness came, the party from the Pecos proceeded on to Lincoln, entering the town cautiously, for it was supposed to be garrisoned by McSween supporters. Some ten or twelve of the Pecos men slipped through to the west end of the town and concealed themselves in the Dolan store. The remainder halted at the eastern outskirts, although five of them penetrated to the center of the town and reached the house of Captain Baca, just east of the Tunstall store. They asked permission to station themselves in his house, explaining that they wanted to serve McSween himself and several of his adherents just as Brady and Hindman had been served. This murderous design, however, was prevented by Captain Baca's refusal to lend his house to such a purpose.

The program of the Pecos men was to stage a fight if any considerable number of McSween men were in Lincoln. The first step was to be an attack on the Ellis store, now a rendezvous and supply depot for the McSween crowd, although neither Isaac Ellis nor any of his sons ever took actual part in any of the fighting. They found, however, the McSween men at the Ellis place had made ready for an attack, and the tightly shut doors and window shutters so impressed the Pecos men that, when the early morning sun made visible the preparations, they did not venture an attack. Instead, they fell back on their subterfuge of assisting Copeland and sent word to him about breakfast time that they were on hand and ready to help make arrests of those connected with the killing of Brady and Hindman. Copeland promptly answered that he did not want their aid; but, fearing that scorning their proffered help might bring about an attack on the town, he sent a messenger to Fort Stanton with a written request to Colonel Dudley for aid in keeping down an outbreak of hostilities.

Before any answer could arrive, trouble had started. Towards noon, George Coe, who was stationed on the roof of the Ellis store, caught a glimpse of a man sitting on a cow's skull in a field a long distance away. Remarking to Henry Brown, who was also on the roof, "See that fellow way off yonder? I am going to take a shot at him," he aimed and fired. The man jumped up, but immediately flopped to the ground. As he was evidently too badly wounded to run, George Coe desisted from shooting at him again. The man turned out to be Charlie Kruling, or "Dutch Charlie," with whom Coe was usually on friendly terms. His ankle was badly enough shattered to keep him in the hospital at Fort Stanton for nearly four months.

Coe's shot was the curtain-raiser. Soon afterward, the two factions were firing at each other's positions in lively fashion. Lincoln seemed on the verge of a more bloody battle than anything that had yet occurred. But the soldiers arrived from the Fort, fourteen men under Lieutenant G. W. Smith and their presence brought a prompt cessation of hostilities. The Pecos men decided that their best course would be to surrender, and they did so, with the understanding that they would be taken to the Fort. For good measure, Copeland added to this batch of prisoners some from Lincoln, among them Dolan himself.

A few days later the *Cimarron News and Press* carried an account of the fight at the Fritz ranch and its sequel, the attack on Lincoln. It was dated from the Indian agency and signed, "Soapweed." If the pen name is carried back to the code found in Riley's memorandum book dropped at McSween's at the time of the Tunstall killing, the authorship can be plausibly attributed to Morris J. Bernstein, the agency clerk. The fact that an outsider voiced the feeling that the Dolan sympathizers (as the Pecos men really were) were resorting to measures high-handed and unwarranted is a strong indication of the general feeling in Lincoln County over the recent developments.

Indian Agency, Blazer's Mill
May 1st, 1878

News and Press. — Last Monday evening Lincoln was enjoying peace, not knowing the fearful deed that had been committed eight miles from the plaza. It was known that the notorious bandit Kinney had organized a force with which to make war on the people in behalf of "the House," but from what quarter the attack would be made was kept a profound secret. Messrs. Sanders and Coe left Lincoln for their ranch in company with Mr. Mcnab, who was going to Hunter's ranch on the Pecos. When they reached Fritz' ranch, they were fired upon by concealed parties, killing McNab and wounding Sanders. They captured Coe and took him as hostage to Lincoln. They took Mcnab's horse and arms, as also those of Messrs. Sanders and Coe, having killed the horses of the latter. They compelled the U.S. mail driver to keep behind them all day for fear that he would inform the people of Lincoln of their coming. Sanders and Coe are two of the hardest working men in this country, yes, in the whole territory. Their character is above reproach. NcNab was serving Col. Hunter in the capacity of detective, and as such had made startling discoveries; this was pretty well known by the rising (barometer) "cattle kings."

The names of the murderers, so far as I have been able to learn, are G. W. Peppin, J. B. Mathews, J. Hurley, J. Galvin, Dutch Charley Kruling, W. Olinger, the Beckwiths, L. Paxton, J. Nash, J. Long, T. Cocoran, T. Green, Dick Lloyd, C. Martin, S. Perry, Buck Powell, Pearce and others, numbering in all thirty-five men, among whom were the "fag end of creation," including ten of the Tunstall murderers.

Our District Attorney failed to have the clerk issue warrants for the arrest of those indicted for the murder of Tunstall, but then, I suppose he wanted to help, in this way, the fugitive "house." Is any other proof wanted of this man's impartiality?

Eighteen of these men stationed themselves near the store of Isaac Ellis and Sons, others stationed themselves above McSween's dwelling house, at which places attacks were to be made simultaneously so as to distract the people. Firing was heard at Ellis', but no sooner did it commence than the party near McSween's decamped in confusion. In their precipitate flight they overlooked Frank Coe, and he thus escaped. Firing now became very lively, and two of the murdering filibusters were wounded. Sheriff Copeland had sent a courier to Fort Stanton for soldiers. In three or four hours all the warriors made a junction. Pretty soon Lieut. Smith with 14 soldiers came in sight. The sheriff took all prisoners. Six of the "Boys" were seriously, perhaps fatally, injured.

They were all taken to Fort Stanton last night, and will be examined before some J. P. before Gov. Axtell can possibly come down and remove him.

These men claim to be acting under orders from the late Sheriff Brady. Peppin and Mathews claim that, as his deputies, they have warrants for Brewer and party for arresting the late Morton and Baker!! Mathews is the "deputy" who manipulated the murder of Tunstall. Kinney and McDaniel and a few more are still at large, but the Regulators are on their tracks, and want them to settle in this county and thus ease Doña Ana County. This is the grandest victory yet won by the people.

I forgot to state that the Regulators cut the Kinney party off from their horses, and in this way prevented their escape until the soldiers arrived. Mexicans and Americans did nobly.

I just learned that James Chisum was killed by this party before they came up here.

Writing to your paper from this county appears to be a reigning passion. Now that the last grand jury have disgraced our "Hampton," and a splinter from a circular-saw struck "Warwick" and knocked the bottom out of "Box," I fear that I will be struck by lightning. I have done much in the "tree" business and washed everybody to the satisfaction of the powers at Washington. The water is now filling the ship and as every rat is leaving it to save his own life, I do not wish to be left behind, and as a mark of my earnestness I write you.

Soapweed

Two days later, on May 3, McSween attempted to set the agencies of law into motion again, this time in connection with the attack on Macnab, Frank Coe, and Sanders. As no justice of the peace was at Lincoln, "Judge" Wilson having been deposed by Governor Axtell nearly eight weeks before, McSween turned to J. G. Trujillo, justice of the peace for Precinct no. 2, which centered around San Patricio, and made affidavits charging R. M. Beckwith, W. H. Johnson, and the rest of the Pecos men with the murder of Macnab and the wounding of Sanders. Warrants were issued and placed with Copeland to serve. He proceeded to the Fort and formally arrested those for whom he had papers, notifying them that a preliminary hearing before Squire Trujillo was set for Monday the sixth.

A later letter to the *Cimarron News and Press*, by "Soapweed," will give an insight into the developments incident to the arrest of the crowd from the Pecos. The significant matter now was the attitude the military at Fort Stanton were taking. Colonel Dudley and his officers were beginning to show a bias toward the Murphy-Dolan side.

They also seemed determined to corral the McSween following and place them in the guardhouse.

Indian Agency, Blazer's Mill
May 4th, 1878

News and Press. — I stated in my last that a party of thirty-five men — Murphyites without the blue ribbon — murdered Frank McNab, wounded Mr. Sanders, probably fatally, and took and held Frank Coe as hostage after they had done their best to murder him. By actual count, 22 of these men were taken prisoners by Sheriff Copeland, aided by a posse of soldiers, and taken to Fort Stanton. Seven of the 22 were participants in the Tunstall murder and it is pretty certain that they, with others, were indicted by the last grand jury, but, owing to the District Attorney's impartiality (?), no warrants were issued for them.

After Copeland reached Fort Stanton he found himself unable to disarm these men. They were assigned quarters elsewhere than in the guardhouse, so as to save their feelings; they merited consideration, being murderers, thieves and "rising cattle kings."

The morning after they were taken there a warrant issued by J. G. Trujillo, J. P., of San Patricio, for their apprehension, commanding the sheriff to bring them before him, to be dealt with according to law. Of the 22 taken prisoners five were unknown, and, as usual in such cases, Copeland formally made the arrests and turned the prisoners over to Capt. Purington, officer of the day, as I am informed, whereupon the five whose names as stated in the warrant as unknown were liberated! Thus, if I see a man murder Jones, I cannot have him arrested because I do not know his name!

As soon as Copeland had formally made the arrests he asked for an escort to take the prisoners to San Patricio.

This escort was refused him unless he would first arrest 12 or 15 of the people of Lincoln. The sheriff informed the officers that he would arrest any and everybody for whom he had warrants. At once Murphy's affidavit men, G. W. Peppin and J. B. Mathews, made oath before some officer of the post, that 12 or 15 men, Isaac Ellis and Sons and A. A. McSween among the number, had made an assault with intent to kill. Thereupon a military courier was sent here for the purpose of getting our Justice, Easton, to issue warrants, which he did. On Thursday night Copeland reached San Patricio with 25 soldiers. Here he found McSween and others who were there as witnesses. Lieut. Goodwin placed Mr. Dow under arrest because he would not, and could not, tell Mr. Goodwin where men were whom he wanted. He was sent with Copeland to obey orders, but instead of that he gave orders and refused to allow the sheriff to make any arrests unless certain parties against whom he was incensed were taken to Stanton! Poor, little fellow! He had an opportunity to vent his spleen and show his partisanship and made the most of his opportunity.

Ellis and Sons, in company with others, were taken to the guardhouse and there confined, while those of the 22 elsewhere spoken of, were enjoying the liberties of the Post armed. On Friday evening these were disarmed but permitted to go where they pleased. With the accusation of double murder against him, J. B. Mathews was allowed to go to Murphy's ranch after cattle to fill the beef contract at the Post, and this without the knowledge or consent of the sheriff. Suppose the charge against the residents of Lincoln confined in the filthy guard-house, that of "assault with intent to kill," to have been true, was there any reason why they should be treated worse than those charged with, and indicted for, murder? The "assault with intent to kill" consisted in the men charged with it having, under the direction of the sheriff, taken measures to protect their lives and property from the rapacity of these privileged prisoners, the majority of whom are of the famous Jesse Evans' band.

By virtually releasing the balance of the 22 the sheriff was enabled to secure the citizens confined in the guardhouse the privilege of an examination before a Justice on the charge of assault, etc.! The 22 came, as they expressed it, to kill Ellis, McSween and Copeland; they failed; and notwithstanding the military may aid the oppressors, the people are true to themselves and are determined, when they say, they will no longer be oppressed.

Soapweed.

The other side of this confusing and somewhat *opera bouffe* affair may be had from a letter to the Santa Fe *New Mexican* from someone who signed himself "El Gato."

Fort Stanton, N. M., May 10, 1878

Editors *New Mexican:*

There is at present a lull in the tempest, and although it is not considered even probable that the war has reached an end, yet all are thankful even for a few days' respite. The last fight was the affair in which Johnson with about twenty-two men, all of whom are said to be property owners and he himself a married man, came from their ranches on the Pecos to Lincoln to report to our new and inefficient sheriff, John Copeland, to aid and assist him in serving the warrants he held in his possession against the murderers of Brady, Hindman, Roberts, and others. Johnson was one of Brady's deputies, and held at the time warrants for the arrest of a number of men, among others one for McNab. Before reaching Lincoln they met McNab, Frank Coe, and A. Sanders (the two former were of the fourteen who so gallantly attacked and murdered Roberts at the Indian Agency).

On attempting to arrest McNab they were fired upon, and returning the fire, concentrated it almost entirely upon him; he fell riddled with bullets. Frank Coe and Sanders were captured, the latter severely wounded. The prisoners, having in view the actions of their party when they captured Morton and Baker, and fearing the just punishment of their crimes, begged like dogs for their lives. This, however, was unnecessary; their captors were no hired assassins fighting for pay. No, on the contrary, they are the men whose names head the tax list of this unfortunate county; men who leaving their families, their homes, and their properties, have come over a hundred and fifty miles, willing to sacrifice their lives in order to restore peace to this distracted section of the territory.

On arriving at Lincoln they found the new sheriff in town carousing with the very men whom he was bound to arrest under writs issued by the court on indictments which even McSween's grand jury was compelled to find. At this sight their indignation knew no bounds, but with a praiseworthy desire to respect the law, they sent to Copeland and placed their lives and services at his disposal, should he attempt to do his duty and serve his warrants which he at that time carried in his pocket. To use a vulgar phrase, "he was having a good time," and it would be ingratitude of the blackest kind should he arrest and confine the gentlemen who were providing him with amusement.

He immediately gathered McSween's band of assassins and led them to the attack, having in the meantime sent for U.S. troops. Johnson and his men were unwilling to fight the authorities and more unwilling to surrender to McSween's butchers; and retreated to the mountains until the arrival of the troops, when they immediately surrendered to Lieut. G. W. Smith, 9th Cavalry. On their arrival at Fort Stanton they immediately made affidavits and had warrants issued against the men who fired on them when they entered the town. These warrants were issued by the justice of the peace at Blazer's Mill, Mr. Easton. Some of them were served nominally by Copeland with the assistance of the military, but in reality by the officers in command of the detachment. Copeland was compelled to accompany this expedition by the firm and determined action of Colonel Dudley, commanding Fort Stanton, and this alone can account for the fact of his once having attempted to do his duty. When the day arrived for the trial of these cases Mr. Easton, from motives unknown to your correspondent, handed in his resignation and refused to try the cases. Both parties who had until now been under arrest were therefore released.

This is the state of affairs at present; the two parties are at liberty, and a desperate fight is daily expected. As a natural consequence of the present state of affairs, there are a thousand and one rumors afloat; among the principal are the following:

1st. That McSween had paid John Copeland $3,000 for acting as sheriff.

2nd. That McSween had paid various sums to procure false evidence against Dolan and Riley.

3rd. That McSween has hired the services of a Presbyterian minister to give his actions a religious flavor.

These rumors I give with all due reserve. The only one corroborated is the first, and that is, as far as I can learn, grounded on a statement to that effect made by Copeland while under the influence of liquor. "In vino veritas."

El Gato

While all this incident to the attack on Lincoln was taking place, McSween received an answer to a letter he had sent Rynerson, asking that the district attorney place in Copeland's hands warrants for those indicted for the killing of Tunstall at the recent term of court. Rynerson, evidently displeased by McSween's letter, did not hesitate to taunt him "with the license of ink," in a manner unbecoming to the district attorneyship.

Las Cruces, N. M.
May 2nd, 1878

A. A. McSween, Esq.
Law Office of McSween & Shield
Lincoln, N. M.

Dear Sir:

I am just in receipt of yours of the date of the 27th ulto., directed to me, in which you say, "If the parties have been indicted by the last grand jury for the murder of John H. Tunstall, I wish to ask you to place warrants in the hands of our sheriff for their arrest. Please reply."

In reply I have to say that I shall discharge my duty without let or hindrance from any one, and when warrants are necessary, in every case they will be issued and placed in the hands of the proper officer. Just whom you mean by "our sheriff" is not clear to me, as in the past few months it is said you have had some interest in more than one sheriff. You may mean Martínez, you may mean Barrier, or you may mean some one else whom I do not know, whom you have reduced to possession and are pleased to designate as "our (your) sheriff;" and since you have undertaken the task of directing me in my duties, I may be permitted to suggest that you seem to have forgotten to dictate or direct as to what should be done as to the warrants "if parties have been indicted by the last grand jury" for the murder of Sheriff Brady, George Hindman, A. L. Roberts, and others in Lincoln County. Passing strange!

Very Resp'y,
W. L. Rynerson,
Dist. Atty.

The petulance and sarcasm coloring this letter betrayed Rynerson's inveterate hostility toward McSween. The position taken in regard to arresting those indicted for the killing of Tunstall bore out the popular impression that the district attorney was a strong sympathizer of the Dolan faction, if not a full-fledged partisan. At any rate, he was taking no steps towards the arrest that the grand jury indictments demanded.

The preliminary hearing at San Patricio on May 6 brought about a peculiar attempt on Colonel Dudley's part to turn the tables on the McSween faction. Knowing that McSween himself would be there, with several others as witnesses, he sent Lieutenant M. F. Goodwin and G. W. Smith with twenty-five soldiers over to San Patricio. Copeland, the sheriff, was taken along ostensibly to do the actual arresting, but the whole affair was managed and directed by the military authorities. Colonel Dudley evidently had concluded that Copeland would not make arrests among the McSween faction. He had even lectured Copeland severely, and now was putting him to the test. Handing him a batch of warrants, obtained through affidavits that Peppin, Mathews, and an army officer made before Dave Easton, justice of the peace for precinct no. 3, which centered around Blazer's Mill, Colonel Dudley said to Copeland, "Now let me see if you will do your sworn duty as sheriff and make these arrests. Here are warrants charging several of the McSween crowd with assault with intent to kill, growing of the fighting a few days ago at Lincoln. I am giving you a detachment of soldiers. Let's see if you will now do your duty."

Copeland had no zest for this task, but the army officers were relentless. At Lincoln, on the way to San Patricio, they forced him to arrest Scurlock, Widenmann, Scroggins, George Washington,

Ignacio González, Isaac Ellis and his son Will, Steve Stanley, and Sam Corbet. When the party reached San Patricio, Copeland demurred strenuously at arresting McSween and the others, but he was not allowed to dodge the issue. McSween made no attempt to avoid arrest, although he was not conscious of any reason for it. Lieutenant Goodwin, wanting to bag several more, demanded of McSween in a very overbearing manner information as to where to find Billy the Kid, Bowdre, Middleton, and one or two others of the Regulator group. When McSween replied that he had not seen any of them lately and knew nothing as to their whereabouts, Lieutenant Goodwin angrily retorted, "I know for a certainty that you have been with them this very day and paid for their dinners at Dow's store right here in San Patricio." McSween, taking this remark as a reflection on his truthfulness, protested strongly against such gratuitous insults, especially from an army officer.

The whole affair of the military going down to San Patricio had a theatric flavor. The outcome was that after two days in the guardhouse, McSween, Ellis, and all the others were released about as flagrantly as they had been taken into custody. Any effort to take them before Justice of the Peace Dave Easton at Blazer's Mill had been frustrated by Easton's abrupt resignation. Squire Trujillo at San Patricio would likely set them free, if he had the chance. Since there could not be created a valid reason for holding them, they all were released. The effort to do anything with the Pecos men also collapsed and they were also freed, and the guardhouse at Fort Stanton was cleared of its horde of civilian prisoners.

Curious as these moves and countermoves were, they revealed a new state, especially in the part the military was to play. Gone now was the amity and cordiality that had been displayed after the adjournment of court a few weeks before. The McSween sympathizers, who had then applauded the military, now reviled them. They believed Dolan, using his adroitness and persuasiveness, had won over Colonel Dudley and certain others of the Fort Stanton officers. Whether there was any truth in this, one thing did happen: the Dolan faction was galvanized into activity. With the aid and comfort derived from Fort Stanton, they harassed the McSween faction more strongly than before. They even revived some of the old charges which the court had seemingly settled. In the case of McSween, they brought forward the embezzlement factor by means of an alias warrant and forced him to make a new bond. This time Rynerson was much less arrogant and allowed a bond with much more readiness. The new bond carried securities that totalled only $10,000, when barely sixty days before a bond had been refused, although its securities ran to four times that sum. In the case of Barrier, Dolan also tried to stir up activity. This deputy sheriff from San Miguel County had loyally stood by McSween, even to ignoring Judge Bristol's order to turn McSween over to Brady, as he believed that doing so would mean the end of McSween. A visit of Dolan to Mesilla resulted in an order for the arrest of Barrier for contempt of court, even though Barrier had departed for his home in Las Vegas when the term of court had produced an exoneration of McSween.

25. Raid on Dolan and Riley's Cow Camp

ON MAY 14 SEVERAL of the Regulators staged a raid on the cow camp of Dolan and Riley on the Pecos in the vicinity of Black River. The party, numbering eighteen or twenty, included Scurlock, Bowdre, George Coe, Brown, Scroggins, two other Anglos, one of whom probably was Billy the Kid, and eleven Mexicans. Accounts disagree as to the leader on the expedition, some saying it was Joscita Chávez, others stating it was Scurlock. Very probably Scurlock was the guiding spirit, whether the titular leader or not. Scurlock was now one of Copeland's deputies, a position that tended to give some legal pretext for going to the Pecos. As an item in the Cimarron *News and Press*, June 6, 1878, states, they were seeking to arrest Mathews, Peppin, Kinney and others in the crowd that had killed Macnab and wounded Sanders two weeks before. Indeed what occurred at the cow camp implies a considerable element of reprisal about the visit. The Seven Rivers contingent had been gradually accumulating horses, some probably Tunstall's taken from Brewer's ranch the preceding September. Other horses, more recent acquistions, were certainly those taken from Macnab, Sanders, and Coe. The recovery of horses was at least part of the business that took this group of Regulators down into the Pecos country.

Details about the raid are now meager and hard to obtain. It seems, however, that the Regulators descended upon the cow camp when it was in charge of a small number of herders, all of whom promptly took flight. Two of the fleeing ones were wounded and a a third killed. "Indian" was the only name recorded for the latter, but he seems to have taken a conspicuous part on the Dolan side. The Cimarron *News and Press* item gave his history as follows:

> The deputy sheriff (Scurlock) had a warrant issued by the district court for the arrest of this Indian, charging him with having murdered a man on the Rio Grande. The Indian, it seems, admitted being at the murder of Tunstall, and being one of the foremost in the killing of McNab.

Scurlock's party gathered up the horses they were after, probably getting some at the cow camp and others at Beckwith's ranch. Carrying off these horses significantly affected the subsequent course of events by bringing into activity the influential agencies at Santa Fe connected with the Dolan-Riley faction. When the news reached Lincoln, Riley, who had returned from a sojourn of a few weeks at Las Cruces, promptly notified Fort Stanton and asked Colonel Dudley to send a detachment of soldiers to aid in the recovery of the horses. The plea he thought would influence Colonel Dudley most strongly was that if he did not get back the horses, the Dolan store would be unable to drive in their cattle to deliver on government contracts. Colonel Dudley could not respond even to that appeal, so strict just then were orders from the War Department. Soldiers were not to be used upon request of private individuals; they could be sent only when the sheriff or some other important official applied.

Riley shifted his tactics. The horses taken might be said to belong to Catron, since he had foreclosed on all the property of J. J. Dolan & Co. What could be more effctive than to send word to Catron at Santa Fe and have him exert his well-known high-powered influence? Two letters reveal how adequately the scheme worked. In the first, Catron cracked the whip over Governor Axtell:

> May 28, 1878
>
> Gov. S. B. Axtell,
> Dear Sir: ⊚
>
> I am just in receipt of a letter from Mr. Thornton, my law partner, who is at present in the county of Lincoln, where I have a herd of cattle and 25 horses and 2 mules, the horses and mules being used for herding and driving the cattle.
>
> Mr. Thornton informs me that a few days since, a party of men under the charge of a man claiming to be deputy sheriff, went to the ranch where my cattle were, and killed the herder and wounded two other men, and then drove off all the horses and mules, leaving my herd entirely unprotected and uncared for. I

had just ordered my agent (E. A. Waltz) to go there and round up and brand the cattle and calves, and this seems to have been done in order to prevent that.

There are a band of outlaws there estimated at from fifteen to a hundred, well armed, who have the whole country in terror, and those who took my horses are the same ones, or a part of them.

I also learn that all the stock men on the lower Pecos living near my cattle have been compelled to abandon their stock and go to the mountains where they are now awaiting an attack.

There seems to be no authority in the county of Lincoln to compel people to keep the peace or obey the law, and there seems to be an utter disregard of the law in the county, as well as of life and private rights.

I would most respectfully request that some steps be taken to disarm all parties there carrying arms, and that the military may be instructed to see that they keep the peace.

I am informed that the sheriff keeps with his deputies large armed posses, who are of one faction only and who take occasion at all times to kill persons and take property of the other faction whenever they get an opportunity.

There is no power, from what I can learn, that can keep the peace in the county except the military, of whom both parties have a healthy dread.

Hoping your Excellency will take such steps as will insure peace and preserve the lives and property of citizens and persons in that county, I am,

> Very respectfully,
> T. B. Catron

A request from such a source stirred Governor Axtell into action. He forwarded to Colonel Hatch a strong letter in which he pointed out that the property of Catron was endangered, and "he is now prevented by violence from rounding up and taking care of his cattle, some two thousand in number." He urged that soldiers be dispatched to Roswell and kept there for a time. He advocated trying the disarming procedure suggested in Catron's letter. But the startling feature of the Governor's letter was its closing paragraph:

> By authority of law, I have removed John H. Copeland from the office of sheriff of Lincoln County, and have appointed in his stead, George W. Peppin, who is now sheriff.

Governor Axtell's action was a flagrant violation of a law which he himself had signed.

At the same time, the territorial newspapers displayed a proclamation:

Thomas B. Catron, U.S. District Attorney, was virtually a dictator of New Mexico. He exerted his dominance in part through making substantial loans and investments, particularly in Lincoln County, and usually through such agents as Murphy and Dolan in their Lincoln mercantile firm.

PROCLAMATION BY THE GOVERNOR

For the information of all the citizens of Lincoln County, I do hereby make this public proclamation:

First — John H. Copeland, Esq., appointed a sheriff by the county commissioners, having failed for more than thirty days to file his bond as collector of taxes, is hereby removed from the office of sheriff, and I have appointed George W. Peppin, Esq., sheriff of Lincoln County. This has been done in compliance with the laws passed at the twenty-second session of the legislative assembly relating to sheriffs.

Second — I command all men and bodies of men now under arms and traveling about the country to disarm and return to their homes and their usual pursuits, and so long as the present sheriff has authority to call upon U.S. troops for assistance, not to act as a sheriff's posse.

And, in conclusion, I urge upon all good citizens to submit to the law, remembering that violence begets violence and that they who take the sword shall perish by the sword.

S. B. Axtell
Governor of New Mexico

May 28, 1878

The reason given for the removal of Copeland was pretty thin. The Governor had taken advantage of pure technicality, not to say subterfuge. The real reason for a change was that Copeland was offensive to the Dolan faction. All they could bring forward by way of objection was that he was zealous in his devotion to the McSween side. The new appointee, Peppin, unquestionably was just as strongly devoted to the Dolan faction.

George W. Peppin always had been hand in glove with the Murphy firm. He, too, was of the ex-Civil War soldier group. In 1862 he had come to New Mexico as a private with the California Column. A stonemason by trade, he had been drawn to Fort Stanton by the rebuilding which started in 1868, and when that terminated he had settled on a small farm just west of Lincoln. With his family he continued laying adobe when there was a demand, building two structures at what was to be known as Roswell, and putting up the walls of L. G. Murphy's two-story building at Lincoln. Hence on many grounds, both of circumstance and reason, Peppin was dedicated to the Dolan side. In the first stages of hostilities, Brady had used him as a deputy; thus he had become rather active in the altercations. No wonder, therefore, that his appointment was taken as conclusive evidence that Governor Axtell was again giving the Dolan side all the aid possible.

Governor Axtell's request for troops bore fruit. A large detachment, fully equipped for field duty and prepared to make a long stay, started down to Roswell on June 7. Captain Purington was in command, and the men were from his company, "H" of the 15th Infantry. All this presaged a larger activity by the soldiers in Lincoln County affairs than heretofore. It also indicated that when the right ones petitioned, the soldiers could be brought into use. If the shoe that pinched had been worn by someone else, John Chisum, for example, would there have been such a notable effort at relief as when the sufferer was T. B. Catron? Naturally there followed a prompt protest from the McSween side. Someone signing himself as Pecos wrote to the *Cimarron News and Press* the following sarcastic letter:

Roswell, N. M.,
June 17, 1878

News and Press: A detachment of cavalry, under the command of Captain Purington and Lieutenant Smith, is here to "round up" for T. B. Catron, Esq., U.S. Attorney for the territory of N. M. By all means let the army be increased. Quite a number of its rank and file can be employed here in herding, marking and branding cattle. At first the experiment may not prove profitable, but it affords an excellent opportunity to exhibit the efficiency of our army. As Uncle Sam furnishes horses, forage, men and rations, need we growl? I am told they are better hands to scatter than to gather cattle. Captain Purington is too slow in his movements for a Texas cow; Lieutenant Smith is too impetuous; the soldiers will not head the infuriated cow without fresh orders! In this way time is wasted and horse flesh used up without any particular benefit to Mr. Catron or anyone else. These military gentlemen can manipulate guns and sabers, but they lack the alertness of the cowboy. For the sake of their families, I trust that nothing serious will happen to these gallant sons of Mars whilst in the cow-punching business, but should any mishap overtake them, surely our government would not be slow to recognize their services to the U.S. Attorney for New Mexico by pensioning them or their survivors!

Several of us here are going to apply for soldiers and officers for the same purpose for which "Bishop" Axtell secured them for U.S. Attorney Catron. We expect to have lively times here this summer.

While these portentous happenings, both in Lincoln County and at Santa Fe, were taking place during May, the Las Vegas *Gazette* was misled into the belief that Lincoln County was quieting down.

Under the title "All Quiet On the Rio Bonito" it indulged in a quotation from a private letter from Lincoln to C. Simpson. Simpson had been at Chisum's in March and had been a member of the party which went up to Lincoln and arrived the day Brady was killed. The item in the *Gazette* was as follows:

> Everything is quiet in Lincoln County. A truce seems to have been tacitly agreed upon. The telegram to the *New Mexican* reporting the death of Sam Smith, Newcomb, Widenmann, and others, was a canard. Easton has charge of Murphy, Dolan, and Riley's house. McSween is at Chisum's ranch. W. H. Johnson and his party from Seven Rivers are at the Indian agency. Murphy has sold his ranch at the Carrizo Springs to the Hall Brothers, young Englishman with capital, for the sum of $18,000.

Whoever wrote so optimistically was unaware of the fomenting turmoil that was developing and which would slowly grow throughout June to arrive at its culmination in July.

26. A New Sheriff Takes The Field

HAVING QUALIFIED as soon as possible as sheriff, Peppin started an energetic campaign against the McSween party. His first step was to appoint a staff of deputies, the selections including John Long, Buck Powell, Marion Turner, and José Chávez y Baca. Long and Chávez y Baca, both associated with Lincoln, might be regarded as appointees from the Dolan party in its more local aspect; Buck Powell and Marion Turner, Dolan adherents from Seven Rivers and Roswell respectively, might be considered appointees in the Pecos area.

June 18 Peppin was ready to launch a masterstroke, the aim of which was nothing less than to arrest the leading members of the McSween faction. As Peppin had also been appointed a deputy U.S. marshal, he was in a position to undertake the execution of a sheaf of federal warrants, including one or more for nearly the whole of the old Regulator group issued in connection with the Blazer's Mill fight, on the ground that the killing of Roberts had been on the Indian reservation. The loophole, however, in the argument was the fact that Dr. Blazer's house was not actually a part of the reservation even though in the reservation. When the tract was set aside for the Indians, Dr. Blazer and other settlers who had acquired property rights were not disturbed. Thus Roberts had not been killed on land belonging to the government; however, that fact did not deter the issuing of warrants which might be used to accomplish the arrest of members of the McSween party.

The federal warrants were potent in securing help from the army. Amid all the vacillating about the use of soldiers in civil matters, one firmly settled matter was that soldiers might be called upon to aid in the execution of United States warrants. Thus, when Peppin was ready to start forth with his posse, he made a formal request in his capacity of deputy United States marshal for aid from Fort Stanton in arresting some of the McSween crowd supposed to be in Lincoln at the McSween house and the Ellis store. Promptly honoring the request, Colonel Dudley sent twenty-seven men, in charge of Lieutenant Goodwin.

As the soldiers were going toward Lincoln, they were met by Peppin with the posse he had mustered, numbering about twenty. In it were the notorious John Kinney, and several of his "Rio Grande Posse." One of the current beliefs about Kinney was that he expected to give service rendered under an offer of $500, some said $1,000, for killing McSween. At any rate, the general reputation of Kinney and his following was so malodorous that Lieutenant Goodwin, highly partisan though he might be, grew squeamish about mingling his soldiers with a posse that included some of the most notorious renegades in southern New Mexico. Peppin was bluntly informed that he must purge the posse of such as Kinney before the soldiers would cooperate. Peppin promised to get rid of the offensive element just as soon as they reached Lincoln, and the two groups, soldiers and civilians, moved on towards Lincoln.

The masterstroke, however, failed to materialize. News of the attempt had reached the McSween crowd and all had left Lincoln for their old refuge at San Patricio. In fact, Peppin's activity had caused a general exodus from Lincoln, not only of those in the McSween crowd who did the fighting, but of those who were the guiding spirits. Even Juan Patrón deemed it expedient to leave, for the Dolan set were supposed to be about as eager for his death as McSween's. He sought protection at the Fort, claiming that Jim Reese, a member of the Kinney gang, had come to the door of his house and would have killed him but for the timely interference of Colonel Micky Cronin, a resident of Lincoln. McSween also at this juncture made his third flight from Lincoln. His friends realized his danger, which seemed to grow greater with each day. His plan at first had been to go back to Chisum's ranch, which had served him well before, but that idea was given up. Possibly John Chisum's absence (he had gone to St. Louis, ostensibly for treatment of a leg injured by a horse's kick) may have had something to do with the change of program. At any rate, McSween chose to go to San Patricio and be with those of his followers who were doing the fighting. Indeed, they had virtually become his personal bodyguard.

While he abhorred violence, McSween was no mollycoddle or coward, as his conduct in these trying times proved. Now that he was associated so directly with his fighting men he may have begun to carry fire-arms. The Cimarron *News and Press* indicated this in an obituary published later in the summer:

> There was no bluster or bravado in his character, but he was a man who loved peace and order, and who never carried a weapon until the last few weeks, when he with other good citizens was obliged to shoulder his rifle in defense of his life against the murderous band of horse thieves and cutthroats whom Axtell's bushwhacking sheriff had imported, and who without warrant or authority hunted him throughout the county, thirsting for his blood.

The arrest of McSween in June on the charge that he had assaulted John Long with a deadly weapon is, however, no proof that he had personally taken part in any shooting, though he was certainly present when someone in his group shot at Long and killed the latter's horse.

The story back of this arrest is as follows. For some reason Peppin had not immediately followed the McSween crowd into their refuge, San Patricio. He had contented himself with possessing Lincoln, feeling so secure that he had sent the soldiers back to the Fort. A few days later he renewed the effort to capture the McSween party, this time inclined to dispense with the help of the military. But just as he was about to start, his courage weakened to such a degree that he applied for a detachment of soldiers. Colonel Dudley, who seems to have lost patience with Peppin on account of hesitancy and vacillation, refused the request with the curt reminder that as Peppin already had a posse of twenty or more, he saw no special need to reinforce it with soldiers.

Peppin then decided to send a part of his posse to San Patricio in charge of his deputy, John Long. On June 27, Long and his men had a minor encounter with eleven of the McSween crowd, among whom were McSween, Copeland, Billy the Kid, Waite, Bowdre, French, Scroggins, "Dirty Steve" Stephens, Jesús Rodríguez, Atanacio Martínez, and Esequio Sánchez. The McSween side, apparently not anxious for a fight, preferred to get away into the mountains. The skirmish, therefore, produced no damage to either side except that Long's horse was shot from under him. Long was able, however, to recognize several, among them McSween and Billy the Kid. So when he returned to Lincoln he made affidavits against them, charging assault with intent to kill. Probably he had really seen McSween among the attackers and had noted that he carried a rifle, but whether McSween had made any use of it, is another question altogether.

The McSween men made their retreat from San Patricio in the direction of their old sanctuary on the Pecos, in the vicinity of Chisum's ranch. When Colonel Dudley heard of their departure and learned what had happened at San Patricio, he felt he ought to take a hand in the proceedings independently of Peppin. He started Captain Carrol with thirty-five men towards San Patricio in order to curb any large outbreak between the two factions. Though Carrol's mission was not directly to support Peppin, but rather to intervene if necessary to protect life and property, he could not resist giving pursuit to the McSween group. He followed them a considerable distance into the mountains south of San Patricio when he was suddenly recalled by Colonel Dudley.

Colonel Dudley had received new orders just issued by the War Department to make effective a recent enactment of Congress regarding the use of soldiers in civil affairs. On June 18 an amendment to the army appropriations bill had been passed, prohibiting the use of any part of the army as a *posse comitatus*, or otherwise, for executing the laws, except in certain cases expressly authorized by the Constitution or acts of Congress. The new orders that came to Colonel Dudley from Colonel Hatch's office in the wake of this enactment were so stringent that he immediately sent a recall to Captain Carrol. This trick of fate probably saved the McSween crowd from capture, for Carrol was much in earnest about the pursuit and had a detachment large enough to obtain results. Peppin exhibited no inclination to go on with the pursuit with his civilian posse. So the McSween contingent were allowed to make their way down to their old refuge on the Pecos. Lincoln was again in the hands of the Dolan side. Peppin with a force of about fifteen proposed to hold the town in spite of the McSween men, if they should come back from the Pecos.

27. A Federal Probe

DURING JUNE, with its clashes and skirmishes, Judge Frank Warner Angel had been conducting an investigation as a special agent for the Department of Justice. He was under instructions to concentrate on two matters: the murder of Tunstall, and the improper management of the Indian agency. Letters galore had gone to Washington. Dr. Leverson had written directly to President Hayes and to Secretary Carl Schurz. Others had written, too, so many in fact it is difficult to say whose letters were the most influential. Even Widenmann had indulged in some letters, as his family were natives of the same town in Germany as Carl Schurz. Widenmann used this as leverage with a certain degree of success. He greeted Judge Angel's arrival with a letter published in the Cimarron *News and Press* appealing for cooperation in Angel's efforts to go to the bottom of the troubles besetting Lincoln County.

> Frank Warner Angel, Esq., of New York City, is here to investigate charges against U.S. officials and also the murder of J. H. Tunstall.... If the iron heel of the "ring" is to be removed from the necks of our people; if monopolies are to be broken; if the blighting, despotic, and pernicious power and influence of officials in New Mexico are to be brought to an end and authoritatively exposed, the people must come to the front. Every man and woman in New Mexico, knowing the damaging facts against U.S. officials should disclose them now to Mr. Angel ... The cry from New Mexico has become so loud, strong and consistent that the administration has sent Mr. Angel to hunt the cause; the people who are familiar with the game must now guide the hunter ...

If you have any charges to make against federal officers, now is your time to make and substantiate them, or forever hold your peace. You are in duty bound to presume that Mr. Angel will do his whole duty, so you cannot excuse yourself from the discharge of yours by saying that you have no faith in investigations. If you have any testimony, disclose it to him and then wait and see whether or not he does his duty. He certainly is willing to perform the preliminary part of his duty — he is ready and willing to take testimony and go anywhere to get it. He shows no disposition to waste his time in sporting — he appears to be a hard and willing worker, always ready with his pen and paper. You have been loud in your complaints; come forward now and sustain them. The people of New Mexico are said to be downtrodden; now or never is the time to stand up.

Decidedly cold towards Judge Angel were the dominating politicians in New Mexico. Their newspaper mouthpiece, the Santa Fe *New Mexican*, directed at him editorials tinctured with mild personal defamation. He was nicknamed "Sleeve Buttons," an epithet that recalled some gossip five years old. Judge Angel, then on a similar mission in the territory, had been accused of receiving presents and bribes for his influence with government officials at Washington. "This man," so one editorial said, "has now commenced playing the role of informer and mud dauber, misrepresenting and perverting facts; he is the man who puts himself forward as the champion of outraged law; that wants certain things exposed, and who says he will fight openly now where he was fighting formerly under the guise of friendship. 'Sleeve Buttons' has an idea that he is a lawyer — that he would make a good attorney general or district attorney; he wants office, and wants it badly. But it won't do, Mr. 'Sleeve Buttons.' You are known, your dirty acts are known, and your blackmailing proclivities are known."

The motive back of such comments and slurs was so apparent as to take the edge off them. Unquestionably there were some scared political leaders and territorial officials in New Mexico when Judge Angel arrived and commenced the investigation. McSween hoped that the truth about the murder of Tunstall would be revealed, and wrote Tunstall's father to that effect in the letter given below. He also included a sort of balance sheet of factional casualties, which may be deemed official, up to the date of the letter.

Lincoln, New Mexico, June 5, 1878

Dear Mr. Tunstall:

We have succeeded in getting the U.S. government to appoint and send out here a gentleman from New York to inquire into the murder of John. For the past week or ten days I have been very busy in taking testimony. Parties for years in the employ of Murphy have testified that sentence of death had been passed on your son and myself long before he was killed. One man testified that [a member] of the Murphy & Co. party, before John was killed, offered him $1,000 if he would kill me as I was leaving my house in the morning for my office. It's notorious that I have never owned or carried a more formidable weapon than a penknife, and it would be an easy matter to kill me.

I have no doubt but that the United States government as a result of this investigation will be obliged to award you a large sum for your son's death. The testimony will be as full as it can be made. On their side there has been killed on account of John's death Morton, Baker, Roberts, Hill — Evans crippled and now in U.S. hospital — Brady, Hindman, and two others whose names are unknown, but *helped* murder John.

Full particulars of the trouble, cause and result, will shortly be published by the officers of this county and will be sent you. There is not much use in sending newspapers having exciting paragraphs for the purpose of making them [illegible] and spicy when they are ignorant of the status of things here.

On our side were killed Brewer and McNab; wounded badly, Middleton, [George] Coe, Antrim [Billy the Kid], French, Bowdre, and Sanders.

I think the estate is above, not under, what I represented. I have not received a dollar from anyone yet. I furnished everything and so continue to do. Mr. Ellis is in business and is not in a condition to advance anything. It takes time to realize on assets here with profit, consisting as they do of stock and produce.

Yours very truly,
A. A. McSween

P.S.

Mr. Widenmann has the sole management of the estate. By way of advising, I'll do all I can.

Will try and send particulars of Brewer's death by next mail and will also write my ideas about a monument for John.

About three weeks later, on the eve of his departure from Lincoln for safety's sake, McSween wrote again to Tunstall's father:

The evidence in regard to the murder of John has been taken and I have no doubt that it's of such a character as will entitle you to an indemnity. Mr. Angel, the commissioner, called upon me today and said that Mr. Tunstall was killed by a mob. Many of the old mob have come in again and are determined to kill me. In view of this, Mr. Angel and other friends here advise me to leave for a while. I'll go off about 65 miles from here, where I think I'll be safe.

Judge Angel's search was thorough. He went to Lincoln, and with the assistance of McSween and others gathered affidavits from all who were in any way implicated in that matter. Although the testimony was highly conflicting, Judge Angel was able to simmer it down to the following report which was completely fortified at every point with affidavits.

To the Honorable Charles Devens,
      Attorney General,
Sir:

In compliance with your instructions to make careful inquiry into the causes and circumstances of the death of John H. Tunstall, a British subject, and to ascertain whether the death of said Tunstall was brought about through the lawless and corrupt conduct of the United States officials in the territory of New Mexico, and to report thereon, I have the honor to submit the following report in relation to the premises.

First, as to the cause of the death of John H. Tunstall. Mr. John H. Tunstall by his straightforward and honest business transactions with the people of Lincoln county, New Mexico, had almost overthrown a certain faction of said County who were plundering the people thereof. He had been instrumental in the arrest of certain notorious horse thieves. He had exposed the embezzlement of territorial officers. He had incurred the anger of persons who had control of the county and who used that control for private gain. He had introduced honest and square dealings in his business, and to the enmity of his competitors can be attributed the only cause of his death.

Second, as to the circumstances of John H. Tunstall's death. An attachment had been obtained against the property of one Alexander A. McSween. It was claimed that said Tunstall was McSween's partner. The sheriff in order to attach certain property, viz. stock and horses alleged to belong to McSween and Tunstall, sent his deputy to Tunstall's ranch to attach the same; when said deputy visited said ranch and was informed that he could attach the stock and leave a person with it until the courts could adjudicate to whom the stock belonged, he left without attaching said property and immediately assembled a large posse among whom were the most desperate outlaws of the territory. They again started for Tunstall's ranch; in the meantime Mr. Tunstall had been informed of the action of the sheriff, and believing that the real purpose was to murder and not to attach, he left his ranch, taking with him all the horses, and started for Lincoln, the county seat.

Directly after Tunstall had left his ranch, the deputy sheriff, and said posse arrived there, and finding that Tunstall had left with the horses, deputized Wm. Morton, who selected 18 men and started out ostensibly to capture the horses. After riding about thirty miles, they came up to Tunstall and his party with the horses and commenced firing at them. Immediately Tunstall and his party left the horses and attempted to escape — were pursued and Tunstall was killed some hundred yards or more from his horses.

Who shot Tunstall will never be known. But there is no doubt that Wm. Morton, Jesse Evans, and Tom Hill were the only persons present and saw the shooting, and that two of these persons murdered him, for Tunstall was shot in two places — in the head and breast. Of these persons Morton and Hill were afterwards killed, and the only survivor is Jesse Evans, a notorious outlaw, murderer, and horse-thief. Of these persons Evans and Hill had been arrested at the instigation of Tunstall. They were at enmity with Tunstall, and enmity with them meant murder.

There was no object for following after Tunstall except to murder him, for they had the horses which they desired to attach before they commenced to pursue him and his party. These acts together with the bitter feeling existing against Tunstall by certain persons to whom he became obnoxious, and the deputy allowing those notorious outlaws to accompany him, lead me to the conclusion that John H. Tunstall was murdered in cold blood and was not shot in attempting to resist an officer of the law.

Third, was the death of John H. Tunstall brought about by the lawless and corrupt action of the United States officials? After diligent inquiry and examination of a great number of witnesses, I report that the death of John H. Tunstall was not brought about through the lawless and corrupt conduct of the United States officials in the Territory of New Mexico.

All of which is respectfully submitted.

> Frank Warner Angel,
> Special Agent.

The other matter that Judge Angel looked into was the conduct of the management of the Mescalero agency. There were three angles to this inquiry: first, had the agent, Godfroy, disposed of government property to individuals or firms? second, had he knowingly accepted flour of lower grade than contracted for? and third, had he "padded the rolls" in regard to the number of Indians receiving rations?

Both Dolan and Riley admitted that when they forwarded supplies of beef and flour, the teamster making the deliveries frequently brought back a load from the agency warehouse. They claimed that sugar, coffee, tobacco, and *manta* thus procured were merely borrowed, and were eventually replaced, although they admitted that no written records existed to show anything about the transaction. Testimony about the quality of flour was highly conflicting, Dolan claiming it was of "quality at least equal to the quality contracted for; in some instances it has been superior." But others described it differently. James H. Farmer spoke of it as follows: "The flour I hauled from the store of Dolan & Riley at Lincoln was wheat meal ground in a Mexican mill. I did not consider it flour. I would not have bought it for myself or my help. It was unbolted flour. I once got out of flour on the road and tried to use some, but could not. It was gritty, very poor." To determine the number of Indians drawing rations, Judge Angel went to the reservation and made a count. Only 375 Indians put in appearance, although the conditions were, as he admitted, unfavorable. This tended to substantiate testimony from Captain Henry Carrol that when rations were issued in October, 1877, there were about 250 present, although ration tickets mounted up to 901.

While irregularities seemed to exist, Judge Angel was inclined to think that leniency might be shown, especially in view of the fact that Godfroy seemed to be controlling and training the Indians better than almost any other agent. He was later permitted to resign without criminal prosecution.

28. The Five-Day Battle

JULY, THE MIDDLE of which was to bring matters in Lincoln County to a decisive issue, opened with an inconclusive collision at Chisum's ranch. As soon as the presence of the McSween group on the Pecos became known to Marion Turner and Buck Powell, Sheriff Peppin's deputies, they started to muster the Pecos men. They quickly assembled a posse at Seven Rivers and headed for Roswell, which became their headquarters for the time being. The McSween men were in camp near where the Rio Hondo empties into the Pecos, but they went back and forth freely between that place and the Chisum ranch some six miles south. Though John Chisum himself was away, his brother, Jim Chisum, accorded the McSween men the same reception "Old John" would have given, the ranch store being their chief source of supplies. If the men did not have money to pay, McSween could be expected to foot the bills. Was not the purse of the Tunstall family open to McSween? He had repeatedly declared that he would spend every dollar he had in this cause; but, as his own money was not inexhaustible, the purse of the Tunstalls must be utilized to pay for food and ammunition, as well as possibly a per diem for the men. The Ellis store at Lincoln was the place of supply when the band was in that vicinity, as a bill for $961.53 rendered against the Tunstall estate shows; in like manner the store at Chisum's ranch was the source of supply now.

Early in July a part of the McSween party, twelve or fourteen perhaps, at Chisum's ranch were attacked by Buck Powell and fifteen Pecos men who hoped to capture them. This, however, proved impossible for they had stowed themselves in the stronghold the Chisum's house could become in time of warfare. The structure was built of adobe, enclosing a court or patio. The roof was provided with the usual parapet, high enough to shield sharpshooters posted behind it. All that Powell could do was to surround the Chisum house with his force and keep up a desultory fight with the McSween men, all during July 4 and the night following. On the morning of the fifth Powell gave up his attempt and withdrew toward Seven Rivers.

A day or two later he came back reinforced by Marion Turner with additions from the Pecos men, who now expected to stage a fight to the finish. The McSween men, however, had given them the slip and were on their way back to their old haunt at San Patricio. McSween himself had come more and more strongly to realize the inevitable and, having grown tired of being a refugee, was ready to go to Lincoln and stay there or be killed. As a blind, the McSween party made a feint of going up the Pecos as though their destination might be Bosque Grande or Fort Sumner, but a few miles north of Roswell turned and went in across the county in the direction of Lincoln. In passing through a small Mexican settlement on the Berrendo, they added a few recruits.

When the flight of the McSween party became known, Marion Turner and Buck Powell led their men rapidly toward Lincoln. They, too, anticipated a desperate encounter shortly and proposed to go to the aid of Peppin, whose small posse at Lincoln would be somewhat outmatched by the McSween band, which now had enlisted a number of native New Mexicans who held grievances against the Murphy-Dolan organization.

The news quickly reached Lincoln that the McSween party had returned to the vicinity of San Patricio. About the tenth of July a part of Peppin's posse went thither. José Chávez y Baca was the deputy in charge and with him were John Hurley, Juan José Parado, Lucio Montoya, Pantaleón Gallegos, George Davis, John Kinney, and possibly a few others. Dolan accompanied them quite unofficially, but as usual directed things. The posse ransacked the town most ruthlessly and brutally. They searched several houses without showing any warrants or claiming to have them. When doors were not opened, they battered down with rifle butts. Vile and insulting language was used toward both men and women citizens.

Someone signing himself "Lincoln" sent the Cimarron *News and Press* a rambling account of the ransacking of San Patricio, together with the sidelights on recent developments in Lincoln County, which was published in the issue for July 25:[3]

---

3. Although this letter is dated at Lincoln, July 11, and McSween did not return there until the fourteenth, it was understood that he composed the letter signed "Lincoln."

LINCOLN COUNTY
THE PEPPIN MOB ROBBING CITIZENS
AND DESTROYING PROPERTY
Kinney, the Bandit, the Right Bower
of Axtell's Sheriff.
Lincoln, N.M.
July 11, 1878

News and Press: Headed by Axtell's sheriff and J. J. Dolan the Rio Grande posse killed and stole horses in San Patricio last week; and at the same time and place, they broke windows and doors, smashed boxes and robbed them of their contents; from an old woman who was living alone they stole $438. They tore the roof off of Dow Bros. store; threw the goods out on the street and took what they wanted. Towards women they used the vilest language. Citizens working in the fields were fired upon but made good their escape up the river. Dolan and Panteleón Gallegos, late clerk to the "House," killed a horse lariated near the town because the owner was supposed to sympathize with the Regulators. Dolan informed the people that there was no law in the county that he could recognize and that when certain Regulators and sympathizers were killed, he would leave the d — d country. Kinney, who was present, remarked those were his sentiments. Kinney said in town that he was employed by the Governor and that he and his men would have to be paid $3.50 a day by the county, and that the sooner the people helped him arrest the Regulators, the sooner their county would be relieved of this expense; Dolan endorsed this speech. Peppin stated that he would turn those who sympathized with the Regulators out of their houses, that he would take all of their property, that he had power to do as he pleased. Dolan and Kinney enthusiastically endorsed this sentiment.

The Dolan party saw eight Regulators the other day and pursued them. The latter being outnumbered five to one, made for the mountains under a heavy shower of bullets, returned with some effect by the pursued. Result: one Dolan and Peppin man wounded — not fatally — and two horses killed. Peppin and Dolan with their Rio Grande posse went to the Coe and Sanders ranch and stole all the vegetables they were able to find, and plundered the ranch of a suit of clothes, shirts, etc.

The Regulators now number over 200 able-bodied men, well equipped. They have now detailed 50 of their number to harvest each other's wheat. Of this number six are detailed to herd the horses and sound the alarm. The "House" has said that anyone opposed to it could not harvest this year, but the people have shown how easily even a Ring can count its chickens before they are hatched. On the heels of the army of reapers follows Coe and Sander's matchless threshing machine, though the Peppin-Dolan mob lately said that the machine would be burnt if an effort was made to use it.

'Lawrence G. Murphy' has written Judge González an extraordinary letter in relation to the petition sent by the people to Governor Axtell asking the removal of Peppin. Major Murphy says that unless the Judge promptly denies the signing of the petition, he will publish him throughout the county as a base liar. He says that if the Governor was disposed to remove Peppin he could not do so. No doubt he knows whereof he writes. Judge González had been informed that he too is on the black list; so he has applied to Colonel Dudley for protection. His abode, in consequence, will be at Fort Stanton for some time. Hon. J. B. Patrón is enjoying military protection at Fort Stanton.

Every one of the Peppin posse, from Kinney to Dolan, claims to be regular deputies. They roam around in gangs and take horses and arms, provisions, etc., by order of the sheriff. They claim to have orders to take all horses or kill them if resisted. Farmers on the Pecos are prepared to receive Peppin's party; several efforts have been made by latter lately to take the farmers' stock, but without success. All of those, living, who aided Peppin in the murder of McNab are deputies. One of them, Marion Turner by name, called upon C. Sedillos, constable for precinct no. 6, lately for his authority to act as constable. Sedillos showed his commission. Mr. Turner tore it up, saying he was authorized by Peppin to act [as such]. He warned Sedillos not to act after that revocation. Thus Mr. Turner is well qualified to perform and do all that his principal could do if he were personally present. Three years ago he murdered a Mexican "to see," as he afterwards stated, "how a damned greaser would kick." After this exploit he left unmolested for Texas. Subsequently he was indicted by the grand jury. He returned here nearly a year ago, but no steps were taken to arrest him. He settled and filed upon the Van C. Smith place at Roswell, a proceeding very unpalatable to the "House" and Mr. Catron, the latter holding a mortgage on the place amounting to $2,000. Now that Turner has accepted a deputyship, I presume that the misunderstanding growing out of the filing business has been "fixed up."

The women of San Patricio made complaint to Colonel Dudley of the outrageous conduct of Peppin, Dolan, Kinney, and party. He sent Captain Blair to view the damage done in the name of the law.

I have no doubt but that unless Peppin is removed and posse withdrawn there will be a fearful destruction of life and property. The people are counselled on every hand to be patient, but there is a limit beyond which patience ceases to be one of the virtues. If the people give vent to their wrath once, the work will be short and terrible.

Peppin and posse have turned a tower belonging to McSween into a jail. They took adobes belonging to him and built a room on top for their convenience. Prominent Americans and Mexicans have prevailed upon McSween to leave his home so as to escape death at the hands of this sheriff's posse. He is in daily communication with his friends.

Some of the Kinney band say they are to be paid by the parties in Santa Fe. Wonder who the parties are?

The situation at San Patricio as presented in the foregoing letter found ample substantiation in Captain Blair's report to Colonel Dudley. On July 11 he had visited San Patricio and gathered with the aid of Juan B. Patrón as interpreter full insight into the ransacking of the place. He summed up the affair as follows:

From what I saw and heard it appears that the sheriff's posse under Baca, acting to some extent (exactly how far does not appear) under Mr. Dolan's instructions, tore down a portion of a house, forced and tore open a number of doors, and searched houses without showing or claiming to have any legal warrants for so doing, that the searches were conducted in a discourteous, uncivil, and even rude manner. The residents of the houses so entered and searched claim that they are wholly unpartisan, took no part in the fray and that no shots were fired, or offensive demonstrations made from their houses.

This incursion upon San Patricio aroused the McSween crowd to the point where one of them wrote the threatening letter to Walz, the agent of Catron in the management of the affairs of J. J. Dolan & Co., a notice of a tit-for-tat policy which went as directly as possible to the representative of Catron and contained a reference to the raid on the Dolan and Riley cow camp a short time before. This occurrence had brought Catron more into the open than heretofore as a factor in Lincoln County's disturbances.

In Camp, July 13, 1878

Mr. Walz — Sir,

We all are aware that your brother-in-law, T. B. Catron, sustains the Murphy-Kinney party, and take this method of informing you that if any property belonging to the residents of this county is stolen or destroyed, Mr. Catron's property will be dealt with as nearly as can be in the way in which the party he sustains deals with the property stolen or destroyed by them.

We returned Mr. Thornton [Catron's partner] the horses we took for the purpose of keeping the Murphy crowd from pursuing us with the promise that these horses should not again be used for that purpose. Now, we know that the identical horses returned are used by the party with whom you are all clearly identified.

We know that the Tunstall estate cattle are pledged to Kinney and party. If they are taken, a similar number will be taken from your brother. It is our object and efforts to protect property, but the man who plans destruction shall have destruction measured him. Steal from the poorest or richest American or Mexican, and the full measure of injury you do, shall be visited upon the property of Mr. Catron. This murderous band is harbored by you as your guest, and with the consent of Catron occupies your property.

Regulator

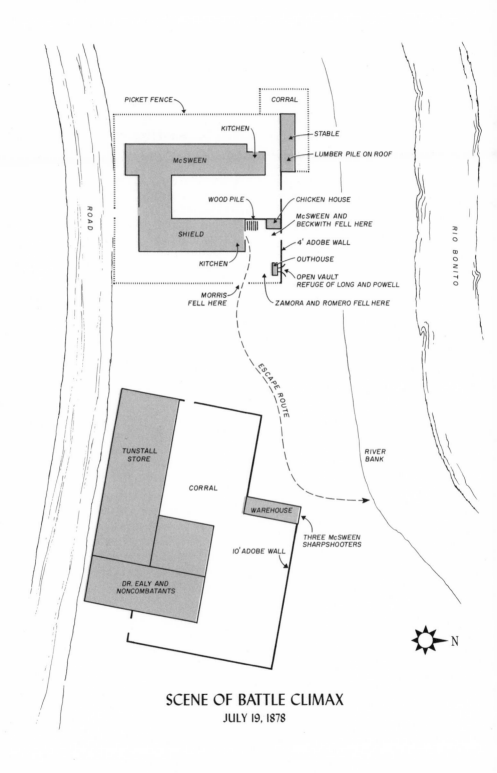

SCENE OF BATTLE CLIMAX

JULY 19, 1878

29. Four Days of Fighting

SOME TIME DURING the night of Sunday, July 14, the McSween forces numbering fifty or sixty rode into Lincoln and distributed themselves in three strong adobe buildings. The largest division, composed of twenty or twenty-five Mexican adherents commanded by Martín Chávez, used the Montaño store. Another group established themselves at the Ellis place, from which they might control the eastern entrance into the town. In the McSween house itself were McSween and about fourteen of the pick of his men-at-arms, divided about equally between Americans and Mexicans. The names of these, as far as the list can be made, were Jim French, Billy the Kid, Tom Cullins (alias Joe Bowers), Tom O'Folliard, Harvey Morris,[4] Joseph J. Smith, José Chávez, Francisco Zamora, Eugenio Salazar, Vicente Romero, and Ignacio González. The number of men, as well as their strategical distribution, indicated that the McSween faction had come back determined to repossess the town and hold it against all hazards. The decisive conflict, which had been long brewing, was evidently at hand.

The arrival of the McSween group took the sheriff completely by surprise. Most of Peppin's men were out of town watching San Patricio under the belief that the McSween crowd would almost certainly appear at that much-used rendezvous. The garrison at Lincoln consisted of only five or six, stationed in the "Indian tower," as an old *torreón* was called. Besides Peppin, there were Billy Mathews, Jim Reese, Sam Perry, Jim McDaniels, and "Dummy," a man so nicknamed because he was deaf and dumb, or supposed to be. As this force was entirely too small to cope with the McSween force, Peppin dispatched a messenger to San Patricio with an order recalling members of his posse who were

---

4. Harvey Morris could hardly be classified as a combatant. He was a young man who had recently arrived from Kansas, suffering from a lung ailment, and who had been "reading law" in McSween's office.

over there. In the meantime, the McSween men fortified their buildings. They barricaded windows with adobes; they piled bags filled with dirt against doorways; they drilled portholes through walls. Their positions were indeed so nearly impregnable that the ensuing fight gave promise of becoming a long-drawn-out siege.

On Monday morning, the fifteenth, one of the first moves by the McSween faction was to try to empty the Indian tower, which Peppin's men were converting into a hornet's nest. In clearing the tower, McSween first tried negotiation. The men in it used Captain Baca's house as their base for supplies, going back and forth freely. The Baca house also was in such a location as to make a good screen for anybody trying to get close to the McSween house. The Baca house stood on land belonging to McSween, though the house itself was claimed by Baca. He decided to compel Captain Baca to vacate the property, as the following communication shows:

Lincoln, N.M., July 15, 1878

Captain Saturnino Baca,

Sir: I want you to vacate the property now occupied by you at once. Unless you leave the house within three days proceedings will be instituted against you without further notice.

You have consented to so improper use of the property by murderers for the purpose of taking my life, and I can no longer consent to your occupancy thereof.

Respectfully,
A. A. McSween

This notice threw Captain Baca into a high pitch of both indignation and fear. At once he sent a frantic appeal to Colonel Dudley stating that his wife with a child but a few days old could not stand removal. He also reminded Colonel Dudley at length that he had been a soldier in the New Mexico volunteers from 1863 to 1868.[5] Dudley, however, was powerless to do anything directly in answer, for his hands were still completely tied by the new orders relating to using soldiers in civil disturbances. He did, however, go so far as to send to Lincoln the post surgeon, Dr. Appel, to investigate.

Dr. Appel called on McSween and found him disposed to be reasonable in the matter. If the Peppin men would leave the tower and not attempt to use it, Captain Baca might remain; but if the men continued to occupy the tower, they must be eliminated. As a step towards that end, Captain Baca must leave or be driven out. Appel next went to see the Captain and found him afraid to ask the men in the

---

5.   Military records indicate that Baca's army service commenced in 1861.

tower to leave it. He spoke of McSween men being on both sides of his house, and considered himself as left to their mercy if Peppin withdrew his men. He declared that reports had it that the McSween men were threatening to burn his house down if he would not leave.

Dr. Appel also interviewed the Peppin men in the tower. Naturally they did not favor the suggestion about leaving, but were willing to do so if there could be some guarantee that the McSween men would not step into the tower as soon as they were out of it. They proposed that some soldiers be put in charge, who could keep it neutral ground. When Appel returned to McSween and discussed this proposal, he found him willing to accede to it, provided the presence of the soldiers would positively mean that neither side would have the use of the tower or any part of the Baca premises. The neutrality of the military was evidently suspect with McSween, and he wished to leave no loophole by which the tower might fall back into the hands of the other faction.

The situation concerning the tower seemed to have reached an *impasse*, and Dr. Appel had to return to the Fort with negative results. He also carried back information about the deplorable state in Lincoln. Most of the population who could do so had left town in order to be entirely out of the fighting zone. Only about twelve families remained of the thirty or forty usually there.

Later in the day, probably in the early afternoon, Peppin went through the formality of attempting to serve warrants upon certain ones in the McSween crowd. John Long, one of his deputies, was ordered to go to the McSween house with warrants for McSween, Scurlock, Bowdre, Billy the Kid, Henry Brown, Frank Coe, George Coe, and several others and demand that they give themselves into custody. As he approached the house, he was fired at several times but did not fire in return. His demand for surrender was completely ignored, and Long returned to the Wortley Hotel, the chief assembling place for the Dolan forces.

The rest of Peppin's posse arrived from San Patricio in the afternoon, entering the town from the west so as to avoid passing any of the three buildings containing McSween men. They were joined en route by the Buck Powell-Marion Turner band from Seven Rivers, which had camped overnight in the Capitan foothills after their unsuccessful attempt to capture McSween at Chisum's ranch. The Dolan force was now numerically about equal to that of the McSween supporters and included Robert and Wallace Olinger, John and Robert Beckwith, Andrew Boyle, Milo Pierce, Tom Cochran, James Reese, Samuel Perry, James McDaniels, R. L. Bryan, John Hurley, Jesse Evans, Billy Mathews, Sam Collins (Caleb Hall), George Rose, Joseph Nash, John Galvin, John Chambers, James Irvin, Charles Crawford

("Lallacooler"), Ed Hart, as well as John, Jim, Bill and Tom Jones.[6]
There was also a sprinkling of native New Mexicans, including Lucio
Montoya, José Chávez y Baca and Pantaleón Gallegos.

As soon as the reinforcements were strategically deployed, an
outbreak of heavy firing began. Toward the close of the afternoon
came another flurry of shooting, lasting about half an hour, brought
on by some of the McSween men attempting to leave the Montaño store
and go over to the McSween house. To do so they had to pass within
range of the tower, which still harbored five or six of Peppin's men.
The McSween men were ordered to halt, but gave their answer with
rifle shots. The Peppin men answered in kind, and the firing soon
became general. But the casualties of the first day were slight. For
all the expenditure of ammunition, only a horse and a mule were hit.

The few residents of the town kept under cover closely. The
street was as empty as though the town were deserted. Mrs. McSween
had determined to remain in her home with her husband. She fully
knew there would ultimately be a severe onslaught upon this house
since the most prominent members of the faction composed its garrison.
The McSween dwelling was virtually a double one, the west wing being
occupied by the McSweens, and the east wing by the Shield family.
Mrs. Shield, with her five small children, remained in their part of
the house. A stone's throw to the east, in the Tunstall building, were
other noncombatants, Dr. and Mrs. Ealy, their two children and Miss
Gates. These likewise deemed it best to remain where they were
and await developments, although they realized fully their exposed
situation.

During Tuesday, July 16, firing was intermittent most of the time
between the two groups. Peppin's men were inclined to be more
aggressive than on the previous day. Peppin still had six in the Indian
tower and kept the rest assembled at the Wortley Hotel. The McSween
men made a good deal of trouble for the Peppin men during this third
day by effective sharpshooting from the roofs of the buildings they
occupied. Particularly was this true at the Montaño store, which had
among its garrison several excellent marksmen. In an attempt to check
this shooting Peppin sent five of the best shots among his men out
upon the rocky hillsides to the south of town with instructions to drive

---

6. "Tom Jones" listed in reports of the fight was probably an alias, as no doubt
    were some of the others; he should not be confused with Tom Jones, brother
    of John, James, and William, sons of Heiskell Jones. Tom was only eleven
    years of age and was with his mother at Seven Rivers at the time of the fight.
    Nor was Heiskell Jones' thirteen-year-old son, William, active in the shooting,
    although according to family tradition he helped mold bullets and load guns
    for the men.

the McSween men down from the roof of the Montaño store. A good deal of shooting was required to get this done, but finally it was accomplished without casualties on either side.

Peppin also endeavored to get aid from Fort Stanton. In a note to Colonel Dudley he emphasized the fact that in trying to serve United States warrants on certain persons being protected by McSween he was meeting with resistance. "If it is in your power," so the note read, "to loan me one of your howitzers, I am of the opinion that parties for whom I have warrants would surrender without a shot being fired. Should it be in your power to do this in favor of the law, you would confer a great favor on the majority of the people of this county, who are being persecuted by a lawless mob."

Colonel Dudley was unable to be accommodating about the cannon. He wrote:

> My sympathies and those of all my officers are most earnestly and sincerely with you on the side of law and order. Up to the present time I have endeavored in all my official acts to avoid in any possible way by act or expression to act otherwise than in an impartial manner towards both factions in Lincoln County, but I do not hesitate to state now that in my opinion you are acting strictly within the provisions incumbent upon you as deputy U.S. marshal and sheriff, and were I not so circumscribed by law and orders, I would most gladly give you every man and all the material at my post to sustain you in your present position, believing it to be strictly legal.

In connection with the dispatching of this answer an incident occurred which became part of Colonel Dudley's pretext for marching down to Lincoln. The courier, a Negro soldier named Berry Robinson, had an adventurous trip. When he reached the Double Crossing on the Rio Bonito he was stopped by several men, guards posted there by one or the other of the factions, since this location made possible a control of getting in or out of Lincoln. These men contented themselves with a little fun at Robinson's expense and, after catechising him about his purpose in going to Lincoln, let him go on his way. The adventure, however, was a mere preliminary to another. As he was approaching the Wortley Hotel a shot was fired in his direction. It did not hit him, but it had significant results.[7]

---

7. In 1927 Mrs. McSween (then Mrs. Barber) assured the writer that she was positive there was no shooting at this hour of the day except that a shot, someplace to the west, was heard by those in the McSween home shortly before a soldier was seen riding up to the Wortley place. She pointed out that the McSween men, believing the Fort Stanton officers to be allied with the Dolan faction, would hardly have been foolish enough to shoot at a U.S. soldier and thus furnish an excuse for the military to intervene.

Peppin took immediate advantage of this shooting at a soldier. Here might be a means to alter the "hands off" policy Colonel Dudley complained about in the note Berry Robinson had delivered. The following note went back to the Fort:

Lincoln, N.M., July 16, 1878

Colonel N. A. M. Dudley,
   Comdg, Fort Stanton, N.M.

Colonel:

I have the honor to acknowledge the receipt of your very kind favor of date. Am very sorry I can't get the assistance I asked for, but I will do the best I can. The McSween party fired on your soldier when coming into town. My men on seeing him tried their best to cover him, but of no use. The soldier will explain the circumstances to you.

I take this opportunity of thanking you for your kindness in the name of all my posse.

Respectfully
Your obet. svt.
George W. Peppin
Sheriff

Thus, Tuesday closed without casualties, although the Berry Robinson incident might grow into something serious. Could it be wrenched into an excuse for sending soldiers down to Lincoln, Colonel Dudley would undoubtedly use it.

On the third day, Wednesday, July 17, the struggle assumed a grimmer aspect. So quietly did the day start out around the building occupied by the McSween following that some of the men Peppin had posted on the hillsides concluded that the McSween men must have evacuated during the night. Accordingly, they started back to the Wortley Hotel under such a sense of security that they did not take care to make their way under protection of the boulders scattered along the sides of the hills. Thus, they became an inviting target for the men in the Montaño house. Fernando Herrera, one of the best shots, fired at Charlie Crawford, ("Lallacooler"), and wounded him so badly that after he dropped to the ground he was unable to crawl to a protecting rock. Crawford's companion, Lucio Montoyo, sped away to cover, but Crawford was left lying in the open for the rest of the hot July morning. Not a man of Peppin's was willing to risk his life in going to Crawford's aid.

About midday the shooting at Berry Robinson began to bear fruit. Several officers, composing a board of inquiry, came down from Fort Stanton, escorted by a detachment of cavalry. After gathering testimony from the men at Wortley's Hotel they visited McSween, whose statement directly contradicted what the men at Wortley's had said. McSween was emphatic in his denial that any firing had taken place from his house after six o'clock the day before. The board concluded its investigation by obtaining statements from Peppin's men in the tower, which contradicted McSween's testimony. They declared that they had heard firing from the McSween house just about sundown, and occasionally even up to midnight. Considering the officers' friendship with Dolan and his associates, and their open hostility to the McSween faction, their findings are not surprising:

> After considering all the evidence before it, the board finds that Private Berry Robinson, Company "H," 9th Cavalry, who was ordered to Lincoln to carry a dispatch to special deputy U.S. marshal and county sheriff Peppin, had, as he approached the town and when within 500 yards of it, several shots fired at him by parties concealed within Mr. McSween's house. Said Robinson was in uniform, and it was broad daylight.

While the members of the board were in Lincoln, Dr. Appel and others of its personnel performed a humane service. When they learned that Crawford was still lying out on the hillside, badly wounded, they determined to go to his aid and if possible bring him down from this exposed situation. Captain Blair and two of the enlisted men joined Dr. Appel in the rescue of Crawford. The only thing that marred it was a shot fired at them, presumably by one of the McSween men. Dr. Appel completed his humane work by getting an ambulance sent down from the Fort and conveying Crawford thither. His wound in the left hip was a serious one, and he was considerably exhausted by exposure, but he managed to survive until August 24.

In the fourth day of the fight, Thursday, July 19, both sides were comparatively inactive, at least so far as firing was concerned. Nevertheless, the day had its spasms of excitement. Peppin's attempt to procure a howitzer had generated a crop of wild rumors, one of which was that the McSween men were seeking to procure a cannon. John Chisum was supposed to be coming to aid of McSween with a 16-pounder, although the rumor did not bother to explain where he had obtained it. Neither was it apparent why the McSween crowd needed assistance when clearly they had the upper hand for the time being.

Had there been a fight in the open at this point they would probably have won the victory, since numerically they equaled their opponents and in fighting skill had the odds in their favor. But Peppin, advised by Dolan, was not seeking a contest of that kind. Their policy was to break down the morale of the McSween men by getting the military into the town. This, they believed, would terrorize the McSween crowd into surrendering; at least the impressionable Mexican group would almost certainly be affected by the appearance of the soldiers. Colonel Dudley, they knew, chafed to enter the struggle. To urge him into action they caused a flow toward the Fort of a stream of notes from terror-stricken Mexicans who pictured their danger and begged protection. Possibly a decisive pretext might be found under the guise of protecting noncombatants and saving property from destruction.

Colonel Dudley was in a quandary. His board of inquiry had expressly recommended action in the Robinson matter, but it was not easy to decide what course to follow. In the afternoon Dolan came to the Fort and tried to help Dudley make up his mind. The purport of their long conference can only be judged by subsequent developments. As soon as Dolan left, orders were given to have all available pieces of artillery put into condition for use. All the officers were summoned to a consultation at the quarters of the commanding officer. The outcome of the meeting was a document signed by five officers, which strongly supported Dudley's determination to go to Lincoln. Such a document might serve to clear Colonel Dudley's skirts if he should be taken to task for overriding orders.

> General N. A. M. Dudley having asked the undersigned officers their opinions and advice as to the advisability of placing soldiers in the town of Lincoln for the preservation of the lives of the women and children, and in response to the numerous petitions received from persons in that town, do hereby place on record their concurrence in the measures adopted by General Dudley, believing them to be in the cause of right and humanity.

> George A. Purington,
>   Capt. 9th Cav.

> D. H. Appel,
>   Asst. Surgeon, U.S. Army

> Thos. Blair,
>   Capt. 15th Inf.

> M. F. Goodwin,
>   2nd Lieut., 9th Cav.

> Samuel S. Pogue,
>   2nd Lieut., 15th Inf.

> Fort Stanton, N.M.
> July 18, 1878

During the morning Dr. Ealy became the chief actor in a bit of heroism that matched Dr. Appel's the day before. Late in the afternoon of the previous day, Ben Ellis had been hit by a stray bullet while tending the horses in his father's corral. As the wound in the neck seemed serious, two of the McSween men quartered in the Ellis store undertook to get Dr. Ealy to come down from the Tunstall building, where he lived, and give young Ellis proper medical attention. They waded up the Bonito, then crawled up to and over the wall of the store corral, and so got to the back door of the apartment occupied by the Ealys. Several shots were fired at them by the Peppin men in the tower, but none hit. Dr. Ealy attempted to go back with them but did not succeed in doing so. Wading the stream was rather too much for him, especially when the men in the tower directed their shots at the party. The next morning, however, he courageously renewed the attempt. With him he took Mrs. Ealy and the two children; he felt that both groups would respect women and children, while they might not himself, even though he was not active in the fighting. They walked into the street and down past the tower, without a shot from the Peppin men. On they went past the Montaño store, without a shot from the McSween men. Thus they reached the Ellis house where Dr. Ealy dressed Ben Ellis' neck.

30. July 19 – A Fateful Day

On Friday, July 19, the fifth day of the conflict, firing commenced about seven in the morning. The men in the McSween house engaged in a warm exchange of shots with the members of the Peppin posse concentrated in the Wortley Hotel. During the night John Long, one of the most aggressive of the Dolan fighting men, left the tower where he had been since the beginning of the fight and joined those at the Wortley Hotel. Andy Boyle, slipping down to the tower under cover of darkness, had tipped him off that the climax was likely to come the next day. The program was to surround the McSween house and then resort to the most forcible, not to say savage, means available to dislodge McSween and the men with him. Long had insured his chance to participate by going up to the Wortley Hotel.

At this stage, the McSween men were highly sanguine about winning. On Friday morning one of those with McSween, Joseph J. Smith, wrote a letter which was almost a song of victory. He addressed a Mr. Capper, probably his ex-employer:

> I thought I would write you a few lines to let you know what the people are doing up here. We have taken the town. One was killed day before yesterday, and one wounded. Ben Ellis was shot through the neck by one of the guards. Everything is fair in war. Seen Jim Reese the other morning walking down the street. I heard Jim Reese cried because he was on the wrong side. He says he is in it and can't get out of it. All of them have taken an oath to stand by each other until death. So I guess we will get to

kill a lot of them before they get away. Capper, you must not think hard of a fellow for quitting you. But I wanted to go; so I went. The U.S. troops have stepped aside and given us full swing. There is forty-five of us citizens have turned out. I tell you it makes a fellow's hair stand up when bullets come whistling through the air. I don't mind it much. Best respects to Sam. Harvey Morris sends his respects to all. Had a little excitement yesterday evening. The Murphies told some woman in town that they got a condemned cannon and was going to bombard the town. Tried to scare us out, but we didn't scare worth a darn. Well, I must quit writing. Good luck to you.

Had Joseph Smith written a few hours later he would have modified greatly his statement about the soldiers having "stepped aside." At 10:30 Colonel Dudley appeared at the head of a body of thirty-five enlisted men and all the officers at the Fort except Lieutenant Pogue, who had been left in command. A Gatling gun, with 2,000 rounds of ammunition, had been brought along, as well as a mountain howitzer with an ample supply of its ammunition. The expedition down to Lincoln was equipped with rations and other supplies for a three days' stay if that length of time should be needed.

The detachment, leaving the Fort at eight o'clock, made the trip to Lincoln rapidly. At the top of a hill about a mile from town, Colonel Dudley ordered a halt for a short rest, giving him an opportunity to further a plan he had contrived for plaguing McSween in connection with the Berry Robinson affair. The Colonel sent over to a house nearby, in which "Judge" Wilson was refugeeing, and ordered him to come at once to where the soldiers were halted. When Wilson appeared, he was brusquely told he must go to Lincoln and issue a warrant for McSween, based on affidavits from the officers who had composed the board of inquiry. Wilson agreed to carry out this demand. Just as Dudley's command was about to resume its course, vigorous firing was heard from the direction of the town. Clearly the struggle was still on.

On reaching the outskirts of the plaza, Dudley prepared for an impressive entry, the men from the cavalry in front and the men from the infantry, who had been riding in wagons, marched in the rear of the cavalry down the street of Lincoln. At the Wortley Hotel, Dudley called a halt and summoned Peppin forth. In an oracular manner he addressed the sheriff and such of the posse as were around, impressing upon them the fact that he had come not to assist them but because of numerous petitions from women and other noncombatants for protection. From the headquarters of the Dolan faction the troops marched down the road past the McSween home without stopping until they reached their campsite. There were many vacant plots in Lincoln but Colonel Dudley, experienced in military strategy, selected one between two of the places held by McSween — the Ellis place east of the campsite and the McSween house to the west — and almost directly across the road from the third position occupied by McSween supporters, the Montaño store.

Dudley gave his first attention to the Montaño store. He called for Martín Chávez, who commanded this division of the McSween forces. To him he delivered an ultimatum tinged liberally with threats to the effect that if any of the men in that store fired into his camp or at any of the soldiers anywhere he would turn loose his cannon on the whole building. As there were some women and children in the building, he concluded the harangue with an appeal to them to leave if the men continued to use the house as a stronghold.

Colonel Dudley's next step was to send Dr. Appel down to the Ellis store, about 300 yards eastward of the camp, to explain to Isaac Ellis why the soldiers had appeared on the scene. Appel decided on the way, however, that it would be better for Isaac Ellis to hear the explanation from Dudley himself, and he simply informed Ellis that Colonel Dudley wished to see him at the camp. At Ellis' Appel found several prominent McSween men — Bowdre, Scurlock, and Middleton — whom he could not invite to go with Ellis, so he had to announce to them that the troops had not come to assist either party and to warn them not to shoot toward the soldiers under any circumstance.

Isaac Ellis and Dr. Appel returned to the camp and found Dudley impatiently awaiting Peppin, for whom he had sent. When Peppin came, escorted by three or four soldiers, Dudley reiterated to him, as the leader of one side, and Ellis, as a prominent adherent of the other, that he firmly expected to fire on either or both of the factions if they fired into his camp or injured any of his troops. He repeated his declaration that he had come not to assist the sheriff's or the other party but solely to protect children and noncombatants and to prevent destruction of property. When Ellis went back to his house, Dr. Appel returned with him to dress the wound of Ben Ellis. He heard Ellis go to the McSween men and tell them very emphatically that they must not fire from his house. He also heard them reply that it was all right with them, as they were going away shortly.

At this point a messenger from Colonel Dudley ordered Dr. Appel back to camp immediately. He was needed to sign the affidavit upon which Wilson was to issue a warrant for McSween. Dudley had decided that the warrant should be made out for McSween individually, although just why is difficult to understand. Obviously Dudley was sharply antagonistic toward McSween; in fact, under the questioning of Judge Angel when the management of the Indian agency was under investigation, he had expressed himself very positively about McSween. He admitted that his personal knowledge was limited, yet from what Judge Bristol and some others had told him he felt that McSween was a very dangerous man, not to be believed on oath. On this visit to Lincoln, Dudley deliberately ignored McSween, summoning Ellis to hear what he had to say to the McSween faction. Issuing a warrant for McSween went against the grain with Wilson, and he tried evasion by arguing that as a justice of the peace he had no jurisdiction where a soldier was involved and the matter had better be handled through a United States commissioner. Dr. Appel urged in rebuttal that he and his fellow officers had not bartered away their rights as citizens by going into the army and, therefore, were just as much entitled to take legal steps in this matter as anybody else. He even went the length of promising to assume the consequences if there should be any. Colonel Dudley's contribution to the coercing of the recalcitrant justice of the peace was a blustering threat that if he did not issue the warrant he would have him made prisoner and placed in irons. Under this combination of argument and browbeating Wilson yielded and made out the warrant.

THE CALL TO SURRENDER

While this was going on at the camp, some excitement developed at the Ellis house. There was mounting of horses in the corral and evidences of departure. The Montaño house group decided to evacuate now that the camp of the soldiers was so close as to render them impotent in the fighting. The whole party of twenty-five or thirty passed down the street directly in front of the camp and on to the Ellis house, where they proceeded to get their horses from the corral. Soon afterwards they rode across the Rio Bonito and disappeared in one of the canyons in the hills to the north, along with the men from the Ellis house. Peppin dashed down to the Ellis place with a few of his men and called to the McSween men to surrender. They paid no attention to him and kept on their way, too far by then for shots to have any effect. The exodus was a serious blow to the McSween faction, for it meant the loss of nearly two-thirds of its fighting men. The Mexican contingent had been badly scared, as expected, by the soldiers and Colonel Dudley, but it is hard to explain the defection of such redoubtable fighters as Bowdre, Scurlock, and Middleton, who went across the Bonito with the Mexicans.

In the meantime Wilson was attempting to find someone as constable to execute the warrant for McSween. Apparently no one wanted the job, and finally he turned it over to Peppin, who selected Marion Turner as the deputy to make the attempt. Turner, with a bodyguard of four or five of the posse, approached one of the windows in the front of the McSween house and shouted to those inside that he held warrants for McSween and several others. Someone inside called back, "Yes, and we hold warrants for some of your men." This nettled Turner and he replied, "Well, why don't you come out with them?" From someone inside the house came the answer, "Our guns are our warrants," leaving nothing for Turner to do but return to the Wortley Hotel and report that McSween and his associates had refused his demand to surrender.

Shortly after, Colonel Dudley received a note from McSween protesting the presence of the soldiers. As they moved to and fro in the vicinity of the house, especially up and down the street, the Peppin men had opportunities to fall in with the soldiers and get closer to the McSween house than they could otherwise. The McSween men did not dare to fire when there was the least possibility of giving even the appearance of shooting at soldiers. The note, delivered at Dudley's camp by Minnie, one of the Shield children, was as follows:

LAW OFFICE OF
McSWEEN & SHIELD

Alex. A. McSween
David P. Shield

Lincoln County Bank Building
Lincoln, N. M., 7/19/1878

Colonel Dudley, U.S.A.

Would you have the kindness to let me know why soldiers surround my house. Before blowing up my property, I would like to know the reason. The constable is here and has warrants for the arrest of Sheriff Peppin and posse for murder and larceny.

Respectfully,
A. A. McSween

Colonel Dudley returned through his adjutant the following, using the same little girl as messenger:

I am directed by the commanding officer to inform you that no soldiers have surrounded your house and that he desires to hold no correspondence with you; if you desire to blow up your house, the commanding officer does not object, provided it does not injure any United States soldiers.

Dudley's brusqueness was evident enough. McSween's note showed that it was written under considerable excitement and haste by a man worn out by the ordeal he had been passing through. The second sentence contained an ambiguity, which Colonel Dudley took as an opening which would give him the chance to bestow on McSween a slap on the face. When McSween penned "before blowing up my property," he probably was thinking of the mountain howitzer; but Dudley chose to construe the passage into a threat on McSween's part to blow up the house himself.

There is some indication of another exchange of notes between McSween and Dudley, either before or after the one just cited. It crops out in the traditions and even presents itself in contemporary accounts. Sam Corbet, for instance, in writing of the events of this momentous day to Tunstall's father probably speaks of the other note, when he says, "Mr. McSween wrote Colonel Dudley a note saying that he would surrender to the military, but did not want to surrender to a mob. Colonel Dudley sent him word that he had nothing to do with it, he only came to protect women and children." Mrs. McSween used to say that McSween made an offer of this kind, only to have it spurned by Colonel Dudley as outside his province. McSween very probably would take such a position since he was fearful of letting himself get into the hands of Sheriff Peppin. He had felt that way about Brady and now he saw no reason to have any greater confidence in Peppin.

As noon approached, Peppin and his men became eager to set fire to the McSween house as a means of driving out the inmates. The presence of Dudley had emboldened them to a high degree, and they became so elemental as to give no heed to the fact that women and children were inside the house. What was uppermost in the minds of nearly all was that the crucial time had come. The McSween strength was decidedly weakened by the withdrawal of Martín Chávez and the twenty or thirty men with him and the departure of the McSween supporters from the Ellis house. Only the ten or twelve inside the McSween home remained to reckon with. As for the soldiers, while nominally neutral, they gave a great amount of morale to Peppin's men.

As a preliminary step to firing the house Peppin distributed his men among the houses in the vicinity of the McSween place so as to have a cordon around it. Some were in the Steve Stanley house directly across the road to the south, while others were in the Mills and the Chávez houses, to the west of the McSween home. Some were even placed in the stable in the northwest corner of the McSween lot. With everything arranged, John Long, accompanied by "Dummy," slipped around to the rear of the east wing of the McSween house, in which the Shield family were staying and, with a can of "coaloil" procured from the Ellis store under compulsion, tried to start a fire in that part of the building. They got the door open, and as Long poured the kerosene on the floor Dummy brought in stove wood from the stack near the kitchen door and piled it on the kerosene-soaked floor. They worked rapidly but thoroughly. Soon a fire was underway that seemed to spell the destruction of that part of the house. The strong wind blowing from the east would fan the flames briskly along the east wing, thence around the front and into the west wing where the McSween men were. Just as Long and Dummy were making their exit, little Minnie Shield opened a door into the kitchen and, seeing the blaze, gave the alarm. Mrs. Shield rushed in and with the meager supply of water in the house managed to extinguish the fire.

Not only was this incendiary effort brought to nought, but Long was ingloriously deprived of the opportunity of participating anymore that afternoon. During the first days of the struggle, George Coe had been in the Montaño store, but prior to the last day had established himself, together with Henry Brown and Joseph Smith, in the warehouse back of the Tunstall store. Toward the top of the building were ventilating openings in the adobe walls which served admirably as portholes and were being adapted to that end by Coe and his companions. As Long and Dummy were leaving the yard back of the east wing of the McSween house, Coe opened fire. His two companions joined in and Long ran for shelter with Buck Powell, who had also been crossing the yard. The first available cover happened to be a privy standing on the extreme edge of the McSween lot with its vault dug in the Bonito embankment. No time was it for squeamishness, and Long and Powell without hesitation "forted up" in the vault. The bullets from the three men in the Tunstall store kept them in those mephitic surroundings all afternoon, for not until dark did they dare leave.

About half an hour after Long's frustrated attempt to set the house on fire, Andy Boyle gave his services to the same mission. From the stable where he was stationed with five or six others, he managed to reach the west wing carrying shavings and chips as kindling. Helped by these and planks ripped from the top of the stable, he succeeded in getting a fire well started against the back door of that wing. When the McSween men discovered what had happened they tried to put the fire out, but Peppin's men in the stable and the two houses west of the McSween lot sprayed too steady a stream of bullets for them to accomplish anything toward extinguishing the blaze. The fire was let run its course. Several hours would be required for it to make its way through the building. The wind from the east would retard rather than accelerate its progress. Moreover, an adobe house had but little woodwork for the flames to feed upon — simply the flooring, rafters, doors and windows. So the inmates cheered themselves with the prospect of being able to remain in the house, or at least some remnant of it, until nightfall. Then under cover of darkness they would have a chance to make a dash for safety down to the brush-covered banks of the Bonito, just below the rear of the McSween lot.

At this juncture Mrs. McSween joined her sister, Mrs. Shield, in an effort to reach safety. Now that the worst had come and threats about burning the house were being made good, it was clearly best for the women and children to leave. Recounting this experience, Mrs. McSween wrote to Tunstall's father as follows:

> My sister and myself, with her little children, made our escape from one end of the house, whilst the other was in flames. Even whilst we were fleeing for our lives, some of those men were pouring oil on the floor and setting fire to it. These men were protected by soldiers sent with them by Colonel Dudley, and this mob was stationed all around the house in secreted places, shooting into every door and window of it during all this.

But Mrs. McSween changed her mind about leaving the house. As she went on to say in her letter to Tunstall's father:

> I returned to the house thinking I could be a protection to my husband; and then I went down to Dudley's camp and asked him for protection to take from the house some clothing and articles of domestic use. But he would not grant it. So I returned again with a heavy heart to tell Mr. McSween, and remained with him until the last room was on fire. Bullets were flying all around me that day. I feared nothing.

The appeal to Colonel Dudley mentioned by Mrs. McSween is one of the striking incidents of this tragic nineteenth of July. It therefore requires a larger part in the picture than the foregoing bare version would give. As time passed, those inside the McSween house realized their situation and discussed what measures should be taken. Mrs. McSween believed that Colonel Dudley could be persuaded to intervene and at least save their lives, although her husband, disheartened by the communication from Dudley, had little faith that he could be moved.

Crawling on hands and knees to the front door because of danger from bullets, Mrs. McSween went out into the street. Outside the danger was not so great, for both factions had shown a disposition to stop firing when a woman might be hurt. But in the case of Mrs. McSween that rule of conduct might be forgotten, since her energetic actions and words in support of her husband had earned for her a large amount of dislike among the Dolan element. Nevertheless, she proceeded down the street without molestation in the direction of the camp. As she passed the tower she saw Peppin standing outside and called out to him pleadingly, "Peppin! Peppin! what does this mean? Why have you set our house on fire? Why are you letting it and all we have in it be burned up?" Peppin's answer was simply a reiteration of the formula he had used several times that day to the effect that he proposed to get McSween and all the others he had warrants for, even if it cost the lives of everyone in both the posses.

When she reached the camp, she was readily accorded an interview by Colonel Dudley. She plunged *in medias res* with the question, "Colonel Dudley, what do you mean by having my husband's house surrounded by your soldiers?" Colonel Dudley disclaimed any knowledge that such was the case and proceeded to set forth his purpose in coming to Lincoln, using the same language that he had at other times: "I have come to Lincoln with my small command solely for the purpose of giving protection to women and children and such others as may care to avail themselves of it. I do not intend to take sides in the fight, nor shall I permit any of my men to do so."

Mrs. McSween then commented on the howitzer she saw in the street. "Why, then, Colonel Dudley, do you have that cannon pointed toward our house, if you do not intend to take sides in the fight?" Colonel Dudley became so amused at her ignorance of the ways of howitzers that his customary pompousness vanished in a laugh as he said, "Madam, if you will take a careful look, you will find that gun is not pointed towards your house at all, but in exactly the opposite direction. I intended using it, if needful, on the men I found this morning in Montaño's store. I expected trouble, but they took the hint and vamoosed."

Mrs. McSween then shifted the topic to Peppin and his posse, expressing her unvarnished opinion of the ruffians and tough characters he was using. Colonel Dudley retorted, "The men in your party seem to be about the same grade." Mrs. McSween admitted that such was the case. The next turn in the conversation brought up the burning of the house. "Colonel Dudley," she asked, almost weeping, "why have you allowed Peppin's posse to try to burn our house?" Dudley replied, "I am not aware, madam, that your house has been set on fire by Peppin's men. A few hours ago I received from your husband a note saying that he was going to destroy his house. How am I to know that he had not carried out that intention, and that is the reason the building is on fire?"

This answer aroused Mrs. McSween's indignation. She declared that McSween had made no such declaration, and when Dudley insisted that he had she said with vehemence, "I don't believe you have any such statement from McSween." "Indeed, I have," answered Dudley, "and to prove it to you I will produce it." With that he reached into his pocket and drew out the note. At this point Mrs. McSween became greatly excited and tried to snatch that letter from his hand, saying, "Give me that letter, sir." "Hold, madam, hold," replied Colonel Dudley with some display of temper, "if you try to snatch that letter, I will call the guard, and have you escorted from the camp."

By this time Mrs. McSween, realizing the futility of any appeal to Dudley, ended the visit with a heartstricken but vindictive peroration: "You are a cruel and hard-hearted man, Colonel Dudley, to sit here in your camp and allow Peppin and his men to do what they are doing. Some day these deeds will recoil on your head! If I live, I will do all in my power to bring that about." She then made her way back to the burning house in utter disappointment and bitterness of heart.

When she returned with the report that her appeal to Dudley had been without avail, the inmates of the house held a council to see what course was best. All agreed that the house was doomed, and in a few hours they must choose between being burned to death in the building, or leaving it through a rain of bullets. McSween by this time was completely apathetic; in fact, he was so overworn from the long strain that he was virtually in a state of collapse. Under the need for emergency leadership Billy the Kid, possibly the youngest of the crowd in years but with nearly six months' veterancy in the McSween cause, came to the fore. Previously he had somewhat taken a back seat; at any rate he had not stood to the front as a leader, although recognized as being so full of coolness and derring-do that it was only a question of time until he might become the leader. Dick Brewer and Frank Macnab had each had his term at the rank and then had been removed by death. For two months the old Regulator organization had been without a definite leader, although there were indications that Jim French might succeed to that position. He was also in the McSween house at this time, but Billy the Kid ranked ahead of him. To his companions he said, "We can stick it out, if the fire does not burn any faster than it is now. Some of us are certain to get hit, but most of us can make it across the river. It's only a few hundred yards, and, if we run fast and shoot fast, we can hold off Peppin's crowd so they can't do us much damage." Then turning to Mrs. McSween he said, "I expect, ma'am, you had better leave before; a dress ain't very good to make a run in." Mrs. McSween insisted that she would stay as long as it seemed at all safe, but agreed to leave early enough so as having to look after her would not impede the others in their sally from the back door. It was agreed that Billy and two or three volunteers would run out first, drawing the fire of the attackers. Then McSween and the others would slip out into the darkness while the attention of Peppin's men was thus diverted.

All seemed to have enough courage left to carry out this plan, highly dangerous though it was, except Ignacio González, who, although ordinarily a rather seasoned fighter, had reached the last level of courage. A wound in the arm that morning had turned him completely craven. He whimpered something about its being best to surrender then and there, but Billy the Kid, exhibiting the sternness of which he was capable, snapped at him, "You damn cowardly greaser! I've got a great mind to hit you over the head with my pistol. We are all going to stick here until dark. Brace up and behave like a man."

As the afternoon wore on, the firing became more vigorous about four o'clock. The cause was the attempted return of Martín Chávez and his twenty or thirty men. They had come out of their panic and attempted to get to the aid of their comrades in the burning house. The cloud of smoke had apprised them of what was taking place. They came down as far as the north bank of the Rio Bonito and used up a quantity of ammunition in shots at the Peppin men. The distance, however — 800 yards or more — prevented the shooting from being effective. Finally, realizing the hopelessness of the attempt, they retired again into the canyons and left their comrades to whatever fate might be in store for their beleaguered house.

When the outbreak of firing had ceased, Miss Gates, the young schoolteacher living with the Ealys, undertook to carry a communication from Dr. Ealy to Colonel Dudley. It seemed probable that the Tunstall store, in the east end of which the Ealys were living, might undergo the same fate as the McSween house. The three sharpshooters — George Coe, Henry Brown, and Joe Smith — located in the warehouse, were among those Peppin held warrants for and his next move would be to compel them to leave. Dr. Ealy realized this and wrote an appeal to Dudley with which Miss Gates made her way to the soldiers' camp. Colonel Dudley immediately directed Lieutenant Goodwin and Captain Blair to take three enlisted men and go to the help of the Ealys. He also sent an army wagon to transport their household goods to some safe place. But Dudley's well-known irascibility asserted itself while the assistance to the Ealys was going on. Having heard that Dr.

Ealy had spoken sharply and contemptuously to the soldiers about something, he countermanded his order about the rescue work. Mrs. Ealy, however, eased the situation by a note of apology seasoned with thanks for the aid already given, and Colonel Dudley allowed the removal of household effects to be resumed.

It was now growing dark rapidly and the fire had eaten its way almost to the last room of the McSween house. When Captain Blair and the others began to aid the Ealys, Mrs. McSween had come over and asked if she and the Shields were also eligible for protection. Captain Blair told her that they would be if they came over and joined the Ealys but he could not give them any aid if they remained in her own house. She had then gone back and gotten Mrs. Shield and her five children. When they were all assembled, Captain Blair escorted the party of noncombatants to the Juan Patrón house, which was vacant, and installed them in it together with what household goods had been saved. This house was thirty yards beyond the camp and relatively outside the firing zone.

31. The Big Killing – Exit McSween

In writing to Tunstall's father, Mrs. McSween gave her brief but comprehensive account of the tragic incident of this terrible July 19:

> In the evening my husband and his friends blinded with smoke, wearied by battling the flames and the no less remorseless enemies outside, driven from room to room as the fire increased in fury till the last room was consumed, at last sallied from the house and — Oh God, my heart almost did fail me to write it — was shot down like a dog on his own threshold, and when he had fallen upon his knees, calling out "I surrender, Oh, my God save me. Oh, Lord, Lord, save me." And after he fell, they tore up burning boards and piled them to his body and left it to burn. Oh, how can I live through this. I hope you all pray for me. I need your sympathy so much; my burden is so heavy. I am left homeless, and almost clothesless, and defenseless, and with nothing but the memory of a kind and loving husband to sustain me. What they didn't burn up, they stole.

Mrs. McSween was also able to learn from one of the survivors something of what had transpired during the last hours in the besieged house. It was Billy the Kid who proposed a desperate strategy for escape. He volunteered to lead two or three others in a dash across the yard and through the gate in the plank fence which formed the east boundary of the McSween premises; while the attention of the attackers was occupied with attack and pursuit of these, McSween and the others were to make their getaway through the gate in the

[270]

adobe wall bordering the north side of the yard. In New Mexico the sun in July sets about eight o'clock in the evening, and the men trapped in the burning house had to wait until nearly nine before darkness grew deep enough for the attempt. They huddled closely about the rear door of the kitchen in the east wing, the part used by the Shield family, and watched the disappearing daylight. Then Billy the Kid, Jim French, Harvey Morris, and perhaps another, made their move. Morris was killed instantly as he crossed the yard. The others managed to dash safely through the east gate and on to the rear of the Tunstall warehouse where they were soon enveloped in the underbrush along the bed of the Bonito. In the darkness random shots from the Peppin men failed to prevent their escape.

But McSween and the others who had remained in the house waited too long. By the time they emerged, firing at Billy the Kid and his companions had ceased and was quickly turned on the McSween group. They were driven back into the yard, some even trying to dodge back into the burning building. McSween, Francisco Zamora, Vicente Romero, and Francisco Salazar sought safety behind the woodpile in the corner outside the kitchen door. Others concealed themselves in the chickenhouse beside the west wall of the yard. Ten minutes passed. McSween and the three with him left their protecting corner and started again toward the north gate, but found that exit guarded by Andy Boyle, Joe Nash, Bob Beckwith, John Jones, Marion Turner, and the man known as Dummy. Such a group was an effective barrier to escape and the entrapped four were forced back into their corner.

At this juncture someone in the back yard — no one can positively say who, whether one of the men with McSween or one of those at the chickenhouse — called out, "We want to surrender. Is there anybody who will receive our surrender and protect our lives?" Bob Beckwith, as one of Peppin's acting deputies, replied, "Yes, I can receive your surrender," and followed by John Jones, Joe Nash, and Dummy started into the back yard. Barely had these four got through the gate and into the yard than the firing broke out afresh. In a second or two Bob Beckwith, McSween, Romero, and Zamora were killed, while Salazar lay on the ground unconscious from wounds.

What caused this final outbreak of shooting is one of the insolubles of the Lincoln County War. As usual, there are several versions, in bewildering contradiction. Some allege that Ignacio González, who had been severely rebuked by Billy the Kid in the afternoon for a display of cowardice, was the one who called out an offer to surrender. When Bob Beckwith came forward, someone who did not approve that course fired at Beckwith's group. Naturally they returned the fire,

converging it on the group in the corner. Another account has it that
John Jones, ruthless and reckless, was the main instrument in the
slaughter. As he and Bob Beckwith advanced into the yard, they
caught sight of McSween in the corner. With the chief person of the
McSween aggregation at close range, John Jones could not resist lift-
ing his rifle. Beckwith, realizing that John Jones was about to shoot
down a man in the act of surrender and not wishing to countenance
so atrocious a deed, threw up his hands to grasp the rifle and deflect
the aim. Beckwith, however, was only luckless enough to contribute
to his own death. When Jones pulled the trigger, the bullet went
through the wrist of Beckwith and on into his head. After this shot,
different ones on both sides began firing.

The most reliable eyewitness testimony on this moot point of
how the denouement was brought on is perhaps that of Joe Nash, given
nine or ten months later at the court of inquiry that investigated Colonel Dudley's conduct. As Joe Nash related it, the occurrences in the
back yard were as follows:

> After the first party left, myself, Robert Beckwith, John Jones,
> and Andrew Boyle stood at the gate north of the east L of the
> house to guard that portion of the premises, and if possible to
> prevent any man of the McSween party from escaping. While
> there, some one of the McSween party called out to us to know
> if we would take them prisoners and Robert Beckwith replied that
> he would, that he came for that purpose only except it was neces-
> sary to kill them while taking them. Then the man we called
> "Dummy" came up, walked in where those parties that asked to be
> taken were. John Jones, Robert Beckwith, and myself followed.
> When we got up to those parties that asked to be taken, we were
> fired upon by some of them secreted in a small chicken house. Bob
> Beckwith was killed. McSween and the others made a break to get
> away. We commenced firing at them as they ran. McSween was
> killed. Three Mexicans also, and one Mexican wounded at the
> time Bob Beckwith was killed. John Jones and "Dummy" jumped
> behind the corner of the McSween building, I jumped back to
> the gate, and we continued to fire at McSween and his party as
> long as there were any of them left, they doing the same at us.
> Some of the McSween party got away, some two or three more
> stayed in that chicken house and continued to fire at myself and
> the others of our party. I came nearly being hit in the neck by
> some one shooting from the chicken house. Then myself and
> Andrew Boyle went around to the back of the chicken house,
> punched a hole through the adobe wall with a log, and called out
> to the parties in the house to surrender. They said they would not

and had never intended to. Then Andy fired two or three shots into the chicken house through the hole that Andy and myself had made. Then we went back to where McSween and Bob Beckwith were lying dead. By that time the house was nearly burned up. So I dragged McSween out of danger of being burned, and some one of the boys in our party carried Robert Beckwith away.

Regarding the death of McSween, the same conclusion is to be made that Judge Angel was compelled to give about the death of Tunstall: who shot McSween will never be known. But there is no doubt that Robert Beckwith, John Jones, Joe Nash, and Andy Boyle were inside the yard and doing the shooting towards the group in the corner. The "shaking up" of McSween, which Rynerson, the district attorney, had advocated in his letter to Dolan and Riley was accomplished. For nearly six months Alex McSween had undergone the ordeal with courage and fortitude. He had returned to Lincoln at the beginning of the tense week accompanied by a large number of his friends and sympathizers who chose to help protect him. His own attitude, however, was one of resignation. "I am tired of being a refugee," he had said to Mrs. McSween when he returned to Lincoln. "I want to die in my own home." Under the trials of the successive weeks he had borne himself courageously and clung to Scriptural idealism to the end, refusing to shoulder a rifle or strap a revolver about his waist. No contemporary record, however, shows that he became at the last totally disqualified and unmanned by panic and fear. He did possibly sense the uselessness of further contest with the inevitable. In the long-drawn contest with his enemies, zeal may have outrun discretion, especially in his fervid determination to avenge the death of Tunstall. The verdict of Judge Frank W. Angel about the merits of the two parties presents the case completely. "Both have done many things contrary to law; both violated the law. McSween, I firmly believe, acted conscientiously; Murphy & Co. for private gain and revenge."

When the Peppin men realized that the consummation they had so devoutly wished in the death of McSween had come, they gave themselves over to celebration during the remainder of the night. In all this hilarity the killed and wounded were forgotten. The sheriff's posse hurrahed, they danced, they sang. The soldiers came down from their camp, and, if not actually participants, were at least spectators of the carnival, improvised against a background of smoke-begrimed house walls which kept vigil over the dead.

For rejoicing in their victory, the Peppin crowd immediately commenced possessing themselves of the spoils. They battered down the doors of Tunstall's store and looted its shelves and showcases.

They helped themselves to groceries, clothing, blankets, guns, ammunition, or whatever else their fancy dictated. Some of greater shrewdness than the rest tore their way into the room used as the bank and carried off what money they found.

Beckwith's body was removed from where it had fallen over that of McSween, but the bodies of the others lay where they had fallen until the following day. The legal formalities were carried out punctiliously. A coroner's jury held an inquest over the five bodies and embodied the grim facts statistically and laconically in the following report:

> The Territory of New Mexico, County of Lincoln.
>
> Proceedings of the coroner's jury over the bodies of A. A. McSween, Harvey Morris, Francisco Zamora, Vicente Romero, and Robert Beckwith, whose bodies were found at Precinct No. 1 in Lincoln county of July 20, 1878, A. A. McSween with 5 shots in his body, Harvey Morris with 1 shot in his body, Vicente Romero with three shots in his body and leg, and Robert Beckwith with 2 shots, 1 in the head and 1 in the wrist. The Coroner's jury after examining all the bodies above mentioned, and from the best evidence they could obtain, render the following verdict, to wit:
>
> We, the coroner's jury, under our oaths do say that A. A. McSween, Harvey Morris, Francisco Zamora, and Vicente Romero came to their deaths by rifle shots from the hands of the sheriff's posse, while they, the above persons, were resisting the sheriff's posse with force and arms, and that Robert Beckwith came to his death by two rifle shots from the hands of the above named persons, of A. A. McSween, Harvey Morris, Francisco Zamora, and Vicente Romero, and others, while they were resisting the sheriff's posse as aforesaid with force and arms, he (Robert Beckwith) then and there being a deputy sheriff and in the discharge of his duty as such, and trying to arrest the parties for whom he had warrants to arrest.
>
> This being done at Precinct No. 1 in Lincoln county, New Mexico, this July 20, 1878.
>
> | | |
> |---|---|
> | Felipe Miranda | Octabiano Salas |
> | José García | Felipe Mes |
> | Maximiliano Chávez | José Serno |
>
> Coroner's Jury
(Citizens of the
County of Lincoln)

This document gives the casualties officially accepted but at the time many persons believed that others had been killed. The usual rumors were flying about and some said that José Chávez, Billy the Kid, Jim French, and several others, who could not be accounted for just then, were among the dead and possibly buried in the ruins of the McSween house. But all of these eventually reappeared and manifested much aliveness. Another piece of gossip was to the effect that one of the McSween men had been killed in the earlier part of the fighting and buried under the floor of one of the rooms of the house. This was probably a canard pure and simple. The only possibility of other deaths that may be off the record seems to lie in a statement about Andrew Boyle's knocking a hole in the wall of the chickenhouse where some of the McSween men had taken refuge, and then thrusting in his rifle and firing shots.

The disposal of the dead was done officially through Peppin. He turned the bodies of the two Mexicans over to their relatives, who bore them away for burial in one of their graveyards. The body of Bob Beckwith was carried to Fort Stanton and buried under the auspices of the military in the cemetery there. Peppin, however, was not allowed to have anything to do with the burying of Harvey Morris and McSween. When he sent an oral inquiry to Mrs. McSween by her nephew, one of the Shield children, as to her wishes about their interment, she returned an emphatic order that he was not so much as to touch the body of either, and Peppin accordingly left the matter in her hands entirely. As she felt it unsafe to venture out publicly when the Peppin men were controlling the town, she let the two Negroes employed by the McSweens, George Washington and George Robinson, attend to the burials. Graves were dug in the plot of ground near the corral at the Tunstall store, close to the grave of Tunstall, and in them were laid the two most recent victims of the feud. Minimum rites were necessary because of the condition of the bodies and the possible disinterment by the vandals and ruffians that were swarming over the town.

Early that morning Dr. Appel sought out Eugenio Salazar, who had been badly wounded while trying to escape from the McSween house. At the time he was supposed by the sheriff's men to be dead, so completely unconscious was he, and for that reason he escaped a *coup de grace*. On recovering consciousness he had managed to crawl away, while the Peppin men were in their revels, and get to the house of a relative a half mile or so away. When Dr. Appel received a message that Salazar needed attention, he went with his usual willingness to help the wounded without regard for their affiliations in the feud. On this occasion, however, he went reinforced by a hope that he might obtain a firsthand account of the death of McSween. What Salazar told him varied from the other accounts as to the time element, the number of men in the McSween home, and the death and burial of Chávez and Bowers, according to Appel's official report:

> A short time after sunrise on the morning of the 20th inst. I awakened and learned that the fighting had ceased. I was called to see a Mexican, Eugenio Salazar, who had been wounded. On the way to the house in which he was, I passed Ellis's and saw the sheriff's posse removing a number of saddles and other property belonging to the McSween men. I learned that they found thirteen saddles there, and among others that taken from Morton when he was killed. I then went to see the Mexican, and he said he was in the house of McSween, and left with him. [He was] one of the last party of five who left there. He made an affidavit that there were fifteen men there, giving the names of all, and said that two, José Chávez and Thomas Cullens (or Joe Bowers), were buried in the ruins, and the other thirteen had escaped from the house. His party first offered to surrender, and when Robert Beckwith came up, one of the party fired at and killed him, and they were then fired at. He hugged the adobe wall in the rear of the burning house and received two wounds. I found one passed through the back (not a very serious wound), and another entered his right shoulder, passing downwards and to the left, and the ball had not come out. He fainted away after being wounded, and about 9 o'clock, he returned to consciousness, made his way to the house in which I found him, reached it about midnight, it being about 1,000 yards from McSween's house.[8]

About four o'clock in the afternoon Colonel Dudley departed for Fort Stanton accompanied by all the soldiers except a noncommissioned officer and two privates, whom he left as a "picket" for the protection of Captain Baca's house. Nobody could tell what the next move of the McSween adherents might be, but very likely they would attempt some retaliation on Captain Baca, who was generally credited with having been largely influential in getting the military to appear in the town. Before departing, Dudley made a general offer to the

---

8. Fifteen-year-old Eugenio Salazar's report to Appel of the death of Joe Bowers was afterward proved to be in error, although accepted at the time by Dudley and included in his official report. Bowers is known to have later, on September 7, participated with Sam Smith and others in a raid on the Fritz ranch, driving off 17 horses and 180 head of cattle. By some accounts he was a witness to the murder of Chapman, February 18, 1879. In March, 1880, at Rancho Grande, Kansas, John Middleton wrote to J. P. Tunstall in England, mentioning his old friend Joe Bowers and saying that Bowers was then a foreman on the Hunter & Evans ranch in Kansas.

people of Lincoln to take to the Fort any wishing to go there for safety. Dr. Ealy and his family, as well as Mrs. Shield and her children, went with Dudley. Mrs. McSween chose to remain in Lincoln in spite of the open threats on her life. Her bitterness toward Dudley, which was to become more and more virulent with the succeeding months, had on the day following the killing of her husband reached such a degree that she refused to place herself under any obligation to him. Her remaining in Lincoln contained an element of consecration to a cause. She wished to save what she could of the property her husband had been amassing, not merely for her own sake but rather to use to bring the hand of justice upon those responsible for the great damage and grief brought upon her.

That night at Fort Stanton, Colonel Dudley sat up late finishing a report to district headquarters of what had taken place at Lincoln on the momentous day. He could not refrain, this professional soldier and veteran of much fighting both in the Civil War and in Indian campaigns, from recording the thrill he felt at the heroism displayed in this contest, waged in an insignificant town, located in a remote section of New Mexico. With impartial hand he distributed praises, accompanied by the prophecy that the end was not yet.

> Men who have the reckless courage to attack a building in bright mid-day, its walls forming a perfect protection against any modern musketry to its inmates, pierced as this castle of McSween's was with scores of loopholes for rifles on every side and angle, to say nothing of the flat roof protected by a perfect wall of defense, and for hours hugging the walls, exposed to the fire not only from the loopholes but from the roof and adjacent buildings held by McSween's men for a distance of nearly 300 yards, are not of a character to be easily induced to abandon a course they believe is only half completed.
>
> A similar remark can be made of the party holding this structure, who held the same fortification for five days, the last nine hours gradually retreating from one room to another as the heat compelled them to do what no amount of leaden missiles from the rifles of the attacking party could do, and for one hour finally all huddled in one room nearly surrounded by the flames, some, as it is claimed, preferring to be burnt rather than surrender to the sheriff's posse. More desperate action than was exhibited on this unfortunate day by both sides is rarely witnessed.

The next day Sam Corbet, always faithful to the affairs of the Tunstall store, reported the terrible happenings to Widenmann, who was in Mesilla, where he had gone the early part of July to be on hand at the Doña Ana session of court.

Lincoln, 20 July 1878

Dear Rob,

Yesterday morning Genl. Dudley, Capt. Purington, Capt. Blair, and Lieut. Goodwin with a detachment of cavalry and a detachment of infantry and a cannon marched down to the Plaza. Just as soon as they came in sight, Peppin and his posse got themselves ready for a fight. Peppin's posse went to Mr. McSween's and told them to surrender, which they refused to do. They then set fire to the house and burned everything Mr. McSween and Mr. Shield had. Killed McSween, Harvey Morris, Vicente Romera, and Francisco Zamora. These have been found; I do not know if any more were found or killed. Last night or soon this morning the store was busted open and everything taken that was wanted. I went to Peppin and talked to him; he said he was not responsible for anything in the store. I nailed it up the best I could but think it will be opened again or burned. I don't know what to do; I am liable to be killed at any moment.

Have not heard from you since court adjourned. Why don't you write to me? I have written three letters and received no answer. Mrs. McSween and Mrs. Shield have not a change of clothing left. Dr. Ealy is going to leave; he is going straight to Washington. He has gone to the Fort now. I will not describe the conduct of some gentlemen but you will find it out soon. For God's sake don't make anything I say public. God knows what will turn up next. I am still stopping at Ellis's. The cattle on the Felix is liable to go any day. Please let me hear from you.

Your obt. servent
S. R. Corbet

Even more eloquently than Colonel Dudley's rhetorical passages, the unstudied simplicity of young Corbet's letter depicts the tragic end of McSween and his friends and the stricken plight of the little community of Lincoln.

PART IV

Embers Blaze Again

32. The Killing of Bernstein

THE TWO OR THREE weeks succeeding the Five Days Fight were a lull after the storm, although symptoms of uneasiness and disorder still continued in Lincoln. The death of McSween would hardly fulfill the plotting of his enemies, for Mrs. McSween remained to instigate retaliation. As long as she was alive the Dolan faction could never feel completely triumphant or at ease. Barely two days after the night of July 19, Mrs. McSween began to receive unquestionable indication of what fate might overtake her.

While she was superintending a search among the blackened ruins of her home with the aid of the faithful Negroes, George Washington and Zebron Bates, hoping to recover something from the wreckage, Andy Boyle and John Kinney came by and watched her efforts for a few moments. When they saw her pick up a partially burned roll of what had once been a valuable carpet, Andy Boyle said roughly, "What's the good of trying to save that? By God, we've killed McSween and we'll get you next!" Mrs. McSween answered this threat with, "Well, kill me! You have already taken away all that was precious to me, my husband and my home. I'd just as soon you'd take my life." Then, pointing to the carpet, she reviled them with, "I'll not leave that for you vandals to carry off. I'd rather see the Mexicans get it than you." This angered John Kinney to the point that he threatened to kill Mrs. McSween then and there. She did not quail under the threat, even though it came from the formidable John Kinney; she went on with her tasks while Boyle and Kinney hung around a few minutes more and then went toward the western end of town, still the head-quarters for their faction.

Another storm center in Lincoln was Captain Saturnino Baca. The survivors of the McSween faction were likely to even the score with him somehow for the support he had given the Dolan faction during the Five Days Fight. Nothing, however, developed during the next ten days or so and by July 31 things had quieted enough for Colonel Dudley to withdraw the guard of soldiers left at the Baca house. The very next day, however, it had to be replaced. Almost as soon as the guard was removed two mounted men appeared and behaved in a suspicious manner. Then during the night Jim French and Charlie Bowdre had turned up in Lincoln making threats about burning Captain Baca's house in retaliation for the McSween home. This threw the Captain into another fright and caused him to appeal to Colonel Dudley for military protection, which was given.

The first overt renewal of hostilities between two factions, however, was not at Lincoln but at the Indian agency. The McSween men had reorganized and assembled on the Ruidoso in the vicinity of San Patricio. Major Godfroy, the Indian agent, had been so much hand-in-glove with the Murphy and Dolan organization that he felt uneasy at hearing of this, and he hastened to get a guard of soldiers. One reason he and others were in great concern was general uncertainty as to the whereabouts and designs of this considerable remnant of the McSween faction. Sheriff Peppin, with a posse of about twenty-five, was down in the Pecos section, clinging to the theory that they had returned to the vicinity of Chisum's ranch. Major Godfroy, who felt that Billy the Kid wanted to kill him, had heard a contrary rumor that several of the McSween men, including such fighters as Scurlock, Henry Brown, Billy the Kid, George Coe — in fact, almost all the old Regulator group — were in the mountains south of San Patricio, a location uncomfortably close to the agency. Major Godfroy's application for a guard, therefore, was so imperative that a small detachment under the command of Lieutenant Smith arrived at once from the Fort.

PEACE NOT SECURED

The presence of the soldiers, however, did not insure peace. On August 5 near two in the afternoon, about twenty McSween partisans rode out of the timber on the hill east of the agency en route, by most reports, to Tularosa in the hope of overtaking Frank Wheeler's band of San Nicolas Spring rustlers who had made off with a herd of horses belonging to the Tunstall estate. The McSween men were immediately spotted by a party of Mescaleros who opened fire on the approaching horsemen, apparently assuming that the visitors had designs on the small herd of Indian ponies which the Mescaleros had taken to graze along the banks of the creek. Agent Godfroy and his clerk, Morris J. Bernstein, were giving out supplies in the agency issue room when they heard the firing. Disregarding Godfroy's warning to be careful, Bernstein started to investigate. He mounted his horse and dashed toward the scene of the firing. Major Godfroy followed, but Bernstein outstripped him and became lost to sight beyond the crest of the hill. Before Godfroy could reach the top, he saw Bernstein's horse returning riderless and knew that Bernstein was probably killed. Nevertheless, he kept on to find out definitely. He could see nothing of Bernstein but he did observe one of the strangers shoot an Indian who was pursuing him. Another of the visitors, seeing Godfroy on the top of the hill, took a shot at him but missed, although the ball went close to the Major's head.

All this happened so quickly that the soldiers, quartered about a mile west of the agency, were unable to immediately reach the scene. Major Godfroy turned back toward the agency but, meeting the soldiers on their way to the fighting, returned with them. When they arrived, some of the shooting was still going on but the invaders departed shortly, taking, by some accounts, some of the horses belonging to the Indians. Bernstein's body was found lying face downward on the hillside with four bullets in him. His gun, pistols, and ammunition all were gone. Even his pockets were rifled and left turned inside out. Those pockets were significant indeed. What had been grim but more or less justifiable fighting was now to descend to a level of pillage and thievery.

When the news of the Bernstein killing reached Lincoln, Dolan and his clerk Panteleón Gallegos hastened over to the agency. This time Dolan came to the scene of trouble not out of a desire to manage events himself, but rather out of friendship for Bernstein. When this young man first came to Lincoln from Santa Fe, he had worked for several months in the Dolan store before being recommended by Dolan for the clerkship at the agency. His death caused a feeling of regret generally, for he had an attractive personality. Like Tunstall, he was originally from London; he had first become a bookkeeper for Speigelberg Brothers, a prominent wholesale firm of Santa Fe. When J. J. Dolan & Co. needed someone in a like capacity, they had induced him to come down to Lincoln. During his employment at the Indian agency he had been conspicuous in recovering horses stolen from the Indians but had done nothing to incur dislike from either faction in the Lincoln

County War. The Jesse Evans gang had no such bitter hatred for him as they did for Tunstall. The Regulator group had received support from him in letters he had sent to the Cimarron *News and Press*. In fact, Bernstein's death was to be attributed chiefly to his own recklessness. He was killed by a member of a party of men who, by their own account, were fired upon when merely passing through the Reservation en route to Tularosa. It is highly improbable that they had designs on the Indian horses which, as was well known, were under the guard of a detachment of soldiers assigned from the Fort. Bernstein, however, had assumed on the spur of the moment that they were after the horses of the Indians and had rushed out to prevent it. He had ridden up and asked, "What do you want?" and immediately fired his pistol at one of the Mexicans in the party. They had returned the fire and Bernstein was killed.

The Cimarron *News and Press*, September 19, 1878, offered the following account:

> When Bernstein was killed at the Indian agency on the Stanton reservation, the Santa Fe agent of the Associated Press and the Ring telegraphed that the McSween men did it. Peppin reported it in an affidavit. Dudley endorsed his statement. Axtell telegraphed it to the Secretary of the Interior, and forwarded it to the President in support of a requisition for troops, which, however, was not granted. Now comes the Mesilla *Independent* and gives a reliable statement of the manner of Bernstein's death, by which it appears, as we have always believed, that the McSween party had nothing to do with it. Here it is:
>
> It is positively asserted that Bernstein was killed by a Mexican who was with a party going from San Patricio to Tularosa to assist in recovering a lot of stolen stock in the possession of Frank Wheeler and others then at San Nicolas. When the Mexicans reached the water along side of the road above the Agency, they stopped to water their horses. Bernstein saw them and probably supposing them to be a party of the "Regulators" attacked them with a party of Indians; he rode up on one Mexican and fired two shots at him; the man took shelter behind a tree. Bernstein still advancing rode close to the tree and fired again at the man, who returned the fire and killed Bernstein. The Mexican says he acted strictly in self-defense and will at any time deliver himself up for trial. His name is Atanacio Martínez.

Another version ascribes the death of Bernstein chiefly to Esequio Sánchez, a young fellow desirous of making a reputation for himself as a killer. Billy the Kid never made claim to the deed himself. The fact remains, however, that the attack at the agency was made by a party numbering twenty or so, nearly all members of the McSween faction in the fight three weeks before. There were veterans of the old Regulator group in Scurlock, Scroggins, Cullins, George Coe, Middleton, Bowdre, Billy the Kid, Henry Brown, Jim French, Fernando Herrera, Ignacio González, Esequio Sánchez, as well as others of later acquisition.

Colonel Dudley became greatly wrought up over this fight at the agency. To have it happen with a detachment of soldiers close at hand was indeed embarrassing. Moreover, it partook of the nature of a direct affront to the government, occurring as it did on the Indian reservation. No wonder then that Dudley expressed himself strongly to Major Godfroy. "Cost what it may," he wrote, "to bring to justice the murderous scoundrels who so wantonly assaulted you, killed your chief clerk, and attacked the Indians of your Agency, I will put forth every activity possible." Lieutenant Goodwin was promptly sent with a detachment of troops in pursuit of the suspected men and Lieutenant Smith ordered to remain at the agency with a guard of ten soldiers. The trespass supposedly having taken place on government land, Dudley now had free rein for the use of the soldiers.

33. Exodus from Lincoln County

AT THE TIME OF the Bernstein killing Mrs. McSween was in Las Vegas, where she had gone for medical attention. Returning to Lincoln a few days later, she found herself in a most precarious situation. Her enemies, not content with threats against her life, had resorted to attacks upon her character. They had even circulated malicious gossip that she and her husband had not been legally married. In Lincoln she had heard jeering slanders from passersby, interlarded with ribald singing. Recently, however, she had taken a step which had stirred her enemies to a higher pitch of hostility. Judge Angel, who was then at Las Vegas completing the special investigations that had brought him to New Mexico, had written to Mrs. McSween for affidavits from herself and others whom she considered competent witnesses about the burning of the McSween house and the killing of her husband. These documents he proposed to forward to Washington as part of the report he was about to send to the Department of Justice. Mrs. McSween had promptly secured five or six affidavits and forwarded them. When her enemies heard of this, they grew louder than ever in their threats against her life.

Jim French, Tom O'Folliard and a few others of her late husband's supporters hastened to Lincoln to protect Mrs. McSween from the threatened violence. Billy the Kid, now staying on John Chisum's range at Bosque Grande, is known to have paid one brief visit to Lincoln where he went on September 1 to help Doc Scurlock move his family and belongings to the safe neighborhood of Fort Sumner. On

August 11 Jim French was charged with stealing a team of mules from José María Aguayo, but the sheriff made no immediate attempt to arrest him; with the McSween men in Lincoln, Peppin prudently stayed out of town, confining himself to Fort Stanton where he held the job of post butcher. The Fritz ranch, below Lincoln, long the stronghold of the Murphy-Dolan contingent, was raided and fifteen horses and 150 head of cattle driven off. French and O'Folliard were charged with leading the raid and the latter was afterward tried for the crime but acquitted.

Despite the presence in Lincoln of a few of the one-time McSween fighting men, the widow found her position increasingly hazardous. A friendly but frightening warning came to her from Billy Gentry, whom she had known only as an enemy of the McSween faction. He had learned that nine of the most desperate men of the Dolan party were planning to attack the house in which Mrs. McSween was living and kill her. Not daring to bring the news directly to her, Gentry relayed it through Dave Easton, who was inclined to be friendly although he was now working in the old Dolan store for the new owner, Catron. Fearing that Gentry's report might indeed be true, Mrs. McSween determined to seek sanctuary at the home of her sister, Mrs. Shield, in Las Vegas, separated from Lincoln by roads totaling almost 200 miles in length. On September 17 she gathered her few personal effects and slipped out of Lincoln on the mail hack, wearing a sunbonnet and coarse dress, this disguise making it seem that the departing passenger was a Mexican laborer's wife rather than the elegant and vivacious Mrs. McSween.

In a letter to Tunstall's father, Mrs. McSween wrote a brief account of her flight from Lincoln:

> I left Lincoln twenty days ago because my life was now threatened on account of having sent the evidence to Washington City. When that party heard that I was making an effort to prosecute the death of my poor husband, they solemnly swore that they would kill me, and started for our town. But I happened to hear of it, and left immediately at the request of my friends. We have now got a new governor, and we have great faith that he will make a great change soon, and they will soon remove all United States officers and put new men in their places. I think the cause of your son's and Mr. McSween's death is very plain to them now in Washington City.

The determination animating Mrs. McSween is shown in another extract from this letter:

I shall work every day I live after him to vindicate his character for him. He was murdered in the most brutal cold blood, and with the assistance of many army officers, and all because he so bravely and nobly tried to prosecute the death of your poor son. These officers were bitter enemies of John, and for no reason unless it was jealousy. Mr. McSween, knowing this, never would go to them for favors or bow to them as the other parties would. Therefore they grew more bitter towards Mr. McSween. I have just sent a large amount of evidence to Washington to Mr. Angel, who has just left this country from having investigated the murder of your poor son, and I pray that it may be favorable. I have also written a letter to General Sherman, the head of our United States army, for an investigation of the murder of my dear husband. He is now expected in this country. I am determined to prosecute his death.

During August there developed in the Seven Rivers section a distressing aftermath of the fight at Lincoln. Hugh M. Beckwith, the owner of the Beckwith ranch around which had centered so much of the troubles over cattle stealing from the Chisum range, had had two sons in the fight at Lincoln, the elder of whom had been killed. The two Beckwith boys had gone up to Lincoln with their brother-in-law, W. A. Johnson, who had been playing a conspicuous role among the Pecos men.

The loss of his son preyed upon old man Beckwith's mind. He put the blame upon Johnson, feeling that if it had not been for Johnson's persuasion Bob Beckwith might have stayed out of the fight. The upshot was that one day about four weeks after the fight at Lincoln the old man took a shotgun and marched over to the house occupied by Johnson and his family. Calling his son-in-law to the doorway, he shot him down as his wife looked on, holding an infant son in her arms.

Loss of life and property had become so widespread, especially following the Five Day Battle at Lincoln, that there began a notable exodus from Lincoln County. Late in August the Las Vegas *Gazette* carried the following news item:

Six wagon loads of emigrants from North and South Spring Rivers in Lincoln County passed through Tuesday going north. They were driven out by the lawless element of the section. They had tried hard to take no part in the conflict and preferred to leave rather than take either side. About twenty horses had been stolen from them. A deputy sheriff rode up with a posse and demanded that they take up arms and go with them and fight. This they refused to do and loaded up and left the country. They left their lands, houses, standing crops, gardens, and everything pertaining to comfortable homes.

The party quitting Lincoln County was the Mormon colony that had settled on a part of Chisum's range in the spring of 1877. The men had come first and put in their crops, then sent for their wives and children under the belief that they were established in the Pecos Valley, but they had had barely a year of undisturbed tenure. When the Pecos men, urged on by Marion Turner and others, were gathering for the march up to Lincoln in the latter part of April, 1878, they had brought pressure on the Mormons but had been unable to get them to take any part in the expedition. A similar effort had been made in the early part of July when Marion Turner was collecting a posse to oust McSween and his followers from their refuge on the Pecos. This second attempt likewise did not succeed in drawing the Mormons into the fight. After the battle in July, Turner and his following had returned to Roswell and indulged in threats toward the colony. Fearing that these threats might be put into execution, the whole group of Mormons left one night for Las Vegas. It was perhaps well that they did for Turner's gang came the next morning to their homes. Had they remained they might have suffered more than they had already from the attentions of the Turner posse.[1]

A week or two later the Las Vegas *Gazette* carried another item indicative of the exodus:

> Hunter & Evans, Wiley, Coggins, Chisum, and all the big cattlemen are leaving the infested district of Lincoln.

Significant indeed was John Chisum's pulling up stakes. Only one interpretation could be put upon his course: his expectation that things would go from bad to worse in Lincoln County and that he was giving up the struggle. In June he had gone away to St. Louis for treatment of an old leg injury and had not been on hand during the crisis in July. Later in the summer he had returned to South Spring River with mind made up to emigrate. He at once started the removal of his cattle (a small selected herd had been retained from the sale to Hunter & Evans) to a new range on the Canadian River in the Texas Panhandle. The South Spring River ranch was practically abandoned. Chisum himself eventually went east on an extended trip, placing the management of his cattle in the hands of his brothers.

---

1. Late in 1881 or early in 1882 the Mormon colony returned and started afresh to establish themselves in the Pecos Valley. After about two years they again became dissatisfied (although not this time on account of lawlessness and insecurity of the county) and left for Arizona.

34. Ravages of Selman's Scouts

DURING SEPTEMBER AND October Lincoln County's plight grew more desperate. Where before there had been simply two factions, each with some claim to acting in behalf of law and order, now there developed several groups of outlaws and desperate characters roaming up and down the county and making no pretense to motives other than selfish greed and desire to fatten off the spoils. Even the casual traveler on the highway was not safe, for he might fall literally into the hands of thieves and robbers, as did a certain farmer living in the Hondo. He happened to meet one of these bands between the Brady ranch and Lincoln and was stripped of his clothing and relieved of the $40 he had on his person. The same band of "Scouts" then went on to the Rio Pecos and added to their booty ten or twelve head of Chisum horses.

The activities of the remnants of the McSween crowd were mild in comparison with those of other groups elsewhere in the county. The two original factions had subdivided until now there were at least four bands. A fresh influx from Texas developed into still another band, although it absorbed some elements from the older groups. Thus about half a dozen gangs of desperate characters were preying on Lincoln County.

Conspicuous among the new arrivals was John Selman, who used the name of John Gunter, sometimes that of John Gross. A vigilance committee at Fort Griffin, Texas, had just ended the career of John Laren, Selman's partner in cattle stealing. Selman had departed for south Texas, but when he learned of conditions in Lincoln County he changed his course in that direction. Being a forceful character, he soon took over the leadership of eight or ten as desperate men as himself, some even recruited from Kinney's Rio Grande gang, and they terrorized the country during the summer and fall of 1878. Dudley frequently mentions the activities of this Selman aggregation, speaking of them as the "Wrestlers," although the correct form must have been "Rustlers." Sometimes the band called itself "Scouts," their claim being that they were under some sort of authority from Sheriff Peppin to guard the approaches to the Seven Rivers section from other bands that might try to inflict retaliations for the part taken in the fighting at Lincoln.

During the latter part of September Selman's group moved up to the vicinity of Lincoln and inaugurated a worse type of terrorism than heretofore known. Some were even daring enough to go to Fort Stanton and try to buy ammunition from the post trader's store. On September 27, part of "Selman's Scouts" rode up to the saloon just off the post limits and tried to induce Will Hudgens, who had charge of it, to become their proxy in purchasing ammunition.[2] When he refused, they sent four others to the Fort where they made the purchase without interference. But they fell afoul of Colonel Dudley. He had them arrested before they were outside the military reservation and conducted back to the post trader's. There they were made to return the ammunition and receive back the money paid for it. Then they were ejected from the post limits with a warning that if they again showed their faces there they would be arrested and would not get off so lightly the second time.

The four concerned in this affair departed in great anger. When they got back to the saloon and told their comrades what had occurred, the whole crowd went on a rampage. Through some inverted reasoning they felt that Hudgens should be the butt of their retaliation because he had refused to be the go-between. They proceeded to wreck the saloon and even went to the extreme of mistreating and insulting his wife and sister. A man named Shepard, who remonstrated against the treatment of the women, got hit over the head with a revolver butt. When they departed, they distributed such liberal and convincing threats about renewing their atrocities at an early date that Hudgens felt it best to go to the Fort for protection. He told Colonel Dudley he had recognized several members of the Dolan crowd. One, he said, was

---

2.   Premises owned by Catron; formerly L. G. Murphy's brewery.

Reese Gobles, an escaped convict from the Texas penitentiary, and another was "John Gunter," or John Selman.

After the affair near the Fort, "Selman's Scouts" started on a return trip to the Seven Rivers section, which became memorable for apparently motiveless deeds of violence. In writing to Tunstall's father on the first of October, Sam Corbet briefly relates what they had accomplished:

> The Dolan party came up again last week. Dolan, Captain Evans [of the Banditti] came up with [them] to Fort Stanton and stopped there where they could get protection from the military, while the "Rustlers," as they called themselves, robbed the citizens. They broke open many houses, taking everything out, breaking dishes and so forth; took blankets, jewelry, stock, and anything they wanted — even stripped women of their clothing. They came down to Mess. I. Ellis & Sons' store to rob it, but we were fixed for them, and stood them off. They went below here to [A. M. Clenny's] store at the Junction, nine miles from Lincoln, and took $800 worth of goods. They killed two men and two boys only about 14 years old, unarmed and in the hay field at work. Rode right up to them and shot them down.

The killing of these four young Mexicans in the hay field on September 28 was one of the most wanton deeds during the Lincoln County uproar. What the Selman crowd wanted was horses, ten of which they took at that time. Because the two Chávez y Sánchez boys "resisted" to the extent of saying that if the strangers wanted the horses they must see the boys' father about them, they were shot down and the horses taken. The two Chávez y Sánchez boys were Cleto and Desiderio; with them in the meadow were Gregorio Sánchez and Lorenzo Lucero, both of whom also were victims of the attackers. No element of reprisal for old scores can be detected in this brutal affair. The father, José Chávez y Sánchez, a Mexican citizen held in high esteem, had been altogether neutral in the Lincoln County War. The perpetrators of this atrocity were, if indictments be any guide, John Gross, alias John Gunter, (i.e., John Selman); Gus Gildea; Reese Gobles; "Rustling Bob;" Charles Snow; James Irvin; William Dyer and a man identified only as Collier.[3]

---

3.   Should probably read Collins. There is no record of any Collier in Lincoln County at that time. A man whose name was Caleb Hall but who used the alias Sam Collins was an early leader of Selman-Gildea-Gobles-Speakes party, but had dropped out of the group some weeks before the Ft. Stanton excursion. Collins is known to have been in Texas during the weeks of Selman's raids in the Rio Bonito area.

These outrages were more than flesh and blood could stand and the people of Lincoln took steps to curb them. As Sam Corbet wrote:

> Some of the citizens, I and Mr. Ellis together with them, got after them, and run them two days and nights nearly to Seven Rivers, but could not get close enough to kill any of them. We captured all the loose horses they were driving back, animals and all their blankets and provisions.

But as this was an inconclusive attempt, another campaign was projected. About this Sam Corbet wrote:

> We are going to start to Seven Rivers Friday with all the citizens that can raise a gun, and try and stop their murdering and stealing. I am satisfied that they will make a desperate fight, and I expect will outnumber us; but we have concluded that it is better to die fighting for our right all in a pile than to be murdered one at a time in our homes. I am satisfied that some of us will never get back to Lincoln, but I am willing to take my chances with the good citizens of the county, although I have nothing to lose but my life, which is as dear to me as any one's but the time has come when we have to fight or leave the country, and some of our best citizens have died for their rights, and the few who have been spared this long might as well go the same way, or stop the murderers at once.
>
> Mr. Ellis went to Fort Stanton to get some cartridges today, and Col. Dudley ordered the post trader not to sell a cartridge without an order from him. We managed to get 8,000 rounds by slipping them out tonight... We have warrants for all the outfit below and are ready to start Friday.

There are reports of the later contests with the Selman crowd. Gus Gildea, who was living in 1935, recalled a fight which may be the struggle between the men of Lincoln and Selman's Scouts:

> I have never seen mention of the long all-day fight made by nine of our men *vs.* from 25 to 30 or more of the "Modocs," both Americans and Mexicans. We fought from near the Fritz ranch to the Martín Chávez ranch, about 35 miles, through every village on the road and finally had to take to the mountains. We got back to the road again, and lost seven of our horses, but no men. We whipped them good and plenty. I heard that Kid, Bowdre, *et al* of his white men were in the last part of it.

Another glimpse of the efforts of residents of Lincoln to protect themselves from the Seven Rivers crowd may be an entry in Colonel

Dudley's report under date of October 5, when he relates that Dave Easton, employed in "Catron's store," as the old Dolan store was now called, had been stopped on his way to Seven Rivers by several mounted men about fifteen miles below Kline's ranch on the Rio Hondo, and told he could go no further. Colonel Dudley explained that these were "good citizens" who were trying to prevent the return of "Rustlers" to the upper part of the county and did not want Easton to convey to Seven Rivers news of their whereabouts.

In truth the whole southern section of the county was terror-stricken. Kline, who had a contract for carrying the mail, frantically appealed for protection for the mail riders between Fort Stanton and Fort Sumner, saying that he believed that whenever any of the various gangs thought news detrimental to them was going through the mail they would not hesitate to take the life of the mail carrier. The same cry went up from Roswell. Ash Upson, the postmaster, wrote that he believed it was unsafe for him to remain at his office without protection, for there had been threats to burn the office and take his life. Captain Joseph C. Lea seconded the request. He had just had an alarming experience himself at Berrendo, the Mexican settlement a few miles northwest of Roswell. The people there were in a state of acute indignation over a raid that had occurred a few weeks before. As the Selman crowd were going into the "upper" part of the county, they had first come up to Roswell, then paid the Berrendo settlement a visit. No definite account of this raid exists, but it was obviously in the usual vein of ruthlessness. At any rate, it roused the ordinarily docile Mexicans; some even determined to visit retaliation on the first *Americanos*, in particular *Tejanos*, that came their way. Captain Lea, all unwittingly, almost became the target of this intense resentment. Happening to be riding in that direction, he was halted by a group of decidedly hostile inhabitants. All that saved his life was the fact that one Berrendo citizen put himself between Captain Lea and the hostile ones, remaining a buffer, until Lea had ridden away.

This incident had alarmed Captain Lea considerably. Race antagonism might possibly create an ugly situation. In an uprising the Mexicans in the vicinity of Roswell would outnumber the Americans, who consisted simply of Captain Lea's entourage, plus Ash Upson and a few others. Any chance for aid from the Chisum ranch had disappeared, for the Chisums had emigrated to the Texas Panhandle to escape the unhappy conditions in Lincoln County. At the South Spring River ranch, where there had once been a hundred or so employees, now only a caretaker or two was left. Captain Lea felt warranted in applying to Colonel Dudley for protection. The mails and the post office were privileged to have protection under the War Department regulations and accordingly a large detachment from Company "F" of the 9th Cavalry, under command of Captain Carroll, was dispatched to Roswell, and remained all fall and a large part of the following winter.

In early October disquieting rumors came down from Fort Sumner about the activity of the McSween men gathered there. One of these reports had it that a party headed by Juan Patrón killed two men somewhere between Fort Sumner and Lloyd's Crossing, a few miles above Roswell. Indefiniteness in regard to the exact locality matched the vagueness as to whom were the victims, reportedly members of the Selman gang. Also, there were reports that one or more of Selman's men had been disposed of by Patrón and his Regulators at Puerto de Luna.

No wonder the whole situation began to get on the nerves of Colonel Dudley. Frantic to make use of his soldiers and fervently believing that the salvation of the country depended on a sharp dose of martial law, he felt hedged in by the restrictions of General Orders #28 C. C. of 1878. In language as strong as he dared use in letters and reports he begged repeatedly to be allowed to effect a quick restoration of law and order by an energetic use of soldiers. Typical is this passage from one of the weekly reports to Colonel Hatch:

> I respectfully ask in the name of God and humanity that I may be allowed to use the forces at my command to drive these murderers, horse thieves, and escaped convicts out of the country. The wives and daughters of quiet and good citizens are being daily insulted by these desperadoes and driven into hiding in the mountains in order to save their lives. This too almost in sight of the garrison.

The particular outrage behind this plea was a revolting occurrence at Bartlett's Mill, some eleven miles from the post. Several of the "Wrestlers" designated generically as "murderers, horse thieves, and escaped convicts" had come to the mill and shamefully abused the wives of two of Bartlett's employees. The women had been taken into the underbrush, stripped of clothing, and used at the pleasure of their captors. As Colonel Dudley's hands were still tied by orders from the War Department, he was forced to decline the request for protection. He honestly thought martial law the only course and used every leverage possible to lift off the clog of departmental refusal. He realized that a resolute desperado with a few followers could defy the local officers of the law and any civilian posse. It seemed anomalous to use soldiers to protect the mails but not to use them to aid officers in capturing the criminals after the crime had been committed. It seemed axiomatic that in new regions like Lincoln County the army should be the chief reliance for protection in any emergency.

Colonel Dudley, therefore, went the length in trying to obtain a removal of these restrictions, or at least some relaxation of them. From Peppin he secured a lengthy affidavit describing conditions as they were and the difficulties the sheriff was having, even to his getting no financial support from the county commissioners although he had taken the sheriffship under an understanding he was to have that as well as military support. The affidavit was accompanied by a letter from Colonel Dudley which pictured the deplorable state of Lincoln County as growing worse with every week. To make this appeal the more impressive, the affidavit and the letter were borne to Santa Fe by a delegation of Lincoln County officials consisting of the probate judge, Florencio González, the county treasurer, José Montaño, one of the county commissioners, Captain Baca, and one of the justices of the peace, George Kimbrell. As the Santa Fe *New Mexican* put it, when publishing both affidavit and letter:

> These officials stated to the governor that in addition to murder and robbery these fiends in many instances added the dreadful and unnatural crime of rape, too — their victims in two instances being mere children. They implored the governor, almost on their knees, for assistance. The governor had forwarded their petitions to President Hayes with a strong request for assistance from the United States to protect the people of the territory from domestic violence. If the governor's request is not granted, it will probably become his duty to convene the legislature.

The governor's letter of transmittal was likewise a strong appeal. He explained that the territory was without militia and the governor without authority to call for volunteers. He pictured the lawlessness of the section, giving as his estimate that there were 200 men in the various bands infesting it. Some of this crop he ascribed to Texas, while others were from Old Mexico. Such atrocious crimes as murder, arson, robbery, and rape were becoming the order of the day. The temper of most of the crowd might be surmised from the answer made by a ringleader in one of these bands when asked who they were. "We are devils just come from hell!"

35. A New Governor and His Program

In SAM CORBET'S letter to Tunstall's father, quotations from which were given in the preceding section, was a sentence of gossip which showed Lincoln agog over the coming of Governor Lew Wallace to replace Governor Axtell. "Mr. Dolan and Captain Evans," so Sam Corbet put it, "stopped in the Fort until yesterday [when] they started to Santa Fe, I suppose to try to get in with the new governor." The suspicion was altogether plausible, although in Dolan's case another purpose might have been assigned, namely that he was going to see his former partner, Major Murphy, who was dying. Major Murphy on March 14, 1877, had sold to his associates, James J. Dolan, John H. Riley, and Jacob B. Mathews, the store at Lincoln and all his other Lincoln County holdings except the "Fairview" ranch at Carrizo Spring. Although a bedroom in the store building was reserved for his use, on only one occasion is he known to have visited Lincoln after his retirement, this in response to summons to appear before the April term of court. From his Carrizo Spring ranch he moved to Santa Fe. His health, some time undermined by constant and heavy drinking, had failed rapidly in Santa Fe and by the first of October the end was simply a question of a few weeks. Dolan's trip to Santa Fe, however, did coincide with the arrival of a new governor, so Sam Corbet probably was largely correct in his surmise.

Behind the removal of Governor Axtell was a chain of events that went back to the letters Dr. Leverson had written on the day of the killing of Brady and Hindman. In them he had directly stated to President Hayes and Secretary of the Interior Carl Schurz that all the territorial officers in New Mexico, with the exception of John Sherman, Jr., the United States marshal, were implicated in the Lincoln County troubles. Washington had previously received sundry mutterings and complaints, especially about Governor Axtell and his part in Lincoln County affairs. In the spring of 1877 his political enemies had made widespread a charge that he was a Mormon elder and in reality an agent of Brigham Young. While such wild accusations almost disproved themselves, they did not add to the peace and tranquillity of the administration. A little later there was another buzzing over the charge that Governor Axtell was a member of the Santa Fe ring, the existence of which all good Democrats of that time strongly believed. Some basis for this conclusion was found in the attitude the Governor had taken toward the private land grants of Spanish times which for so long were a vexing problem in New Mexico. The Governor had proposed that these grants be scrapped and the land restored to the public domain; at once a hue and cry was set up that this would enable him and his friends in the Santa Fe ring to gobble up the land by thousands of acres.

Another of the furors of this stormy administration concerned Colfax County. Governor Axtell had approved a merger of Colfax County with Taos County "for judicial purposes," an expression which meant that all the court activities in Colfax ceased and were transferred to Taos. Soon afterwards the gold mining settlements in Colfax County grew uproarious with crime, a condition the opponents of Governor Axtell were quick to ascribe to the position taken in regard to the courts. They even tried to associate with this merger of the counties the murder of Reverend F. J. Talby, a Methodist minister, which had occurred in September, 1875, on the highway east of "E—Town," as Elizabethtown was called. To Colfax County this murder was as much of a shock as the killing of Tunstall was to Lincoln County.

Though Governor Axtell had seemed to weather all these storms, his part in the Lincoln County War proved his undoing. The Leverson letters were amply confirmed by the report of Judge Angel, and by the first of September President Hayes had reached a decision that New Mexico must have a new governor. Under date of September 4 he tendered the appointment to General Lew Wallace; with little delay General Wallace accepted.

A similar fate overtook the United States attorney, Thomas B. Catron, although less summarily than the Governor's removal. When Catron realized his danger, he tried hard to avert his fate but even the generous batch of affidavits as to his faithfulness, which he procured and sent to Washington, did not save him. Neither did the appeals of his friend and former law partner, Stephen B. Elkins, the territorial delegate in Congress, have their usual success. So Catron read the handwriting on the wall and early in October tendered his resignation, to become effective November 10. The U.S. Attorney General accepted it at once but requested him to continue in office until a successor had qualified. Under this arrangement Catron remained United States District Attorney until S. M. Barnes arrived.

General Wallace became governor on October 1. His appointment carried with it emphatic and plenary instructions from President Hayes himself to bring order and peace to the southern portions of the territory. "If peace and quiet are not restored in Lincoln County in the next sixty days," the new governor announced on arrival, with a tinge of self-assurance, "I will feel ashamed of myself." He had stepped into a role more difficult than he anticipated. The Republican leaders looked askance and treated him coldly. Almost to a man they remained loyal to Governor Axtell and regarded his removal from office as both uncalled for and unjust. Even such strong political antagonism did not deter Governor Wallace from going ahead with the program he had formulated for ending turmoil in Lincoln County.

The general belief was that being a veteran of both the Mexican and the Civil Wars he would rely on military measures to straighten out matters. He had indeed contemplated doing so, for he had come armed with a proclamation from President Hayes as a preliminary to declaring the county in a state of insurrection. The body of the proclamation was as follows:

Whereas it has been made to appear to me that, by reason of unlawful combinations and assemblages of persons in arms, it has become impracticable to enforce by the ordinary course of judicial proceedings the laws of the United States within the Territory of New Mexico, and especially within Lincoln County therein, and that the laws of the United States have been therein forcibly opposed and the execution thereof forcibly resisted; and

Whereas the laws of the United States require that whenever it may be necessary, in the judgement of the President, to use the military force for the purpose of enforcing the faithful execution of the laws of the United States, he shall forthwith, by proclamation, command such insurgents to disperse and retire peaceably to their respective abodes within a limited time:

Now, therefore, I, Rutherford B. Hayes, President of the United States, do hereby admonish all good citizens of the United

States, and especially of the Territory of New Mexico, against aiding, countenancing, abetting or taking part in any such unlawful proceedings; and I do hereby warn all persons engaged in or connected with said obstruction of the laws to disperse and retire peaceably to their respective abodes on or before noon of the 13th day of October instant.

Though the proclamation opened the way to a freer use of the soldiers in controlling lawlessness, Governor Wallace was loathe to use the power thus placed in his hands with any severity. He was reluctant to use martial law in its drastic form and decided to take time enough to try out a seven-point plan, the features of which were:

I. To dispatch all available troops from other posts in the Territory to Fort Stanton and distribute them in temporary camps in Lincoln and Doña Ana counties.

II. To have these soldiers scout thoroughly in these counties to break up all camps and corrals of outlaws.

III. To arrest without fear or favor all persons or bands of persons found in such camps or on the highways in possession of stolen property, or property for the possession of which they could not account satisfactorily.

IV. To hold all such persons until the proper court of the county met and took action according to legal procedure.

V. To have the property taken from such persons placed, if stolen, in safe keeping for identification and reclamation.

VI. If officers were satisfied that any one arrested by them was not deserving of arrest, they might at once release such persons.

VII. Army officers were to be especially careful not to interfere with good citizens going peaceably about their own business, since the object of this whole plan was to secure protection for all such.

This plan, the product of a mind which derived its set from practicing law and commanding battalions, was obviously cumbersome. Several weeks passed before it manifested any semblance of being in operation. Governor Wallace, however, was optimistic and kept predicting the situation would clear up in time without extreme measures. Had he grasped the nettle fast and firmly in the beginning, the course of events in Lincoln County might have been different. Governor Wallace had certain reasons for not embarking on a drastic course. At this particular time his confirmation was pending in the Senate. It was being fought, as he well knew, by prominent Republicans; consequently, he would move gradually and as inoffensively as possible in the Lincoln County troubles.

The outcome of all this mildness was "the governor's pardon," announced about the middle of November by another proclamation, Wallace's own.

For the information of the people of the United States and of the citizens of New Mexico in especial, the undersigned announces that the disorders lately prevalent in Lincoln County in said territory have been happily brought to an end. Persons having business and property interests therein and who are themselves peaceably disposed may go to and from that county without hindrance or molestation. Individuals resident there but who have been driven away, or who from choice sought safety elsewhere, are invited to return under assurance that ample measures have been taken and now are and will be continued in force to make them secure in person and property.

And that the people of Lincoln County may be helped more speedily to the management of their civil affairs as contemplated by law, and to induce them to lay aside forever the divisions and feuds, which by national notoriety have been so prejudicial to their locality and the whole territory, the undersigned by virtue of authority in him vested, further proclaims a general pardon for misdemeanors and offenses committed in the said county of Lincoln against the said laws of the said territory in connection with the aforesaid disorders, between the first day of February, 1878, and the date of this proclamation.

And it is expressly understood that the foregoing pardon is upon the conditions and limitations following:

It shall not apply except to officers of the United States army stationed in the said county during the said disorders and to persons who at the time of the commission of the offense or misdemeanor of which they may be accused were in good intent resident citizens of the said territory, and who shall have hereafter kept the peace and conducted themselves in all respects as become good citizens.

Neither shall it be pleaded by any person in bar of conviction under indictments now found and returned for any such crimes and misdemeanors, nor operate the release of any party undergoing pains and penalties consequent upon sentence heretofore had for any crime or misdemeanor.

In witness whereof I have here unto set my hand and caused the seal of the territory of New Mexico to be affixed.

Done at the city of Santa Fe, this
13th day of November, A.D. 1878

Lewis Wallace
Governor of New Mexico

At first this offer of immunity appeared likely to clarify the situation. The troubles were unquestionably too widespread for the courts. In fact, the fall term of district court, which should have come regularly in October, had already been abandoned. Judge Bristol's court would have its work greatly simplified if the overcrowded docket could be relieved of those who were eligible to the terms of the offer. In a short time several of those who had fled from the state under fear of indictment plucked up enough courage to return. This was especially true in the Seven Rivers section where fear had been acute ever since the July fight and where access to Texas was easy. Among those who returned were Buck Powell, M. L. Pierce, and his partner, Lewis Paxton. Some of those closer to Lincoln also felt a return of confidence. Captain Baca, who had finally become a refugee at Fort Stanton, felt it was now safe enough to return to his home at Lincoln.

36. Dudley Picks a Quarrel

TOWARD THE CLOSE of November bickerings between Colonel Dudley and Governor Wallace threw new fuel on the smoldering embers the new Governor was regarding optimistically as dead coals. The friction between these two went back to about the middle of October when Mrs. McSween, perhaps thinking the arrival of a new governor the opportune time, had started her campaign against those she regarded as most instrumental in the destruction of her property and the killing of her husband. Her spirit is clearly revealed in a letter to the father of Tunstall written from Las Vegas on October 18. Her request for additional funds from the Tunstall family made it necessary for her to offer an explanation in a letter.

> I shall have to use a good portion of this to bring suits against the murderers of my husband & I intend to sue this county for damages & all parties who were connected with those troubles that are property holders, say Dudley & a few others whom we know to be worth something. As our county is now under martial law, I am going to have every man (who was implicated in burning our house & killing my dear husband) arrested & tried for murder. I do think we will come out all right yet, though right is slow in coming. Our new governor appears to want to do what is right. He promises to give me all the assistance he can in bringing those men to justice & I shall never give up so long as I have a ray of hope.

During her stay in Las Vegas Mrs. McSween had employed Houston I. Chapman, a recently-arrived attorney from Portland, Oregon, to assist her in her efforts to avenge her husband's death. Certainly she needed a legal advisor, for her affairs had grown decidedly complicated. Her husband's will, made soon after Tunstall's death and under the conviction that his own might follow soon, had designated John Chisum as administrator. It also stipulated that in case Chisum could not act, then Mrs. McSween should take charge. Since Chisum was temporarily away from Lincoln County by the time the will was probated, Mrs. McSween had qualified as administratrix and assumed the burden.

In addition to this she was concerned about Tunstall's property, as his was bound up with McSween's to a considerable degree. She felt that the Tunstall estate was not being properly looked after. Isaac Ellis had been placed in charge of Tunstall's property on an interim basis but Tunstall's father, impressed by the friendship existing between his son and Widenmann, had disregarded McSween's advice and favored Widenmann as administrator. When his life seemed as much in danger as McSween's, Widenmann had left Lincoln in June and gone to Mesilla. Then with a great flourish he had departed for England to confer with Tunstall's father, and very likely to impress him with highly colored accounts of the part he had played in avenging the murder of Tunstall. Mrs. McSween casually noted the fact of Widenmann's departure in a sentence closing her letter of the 18 of October: "Mr. Widenmann left this place (Las Vegas) for Washington City & your place some days ago." Upon his departure she acted upon her conviction that for the good of both estates Widenmann must be removed and she herself made administratrix.

Mrs. McSween was allowing her resentment towards Colonel Dudley and several others conspicuous in the July fight to grow beyond bounds. She had worked herself into the belief that with the aid of an able lawyer she could carry through to success trials for arson and murder. Her design was aimed most directly at Colonel Dudley but included Peppin, Kinney, and others whom she intended to involve in the series of trials.

Perhaps her choice of an attorney should have lighted on a different type from Chapman. She ought to have selected a lawyer of poise and judgment instead of one who approached the agitator type. Chapman encouraged her obsession about the trials and urged that in order to get the groundwork thoroughly laid they should both go to Lincoln and spend some time there. Mrs. McSween accepted the idea, and Chapman proceeded to make arrangements for the journey. As the situation was still tense at Lincoln, he sought for Mrs. McSween a degree of protection. He wrote to Colonel Dudley asking him to provide Mrs. McSween with a "safeguard," virtually a passport guaranteeing military protection. Colonel Dudley, now as bitter towards Mrs. McSween as she toward him, promptly declined the request. Then Chapman appealed directly to Governor Wallace, not only asking for a "safeguard" but including the complaint that Colonel Dudley was unfavorable to Mrs. McSween and even exploding the charge that the Colonel was involved in the killing of McSween.

This startled the Governor, who had been in New Mexico but a few weeks. He forwarded Chapman's letter to Colonel Hatch, the district commander, accompanied by a letter of his own, in which he insisted that Mrs. McSween be provided with a "safeguard," since she had important business in Lincoln County requiring her personal attention. Colonel Hatch, trying to carry out what he deemed the Governor's wishes, sent both letters — Chapman's and the Governor's — to Colonel Dudley. Result: an uproar from the pompous and choleric commanding officer at Fort Stanton. Had Dudley's nose been tweaked actually, it could not have caused more of a flare-up. The Colonel struck back viciously and by means beneath the dignity of his position. His reply to Colonel Hatch resolved itself into an attack upon Mrs. McSween's character, which he supported by affidavits from several residents of Lincoln, all of whom had been decidedly anti-McSween, and from officers at the Fort who had as a rule taken a partisan stand.

Two days later, that is, on November 9, Colonel Dudley again felt he must let off steam. This time he wrote directly to Governor Wallace, calling his attention to the testimony about Mrs. McSween he had sent Colonel Hatch. He was at great pains to declare that he had always stayed within the absolute letter of the law in all movements the soldiers under his command had made. He closed with a sentence that threw down the gauntlet to all his detractors: "I am not here quietly to submit to and allow such allegations against myself as your Excellency has seen proper to forward to district headquarters, without making an unqualified denial, and I defy proof to the contrary."

Under date of November 16 Governor Wallace answered the Colonel's fiery letter in a placative tone. He did, however, insist that Mrs. McSween was entitled to protection in going about her lawful business no matter what aspersions upon her character. By this time the amnesty proclamation had been prepared, and Governor Wallace enclosed an advance copy for Colonel Dudley asking him to show it to Peppin, the sheriff. "The effect," the Governor wrote, "is to nullify all writs in his hands for violation of territorial laws in connection with the recent outlawry in Lincoln County, except such writs as he may have issued regularly upon indictments already returned."

Colonel Dudley did not answer Governor Wallace's letter immediately. The next letter in the exchange emanated also from Governor Wallace. As a counterblast to opponents who were fighting his confirmation by Congress he had Colonel Hatch open rather freely the files of his office and sent the material thus garnered to the *Rocky Mountain Sentinel*, published at Trinidad, Colorado, to be worked up into an approving article. When the article appeared, Governor Wallace mailed a copy to Colonel Dudley, accompanying it with the following letter, markedly informal and friendly:

> Enclosed you will find half sheet of the *R. M. Sentinel*, in which you will doubtless be interested. Your reports furnished me a perfect answer to the gentlemen in the territory who are fighting my confirmation on the grounds that my proclamation is false and Lincoln County not quieter. Accept thanks for the reports.
>
> Amongst others whom my action has much outraged is the virtuous editor of the Mesilla *News*. Have you seen his last issue? He goes for me in good style because I presumed to include officers of the army in the terms of my amnesty. I had a good reason for that, by the way, which I will explain when I see you.

On the same date, November 30, Colonel Dudley was preparing a new explosion. In an open letter for that strongly anti-administration journal, the Santa Fe *New Mexican*, Dudley's letter was ostensibly an answer to the one from Governor Wallace dated November 16, but was virtually a declaration of war. Dudley construed that sentence in the amnesty proclamation which brought the army officers within its provisions as having some reference to himself.

> Not having asked any leniency for myself, and well knowing that no officer serving in the county has; and as your Excellency cannot very consistently grant a pardon to an individual or a class or body of men who have not committed a crime, I am, with the other officers of my command, at a loss correctly to interpret this part of your proclamation.

Then asserting strongly that his own actions were above faultfinding, he accused the Governor of being unfair.

> Your Excellency alone, without an investigation except an *ex parte* one, without having given the one of the parties thus accused an opportunity to explain their position, is charged with acts seriously affecting their honor and pardoned for the same

in the one document thus promulgated by your Excellency ....

There can be but one construction placed upon the language of the proclamation. It virtually charges myself and the officers of the army who have been here on duty since the 1st of February last with having violated the laws of the territory, and then proceeds to pardon us, classing one and all of us with the murderers, cattle thieves, and outlaws who killed Sheriff Brady, Roberts, Bernstein, Beckwith, Tunstall, and scores of other citizens of the county ....

I earnestly submit that to warrant giving publicity to such defamatory charges in a public proclamation against a body of officers of long service and good repute, it was but just to have allowed them a hearing first; and not to have come to a hasty conclusion based on evidence of a solely *ex parte* character, not even submitting to them a synopsis of the charges for which they are pardoned ....

I respectfully request to be informed of what offenses I am charged with and who my accusers are. I shall have no trouble in exhibiting their characters in a similar light to that you have had of the woman who solicited and obtained a safeguard. It is my right to be so informed, and until I am found guilty, I respectfully decline accepting a pardon at the hands of your Excellency ....

I am aware that it is not within the province of an officer of the army to make suggestions to a civil functionary occupying the high position held by yourself, much less criticize his official course; but when false and unjust accusations are made against either myself or the gallant officers of the command, it becomes my duty to demand for them and myself a hearing, and not to allow a general pardon to be promulgated for them or myself for offences that we know not of and of which we feel ourselves guiltless.

A supplement to this letter was a short note signed by such officers of Fort Stanton as had been active in Lincoln County affairs. They all approved the stand of Colonel Dudley and stated that his letter "expressed most fully and explicitly our feelings upon this subject in publicly declining to accept the pardon tendered us by your Excellency."

Whatever the motive, the publication of this letter was highly ill-advised. Colonel Dudley unquestionably accelerated an outbreak of old bitterness of feeling toward him individually and the military in particular. In calumniating Mrs. McSween he used a weapon unbecoming an officer and a gentleman. The net result was that Governor Wallace became firmly convinced that one of the most needed steps in the recovery of Lincoln County was a change in the commanding officer at Fort Stanton.

That Lincoln County was still stricken with the old malady manifested itself casually in Colonel Dudley's reports as published in the *Rocky Mountain Sentinel*. The first in the series were merely single sentence affairs saying that nothing had happened since the last report; but later there came more lengthy ones evidently intended as evidence that the soldiers were alert and on their jobs. There was a recent case of cattle stealing from Pat Coghlin at Tularosa, which Lieutenant Godwin was investigating with some unexpected results. Five men implicated in it had been captured, and the stolen cattle found to be headed for the Indian agency. The Cimarron *News and Press*, quick to smell the rat, came out with the following editorial in the issue for December 5. History seemed to be repeating itself; even though the Dolan store was now in new hands (Edgar Walz was managing it for his brother-in-law, T. B. Catron), the old methods seemed still in use in filling government contracts.

> In its last issue the *Sentinel* prints some interesting information regarding affairs in Lincoln County in the shape of official reports of Colonel Dudley, commanding Fort Stanton. They show that a sort of order prevails there now, in the permanency of which we would have more confidence were it not for the strikingly apparent partisanship of Colonel Dudley. We fear that under his administration the peace will be that of the lion and lamb lying down together — the lamb inside.
>
> One very peculiar fact is disclosed in these dispatches and which the *Sentinel* alludes to in proper terms. It appears that a lot of cattle were stolen from Mr. Coghlin and driven from his range. A lieutenant and a detachment of troops were sent after them, who captured the five alleged thieves and traced the cattle to a place where he found them "with the cattle furnished to the Indian Agency."
>
> Lieutenant Goodwin reported this fact to Dudley, whose ardor for the pursuit at once cooled, and he sent back the following: "The Post Commander had grave doubts whether or not any very considerable number of cattle has been stolen from Mr. Coghlin, they having simply strayed from his herd, he having, as is well known, a drunken man in charge. Unless you are well satisfied that the cattle have been stolen, and you have almost a certainty of recovering them, you will not make further attempts to do so."
>
> This, let it be observed, was just as Colonel Dudley had been advised that the cattle had been traced to the Indian contractor's herd, and it looks very much as if in certain official circles it is well considered no crime to steal in Lincoln County, provided it is done to aid the government contractors in filling their contracts.

From such thefts as these the trouble in Lincoln County originated, and this singular action of Dudley does not impress us with much confidence in the kind of peace he maintains. An impartial administration of military power there we believe would restore permanent peace. Governor Wallace's plan is all right, but we fear the military will render all his efforts unfruitful of lasting results.

37. Chapman Clashes With the Military

I F COLONEL DUDLEY DEPLORED Governor Wallace's reliance upon "*ex parte* sources" for impressions of conditions in Lincoln County, attorney Chapman was equally positive that the military were busily pouring misinformation into the governor's ears. As spokesman for Mrs. McSween, he felt called upon to enlighten the governor; so he forwarded to Santa Fe two extraordinary letters. Both were shot through with Chapman's immoderate temperament, as well as his proclivity for stirring up trouble.

In the first, written November 25, Chapman complained that much of the continued unrest in Lincoln County should be laid at the door of Fort Stanton.

> When I was in Santa Fe, you assured me that all persecutions would be stopped and that your proclamation of amnesty should be respected by all parties. I ventured the opinion at the time that the "ring," or Dolan's party, would use it as a convenience to shield themselves, and would continue their persecutions of the McSween men in defiance thereof. Upon my arrival here in Lincoln I found my apprehensions were only too well founded and that Peppin, aided by the military, was pursuing McSween men, while the friends of the "ring" against whom the sheriff held warrants, were granted immunity. I know that this is contrary to your wishes and instructions, and it is hard to produce a different effect from the same causes; and so long as Peppin (who is the tool of the Dolan party) and the military are kept in authority, just so long will Lincoln County be the scene of all manner of outrages and murder.

He expressed contempt for the personal behavior of most of the officers at the Fort, singling out Colonel Dudley's addiction to liquor for strong reprehension. Then he cited a recent occurrence as an example of the way the military treated the citizenry.

> I wish to call your attention to the outrages committed upon unoffending and innocent citizens by the military. A short time since, the store and home of a man by the name of Ballard was surrounded by soldiers, who without one word of explanation arrested Mr. Ballard when he came to the door and marched him out into the cold air in his night clothes and kept him there until chilled through with the cold, from which he is now suffering. A partner of Mr. Ballard's, "Sanger" was arrested and taken a great distance from the store without warrant or authority. A recurrence of such an outrage will certainly result fatally to some one.
>
> In your proclamation you said that "peace and order has been restored in Lincoln County," but I can assure you that it is the calm that precedes the storm. A more deadly strife is liable to commence at any time which will result in the loss of many lives and the destruction of much valuable property, unless something is done to restrain Peppin from continuing his persecutions. I tremble for the result, as the people will submit no longer.

Just four days later, November 29, Chapman wrote a second and even more intemperate letter:

> Today this town was thrown into a panic by two drunken deputy sheriffs charging into town on their horses with their guns cocked and directed at the house of Mrs. McSween. A few minutes afterwards a posse of soldiers under command of Lieutenant Goodwin came riding into town with three horse thieves who had formerly been of Sheriff Peppin's posse, and were brought in for examination before the justice of the peace.
>
> What I have to complain of is the riotous manner in which the military, sheriff and deputies charge about over the country, giving unnecessary alarm and anxiety to peaceably disposed citizens. The sheriff's deputies who were with the military were drunk and had with them a flask of whiskey from which they were continually drinking, and their conduct was anything but that of a peace officer. One of the deputies who accompanied the military fired his gun into the street to the great danger of peaceable citizens, and in fact there was no disturbance except that made by the military and drunken deputies.

After this account of recent happenings, Chapman grew prophetic: "Such outrages by the military, as the one at Ballard's, are becoming too common, and unless a stop is put to it at once serious trouble may be expected." He next showed he was beginning to play the role of agitator:

> Your own proclamation that peace had been restored in Lincoln County supercedes the necessity of further aid from the government and prevents the use of the military to aid the civil authorities in Lincoln County; and I have advised the citizens here to shoot any officer who shall in any manner attempt their arrest or interfere with their rights. I have counseled the people to observe it. While I counsel its observance, I question your authority to grant amnesty before conviction is had, for offenses against the law.

The letter strongly urged Governor Wallace to come to Lincoln in person and gain firsthand acquaintance with the situation instead of long-range impressions.

> I cannot but think that if you visited Lincoln County as you should have done, that you would have acted differently and not have pardoned notorious outlaws and murders. You have been grossly imposed upon by the military who have lied to you in order to shield themselves from the outrages they have committed in this county. There is not an honest man in Lincoln County who would believe Colonel Dudley on oath, yet you rely on him for all your information, and have pardoned him for the murder of an innocent man. I can assure you that the people take no stock in your amnesty proclamation, and they think that you have been derelict in your sworn duty, Governor, in not visiting Lincoln County and acquainting yourself with the true state of affairs. The people of Lincoln County are disgusted and tired of neglect and the indifference shown them by you, and next week they intend holding a mass meeting to give expression to their sentiments; and unless you come here before that time, you may expect to be severely denounced in language more forcible than polite. . . .
>
> I am now preparing a statement of facts for publication which, I am sorry to say, will reflect upon you for not coming here in person, for no one can get a correct idea of the outrages that have been committed here by quietly sitting in Santa Fe and depending on drunken officers for information. A decent respect for the people of this county would have caused you to have come here in person and ascertained who was responsible for all the trouble, and then you should have seen that the guilty were punished. I am no believer in making the laws a convenience or prostituting them for the sake of peace, and the people of this county will not submit to it quietly.

After writing this querulous and lecture-like letter, Chapman went ahead with the mass meeting of which he had spoken. Early in December he posted the following call:

NOTICE

There will be a mass-meeting of the citizens of Lincoln County, on Saturday, December 7th, 1878, at 1 o'clock p.m. at the court house in Lincoln, for the purpose of expressing their sentiments in regard to the outrages committed in this county and to denounce the manner in which the people have been misrepresented and maligned; and also to adopt such measures as will inform the President of the United States as to the true state of affairs in Lincoln County.

All citizens are invited to attend

This meeting did not receive approval from some of the prominent residents of the town who had formerly been McSween adherents. The Ellises in particular, as well as José Montaño, went to Chapman and urged him to drop the idea. They argued that he would simply fan smoldering embers into a blaze. Chapman, however, curiously compounded of self-confidence and hard-headedness, brushed their protests aside and went ahead with the plans.

All details of the meeting seem now lost but the natural inference from all the circumstances would be that it widened the breach between Chapman on the one hand, acting virtually as leader of the McSween faction, and Colonel Dudley and his fellow-officers on the other, counted as the supporters of the Catron-Dolan faction. A direct sequel of the meeting came about a week later in a clash between Chapman and Lieutenant French at Lincoln.

On December 13 a detachment of soldiers, led by Lieutenant French, was rushed to Lincoln because of a shooting scrape in which John Copeland, the sheriff whom Governor Axtell had removed, had shot and severely wounded Juan Mes (sometimes referred to as Maes or Johnny Mace). Copeland's hearing had been set for the next day and as the situation seemed tense the soldiers had been sent into Lincoln. Between eight and nine o'clock in the evening, as Chapman was writing at a table in the former Saturnino Baca house where Mrs. McSween was staying, someone knocked at the door. When Mrs. McSween's servant, Sebron Bates, went to the door and used the cautious preliminary question, "Who's there?," he received the laconic answer, "Soldiers!" The servant opened the door and two Negro soldiers entered. They first turned to Mrs. McSween and delivered a message to the effect that Lieutenant French would be there in a few minutes. Then they took seats by the stove to warm themselves.

A few minutes later one of them stepped over to Chapman and asked his name. "Chapman," he replied curtly. Then the soldier said, "If that's so, I have orders to arrest you and hold you until Lieutenant French comes." Chapman did not protest but merely asked if it would not expedite matters to take him at once to Lieutenant French. "No," said the soldier, "my instructions are to hold you here." In about twenty minutes Lieutenant French came, considerably under the influence of liquor and inclined to be quarrelsome. He had a Mexican boy with him whom he had just put under arrest for carrying a pistol. Wishing to get some statement from him, he turned to Chapman with the request that he put the boy under oath. Chapman replied that he had no authority to administer oaths; but Lieutenant French commanded him to swear the boy. To avoid trouble Chapman went ahead and pretended to administer the oath. This satisfied Lieutenant French and enabled him to go ahead with the maudlin questioning as to where the boy had obtained the gun.

When the examination of the boy was over, Chapman quietly asked by what authority he had been arrested. "By God, sir," Lieutenant French blustered, "if I have any authority, I will show it to you," and seating himself at the table took from his pocket a sheaf of papers and began fumbling among them. Finally he walked over to where Chapman was sitting and said, "God damn you, sir, I'm a better lawyer than you are." Chapman replied with some asperity that such might be the case but he seemed to have a poor way of showing the fact. Lieutenant French ignored the thrust and, returning to the table, resumed his search for some authority for the arrest, muttering that he had warrants for the arrest of several and would see if he had one for Chapman. Almost immediately he wheeled toward Chapman and commenced abusing him as the fomenter of troubles and reviver of old hatreds.

Mrs. McSween tried to head off the violent quarrel by saying, "Lieutenant French, if you have a warrant for Mr. Chapman, show it and he will go with you." The Lieutenant turned toward her with a discourteous, "Please shut your mouth, madam," and then addressing Chapman, "By God, you are the man I'm after. I know that, papers or no papers." Chapman replied that he knew fully his rights and proposed to protect them; if the Lieutenant had a warrant for him, let him show it; if he did not, then let him drop the matter. Lieutenant French retorted that Chapman had not been arrested. Chapman answered "I most certainly was," and indicating one of the soldiers added, "There is the man who arrested me and threw his gun down on me." To this Lieutenant French replied insultingly, "You are a God damn liar, sir."

Mrs. McSween again intervened, corroborating Chapman's assertion that he had been arrested. This drew from Lieutenant French the remark that she was not speaking the truth, almost as bluntly put as was the insult to Chapman. This uncalled-for treatment of Mrs. McSween was more than Chapman could endure. He brought into play his power of sharp retort, especially when incensed, and said, as he pointed to the two soldiers, "Lieutenant, those men, I believe, are more of a gentleman than you." Thereupon Lieutenant French sprang up brandishing his revolver at full cock and shouted to the soldiers, "Stand back, men!" Then turning to Chapman, "God damn you, I'll fix you." Mrs. McSween cried out, "For God's sake, Lieutenant, let's have no trouble in my house!" and burst into tears. Lieutenant French said to her brusquely, "That will do. I don't want any of your tragic behavior. I have seen that played too often back in the states." Then he began to remove his garments, evidently as a step toward fisticuffing with Chapman. When he had removed overcoat, coat, and vest he said, "God damn you, sir, you have got to fight me." Chapman evasively asked, "What authority, pray tell me, have you for cursing me so roundly?" Without answering, Lieutenant French called one of the soldiers and directed him to tie one of his hands behind him, saying, "Mr. Chapman, you are a one-armed man and I want to equalize things by using only one of my hands in the fight."

All this time Chapman, who had made no move toward preparing to fight, stepped closer to Lieutenant French and, barely touching him on the chest, said, "Lieutenant, although you are an officer of the United States army, you must get out of this house. We have had enough of this row." Then stepping to the door he opened it partly. One of the soldiers came over and forced it shut again. Lieutenant French, however, had concluded to depart but at the door paused and said with drunken swagger, "My name is Lieutenant French. I belong to the United States army. I am attached to the 9th Cavalry. I shall meet you again and we shall settle this difficulty." At this point Mrs. McSween fainted, and Chapman, pointing to her, said, "Look there at that lady; see what you have done. Now get out of here!" Lieutenant French looked around and, seeing Mrs. McSween's condition, remarked as he went to the door, "If I have caused all this, I'll go."

When Chapman went out a few minutes later to get the doctor for Mrs. McSween, he encountered Lieutenant French again in the street. He was halted with, "Who goes there?" and when he replied, "Chapman," Lieutenant French asked, "Where the hell are you going now?" When Chapman explained that he was after a doctor, Lieutenant French said, "Pass on. I'll meet you again. I am Lieutenant French of the United States army, Company 'M' of the 9th Cavalry." On his return from the doctor's office Chapman was again halted by this patrol but, on giving his name, he was allowed to go on without further abuse.[4]

ANOTHER DAY'S BRAWL

The next morning, however, the brawling between these two was continued. Chapman, who intended to act as John Copeland's lawyer, went down to the Montaño store to have a conference with him before the preliminary hearing, set for ten o'clock. Addressing one of the soldiers on guard outside of the building, Chapman asked him to inform the sheriff and Lieutenant French that he wanted to see their prisoner, as his attorney. Peppin came out and asked Chapman to step inside the building to wait until Copeland, who was in another room, could be brought where Chapman might talk with the man. When Copeland came, Chapman tried to draw him off into one corner so that their conversation could not be overheard, but Lieutenant French objected. Chapman claimed the privilege of an attorney with respect to his client but Lieutenant French said with a jeering echo of the row the night before, "God damn you, sir, get out of my house." Chapman merely answered, "All right, sir," and started toward the door. Lieutenant French came toward him threateningly, removing his coat and vest and beginning to incite a personal encounter. His "I'll whip you anyhow," implied that this time he would ignore the fact of Chapman's being one-armed. Chapman replied, with strong acrimony, "Don't you lay one of your fingers on me, sir." Lieutenant French shouted violently, "Get off these premises," and turning to some of the soldiers he ordered, "Pull him out."

The clashing shifted to the courthouse a little later. No words were exchanged by them during the hearing before Judge Wilson, but when it was over for the morning and they were outside the building, hostilities were renewed. Lieutenant French left the building first, but when he noticed Chapman had come out he turned and walked back toward him. The exchange of incivilities began with Lieutenant French hurling, "You are the God damnedest meanest man and scoundrel in the country, sir!" and accompanying it with sundry threats. Then he declared himself ready for a fight and willing to equalize matters by having one of his hands tied behind his back. Chapman was in no mood to fight, except with his tongue. "If you do not leave me alone," he

---

4. Details of this incident related to the author by Mrs. Susan McSween Barber, April, 1925.

said, "you will need more arms than the two you have to protect yourself. I do not wish to have any trouble and I advise you to keep away
from me."

Later in the day the two met again. Chapman had gone back in
the afternoon to the courtroom where John Copeland's hearing was to
be continued, when one of the soldiers on guard came up to him and
said he would like to speak to him. Seeing this, Lieutenant French
picked up his rifle and going over to where Chapman and this soldier
were standing thrust the weapon between them, saying, "I don't want
you to speak to any of my men." Chapman replied that he had not
sought the soldier but the soldier him. Lieutenant French reiterated,
"Damn you, I don't want any of my men to speak to you." Chapman
became sharp-tongued and answered, "Anyone that wants to can speak
to me; I am unable to prevent people from speaking with me when
they desire to do so." Judge Wilson interposed to prevent further
quarreling by directing the sheriff to keep order, and Peppin made
Lieutenant French sit down.

The sequel to this series of brawls and word fights was that Chapman swore out a warrant charging Lieutenant French with assault to
kill. The warrant was promptly sent to the Fort by a constable. Colonel
Dudley refused to turn the lieutenant over to the civil authorities but
did go so far as to put him under military arrest. He also sent Dr.
Appel down to Lincoln to investigate. When Dudley learned the particulars he changed his position and allowed the civil authorities to
handle the matter. The day of the preliminary hearing saw Lieutenant
French sent to Lincoln under guard of Lieutenant Dawson and all the
available men of Company "M." Squire Wilson, however, postponed
the case and Lieutenant French was taken back to the Fort. Shortly
the case was dropped altogether in view of the fact that the lieutenant
tendered a full apology to Chapman, putting the blame for his conduct
on his having been drinking.

Such an incident, however, would not pass into oblivion through
the device of an apology, especially in times so full of disturbance.
Chapman would cherish it as another instance of how the military were
riding roughshod over the McSween contingent. The military would
be unified in their feeling that Chapman was an obnoxious man. Lieutenant French had been the mouthpiece for the entire officer personnel
when he said to Chapman that he was the "meanest man and scoundrel
in the country." The officers had their partisans among some of the
roughs whose favor they sought. An inkling that the military wished
to be rid of Chapman was all that was needed. The young lawyer's situation was, to say the least, a perilous one.

38. Sheriff Peppin Gives Up in Despair

BESIDES THE BRAWLS between Chapman and Lieutenant French, December brought another significant contribution to Lincoln County troubles in the resignation of Peppin as sheriff. As his letter to Governor Wallace indicates, he quit in disgust. In all the five months since his appointment by Governor Axtell, so he said, he had not received as much as $5.00 of his salary nor did he hold much hope that the county's empty treasury would ever pay it. He had made considerable outlay of his own money in an occupation not only vain but hazardous. As a matter of fact, Peppin had been for some weeks a mere figurehead in the office. In the face of the hostility and the personal danger that had fallen upon him, he had been living at the Fort, afraid to go beyond its limits without a guard.

When Peppin's resignation became effective, Colonel Dudley promptly notified Captain Carroll and such others of his officers as were scattered about the county with detachments of soldiers and cautioned them about using any of Peppin's deputies, as their appointments were supposed to expire with the resignation of their chief.

With the approach of Christmas Lincoln grew more turbulent and disorderly. To some extent it was because of the season, but it was also because of the impending change in sheriffs. A group of the old McSween crowd, by some accounts headed by Billy the Kid, came down from Fort Sumner and took possession of the town so completely as to make those of the other factions, such as Dolan, Billy Mathews, and John Long, hurry to the protection of Fort Stanton. Young Edgar

Walz, now in charge of the Catron interests, likewise became alarmed and secured from Colonel Dudley a guard of soldiers for the old Dolan store, the ground for granting it being that Walz was virtually beef contractor to the Fort. So extremely was Lincoln now a hotbed of resentment toward the old Dolan group and all their sympathizers, especially the military, that Colonel Dudley, in recalling Captain Carroll from duty at Roswell, instructed him to return to Fort Stanton by some other route than through Lincoln, if possible; in case he must come through Lincoln, his men were not allowed to enter any house, store, or saloon in town.

Details of the re-occupation of Lincoln by the former McSween sympathizers seem almost lacking, yet it seems that Billy the Kid was under arrest for a time. Subsequently, that is, in March, 1879, when he was again under arrest, he is said to have penciled on the door a reference to the fact he had been there "incarcerated first time, December 22nd, 1878," but all the circumstances have faded away, even as to the jail-break that probably was the mode of his regaining liberty. The general insecurity of the Lincoln jail made it child's play for anyone to escape if he wished to. Whether the arrest had anything to do with the old warrants against Billy the Kid, or whether it was some newer, and minor infraction of law and good behavior, it is impossible to determine now.

The first half of January seems to have been a quiet time, but the latter part began to indicate new disorders. Chapman grew even more obsessed with the idea that he was called to be the protector of the people from the harsh treatment of the military. He became more zealous than ever to accomplish the arrest of Colonel Dudley on civil charges of arson and murder. Toward the end of the month he went to Santa Fe in order to get access, at military headquarters, to evidence which he needed. Colonel Hatch, however, refused to let him see any of the reports, orders, or affidavits from Colonel Dudley, unless the Secretary of War should so direct. Chapman then determined to go on to Washington; but before he could start on the trip he had to return to Lincoln to get certain evidence connected with the deaths of Tunstall and of McSween which he wished to carry along.

As Mrs. McSween's advisor in the settlement of the two estates she was administering, Chapman found himself involved in the affairs of the Tunstall estate. In this matter he showed the same virulent and intemperate characteristics that marked his hounding Colonel Dudley. While staying a short time at Las Vegas on his return from Santa Fe, Chapman wrote the following letter to Tunstall's father about the Tunstall interests in Lincoln County.

Las Vegas, N. M.
Feby. 10th, 1879

You will please pardon me for presuming so much upon an entire stranger, but as the subject of this letter is in regard to your interest as well as that of Mrs. McSween, I have taken the liberty of writing to you.

As attorney to Mrs. McSween I have had an occasion to make myself familiar with the business relations that existed between your son and Mr. McSween during their lifetime, and also as to the estate left by your son. I have been busily engaged during the last three months collecting evidence in regard to the murder of your son and McSween, and to the robbing of your son's store with a view to bringing guilty parties to trial, and I feel quite certain that I will be able to convict the men who committed the murders at the next term of court which will convene in April. Mrs. McSween had expended considerable money in collecting evidence and is very determined to have the murderer punished. I think that for a foul murder that of your son is without parallel, and the general public demand that his murderers should be punished.

I desire to call your attention to the estate of your son, that you may take such steps as will protect it. In company with Mrs. McSween I went to Lincoln County in November last for the purpose of probating her husband's will, and upon our arrival there we found that Mr. Widenmann's bondsmen had commenced proceedings to have the letters of administration granted to Robert A. Widenmann as administrator of your son's estate be revoked, and that Mr. Widenmann had given his bondsmen a mortgage on the whole estate in order to secure them, and that under this mortgage they were going to take charge of the estate. The mortgage that Mr. W. gave had no effect in law only as against yourself but not against creditors. After examining into matters I advised Mrs. McSween to take charge of your son's estate and had her appointed administratrix, believing this was the only way to protect your interest and those of Mrs. McSween as much of the property was owned jointly by your son and McSween.

I find that your son was owner of over 2,500 acres of land entered under the Desert Land Law, all of which is in the names of other men, and unless immediate steps are taken, all or most of this land will be lost. I think that Mr. Widenmann was derelict in his duty in not appointing some one to look after your son's estate in his absence. Several thousand dollars might have been saved to the estate had there been some one to look after the property. Under the laws of this country the administrator or administratrix had no control of the real estate unless a sale is ordered of the property. The charge and management of the real estate remain with the heirs and if you desire to have the title to the land claimed by your son perfected, you should send power of attorney to Mrs. A. A. McSween authorizing her to take charge of the land for you. I am certain that you could not entrust the management to a more competent and careful person, and one [who] was a true and devoted friend to your son. Mrs. McSween is so very popular in Lincoln County and can do more towards settling your son's estate than any other person. Your instruction will be strictly followed in the matter of your son's estate.

We have taken steps to have Dudley tried for the part he took in the murder of McSween and the robbing of your son's store, and I am confident of convicting him, which will make the Government responsible for the value of the goods taken from your son's store. It is necessary to convict Dudley and Peppin in order to make the Government responsible.

I also desire to call your attention to the circumstances in which are the men who fought for your son and done all in their power to avenge his murder. They have been indicted for the killing of some of the murderers of your son, and are without any means of defending themselves when the trial comes on. They were promised by both McSween and Widenmann that they should receive pay for hunting down the murderers of your son, but they do not ask any pay, but think that something should be done to assist them out of their present trouble, as it would be a vindication of your son. If you can do something for them, I think that they deserve it. They have requested me to write you and explain their situation, and you can take such action as you may think proper.

I shall leave here tomorrow for Lincoln and shall do all in my power to protect the estate of your son. I hope that you will not delay in answering this letter and advising Mrs. McSween what to do. Many fraudulent claims have been presented against the estate which we hope to defeat. The land (2,500 acres) owned by your son is very valuable, and if the title is perfected, which will require the payment of the remaining one dollar per acre to the government, will be worth at least $20,000 as it is the very best of agricultural land, and controls a large stock range.

Hoping to hear from you as soon as possible, I remain

Yours very truly,
H. I. Chapman

P.S. Address all letters to Lincoln

About the same time, Mrs. McSween was going ahead as administratrix, to recover what she could of the Tunstall cattle. For several months the herd had remained on the Rio Feliz ranch where they had played a part in the ill-fated attachment proceedings, but after the July fight at Lincoln, they had become part of the spoils of the Dolan crowd, especially the Seven Rivers section. A party of the latter had almost immediately gone over to the Feliz and taken possession of the cattle, easy enough with only "Dutch Martin" Martz and the cook, Gauss, to overcome. They had even forced Martz to accompany them to Seven Rivers and help drive the herd. During all this time Widenmann was nominally administrator of the Tunstall estate, but he fled the country — "Mr. Widenmann has left without giving anyone charge of anything," — as Isaac Ellis recounted in a letter to Tunstall's father.

Mrs. McSween, not daunted by the chaotic and indeed dangerous task confronting her as administratrix, had set about getting back what was left of the cattle. The herd was supposed to number 200 and be worth $2,500, a sizable addition to the assets of the Tunstall estate. In order to determine the whereabouts of the herd, she hired Charles D. Scase as detective. He succeeded in the risky business of going to Seven Rivers and learning that a large portion of the cattle was now in the possession of Robert Speakes. But as Speakes was a formidable outlaw, being prominent in the Selman crowd, Mrs. McSween could take no further steps about getting the cattle without high-powered aid. So in spite of her dislike for Colonel Dudley she had to appeal to him for help. She wrote that Speakes was on the verge of driving the cattle out of the country and likely would take them into Mexico.

Colonel Dudley, possibly suspecting some trap in this request from his arch-enemy and troublesome gadfly, met the situation adroitly. He replied that if Mrs. McSween would make out the necessary legal papers and secure from the sheriff a requisition for troops, he would then furnish a detachment to go after the cattle. In the meantime, he felt he was doing all he could when he forwarded the information about the cattle being driven into Mexico to the commanding officer at Fort Bliss, with a request that he take steps to prevent this. For good measure, Colonel Dudley wrote a certain person of his acquaintance with influence at the headquarters of the Texas Rangers and asked to enlist their help. Markedly different in content and tone was this letter from those Colonel Dudley had written about Mrs. McSween in November. For all his pompousness and self-esteem, Colonel Dudley was no fool, keeping his head to a greater degree than others at this time. He always managed to stay on the windward side of orders from Washington, and kept so carefully a record of all his activities since taking charge of Fort Stanton in April, that he did not exaggerate when he claimed to Governor Wallace that he could submit a completely documented account of all activities.

39. The Killing of Chapman

WHILE CHAPMAN WAS AWAY on the trip to Santa Fe, George Kimbrell qualified as sheriff to fill Peppin's unexpired term. Originally from Arkansas, he had been in Lincoln County for several years. During the disturbances, he had somehow managed to preserve nominal neutrality, although he served for a time as a deputy under Sheriff Peppin. Those who knew him, including near neighbors to his ranch on the Rio Hondo, thirty-five miles below Lincoln, predicted that he would be faithful to his duty as he saw it regardless of whose toes might be stepped on.

That Kimbrell intended to be active became evident in a short time. About the middle of February Billy the Kid and his crowd appeared in Lincoln and seemed disposed to "run the town." Kimbrell promptly invoked the assistance of Colonel Dudley, asserting that he could find but one man in Lincoln willing to help him make an arrest. The Kid had declared to the sheriff that if the warrant for his arrest was for murder he would not be taken alive. Kimbrell had slipped out of the Plaza and gone to the Fort for military aid.

Up at Santa Fe effort was renewed to bring to trial those under indictment for the killing of Tunstall. Catron as United States District Attorney, had been entirely lukewarm in the matter; his successor, Sidney M. Barnes, was prodded into action by letters from the Attorney General at Washington, reminding him that Judge Angel's investigation had fixed the responsibility upon W. S. Morton, Tom Hill, and Jesse Evans. In the meantime the first two met violent deaths, but since

Jesse Evans still remained alive, Barnes began to put forth a strong effort to have him arrested and tried. Evans, however, was a slippery customer, not easy to catch and harder to hold after being caught. For over a year he had gone in and out of Lincoln County as he pleased, even with an indictment hanging over him for a brutal murder.

The activities of the new sheriff and the United States District Attorney brought the ringleaders of the two factions to see the desirability of burying the hatchet. Probably they were all pretty well exhausted and ready to quit and close up the feud. Dolan and some of his old crowd happened to be in the vicinity of Lincoln just then engaged in delivering cattle to the Fort from the Seven Rivers section. Circumstances seemed to favor a "parley," and overtures were accordingly exchanged. Billy the Kid, it is said, took the initiative of sending to Jesse Evans a proposal that they either make peace or fight it out once and for all. Evans, after consulting Dolan, agreed to the idea of making peace and stated that three of his faction would be in Lincoln on the night of February 18 to meet a like number of the other faction and discuss the details of the truce.

The meeting was stormy at the start. The two most prominent, Billy the Kid and Jesse Evans, had to give vent to their animosities. The *Mesilla Independent* contained a glimpse of their skirmishing in the following passage:

> Evans thought it impossible to treat with such a man as the Kid, and informed that worthy individual that he would have to kill him then and there. Kid said they had met for the purpose of making peace and he did not care to open the negotiations with a fight; and after some further talk "peace" was declared. . . .
>
> The terms of peace . . . were made a document which in an interesting way reflects the times and the men who subscribed to it.
> I. That neither party would kill any member of the other party without first having given notice of having withdrawn from agreement.
> II. That all persons who had acted as "friends" were included in the agreement and were not to be molested.
> III. That no officer or soldiers were to be killed for any act previous to the date of this agreement.
> IV. That neither party should appear to give evidence against the other in any civil prosecution.
> V. That each party should give individual members of the other party every aid in their power to resist arrests upon civil warrants, and, if necessary, they would try to secure their release.
> VI. That if any member of either party failed to carry out this compact, which was sworn to by the respective leaders, then he should be killed at sight.

Behind this agreement were evidently various motives. The April term of district court was to be held a few weeks later. The new territorial officials were energetic and would likely become more so. Some of those in the two factions were really tired and willing to go ahead and stand their trials. Billy the Kid was believed to feel this way. But if the trials were to be undergone, it would be desirable that important witnesses take the stand with closed mouths. In the statement that "no officers or soldiers were to be killed for any act previous to the date of this agreement" there was a grim significance. The rumors, then, about sentence of death having been pronounced upon Colonel Dudley, Lieutenant Goodwin, Dr. Appel, and others among the officers, were not altogether groundless. Possibly the treaty of peace might merely be a blind, intended to throw people off their guard, while the factions, either jointly or separately, went on to new enterprises of lawlessness. Or possibly it was an effort to compromise Bill Bonney.

That treaties of this kind were flimsy enough the sequel showed. On the heels of the parley came a startling renewal of the old lawlessness. The shocking murder in the street of Lincoln of Mrs. McSween's lawyer, Chapman, with the ink scarcely dry on the treaty of peace, had the earmarks of intrigue and desire for revenge that had been exhibited in the Tunstall killing precisely a year before.

Chapman, accompanied by Juan Patrón, had just returned to Lincoln from Las Vegas, where he had stopped for a while on his return from Santa Fe. The weather was bitterly cold, and he was almost half-frozen when he arrived in the early evening. He had first dropped in at Mrs. McSween's in order to get warm and make a report on his trip. Although he had been rebuffed by the military authorities in his attempt to get Colonel Dudley's reports, he was much elated over having secured from Governor Wallace a definite promise to be down at Lincoln soon. This, he told Mrs. McSween, would certainly mean that the governor would move to see that justice was done. A little later Chapman left to go to his sleeping room in the Tunstall store building.

Scarcely had he gotten into the street when he met a group of the high-contracting parties of the peace conference — Dolan, Jesse Evans, and Bill Campbell, of one faction, and Billy the Kid, Tom O'Folliard, and José Salazar of the other — with additions gathered up for the celebration, including Billy Mathews, George Van Sickle, G. S. Redman, Edgar Walz, and possibly one or two more. Grand handshaking was indulged in, drinks had been quaffed by several members of the party, and then the group had gone the rounds of the town. They had made a call at the house of Juan Patrón. This visit proved too much a strain for Bill Campbell, a new face in the Dolan group, but easily the peer of the worst in either faction. Scarcely had the party entered the house than Campbell drew his pistol on Patrón. All that saved Juan was that he jumped behind others. It did not augur well the endurance of the treaty of peace that within an hour of its consummation, a member of the Dolan faction was trying to kill a prominent member of the McSween crowd.

As the group was leaving Patrón's they encountered Chapman. The night was so dark that at first he was not recognized, Campbell asking who it was. "My name is Chapman" came the curt reply. Campbell immediately drew his pistol and punched it against Chapman's breast, saying, "You are the contemptible cur that has come in here and stirred up trouble. But we've settled it all now, and we are going to be friends. Now, just to show you are peaceable too, you've got to dance." Chapman replied that he did not propose to dance for a drunken crowd, and in an effort to ascertain who were surrounding him, asked one of them, "Am I talking to Mr. Dolan?" "No," replied Jesse Evans, "but you are talking to damn good friends of his." The exchange of remarks grew more sarcastic and acrimonious, until two shots were fired. Dolan, it was afterwards admitted, fired the first one; Campbell fired a second later, and Chapman fell, exclaiming "My God, I am killed."

In the March 5 issue of *Thirty Four*, the weekly paper published at Las Cruces, appeared an article dated at Fort Stanton, February 23, and signed simply "Max," which gave a reasonably authentic version of the killing. It related that the leaders of the two parties...

agreed to bury the hatchet. They promenaded the streets of Lincoln arm in arm and had a regular good time. Early that evening Chapman arrived from Las Vegas and put his horses in Mrs. McSween's corral. Then he went to a neighbor's to get some bread to make a poultice for his face. He was suffering from a severe case of neuralgia. He was returning about ten o'clock and met Dolan, Jesse Evans, and Billy Campbell with Billy Bonny (the "Kid") and Tom O'Folliard of the McSween party. Dolan and his party had insisted on their accompanying them and they consented to do so rather than show any unfriendliness.

When they met, one of the Dolan party asked, "Who are you and where are you going?" Chapman answered and told them he was attending to his business. He was told to talk differently or they would make him. He answered, raising a bandage from his face, "You can not scare me, boys. I know you and its no use. You have tried that before." "Then," said Campbelll, "I'll settle you," and fired his pistol, the ball going in at the breast and coming out at the back. As he fell, Dolan shot him with his Winchester. They then set fire to his body. It is thought they soaked his clothes with whiskey to make them burn.

When they first met, "Kid," tried to get away and ran around an angle of the lane wall, but Evans held the other fast and made him look on during the whole affair. Next day a coroner's jury was held but the Dolan party was in town armed and the people were so bulldozed no evidence could be brought out.

These are the facts as near as I can get them, but no one dares to speak of them except in whispers. If it was known I was writing you, my life would not be worth insuring two hours, and I don't think you will be safe to publish this letter. I want to get away as soon as possible and don't want any Lincoln County in mine.

P.S. Chapman was unarmed. He never carried arms.

The correspondent of *Thirty-Four* makes it plain that Billy the Kid and his associates were not implicated in the Chapman killing. In fact they had tried to keep out of possible trouble by withdrawing from the celebration but had been forced to go along. At the beginning of the encounter with Chapman, Billy the Kid sensed a killing and tried to slip away, but Jesse Evans seized hold of him and forced him to remain. This reluctance to be involved in any revival of shooting scrapes must be taken as evidence of the Kid's sincerity in the formulation of the peace conference that had a short while before adjournd.

The killing occurred about nine or ten o'clock at night, but so stolidly did Lincoln take such things that the body was lying in the street when the sun rose the next day. Sheriff Kimbrell had done nothing except send word to Fort Stanton for a detachment of soldiers. Colonel Dudley, realizing immediately that this killing might usher in a violent return of old disorders, sent twenty men under Lieutenant Dawson and included Acting Assistant Surgeon W. B. Lyons, one of the post surgeons. He charged Dawson to make a thorough investigation, for he understood well enough that gossip would link this killing with Chapman's intemperate remarks and activities concerning the military.

Chapman's body lay in the street for more than twenty-four hours, until the arrival of the soldiers at 11:30 Wednesday night, when it was taken to a room in the courthouse for examination by Dr. Lyons. The body was badly burned but whether this came from a shot at such close range that the powder-flash had ignited the clothing or whether it came from someone's having deliberately set fire to the clothing afterwards he could not determine. Many in Lincoln felt that the latter was the most plausible inference; setting the clothing on fire would destroy any letters or papers Chapman's pockets might contain incriminating to those in opposition to him. Others held a slightly different view. Mrs. McSween declared that Chapman had her watch and a valuable chain, a gift from John Chisum, which she had asked the attorney to bring from the bank at Santa Fe, where she had deposited them for safe keeping. At her insistence a careful examination of Chapman's body was made by Judge Wilson in the presence of Lieutenant Dawson and Dr. Lyon, but the investigation failed to disclose the articles.

Gossip-mongers soon clacked their tongues in an effort to lay responsibility for the Chapman killing upon the military. Campbell was said to have remarked as he walked away from the scene of the killing, "I promised my God and Colonel Dudley that I would kill Chapman, and I have done it." The next day, moreover, Campbell and Jesse Evans had gone up with Dolan to the Fort and held a long interview with Colonel Dudley, although that may have been only to get aid and advice. Chapman had been loudly affirming for weeks that he was about to expose the conduct of Dudley and his fellow-officers. The shooting had been done by persons consistently shielded and protected by Fort Stanton. Wagging tongues would make a deduction from this.

A second detachment from the 9th Cavalry, under Lieutenant Millard F. Goodwin, hurried to Lincoln and bustled about the village with Sheriff Kimbrell. Although the citizens were reminded of what had developed after the arrival of the soldiers on the nineteenth of the previous July, this time they seemed inclined to view the soldiers as saviours. Even Mrs. McSween came forward and offered the Tunstall store as a billeting place if needed. As soon as the burial of Chapman was over, a number of residents sent an invitation to Colonel Dudley to come down as the guest of the town. For some time he had been avoiding Lincoln because of evident ill-feeling toward him, as well as threats made by Billy the Kid's crowd. At the invitation, however, his aloofness melted and he went down to the mass meeting. It was nearly the same sort of love-feast between the citizens and the military as that held the preceding April 24, when the town had been in a jubilee over the discomfiture of the Dolan side in the court battles of that session of district court.

At the meeting a formal request was made of Dudley that the detachment of soldiers be continued at Lincoln. The signatures on the document included John B. Wilson, Ben H. Ellis, Sam R. Corbet, Juan B. Patrón, José Montaño, D. H. Gurney, Esteban Chávez, Bonifacio Baca, Saturnino Baca, Dave H. Easton, T. A. Tomlinson, W. H. Wilson, E. A. Walz, A. J. Ballard, Sydney Wilson, John N. Copeland, Lee Kayser, George Kimbrell, G. S. Redman, Sue E. McSween, Santiago Mes y Trujillo, Francisco Romero y Valencia, and Anton José García. As a further gesture plans were made for a ball in Lincoln on March 4, to which Dudley and all the other officers of the Fort were invited by formal resolution.

DUDLEY ADDRESSES THE CROWD

At the mass meeting Colonel Dudley made an address which was well received. After telling of the hopes he had at first about using his soldiers in behalf of law and order, he put the blame for his failure upon legislation in Congress the preceding June which confined their use to a very limited set of violations of the law. Now, he was glad to say, orders had become so relaxed that he could use troops much more freely, and he pledged himself to use them for suppressing lawlessness wherever it might lift its head. His speech closed with compliments on the spirit of the meeting and congratulations on an evident determination to shake hands over the bloody chasm that had rent Lincoln County. Dudley had risen adequately to the demands of the occasion, although secretly he must have suspected that the people of Lincoln might show the same volatility as the spring before. He must have recalled that the McSween faction, which included the great majority of the town, had then lavished compliments which had endured only as long as he used his soldiers in attempts to arrest members of the Dolan faction. Compliments had changed to curses when a few weeks later he put his soldiers to making arrests among the McSween adherents.

In the latter part of February Mrs. McSween recovered the Tunstall cattle, some 138 head, hardly more than half the expected number. Colonel Dudley had finally instructed Captain Carroll, who was stationed at Roswell, to send some of his men to Seven Rivers to get the cattle from Speakes. When the cattle had been brought to Roswell, Mrs. McSween sent Sam Smith down to identify them, but Carroll, under instructions from Dudley, would not let the cattle pass into Mrs. McSween's hands. The position taken by Dudley was that all cattle about the ownership of which there was dispute involving possible legal tangles should be turned over to the sheriff. As Mrs. McSween was determined not to let Sheriff Kimbrell get his hands on the cattle, she endeavored to get Dudley to consent to turning them over to Judge Wilson, the justice of the peace, or to one of the constables appointed by him. Her tactics were a reminder of the artful legal moves her husband had used a year before when attempting to circumvent the lethargy of Sheriff Brady about arresting those implicated in the murder of Tunstall. Dudley turned down Mrs. McSween's proposal, giving as his reason the fact that constables were not bonded officers as were sheriffs.

Seeing no other way open, Mrs. McSween let Kimbrell bring

the cattle from Roswell to Lincoln. Afterwards they were taken to Brewer's ranch and from there moved to Copeland's ranch, where Sam Smith looked after them until Mrs. McSween could sell them in connection with her settling of the Tunstall estate. She ultimately disposed of them to Lee Kayser for approximately $1,000. The sum, however, added little to the assets of the Tunstall estate since the expense of getting the cattle out of the hands of the thieves and having them looked after until the sale about equaled the amount received.

While serving Mrs. McSween, Charlie Scase had an exciting adventure in Lincoln with some of the desperadoes in whose hands the cattle were. Details of the encounter are not now procurable, but the affair was so critical that Scase, realizing the hopelessness of a fight against them, fled to Fort Stanton and sought sanctuary there. Colonel Dudley grudgingly harbored him for a time but offered him only accommodations in the barracks with Negro cavalrymen. This was too much for Scase's race prejudice and he left the Fort after nightfall to hunt a refuge elsewhere. The episode proved embarrassing to Dudley because his enemies immediately shouted that he had been partisan and had refused protection to Mrs. McSween's representative.

40. Wallace's Clean-up

THE CHAPMAN MURDER BROUGHT Governor Wallace to Lincoln County on March 5, expecting to make a complete investigation which would be followed by the drastic clean-up that his findings would make imperative. When the Governor got there, his eyes were opened indeed. He was amazed that in the two weeks since Chapman had been murdered not an arrest had been made, although the persons implicated were generally known and at least three — Jesse Evans, Billy Mathews, and Bill Campbell — were then staying only a day's ride from Lincoln at the old Murphy Fairview ranch. Important witnesses like Billy the Kid were still around, but no steps had been taken to insure their remaining within call. The entire scheme of legal measures seemed at a standstill in connection with the Chapman killing.

The first step by Governor Wallace was to have arrests made. He tried civil means, but nobody was willing to come forward and make the necessary affidavits. All whom he approached, almost with one voice, declined, alleging that to do so would endanger their lives. When pressed for an explanation, they became dumb. When promised a positive protection from the military, they shrugged their shoulders and replied that they had no confidence in the military since Colonel Dudley, who seemed hand-in-glove with the men accused of killing Chapman, would assist and protect the culprits in preference to the citizens.

Finding himself thus balked in starting the civil machinery, Governor Wallace decided to cut all red tape and to make the arrests through the military without formality of warrants. Accordingly, he wrote Colonel Hatch asking him to instruct Colonel Dudley to make the arrests. A day or so later he wrote Hatch another letter in which he made a categorical request for the removal of Dudley. Evidently in the interval Wallace had become completely convinced of Colonel Dudley's active part in the troubles. Charges against Dudley were rife, going back to the killing of McSween and becoming especially abundant in connection with the murder of Chapman. "I beg to say distinctly that I make you the statements as information came to me in a manner to make the giving of the statement and the request which precedes it, a matter of official duty." Such was Wallace's apology for writing of these matters.

The methods of Governor Wallace were a marked contrast to those adopted by Governor Axtell in March of the preceding year. Where Axtell had stayed at Fort Stanton, Wallace made the Montaño store in Lincoln his headquarters. Where Axtell had simply attended to what the inner circle of the Dolan crowd had to communicate, Wallace listened to a mass meeting. The courthouse was again packed with the adult population, perhaps seventy-five or a hundred. The Governor appealed for all who had any knowledge of the accumulated crimes and misdemeanors to come to him with their information. He also made public announcement that he had just requested the removal of Colonel Dudley and believed that this was the most important step possible toward settling the troubles of Lincoln County. Rounds of applause at this statement showed that the people concurred with the Governor's views.

After the meeting the Governor conferred privately with fifteen or twenty of the most prominent men in his room at the Montaño store. From practically all came the same story — dread of Dudley's displeasure and its manifestation through some misuse of his military authority. No one asserted fear of direct violence to person or property; they rather looked for some form of minor injury or detriment which would be distressing or disastrous. The testimony was so unanimous that Wallace was strengthened in his belief that his demand for Dudley's removal was the right course.

THE GOVERNOR'S DRAGNET

Why should he, the Governor, wait longer in the matter? Did he not have the authority to take the reins in his own hands and virtually supersede Colonel Dudley? Having made up his mind that he should become the dictator, Wallace threw out a dragnet for all persons in Lincoln County who had hanging over them charges for murder or cattle stealing, great or small. He furnished Captain Carroll, who had been given command at Fort Stanton for the time being, a list of thirty-six who were to be arrested, if possible, and impounded at the Fort. The list was almost a muster roll of the principals in the feud, reinforced by others who had become prominent in the subsequent lawlessness. Warrants, old and new, were outstanding for all on the list, but no sheriff or deputy had ever done much toward serving them. The list ran as follows: John Slaughter, Andy Boyle, John Selman, Tom Selman, Gus Gildea, James Irwin, Reese Gobles, "Rustling Bob," Robert Speakes, "the Pilgrim," John Beckwith, Jim French, Joe (Doc) Scurlock, "the Kid" (William Bonney), Tom O'Folliard, Charles Bowdre, Henry Brown, John Middleton, Fred Waite, J. B. (Billy) Mathews, Jesse Evans, James J. Dolan, George Davis, Frank Rivers (alias A. L. Mont, known also as John Long), Eugenio Salazar, John Jones, James Jones, William Jones, Marion Turner, Caleb Hall (or Sam Collins), Heiskell Jones, Buck Powell, James Highsaw, Jacob Owens, Frank Wheeler, and Joseph Hall (alias Olney).

In the meantime the Governor also gave special attention to the arrest of those connected with the killing of Chapman, whether as principals, accessories, or witnesses. First taken into custody were Jesse Evans, Billy Mathews, and Bill Campbell, all of whom had been found at Fairview, the old Murphy ranch. Not wishing to run any chance of losing such important prisoners — for, with the exception of Campbell, they were wanted also for the killing of Tunstall — Governor Wallace decided upon a greater rigor of confinement than hitherto. They were held incommunicado except for their attorney, Sidney Wilson of Lincoln. Not fully satisfied by even such drastic measures, Wallace started correspondence with Major Whittemore, commanding officer at Fort Union, for the transfer of these three important prisoners to that post, the most important in the District of New Mexico, where there was less chance of their escaping. The pity of it is that the plan was never carried out. On the night of March 19 Evans and Campbell escaped from the Post accompanied by a soldier known as Texas Jack, who had been held in the guardhouse charged with desertion. About three weeks later a scouting party from the Fort came across the trio in the vicinity of Dowlin's Mill but were able to capture only Texas Jack. Jesse Evans and Campbell abandoned their horses and took to the mountains.

The arrest of Dolan was an easy matter, for he had placed himself under Colonel Dudley's wing immediately after the killing of Chapman. But when Wallace discovered that Dolan was leaving the Post at will to visit Lincoln, he decided that close confinement would be the better policy and sent Captain Carroll the following peremptory note:

J. J. Dolan was down here [Lincoln] tonight. Please arrest him on his return to the Fort, and put him in close confinement for the murder of H. I. Chapman.

Such a step brought Dolan to a realization that his being a prisoner was no *pro forma* matter and he resorted to his old device of writing to the papers. The publication of such an account of the Chapman affair as that contained in the letter of "Max," published in the Las Cruces *Thirty-Four*, prompted the following letter:

Fort Stanton, N. M.
March 12, 1879

Editors *Thirty-Four*,
   Las Cruces, N. M.
Gentlemen:

In your issue of the 5th inst. is contained an article signed "Max" making very serious charges against me which is maliciously false, and I ask you to do the kindness to publish a card in your columns requesting my friends to not notice the statement until the matter is properly investigated by the courts, and the result made known. By attending to this matter you will confer on me a great favor and [it] will be appreciated. Please send me a copy of your paper with the bill, and I will remit on receipt of the same.

Very respectfully,
Yr obt servt,
Jas J. Dolan

At the same time he wrote to the Santa Fe *New Mexican* a similar request:

A CARD

Fort Stanton, March 12, 1879

Editors, *New Mexican:*
   Gentlemen:

In the last issue of the *Independent*, *Thirty-Four*, and other public journals of the Territory are published very serious charges against me. I would ask my friends to refrain from judging me until such time as the matter is thoroughly investigated by the courts.

Very respectfully yours,
Jas. J. Dolan

The Las Cruces paper, however, did not publish a card as requested but indulged in editorial comment displeasing to Dolan. In

the same issue of *Thirty-Four* there was printed the following, written
to some private person:

Fort Stanton, N. M.
March 8, 1879

My dear ——————,

There are some outrageous lies published in the *Independent*
and *Thirty-four* in regard to the killing of Chapman which if continued will create a worse disturbance than ever. It is true, us
meeting the recognized leaders of the McSween party and agreeing to stop matters in relation to the past, leaving all to be settled
by the courts. This meeting was not our wish alone, but of many
prominent citizens who urged the meeting and compromise. In
regard to my shooting the man, it is false in every particular, in
the first place I had no Winchester carbine with me, and in the
next place, I never thought of anything else but making peace
and preventing trouble — the object of my visit to the plaza was
none other. This I expect to prove to the satisfaction of all. True
I was the party accused. Hoping that you will make public this
statement, I remain,

Yours respectfully
Jas. J. Dolan

The hollowness of this protest so impressed the editors of *Thirty-
four* that they indulged in editorial comment upon it. They voiced a
wish that Dolan had been more explicit since people would reject his
flat denial. They felt that Dolan's denial was weak and noted the fact
that his friends in Lincoln had remained silent. They extended the cour-
tesies of *Thirty-four* if he wished to make a statement of facts and
reminded him that evidence was necessary if he would clear himself.
Dolan replied that his request for the publication of a card had been
ignored by *Thirty-four*. To this piece of grumbling the editors in the
issue for April 9 explained that they did not publish the card because
they did not wish to assume responsibility for the wording of it. They
went on to exhibit Dolan's contradictory statements about details of
the Chapman affair. The ending to the editorial was the significant
sentence, "Dolan prejudices his case every time he appears in print."

During his visit to Lincoln, Governor Wallace had heard much
about Billy the Kid, who had become the most conspicuous member of
the old Regulator group now that several were dead and others had
turned their backs on Lincoln County. If Dick Brewer or Frank Macnab
had lived, or if Jim French or John Middleton or Fred Waite, or pos-

sibly the Coes, had remained in Lincoln County, the Kid might not
have become so prominent. When Wallace learned that he had been
present when Chapman was killed, he decided that he must be arrested.
On March 6 he had sent a note to the military authorities stating what
he had learned about Billy the Kid's recent movements and urging his
arrest forthwith:

> I have just ascertained that the Kid is at a place called Las
> Tablas, a plazita up near Coghlin's ranch. He has with him Tom
> O'Folliard, and was going out of the territory, but stopped there
> to rest his horses, saying he would stay a few days. He is at the
> house of one Eugenio Salazar.
>
> You will oblige me by sending a detachment after the two
> men; and if they are caught, send them on to Fort Stanton for
> trial as accessories to the murder of Chapman.
>
> If the men are found to have left Las Tablas, I beg they may
> be pursued until caught.

Some inkling of the hunt must have reached Billy the Kid, for he
moved to put himself in a better position by sending Governor Wallace
the following letter, which though undated, must have been written
the twelfth or thirteenth of March.

To his Excellency the Governor,
Gen. Lew Wallace

Dear Sir:

> I have heard that you will give one thousand ($) for my body,
> which as I can understand it, means alive as a witness. I know it
> is as a witness against those that murdered Mr. Chapman. If it
> was so I could appear at court, I could give the desired informa-
> tion, but I have indictments against me for things that happened
> in the late Lincoln County War and am afraid to give myself up
> because my enemies would kill me. The day Mr. Chapman was
> murdered I was in Lincoln at the request of good citizens to meet
> Mr. J. J. Dolan, to meet as a friend so as to be able to lay aside
> our arms and go to work. I was present when Mr. Chapman was
> murdered and know who did it, and if it were not for those indict-
> ments I would have made it clear before now. If it is in your
> power to annul those indictments, I hope you will do so as to give
> me a chance to explain. Please send me an answer telling me what
> you can do. You can send answer by bearer. I have no wish to
> fight any more, indeed I have not raised an arm since your procla-
> mation. As to my character, I refer to any of the citizens, for the
> majority of them are my friends and have been helping me all

they could. I am called Kid Antrim, but Antrim was my step-father's name.

Waiting an answer I remain,
Your obedient servant,
W. H. BONNEY

Governor Wallace immediately proposed a secret conference in the following letter:

(Saturday)
Lincoln, March 15, 1879

W. H. Bonney,

Come to the house of old Squire Wilson (not the lawyer) at nine (9) o'clock next Monday night alone. I don't mean his office, but his residence. Follow along the foot of the mountains south of the town, come in on that side, and knock at the east door. I have authority to exempt you from prosecution if you will testify to what you say you know.

The object of the meeting at Squire Wilson's is to arrange the matter in a way to make your life safe. To do that the utmost secrecy is to be used. *So come alone.* Don't tell anybody — not a living soul — where you are coming or the object. If you could trust Jesse Evans, you can trust me.

Lew Wallace

How these two, the governor of the territory and a beardless outlaw not yet twenty, met and discussed the proposal Billy the Kid had made was told by Governor Wallace several years later in a newspaper interview.

Billy the Kid kept the appointment punctually. At the time designated, I heard a knock at the door, and I called out, "Come in." The door opened somewhat slowly and carefully, and there stood the young fellow generally known as the Kid, his Winchester in his right hand, his revolver in his left.

"I was sent for to meet the governor here at 9 o'clock," said the Kid. "Is he here?" I rose to my feet, saying, "I am Governor Wallace," and held out my hand. When we had shaken hands, I invited the young fellow to be seated so that we might talk together. "Your note gave promise of absolute protection," said the young outlaw warily. "Yes," I replied, "and I have been true to my promise," and then pointing to Squire Wilson, who was the only person in the room with me, I added, "This man, whom of course you know, and I are the only persons in the house."

This seemed to satisfy the Kid, for he lowered his rifle and returned his revolver to its holster. When he had taken his seat,

I proceeded to unfold the plan I had in mind to enable him to testify to what he knew about the killing of Chapman at the forthcoming session of court two or three weeks later without endangering his life. I closed with the promise, "In return for your doing this, I will let you go scot free with a pardon in your pocket for all your misdeeds."

When I had finished, the Kid talked over the details of this plan for his fake arrest with a good deal of zest. He even ventured the suggestion that he should be kept hand-cuffed during his confinement in order to give a *bona-fide* coloring to the whole proceeding. He did not commit himself definitely to the proposal, but promised to write me in a few days what his decision was.

Five days later Governor Wallace received a favorable answer in the following note, which outlined the scheme to be followed in a pseudo-arrest.

> San Patricio,
> Lincoln County,
> Thursday, (March) 20th, 1879

General Wallace,
  Sir,

I will keep the appointment I made, but be sure and have men come that you can depend on. I am not afraid to die like a man fighting but I would not like to die like a dog unarmed. Tell Kimbrell to let his men be placed around the house and for him to come in alone; and he can arrest us (that is, me and Tom O'Folliard). All I am afraid of is that in the Fort we might be poisoned or killed through a window at night, but you can arrange that all right. Tell the commanding officer to watch Lieut. Goodwin (he would not hesitate to do anything). There will be danger on the road of somebody waylaying us to kill us on the way to the Fort. You will never catch those fellows on the road. Watch Fritz's, Captain Baca's ranch, and the Brewery. They will either go to Seven Rivers or the Jacarilla Mountains. They will stay around close until the scouting parties come in. Give a spy a pair of glasses and let him get on the mountain back of Fritz's and watch, and if they are there, there will be provisions carried to them. It is not my place to advise you, but I am anxious to have them caught, and perhaps know how men hide from soldiers better than you do. Excuse me for having so much to say and I stil' remain,

> Yours truly,
> W. H. Bonney

P. S. I have changed my mind. Send Kimbrell to Gutiérrez's just below San Patricio, one mile, because Sanger and Ballard are, or were, great friends of Campbell's. Ballard told me yesterday to leave, for you were doing everything to catch us. It was a blind to get me to leave. Tell Kimbrell not to come before 3 o'clock, for I may not be there before.

The details of this voluntary arrest are lost now but presumably Kimbrell consummated it as the Kid had expertly outlined it. A note from Wallace to Purington, upon whom the command of the Fort had again developed, established the fact that Billy the Kid and his side-kick, Tom O'Folliard, a young Texan but recently come into Lincoln County and without as yet much, if any, record of crime, were in the toils of the law, nominally at least:

Lincoln, N.M., March 21, 1879

Colonel G. A. Purington,
   Cmd'g Fort Stanton,
Sir:

Sheriff Kimbrell and a posse of citizens have just come in with the Kid and Tom O'Folliard, captured about a mile below San Patricio. I will keep them under guard for a couple of days; then send them to the Fort.

Respectfully,
Lew Wallace
Governor of New Mexico

In making this arrest Governor Wallace had brought forward a local militia he had organized. One of the drawbacks to law enforcement was the lack of territorial militia. To remedy this partly, Governor Wallace organized a company composed of men in and around Lincoln. This was probably the "posse of citizens" mentioned in the note to Captain Purington, which had taken the designation "Lincoln County Mounted Rifles" but was called derisively, especially by those who disapproved, "the Governor's Heel-flies."

Under the captaincy of Juan B. Patrón, the so-called militia or police force was active in Lincoln County for several months, its membership being civic-minded enough to serve without compensation and provide their own horses, guns, and ammunition, pending the legislature's later voting an appropriation to cover future salaries and expenses. The roll that Governor Wallace finally submitted to the legislature showed that in this company both Mexican and American elements stood shoulder to shoulder in the cause of law and order.

Another interesting revelation is that a large number, possibly the majority, had been adherents of the McSween cause.[5]

Billy the Kid might naturally expect mild and even generous guarding at the hands of these men, many of whom where friends as well as former companions-in-arms. He was much taken aback when he discovered that he was to be kept in the dungeon which served as Lincoln's jail. His protest at repeating the experience with a cell in that jail was given in Pat Garrett's AUTHENTIC LIFE OF BILLY THE KID in the following passage:

> In the twenty-first of March, 1879, Longworth received orders to place the two prisoners in the jail — a horribly dismal hole, unfit for a dog kennel. The Kid said, "Tom, I've sworn I would never go inside that hole again alive."
>
> "I don't see," said Tom, "how either you or I can help it. I don't want to put you there — I don't want to put anyone there. But that's orders and I have nothing to do but obey. You don't want to make trouble for me?"
>
> The Kid walked gloomily up to the jail door and before going in stopped, saying to Longworth, "Tom, I am going in here because I won't have any trouble with you, but I'd give all I've got if the son of a b—— that gave the order was in your boots."
>
> He passed into the hall and had his cell pointed out to him. The door of unpainted pine was standing open, and taking a pencil from his pocket he wrote on it:
>
> William Bonney was incarcerated here first time, December 22nd, 1878; second time, March 21st, 1879, and hope I never will be again.
>
> W. H. Bonney[6]

---

5. Juan B. Patrón (captain), Ben H. Ellis, Martín Sánchez, Camilo Núñez, Elías Grey, Ramón Montoyo, Estalano Sánchez, Trinidad Vigil, Fernando Herrera, Jesús Rodríguez, Juan Pedro Torres, Martín Chávez, Renaldo Frésquez, Florencio Chávez, José Chávez y Chávez, Maximiliano Chávez, Gregorio Girón, T. S. Longworth, Eugenio Maldonado, Pablo Miranda, Manuel Martín, Santiago Mes, Martín Montoyo, Zenón Mora, Trinidad Romero, Manuel Romero, Crescencio Sánchez, José María Sánchez, Esequio Sánchez, Frenio Sánchez y Gonzales, Apolonio Sedillo, Eugenio Salazar, José Salazar, Frenio Sedillo, J. C. Wilkins, George Washington, Alex Rudder, and Ramón Vigil.

6. Obviously Ash Upson was not familiar with the jail at Lincoln when he wrote this part of the book for Garrett. As described by Gregorio Wilson, who as a boy had lived on the other side of the road from the *cárcel*, and also as depicted in construction drawings later discovered by J. W. Hendron, originally there were no cells and no hall in the single room which was actually a deep cellar, its roof supported by a low adobe wall extending a few feet above ground level. The only access was by means of a ladder which could be lowered through a small door in this wall.

The escape of Evans and Campbell on March 19 must have chagrined Governor Wallace and led to stricter confinement for Billy the Kid than had been first intended. However, in a short time he was transferred to the Patrón store where he had the privileges of a star prisoner, if there is truth in the account that Pat Garrett's book gives:

They [Billy the Kid and Tom O'Folliard] were guarded by Deputy Sheriff T. B. Longworth, to whom the Kid had pledged his word that he would make no attempt to escape. Longworth knew him well and trusted him. The Kid and O'Folliard did not betray this trust until they were again placed in jail.

At the house [i.e. store] of Patrón, they led a gay life with plenty to eat and drink, the best of cigars, and a game of poker with any one, friend or stranger, who chanced to visit them. The Kid was cheerful and seemingly contented. His hand was small and his wrists large; so it was difficult to keep a pair of handcuffs on him. When a friend entered, he would advance, slip his hand from the irons, stretch it out to shake hands, and remark jokingly, "I don't want to disgrace you, sir," or "You don't get a chance to steal my jewelry, old fellow."

Governor Wallace himself came down to see Billy and gained not only better acquaintance but a disclosure of the young fellow's secret of success in shooting. The Governor later exposed it to the newspaper man who wrote in the interview already mentioned:

I did not require that the Kid and his companion be kept under strict confinement, and was entirely willing for him to have a good many privileges. I went down one day to see him, and having some curiosity to know whether the stories I had heard about his marksmanship were true, I asked him to give me some exhibition of his skill. After he had shown me what he could do — and it was remarkably good shooting with both the rifle and the revolver — I complimented him and coupled with my praise the questions, "Billy, isn't there some trick in your shooting? How do you do it?"

"Well, General," he replied, "there is a trick to it. When I was a boy, I noticed that a man in pointing to anything he wished to observe, used his index finger. With long use the man unconsciously learned to point with exact aim. I decided to follow suit with my shooting. When I lift my revolver, I ask myself, 'Point with your finger' and unconsciously, it makes the aim certain. There is no failure. I pull the trigger and the bullet goes true to its mark. That's the trick, I suppose, to my shooting."

The results of his visit to Lincoln must have given Governor Wallace satisfaction. If nothing more had been gained than the removal of

Colonel Dudley, the trip was worthwhile. Dudley, however, remained at the Fort for two weeks awaiting orders. His presence was a source of concern and Governor Wallace breathed with relief when Dudley left for Fort Union on March 21, the same date as the arrest of the Kid. If the plan the Governor hoped to put through with the cooperation of the young outlaw went along smoothly, he might soon have another feather to wear in his cap because of the conviction of one or two more of the prominent mischief-makers, especially on the Dolan side. Little did it matter to him that exception was taken to his procedures. A typical comment was that sent to the Mesilla *Independent* by some correspondent at Fort Stanton:

> The troops of this post are nearly tired out; not a day passes but two or three squads are following some deputy of Governor Wallace in making *ex-parte* arrests; the boys don't like this business, and wonder when it will cease. The guardhouse here is a "Bastille" crowded with civil prisoners.
>
> The governor is no doubt correct in doing his duty to abate lawlessness in Lincoln County, but as martial law has not been declared, soldiers — both officers and enlisted men — dislike this thankless duty which gains them enemies in the Democratic Congress.

Although some of the soldiers at Ft. Stanton and the entrenched politicians at Santa Fe may have been unhappy, one fact remains: at long last the first step had been taken in a program which gave promise of firmly establishing law and order in troubled Lincoln County.

PART V

Sparks Are Extinguished

41. Spring Term of Court, 1879

On Monday, April 14, 1879, district court again convened in Lincoln after the lapse of a year. The fall term, ordinarily held in October, had been pretermitted on account of the general confusion. With no court in the tumultuous twelve months intervening, Judge Bristol had a heavy docket, but evidently he was now in a different attitude. His grand jury charge was mild in comparison to the denunciation of McSween delivered a year before. Now he contented himself with a simple review of the troubled state of the county as background for a plea to give the court every aid possible in apprehending wrongdoers. Salting the whole, however, was some moralizing on the futility of violence and lawnessness, of which the following is a sample:

> From the character of the public disturbances in the county one would be led to suppose that the people had abandoned all idea of having their differences settled and their wrongs redressed through the courts, but had resorted to violence for this purpose. Now let me ask any fair and candid man among you if the experiment of redressing wrongs and grievances in Lincoln County by violence — by the rifle and the revolver — by the shedding of blood — has not been pretty thoroughly tested? What are the results of this method? Is any fair-minded citizen satisfied with them? Does he expect any better results by continuing this experiment? Take, for instance, the survivors of either party who were instrumental in the inauguration of these disturbances and who at the beginning of the conflict were so eager and active in resorting

to deadly weapons to settle actual or pretended grievances. Have
they bettered their condition? To use a common and homely
phrase, "has it paid?"

What has transpired in this county furnishes a marked example
of what the results will always be when any considerable portion
of the inhabitants of a county determine to break away from the
restraints of the law and to adjust their differences by violence and
bloodshed. Many who otherwise would have been innocent are
brought into the conflict through sympathy or otherwise and
made to suffer until the public disorders become widespread — the
most appalling crimes are committed — the lives of the innocent
imperilled and their property made insecure. Now, it must be
evident to the minds of everybody that the sooner this barbarous
and criminal mode of regulating matters is suppressed the better
it will be for the public interests of the county, as well as the
private interests of every citizen.

The grand jury was composed of substantial men who would give
heed to Judge Bristol's appeal. Isaac Ellis was foreman, and the others
were A. M. Clenny, Frank McCullum, John Newcomb, Francisco
Romero y Valencia, George Van Sickle, Juan Córdova, Martín Chávez,
Trinidad Vigil, Juan Trujillo, Manuel Romero, Francisco Romero y
Severos, Martín Sánchez, Charles Fritz, and James H. Farmer. This
body, working vigorously, made an unprecedented record by turning
in some two hundred indictments, at least half of which were in some
way connected with killings. The Dolan faction received the greater
number, but McSween followers came in for their share. The foreman,
Isaac Ellis, had been a staunch supporter of the McSween cause; Martín
Chávez had taken up arms for it; still others had been merely approvers
and well-wishers. George Van Sickle, Charles Fritz and possibly others
were known as affiliating with the Dolan group. Nevertheless, they
were among the best citizens the county could offer and had been
selected under the supervision of Judge Bristol and District Attorney
Rynerson, neither of whom could be suspected of hostility toward the
Dolan cause.

During the three-weeks term, a considerable number of important
cases were taken up and disposed of in some manner. Billy the Kid
appeared and pleaded not guilty to old indictments, particularly those
for the killing of Brady and Hindman. At the request of Rynerson, a
change of venue to Doña Ana County was ordered. The Kid's associates, John Middleton and Henry Brown, wanted for the same killings,
did not appear and their cases were continued. They had both gone
back to Kansas in the fall of 1878 and there was slight possibility of
their ever turning up in Lincoln County again.

As those previously indicted for the Tunstall killing — Jesse

Evans, George Davis, John Long, and Manuel Segobia — were to a man absent, the bonds of all were declared forfeited. The cases of Dolan and Billy Mathews, indicted as accessories, were continued and change of venue allowed to Socorro County. As a precautionary measure, Dolan's bond was increased considerably.

The Chapman killing finally brought forth indictments against Jesse Evans as accessory, and Dolan and Campbell on the direct charge of murder. Dolan secured a continuance, with a change of venue to Socorro County. As neither Jesse Evans nor Campbell were around, nothing could be done except to await their arrest, if such an event should ever take place.

The burning of the McSween house and the attendant killings brought forth a plentiful harvest of indictments, which embraced not only those who claimed to be acting as members of the sheriff's posse, but others who had come up to Lincoln from Seven Rivers and vicinity largely on their own will and for love of a fight. The list included some twenty who had been more or less constantly mixed up in the fighting in Lincoln County: Robert Beckwith, Samuel Perry, George Peppin, John Hurley, Jacob B. (Billy) Mathews, John Long, John M. Beckwith, Joe Nash, M. L. Pierce, Louis Paxton, Buck Powell, Robert Olinger, John Galvin, Thomas Cochran, Charles Krueling, Richard Kelly, Charles Martin, Wallace Olinger, Juan ("Johnny") Mes, and W. H. Johnson. Several of these, notably Galvin, Cochran, Krueling, Kelly and Martín, had changed their residence from New Mexico to Texas, and proposed to remain there until things had blown over in Lincoln County. Others, like Mathews, Buck Powell, John Long, and John Hurley, went to the trouble of having their offenses purged away by pleading what their attorneys, Catron & Thornton, called the "Wallace amnesty." Marion Turner and John Jones appeared to be in a more parlous state than the others, for they had been indicted for the actual killing of McSween.

Colonel Dudley found himself indicted, along with George Peppin and John Kinney, for arson in connection with firing of the McSween house. He was held on his own recognizance for $2,000 until his case could be tried under a change of venue to Socorro County. Kinney was then and there arrested and placed under bond, pending trial at the next term of court. Both Dudley and Peppin might have avoided further trouble had they been willing to shelter under "Wallace's amnesty." But Dudley stood firmly by the position he had taken in the open letter, and Peppin felt that he wanted a complete vindication.

Billy the Kid kept his promise to Governor Wallace and appeared before the grand jury with his account of the Chapman killing. This, he well knew, would likely incur the implacable enmity of Dolan,

Campbell, Evans and their following; henceforth he would have to guard against their attempts to get even. His reliance, however, had been on Wallace's promise of immunity: "I have the authority to exempt you from prosecution, if you will testify...." Hardly did he suspect that Rynerson would question the right of the Governor to make any such a promise, or that the district attorney would even go so far as to fight any plan to let him take the stand at trials of the three persons under indictment. Yet that is what occurred, as the newspapers of the time reveal. In the Cimarron *News and Press*, May 22, 1879, appeared an inkling of the tangle. Referring to an account previously appearing in the *Mesilla News*, mouthpiece of the "Ring," the *News and Press* said:

> The *Mesilla News* states that the Kid, Scurlock, and other warriors of the McSween party have been arrested and that the Governor made the request of Prosecuting Attorney Rynerson that the Kid be allowed to turn state's evidence, and that Colonel Rynerson indignantly refused the request.
>
> The *News* by this little story — which doubtless entirely originated with the editor — endeavors to show partisanship and reflect ridicule on the Governor.
>
> Now the facts are these. The Kid was a very conspicuous actor in the Lincoln County War drama, but has not committed any overt act since the issue of the Governor's amnesty proclamation — at least no such act has been chronicled in the local papers and we have heard of none. Therefore he could properly plead the Governor's pardon. He was, however, an eyewitness of the dastardly murder of poor Chapman, which was committed after the amnesty proclamation, and for which Dolan, Evans, and Campbell have been indicted. And the fact of his being an important witness against the favorites of the *News* fully accounts for the milk in the cocoa-nut.

Colonel Rynerson had been the mainspring in bringing the Kid to trial for the killing of Brady and Hindman. Whether the Kid assumed it would be purely *pro forma*, no one can determine at this date; but very likely he continued strong in his faith that Wallace would nullify any unfavorable verdict. But as the time drew near for the transfer to Doña Ana County, where a change of venue had taken his trial, he seems to have altered his views. At any rate, he escaped from custody in the latter part of June, 1879, just prior to the term of court in Doña Ana County. Getting away was probably not difficult; the various versions regarding it all point to its having been done with the connivance of his custodians. The newly organized militia had the responsibility of keeping him. From the captain, Juan Patrón, down to the lowest private they were almost without exception friendly to him, and they knew his arrest and detention were purely voluntary on his part. One version even has it that Juan Patrón, seeing that the Dolan faction were taking shelter under the Governor's pardon, though no move was being made towards permitting Billy the Kid to do likewise, said to him one day, "Kid, I'll give you a horse and a Winchester. Then let's see if they can capture you." The hint seems to have been sufficient. A morning or two later, so the story goes, he remarked to his guards, "Boys, I'm tired of this. Tell the General [i.e. Wallace] I'm tired." Then slipping off his handcuffs, he walked out of the building and across the street to where a horse was hitched. Swinging into the saddle, he rode away in broad daylight, headed towards Fort Sumner, which, by that time, had supplanted San Patricio as his favorite haunt.

A less generally accepted version of the escape has it that the Kid became dissatisfied over the deputy who was to conduct him to Mesilla. Kimbrell had picked James Redman as escort. The Kid felt he would not be safe with Redman, since there was some sort of enmity between them. This he considered ground enough for leaving the custody of Kimbrell, who doubtless was glad to be relieved of the responsibility. At any rate, the Kid regained his liberty.

The civil docket during this term of court was crowded with old cases, which Judge Bristol let lie over until later terms. The suit of Murphy & Co. against McSween for about $4,000 for "divers goods, wares, merchandise, and chattels," together with some real estate, was continued. So was the suit of Charles Fritz and Mrs. Scholand against him for the $10,000 of the Fritz insurance money. In both, McSween's death made it necessary to let them become cases against Mrs. McSween as administratrix.

In all this mass of indictments, changes of venue, and continuances, only one major criminal case came to trial. It connected but indirectly with the Lincoln County War. This was the long standing case against Lucas Gallegos for the killing of Sostero García. Gallegos had been in the Lincoln County jail on account of this matter in the fall of 1877. Fellow prisoners included Jesse Evans and some of his Seven Rivers gang who were charged with the theft of Tunstall's horses and who had been apprehended by Special Constable Dick Brewer and his posse. When the Evans party had walked out of jail, Gallegos had departed with the others and gone to Texas, but after a year or so he had returned to Lincoln County and given himself up. The services of Colonel Fountain of Mesilla were effective in getting him off with the light sentence of a year in the Lincoln County jail for fourth degree murder. The Gallegos case was evidence that the court was able to function again in Lincoln County, albeit rather weakly.

42. Mutterings at Governor Wallace

WHILE DISTRICT COURT was in session, the newspapers over the state warmed up over Governor Wallace's methods in Lincoln County. His vigorous policing provoked outcries from several different sources. The soldiers resented being sent hither and yon on missions they regarded as outside their calling. The officers were disgruntled because Wallace stepped over their heads and gave his own orders. The politicians, who could see no good whatever in the new governor or his official acts, made a great hue and cry in their newspaper stand-bys. On May 17, 1879, the Mesilla *News*, a Ring paper, displayed on the front page a series of orders and notes from Wallace to various officers at Fort Stanton and bemoaned the Governor's "illegal and monstrous acts."

It will be seen that he ordered and arrested citizens in an unwarranted way; that they in many cases were arrested without warrant or accusation made under oath as required by law; that they were not informed of the nature of the accusations against them; that detachments of the army were dispatched to the ranches of peaceable and quiet citizens for the purpose of carrying out his Excellency's strange instructions to inspect their herds, and if necessary, to arrest the owners of stock, not on oath charging a violation of any law, but simply on instructions of Governor Wallace.

We also find Governor Wallace giving directions and instructions to the military at Fort Stanton as one having authority and as though he were in command of the United States soldiers stationed at some of the posts in New Mexico, even directing as to details. We find him even asking the commanding officers to inspect, break open the mail matter to and from prisoners arrested by his, Governor Wallace's orders . . .

It is true that the military were very properly ordered to aid the civil authorities to execute the laws. They properly could go in aid of the civil offices — sheriffs, constables, etc. — but not to carry out the unwarrantable orders or "instructions" of Governor Wallace. If any offense had been committed, it was no trouble to have gone before a magistrate and made oath of violations of law in criminal cases and procured warrants for the arrest of alleged offenders. Then the sheriff should have called on the military for assistance if needed to make arrests or for serving any process.

A prompt reply came from the Mesilla *Independent*, ready always to support the cause of Governor Wallace, since he was attempting the rout of outlawry which the *Independent* had devoutly wished and sturdily fought for. After referring to Governor Axtell's ineffective efforts, the article continued:

At the time of Governor Axtell's removal as complete a state of anarchy and outlawry existed in Lincoln County as it is possible to conceive of. The civil authorities could do nothing. In fact, there were no civil officers in the county, except possibly Axtell's imbecile sheriff. They had all fled for safety or had resigned. Outlaws from all parts of the country congregated in bands, and so far as the law was concerned, rested in perfect security. It was impossible under the circumstances to hold a court of any kind, and the Governor had not at his command the means to break up this congregation of demons.

This condition of affairs was brought to the notice of the President, and the Governor was clothed with sufficient extraordinary powers, it was thought, to restore civil authority, and to bring the brigands, or such of them as could be found, to justice. It would seem to a reasonable man that the time for extraordinary measures had fully come when not a civil officer was left in the county, and the district judge had informed the Governor that he could not hold regular term of court in Lincoln . . . .

We have carefully watched the course of Governor Wallace and so far as we are able to judge, he has made faithful and impartial efforts to carry out his instruction and to do his whole duty in the premises. He has shown no partisan feeling in the matter and has used his best efforts to punish the guilty and restore order in the county.

In this editorial the Mesilla *Independent* included a paragraph of personalia regarding the Lincoln County unworthies named in the Governor's proscription list and commented as follows:

After reviewing the list, the *News* exclaims, "Let every lover of life, liberty and peaceable possession of property read, then condemn such action." Yes, let every man who loves his own life and the peaceable possession of his own property read the above list of names and then decide whether Governor Wallace "shamefully abused his power" in having them arrested. Some of these men are known to be the most abandoned cattle thieves and outlaws that ever escaped the hangman's rope. Cattle and horse stealing, varied with occasional murder, is their acknowledged trade, and there are few men outside the coterie who control the *News*, who did not feel a relief when it was known they were in prison. Yet we are asked to believe the Governor committed a grave offense in using the means at his command in bringing them to justice . . . .

If then we are to believe the *News*, the Governor's "gross abuse of power" consists in his efforts to suppress the outlaws in Lincoln and restore the supremacy of law; to bring murderers to justice and compel respect to legally constituted authorities; and it is to be regretted that in his efforts to enforce the law and give protection of "life, liberty, and the peaceable possession of property," he has met with the bitterest opposition where he should have had, and where he had a right to expect, the strongest support.

The Cimarron *News and Press* lifted its voice in one accord with the *Independent*:

There is a newspaper published in the Mesilla valley styled the *News*. This paper, nourished from its infancy by the close corporation in Santa Fe and its parasites, very naturally espoused the cause of the ring of army and Indian supply contractors who, in connection with their official friends in Santa Fe, were reaping a rich harvest in Lincoln County. It seems that it was necessary for the contractors to keep about them, often in their employ, a set of desperate ruffians who were a terror to the whole country, and who, travelling armed to the teeth, stole horses, committed highway robbery, and for the sake of robbery proved that they would not hesitate to commit murder.

The *News* was a ready champion of these ruffians, whom it familiarly termed "the boys," and of their abettors, and when one of the most notorious of them "Capt." Evans — since indicted for the murder of Chapman — was tried for the murder of Tunstall and acquitted, the *News* could not conceal its satisfaction. The people of Lincoln County were not blind to the evil or its cause, and upon the brutal murder of poor young Tunstall for no cause but his opposition to these contractors and their band of ruffians, the popular indignation burst forth.

It has been a terrible conflict. The firm of Murphy, Dolan & Riley — and its silent partners — was a power. It had made money fast and spent it freely — where it would do the most good — and there were very few officials in the territory who were not the fast friends of this firm. Even Governor Axtell, when cornered, admitted having received pecuniary favors from one of the firm. But the cause of the just is mighty, and it is hard to find a place in the United States where a majority of the people will submit to wrong and persecution. Slowly but surely, in spite of every obstacle, the people of Lincoln became triumphant. The removal of the infamous Axtell and the appointment of Governor Wallace came at a time when the people were sorely in need of the change. The task before the new governor was an exceedingly delicate one. He realized the situation perfectly and fully understood that in doing what was right and for the best interests of that distracted county, he must necessarily incur opposition . . . .

The fact is, the *News* and its backers are opposed to Governor Wallace because he refuses to be a partisan on the side of Dolan and his rascally ring. They have long been accustomed to willing and enthusiastic support from the highest official quarters, territorial, federal and military. With a governor to use the civil and military forces to do their bidding and a U.S. district attorney for a partner it was plain sailing. There were large profits and quick returns, and they were safe in any sort of devilment or crime they saw fit to commit.

With these two important allies, and a facile Indian agent removed, and a governor at the head of affairs who is disposed to see that justice is done though the heavens fall, the career of these gentlemen is cut short in a most disagreeable manner to them. To be prosecuted and punished for the crimes they commit, and not to be able to command the whole civil and military power of the territory and the United States to aid their schemes, is a new sensation, and they begin to yell "partisan," and to vomit forth every sort of abuse at the governor, who does his duty, who goes to Lincoln County, and takes the trouble to see for himself, and listens to the people instead of using the eyes and ears of Messrs. Dolan, and Riley.

Such vilification is a far higher compliment to Gov. Wallace than their praise would be, and he can rest assured that in his course thus far he has gained the confidence and respect of the people as an impartial and fearless official.

The Las Cruces newspaper, *Thirty-four*, made its contribution to the discussion of the governor's course in an editorial appearing May 28, 1879.

The last number of the *Independent* contains a three column leader on "Governor Wallace and the Defenders of Outlaws." It is a well-written defense of the Governor on technical grounds, and as a literary production is superior to anything which has appeared in that paper since the "new management" assumed control. Who is the author it is difficult to surmise, but whoever he may be, he handles the subject very deftly and, with considerable show of reason, attempts to justify the Governor for his exercise of extraordinary powers outside the law. It is just such an argument as his Excellency himself would be apt to use in his own defense.

While we are not disposed to join the hue and cry against the governor but believe he did much good in arresting murderers and thieves; still, with the limited knowledge in our possession it does appear, and the article referred to virtually admits it, that in his zeal to bring criminals to justice he overstepped the legal restraints and attempted to *bend* the law so as to meet the case. We only regret that martial law was not declared to enable him to do legally what he appears to have done in spite of the law.

It is never safe for public officials to disregard legal restraints, even to accomplish desirable ends. Governor Wallace once before thought that it was — when he assisted to count the electoral vote of Florida for Hayes — and in each case a precedent has been established which, if not condemned by the intelligent verdict of the patriotic citizen, may become a dangerous one to the future. In the Lincoln County case we believe he thought the end justified the means; and, judging from his action there, justice to him might incline us to believe that he thought the same in the Florida case. But however that may be, there appears to be little doubt that his zeal to punish outlaws has led him to the commission of a very serious error in Lincoln. There is no power vested in any officer or department of our government to ignore legal methods except in case of martial law; and that itself becomes a legal method when properly declared by competent authority.

It is peculiarly unfortunate for the peace of the neighboring county that the Governor felt bound to *bend* the law. The good he accomplished may all be counterbalanced by having placed himself in a position to require apology for his method. There is a legal way out of the difficulties which afflict the county of Lincoln and we hope the next time an effort is made, whether by Governor Wallace, his successor, or the President of the United States, no blunders will be committed. It is hardly safe to predict, however, that an administration which owes its existence to a disregard of law, or the representatives of such an administration, will hesitate at what they may be disposed to term legal quibbles in the carrying out of a fixed purpose, whether just or not.

We wish for the good of the country that the Governor might be vindicated; but our respect for the majesty of the law leads us to condemn all illegal methods; a respect to which Republican officials appear in too many instances to be strangers, when the law does not exactly meet their own view of the necessities of a particular case.

The next issue of *Thirty-four*, that for June 4, contained a short addition to the discussion under the title "Governor Wallace's Error." It was a crisp reply to some comment made by the *Independent*, taking the position that the Governor had violated Article V of the Constitution. It expressed regret that the Governor had not followed the strict letter of the law and closed with the statement, "What he did was well done, if he had only done it in a legal way."

43. The Ordeal of Colonel Dudley

AFTER THE SPRING term of court in 1879, Colonel Dudley became the center of interest. The order of the day seemed to be investigations and trials, partly upon his own request and partly from Mrs. McSween's implacability. No sooner had he been relieved of the command at Fort Stanton on March 21 than he undertook to secure justification for his actions. He formally requested a military board of inquiry; the request was acted upon so speedily that by April 10 he had returned to Fort Stanton from Fort Union under orders permitting him to remain in order to perfect a defense from his records. The date for the board of inquiry was first set for May 2 but had to be changed to May 25 in order to accommodate Governor Wallace, who was to be one of the most important witnesses.

Mrs. McSween had gone ahead with her efforts to plague Colonel Dudley in the courts. To the long-standing attempt to convict him of arson and murder she now added a slander suit for $25,000 because of the aspersions upon her character made in Dudley's intemperate letters. Chapman's place as her attorney was now filled by Judge Ira E. Leonard, moderate in temperament both as a man and a lawyer. Mrs. McSween had grown thoroughly vindictive toward Dudley and these cases would certainly be carried into the court room, but the methods of Judge Leonard would shear them of much of the fanaticism Chapman would have invested them with had he lived. Leonard had won the complete confidence of Wallace to such a degree that when Rynerson had to be away from his duties as district attorney during the spring terms of court in his district, Leonard had been designated as acting district attorney. Probably the Governor was relieved to have Rynerson off the stage, for he was as heavily tarred with partisanship in the Lincoln County troubles as was Dudley. Nothing, however, had overtaken Rynerson on account of it except at the time of his letter to "Friends Riley and Dolan" about "shaking that McSween outfit," when there were mutterings about disbarment proceedings or some other measure that might end his career as district attorney. Governor Wallace further showed his confidence in Judge Leonard by selecting him as his advisor during the forthcoming examination before the army board of inquiry.

Composing the court of inquiry that began its sessions the last of May were Colonel G. Pennypacker, 16th Infantry (from Fort Union), Major N. W. Osborne, 15th Infantry (from Fort Bliss), and Captain H. R. Brinkerhoff, 15th Infantry (from Fort Bliss). Captain H. H. Humphreys, 15th Infantry (from Fort Bliss) was designated as the recorder. Six enlisted men from Co. H., 15th Infantry, were detailed to act as guards in preserving order. Colonel Edward Hatch, commanding the U.S. Military District of New Mexico, was present as an observer.

Dudley had secured as his attorney Judge Henry M. Waldo of Santa Fe, one of the best lawyers and most astute politicians in the territory, and among those of the Santa Fe clique who had been doing their utmost to annoy the Governor. As attorney general for the territory he had used all his influence to frustrate attempts to prosecute Dudley in the territorial courts. Gossip had it that the Governor was insistent that Colonel Dudley be tried for his part in the Five Days Fight at Lincoln, but that Judge Waldo was vehemently opposed to such a step.

Colonel Dudley faced an elaborate array of charges classified under the articles of war as (A) conduct unbecoming an officer and a gentleman, and (B) disobedience to orders. The first embraced specifications as follows, which reveal the extent to which Colonel Dudley was suspected of having shown partisanship:

I. Conspiracy with the Dolan-Riley party to aid and assist them in measures of violence against McSween.
II. An agreement with one of the parties of the feud to afford them protection and aid against the other party.
III. Allowing the McSween house to be fired, and thus endangering the lives of women and children therein.
IV. Failure to protect these women and children after they had left the burning house.

V. Not preventing the pillaging of the Tunstall store after the burning of the McSween house.

VI. Failure to protect Chapman after the aid of the military had been sought to this end, but referring to him as "one of the murderers, horse thieves and escaped convicts infesting the country," thereby excluding Chapman from the protection of the forces at his command.

VII. Aspersions on the character of a woman.

VIII. The publication of newspaper articles reflecting on policy of Governor Wallace.

IX. The publication with improper motives of certain official documents furnished him to aid his defense before the board of inquiry.

The second general charge — disobedience to orders — merely set forth three instances in which certain specific orders from superiors regarding the interference of troops in civil affairs had been disregarded.

For fully six weeks the board of inquiry dragged, its sessions open to the public except during arguments over the admissibility of evidence or other technical matters. These were frequent, for Judge Waldo battled strenuously for his client. Day after day, now one and then the other of the crowd of more than a hundred witnesses, both civilian and military, took the stand to be examined, cross-examined, and re-examined by the recorder, whose role corresponded to that of prosecuting attorney, as well as by Dudley and Waldo.

One of the first developments was the appearance of Governor Wallace, whose examination lasted a full week. Perhaps nothing in the whole scene was more remarkable than the governor of the territory forced to endure vicious cross-examining on his sincere efforts to quiet the turbulence in Lincoln County. Animated more by personal and political dislike than by valid grounds of objection, Mrs. McSween likewise was subjected to long-drawn-out appearance as witness; her examination was conducted with ungloved hands by those hostile first to her husband and then to her during the crucial stages of the Lincoln County War.

Colonel Dudley had seen to it that those of his fellow officers who had zealously carried out his orders and commissions, such as Lieutenant Goodwin, Dr. Appel, Captain Carroll and others, were on hand to testify in his behalf. He had also several noncommissioned officers and privates who had participated in different occurrences in some capacity or other. The civilian witnesses in his behalf were a motley array of such of the old Peppin posse as could be gathered together. Peppin himself gave his version of the fight, in which he included the positive statement that no soldiers had taken any direct part in it at any time. His testimony was corroborated by his various deputies, Buck Powell, John Long, Marion Turner, as well as by others like Andy Boyle who had assumed prominent if less official parts in the event.

Besides witnesses Dudley had a capacious satchelful of documents. He had not been boasting when he had claimed to have a complete record of all his activities. He had orders, letters, weekly reports, and newspaper clippings, and was prompt to use them as "exhibits" when occasion demanded. The documents, in fact, gave him a strong answer to most of the charges.

Though the McSween side was somewhat smaller, its witnesses were among the stars in the court of inquiry. Billy the Kid, eager now to get on the windy side of the law, and José Chávez told of their escape from the McSween house. Martín Chávez recited how he and his men abandoned the Montaño house and fled across the Río Bonito, leaving their comrades in the McSween house to their fate. Sam Corbet, Dr. Ealy, and a few others were also on the witness stand, their accounts in various ways serving to round out the picture of the terrible nineteenth of July.

A sample of the procedure with the witnesses may be had from the examination of Billy the Kid. Though mainly on the point of whether the soldiers had actually taken part in the firing — a matter that came forward whenever any of the participants of the five days' fight were on the stand — his testimony gave several sidelights on the daring exit he and his companions had made from the McSween house.

The Recorder [Captain Humphreys] — What is your name and place of residence?

William Bonney — My name is William Bonney; I reside in Lincoln.

Q. — Are you known or called Billy Kid? Also Antrim?

A. — Yes, sir.

Q. — Where were you on the 19th of July last, and what, if anything, did you see of the movements and actions of the troops that day? State fully.

A. — I was in Mr. McSween's house in Lincoln, and I seen the soldiers come down from the Fort with the sheriff's party — that is, the sheriff's posse joined them a short distance above there — that is McSween's house. [The] soldiers passed on by [but] the men dropped right off and surrounded the house — that is, the sheriff's party. Shortly after, three soldiers came back with Peppin, passed the house twice afterwards. Three soldiers came down

Billy the Kid, born Henry McCarty and best known as William Bonney. The Kid arrived in Lincoln County toward the close of 1877. Employed as a "herder" on the Tunstall ranch, he was inevitably drawn into the Lincoln County War where he played a relatively minor role. After the defeat of the Tunstall-McSween party he turned to the outlawry which ended with his death at the hands of Pat Garrett.

and stood in front of the house in front of the windows. Mr. McSween wrote a note to the officer in charge asking him what the soldiers were placed there for. He replied saying that they had business there; that if a shot was fired over his camp or at Sheriff Peppin or any of his men he would blow the house up; that he had no objection to [Mr. McSween] blowing up his own house if he wanted to do so. I read the note; Mr. McSween handed it to me to read. I read the note myself. I seen nothing further of the soldiers until night. I was in the back part of the house when I escaped from it. Three soldiers fired at me from the Tunstall store — from the outside corner of the store. That is all I know in regard to it.

Q. — Did the soldiers that stood near the house in front of the windows have guns with them there?

A. — Yes, sir.

Q. — Who escaped from the house with you, and who was killed at that time, if you know, while attempting to make their escape?

A. — José Chávez escaped with me; also Vicente Romero, Francisco Samora, and Mr. McSween.

Q. — How many persons were killed in the fight that day, if you know, and who killed them, if you know?

A. — I seen five killed. I could not swear as to who it was killed them. I seen some of them that fired.

Q. — Who did you see that fired?

A. — Robert Beckwith, John Kinny, John Jones, and those three soldiers — I don't know their names.

Q. — What were the names of the persons who were killed?

A. — Robert Beckwith, Francisco Samora, Vincente Romero, Harvey Morris, and A. A. McSween.

Q. — Did you see any persons setting fire to the McSween house that day? If so, state who it was, if you know?

A. — I did. Jack Long, and there was another man I did not recognize.

At this point in the testimony the recorder stated that he had finished with the witness. Colonel Dudley thereupon proceeded to cross-examine.

Colonel Dudley: What were you, and the others there with you doing in McSween's house that day?

A. — We came there with Mr. McSween.

Q. — Did you not know, or had you not heard, that the sheriff was endeavoring to arrest yourself and others there with you at the time.

A. — Yes, sir. I heard so; I did not know it.

Q. — Had you not been there for two or three days previous?

A. — Yes, sir. I never went out of the house.

Q. — Then you were not engaged in resisting the sheriff at the time you were in the house? — *The Recorder interposed, "I object," and the president, Colonel Pennypacker, intoned, "Objection sustained."* — Colonel Dudley then asked: Were you in the habit of visiting and stopping at the house of McSween before that time?

A. — Yes, sir.

Q. — In addition to the names which you have given, are you now known or styled in Lincoln county as "the Kid"?

A. — I have already answered that question. Yes, sir, I am; but not "Billy the Kid" that I know of.

Q. — Were you not, and were not the parties with you in the McSween house on the 19th day of July last and the days immediately preceding, engaged in firing at the sheriff's posse? *Here the president objected, and Col. Waldo, Colonel Dudley's counsel, argued for the procedure Colonel Dudley was following. The examination of the witness was halted until the president could announce his decision on the point at issue.*

Q. — How many did you see them fire?

A. — I could not swear to that; on account of the firing on both sides, I could not hear. I seen them fire one volley.

Q. — What did they fire at?

A. — Myself and José Chávez.

Q. — Did you not just now state, in answer to the question who killed Samora, Romero, Morris, and McSween, that you did not know who killed them, but you saw Beckwith, Kinney, John Jones, and the three soldiers fire at them?

A. — Yes, sir, I did.

Q. — Were these men, the McSween men, there with you when the volley was fired at you and Chávez by the soldiers?

A. — Just a short way behind us.

Q. — Were you looking back at them?

A. — No, sir.

Q. — How then do you know they were just behind you then, or that they were within range of the volley?

A. — Because there was a high fence behind and a good many guns to keep them there. I could hear them speak.

Q. — How far were you from the soldiers when you saw them?

A. — I could not swear exactly — between 30 and 40 yards.

Q. — Did you know either of the soldiers that were in front of the windows of McSween's house that day?

A. — No, sir, I am not acquainted with them.

Colonel Dudley stated that he had finished the cross-examination.

The recorder then proceeded with the re-direct examination.

The Recorder. — Explain whether all the men that were in the McSween house came out at the same time when McSween did, and the others who were killed by the firing from the soldiers and others?

A. — Yes, sir, all came out at the same time. The firing was not done by the soldiers until some had escaped.

The recorder then stated that he was through with the witness.

Colonel Dudley. — How do you know, if you were making your escape at the time, and the men, Samora, Romero, Morris and McSween, were behind you, that they were killed at that time? Is it not true that you did not know of their deaths until afterwards?

A. — I knew of the death of some of them. I did not know of the death of one of them. I seen him lying there.

Q. — What time of the day was it when you escaped from that house?

A. — About dusk in the evening — a little after dark.

Q. — Whose name was signed to the note received by McSween in reply to the one previously sent by him to Colonel Dudley?

A. — [It was] signed "N.A.M. Dudley;" did not say what rank. McSween received two notes; one had no name signed to it.

Q. — Are you as certain of everything else you have sworn to as you are to what you have sworn to in answer to the last preceding question?

A. — Yes, sir.

Q. — From which direction did Peppin come the first time the soldiers passed with him?

A. — He passed up from the direction where the soldiers camped, the first time I seen him.

Q. — From what direction did he come the second time?

A. — From the direction of the hotel from McSween's house.

Q. — In what direction did you go upon your escape from the McSween house?

A. — I ran towards Tunstall's store; was fired at, and then turned towards the river.

Q. — From what part of the McSween house did you make your escape?

A. — The northeast corner of the house.

Q. — How many soldiers fired at you?

A. — Three.

Q. — How many soldiers were with Peppin when he passed the McSween house each time that day, as you say.

A. — Three.

Q. — The soldiers appeared to go in companies of three's that day, did they not?

A. — All that I ever seen appeared to be three in a crowd at a time, after they passed the first time.

Q. — Who was killed first that day, Bob Beckwith or the McSween men?

A. — Harvey Morris, McSween man, was killed first.

Q. — How far is the Tunstall building from the McSween house?

A. — I could not say how far; I never measured the distance. I should judge it to be 40 yards, between 30 and 40 yards.

Q. — How many shots did those soldiers fire, [those] that you say fired from the Tunstall building.

A. — I don't know.

Q. — Did you see either of the men last mentioned killed; if so, which of them?

A. — Yes, sir, I did. I seen Harvey Morris killed first. He was out in front of me.

Q. — Did you not then a moment ago swear that he was among those who were behind you and José Chávez, when you saw the soldiers deliver the volley?

A. — No, sir; I don't think I did. I misunderstood the question if I did. I said that he was among them that was killed, but not behind me.

On the whole the court of inquiry was a theatrical affair. In spite of all the sound and fury, in a setting of military parade and punctilio, it accomplished little toward getting at the truth. The tactics of those examining the witnesses were evidently cautious. Whenever the questioning reached delicate ground there would come a quick shifting into another direction. A good example of this occurred when one of the officers, Colonel Dudley's right hand man in fact, was asked incisively: "If you were there in the capacity of humanitarians, why did you not carry out that object and prevent the bloodshed and destruction of property that took place on that occasion?" Before the witness could tender an answer, a promptly rendered "I object" relieved him from the embarrassment of having to give a reply.

At the end of six weeks the board of inquiry concluded taking testimony and, following military procedure, forwarded its decision to General John N. Pope, commanding the Department of the Missouri, with headquarters at Fort Leavenworth. He in turn transmitted it to the War Department in Washington. Colonel Dudley emerged covered with a strange mixture of whitewash and tar. The whitewash was bestowed by the board of inquiry, for it exonerated him from any and all wrongdoing. General Pope, however, bestowed the tar by bluntly disapproving the verdict and directing that court martial proceedings be instituted against Colonel Dudley. He was, however, willing for this step to be postponed until after Dudley had gotten from under his trials in the civil courts. The second whitewash came from the War Department. The Judge Advocate General's Office reported to the Secretary of War that while the evidence did not substantiate the principal charges against Colonel Dudley, yet it was to be granted that the presence of the soldiers had given a certain degree of moral support to the sheriff's posse and stimulated them to more drastic measures than otherwise would have been undertaken. As for the minor matters, there was not much proof to support them except the one concerning Dudley's extorting from Judge Wilson a warrant against McSween personally for shooting at the courier. Dudley appeared to have been certainly too violent and arbitrary in that matter, as well as unnecessarily rough in means and intemperate in language on other occasions. The best termination for the whole business, so the Judge Advocate General's Office thought, was to drop it. Further, though Dudley's acts might have been irregular and without sanction from orders, it should be taken into consideration that he was in command of a frontier post in a country overrun with contending bands of outlaws toward whom he could hardly hold a consistently neutral and passive attitude, especially when invoked to protect women and children or other defenseless persons.

Before the final conclusion from the War Department was made public, Dudley had come through his civil trials with flying colors. As the Fort Stanton investigation had cost him a pretty penny — he claimed that he had spent $5,000 in attorney's fees alone — he managed to procure the official services of S. M. Barnes, the United States district attorney, as his lawyer in the civil trials, which came up at Mesilla in the fall term of court (November, 1879). When the cases were called, Colonel Rynerson, whose official duties now forced him to do something in behalf of the old McSween side, found the trial on the arson charge brought to a standstill by Mrs. McSween's failure to arrive. As chief witness for the prosecution, her presence was essential, but her only contribution proved to be a letter giving reasons for her absence. First, her attorney, Judge Leonard, had failed to come to Lincoln and escort her to Mesilla because he had been detained longer than he had expected by business in Colorado; secondly, his protection had seemed necessary now that the journey was especially hazardous because a band of Apaches had just left the reservation and were plundering, it was supposed, in the vicinity of the Las Cruces road. The only move open to Rynerson under such circumstances was to seek a continuance. Judge Bristol took the view that Mrs. McSween was simply trying to impose on the patience of the court and arbitrarily set December 6 as a new date for the trial. He sharply told Rynerson that he must have Mrs. McSween and other witnesses on hand by that time.

When Mrs. McSween received notice of the new date she bravely undertook the journey to Mesilla, accompanied only by her servant, Zebron Bates. At Tularosa she met alarming news about the Apaches under Victorio's leadership having killed several persons just a few days before on the road she was to travel. Because of the Indian outbreak Lieutenant G. W. Smith was at Tularosa with a large detachment of soldiers but, when she asked for an escort, he declared he was unable to spare any men. Mrs. McSween doubtless thought to herself that this was but another instance of the military not helping the McSween cause, but in her reply to Lieutenant Smith she concealed any animus and said simply, "I'll go on. If the Indians kill me, it's just me." No untoward adventures, however, from the Indians or other agents marred the rest of her long 150-mile journey across the Tularosa desert, over the Organ Mountains, and down into the Rio Grande Valley.

Immediately upon Mrs. McSween's arrival, the trial started and was rushed through in an almost continuous session for three days and two nights. The testimony was largely a repetition of that given to the board of inquiry at Fort Stanton six months before. When the case finally reached the jury, only half an hour's deliberation was needed to reach the verdict "not guilty." After this almost *opera bouffe* outcome to the arson trial, the other charges quickly sank into nothing. Rynerson did not press the charge of complicity on the death of McSween, and Mrs. McSween allowed the suit for slander to die a natural death. In spite of all the annoyance, anxiety, and expense connected with the investigation and litigation, Dudley had resolutely stuck to the position taken in the newspaper letter published a little more than a year before, in which he declared positively that he would not cater to the Wallace administration by using the Governor's pardon.

By a strange shifting of alignment Dudley now placed all his "persecution," as he termed it, at the door of the Santa Fe ring, that perpetual target for complainers and malcontents. Partisanship toward the Dolan faction, which had seemed to make him one of the minions of the ring, had undergone a change. Now he was outspoken about being a martyr to the Santa Fe ring. Had he not refused, so he asserted, to allow the quartermaster at Fort Stanton to receive 300,000 or 400,000 pounds of inferior corn furnished by Z. Staab & Co. of Santa

Fe? Had he not also protected the government from exorbitant charges for lumber? Had he not braved the displeasure, not to say the hate, of Catron by refusing to certify as unreliable and unprincipled, some of the persons who had submitted anti-Catron affidavits when the United States district attorneyship was under fire. Had not Catron thereupon vented a threat that he would drive Dudley from the service? Indeed it looked as though the Colonel had been wounded in the house of his friends.

44. Low Ebb to Lawlessness

DURING THE SUMMER and autumn of 1879 Lincoln County seemed quieted down. For some eighteen months the excitement had been acute, but now an improvement might be observed. One of the sources of general unrest, the military at Fort Stanton, had been allayed by the removal of such officers as had been prominent in the disturbances. Governor Wallace had brought it about that all the troops at the Fort except Captain Carroll and Lieutenant Dawson and their companies had been moved to other stations, and in their places had come officers and men entirely disconnected with the past troubles and without bias toward one faction or the other. This change made the section breathe a great deal easier.

Another problem existed in the case of Dolan. For a long time he had seemed immune to any curbs; even when under arrest he seemed a privileged character. Wallace described the situation when he wrote to the Secretary of the Interior while the court of inquiry was in session:

> The people of the county go to Fort Stanton, witnesses on one side or the other of the Dudley court of inquiry, and witness strange sights; they see Dolan, admittedly the leader of the fiercest refractories, at large and busy in Col. Dudley's behalf, although he is under two indictments for murder, one a murder in the first degree. They know that he is not at large by the consent or connivance of the sheriff. They know that the commandant of the fort has my official request in writing to keep him in close confinement. Knowing this, and seeing what they see — Dolan

free to come and go, a boarder at the trader's store, attended by a gang well understood as ready to do his bidding to any extreme — they are further met by threats of bloody things intended when Col. Dudley is acquitted by his court and restored to command of the post, and are afraid, and so constantly as to find it impossible to settle down.

Dolan's arrest by the military created complications, but he succeeded in resolving them in July. Now that he was at last under arrest for the killing of Chapman, he undertook to get release through bail. He maneuvered to be taken to Mesilla under charge of Deputy Sheriff Redman and an escort of six soldiers for *habeas corpus* proceedings. The outcome of the hearing was reported in the Las Cruces *Thirty-four* for July 9 as follows:

> Dolan has been released on $3,000 bail to appear at the next term of court at Socorro. E. A. Walz, Billy Mathews, and others testified. Dolan claimed to have been very drunk and could not have hit Chapman without firing through Walz. Dolan fired, according to his admission, but said he knew nothing of what was happening, and simply fired into the ground "to call the boys off." Campbell said he had promised his God and Col. Dudley to kill Chapman when the party was in a saloon after the killing.

The Mesilla *Independent* discussed the outcome of the examination of Dolan at length, saying in part:

> The examination of J. J. Dolan before Judge Bristol on a writ of *habeas corpus* strikingly illustrates the condition of affairs in Lincoln County. That such fiendish and dastardly murders should be committed in a civilized community, and no arrests or efforts made to bring the guilty parties to justice for weeks after the murders — notwithstanding the guilty parties remained in the town and at Fort Stanton — is strange not to say the least of it. . . .
>
> It will be remembered by those who read the papers that Mr. Dolan once denied over his own signature that he was present when Chapman was killed. He afterwards admitted that he was present but unarmed. He now admits that he was present and that he was armed, and that he fired the first shot but that he fired it to attract the attention of the party. He stood in the midst of a party of eight or ten men and had to fire his pistol in order to attract their attention! Fatal shot! Whether it was fired by collusion with Evans and Campbell or whether he meant it as a signal or merely to attract attention, it caused the death of Chapman. Three seconds after Dolan's shot was fired, Chapman had received a mortal wound.

The Chapman affair had put Dolan in a more critical situation than any other incident of his career. To escape the consequences required all his native adroitness. He kept his usual composure, however; his self-assurance was unbowed. What should he first do with the liberty that came from release on bail but marry on July 13 in Las Cruces Caroline Fritz, daughter of Charles Fritz. In August he was at Socorro where his trial on charges of murder was scheduled. As had been cynically predicted, Catron and Thornton had no difficulty in having the case dismissed. The outcome was unofficially given in a letter by Godfrey Gauss to the father of Tunstall, written November 22, 1879.

> Jimmie Dolan was acquitted of the two murders for which he was indicted by the grand jury. He married the daughter of the farmer Fritz and lives here in town. In this county he would have without doubt been convicted, but he took a change of venue to Socorro, and had not much trouble to find a jury to acquit him. This is law and justice in New Mexico.

In the latter part of August the Seven Rivers section displayed a flare-up. This time it was the Pecos crowd falling upon one another, for those involved had all been participants in the five days' fight at Lincoln thirteen months before. On August 26 John Jones, one of the ringleaders of the Pecos men, quarreled with John Beckwith, brother of Robert Beckwith who had been killed in the fight at Lincoln. The dispute, which occurred in Pierce Canyon on the Black River, was over the branding of a calf; Jones shot and killed Beckwith.

John Jones immediately rode to Seven Rivers and surrendered to the deputy sheriff who gave him permission to return to Pierce Canyon to bury the body of his one-time associate. En route, on the twenty-ninth, he stopped at the Pierce and Paxton ranch house, where he was killed by Bob Olinger. Versions of the slaying differ somewhat, one widely accepted account being as follows:

For some cause bad feeling had developed between Jones and Pierce although they had been comrades-in-arms during the Lincoln County War. For some reason Jones had been outspoken with threats upon Pierce's life. Pierce had told Olinger about the danger, remarking that probably he would have to shoot it out with Jones sooner or later. Olinger immediately tendered his services as bodyguard, saying, "Milo, you know you would not stand much show for your life in a duel with John Jones. Better turn the job over to me." Olinger had also volunteered to stay with Pierce until the difficulty was over. This solicitude was natural; ever since Olinger had been in New Mexico he had lived at the Beckwith ranch, going there when he came from the Indian Territory four or five years before. The recent killing of John Beckwith was a sufficient stimulus to Olinger to even the score with John Jones if opportunity arrived, and the plight of Pierce seemed to present an occasion.

When John Jones reached the camp of Paxton and Pierce a group of the old Seven Rivers crowd — Buck Powell, Jim Ramer, Billy Smith, Bob Olinger, besides Paxton and Pierce — happened to be around the place. Pierce was inside the house lying on a cot, Olinger sitting outside near the doorway. John Jones rode up, dismounted, greeting the group on the outside, including Olinger, and passed into the room where Pierce was. The situation seemed to afford Olinger the cue to act his part of bodyguard. Some accounts have it that Olinger detected Jones in the act of drawing his pistol as he bent over to shake hands with Pierce. Be that as it may, Olinger quickly fired; the bullet passed through the body of Jones, ending instantly the career of that veteran of the Lincoln County disorders. The men were so close together that the bullet struck Pierce in the hip, inflicting a permanent lameness that earned for him the rest of his life the nickname of "Limpy."

The incident carries an additional feature that makes it the root of the animosity between Billy the Kid and Bob Olinger. Although the Kid and the Jones boys had been on opposite sides in the war, he had never given up the friendship he felt for the Jones family, especially for Ma Jones, because of the kindly way they had treated him when he first came to Lincoln County. When he heard of the killing of John Jones, he expressed his willingness to kill Bob Olinger in retaliation. News of this was relayed to Olinger and brought matters to a tension between the two.

During the summer and autumn of 1879 the raids of Victorio's band of Apaches occupied the attention of southwestern New Mexico almost to the exclusion of the Lincoln County troubles. Some notice, however, was given Billy the Kid now that he was at large again. In the Las Cruces *Thirty-four* for July 9 appeared a hint of what he was engaged in. "Kid and Scurlock and others are still in the country. They are reported as getting a crowd together again. No effort is being made to arrest them." In other words, the Kid and his associates were embarking on a career of cattle and horse stealing. In October a party made up of the Kid, Scurlock, O'Folliard, Bowdre, and two Mexicans stole over a hundred head of Chisum cattle from the Panhandle and then sold them to beef-buyers from Colorado. Chisum, however, followed the cattle and recovered them. The story goes that the division of the

$800 received for the cattle did not suit Scurlock, and he severed his connection with the gang and left the country for Kansas.

Fort Sumner became the Kid's stamping ground during these eighteen months. His cattle stealing activities were interspersed with the killing of Joe Grant in January, 1880, which occurred in a saloon at Fort Sumner. Grant was the kind of desperado always full of braggadocio. He was suspected of wanting a chance to shoot the Kid so as to add to his own laurels as a badman. On this particular occasion he was trying to make an impression on the bystanders by shooting at bottles standing on the shelf back of the bar in the saloon. The Kid joined in the fun saying, "Let me help break up housekeeping, pard." In the course of the hilarity Grant found an occasion to give the lie to the Kid and, anticipating trouble, drew his pistol and turned it directly upon the Kid. Grant's weapon, however, failed him. The Kid drew his and sent a bullet through Grant's head.

45. Extinction of the Jesse Evans Gang

UNDER TWO SERIOUS indictments, one for the killing of Tunstall and the other for the killing of Chapman, Jesse Evans ceased to be conspicuous in Lincoln County. After escape from the guardhouse at Fort Stanton on the night of March 18, he made his way down into the Big Bend section of Texas and there was finally captured by the Texas Rangers. In August, 1879, the Las Cruces *Thirty-four* noted that he had been arrested at Fort Stockton. The first news was that he had been killed; thereupon *Thirty-four* remarked, "If true it will save Lincoln County some expense, and justice the shame of another judicial farce." Later information, however, indicated that Jesse Evans was not dead but in jail at Fort Stockton.

The fight with the Rangers came in July of the next year, 1880. He was still "Captain" Evans and had with him three or four others who acknowledged his leadership. Only one of these, George Davis, was a veteran of the Lincoln County War. Others were two brothers of George Davis who had come out from Williamson County, Texas. Another member of the gang was the man known as John Gunter, or Johnny Gross (in reality John Selman), who had been in Lincoln County in the wake of the war during the summer and fall of 1878. This crowd, commonly spoken of as the "New Mexico outlaws," were engaged in stealing cattle and disposing of them at Fort Stockton and Fort Davis. They also turned their talents to robbing stores and depriving individuals of watches and money. On May 19, 1880, they looted the store of Sender & Sieibenbaum at Fort Davis. The proprietors appealed to the Rangers and Orderly Sergeant L. B. Caruthers was sent to the scene. He found the town panic-stricken because the outlaws were still around and might make another foray. During the first few days Caruthers made little headway with his investigation, but the prospects of success grew brighter when the sheriff from the county adjoining Pecos came over and opened the Ranger sergeant's eyes to the stumbling block. Ryan, the Pecos County sheriff, had gotten acquainted with the "New Mexico outlaws" when they came to Fort Stockton and had managed to come to an understanding with them. The terms were that if they would not operate in Pecos County, he would not molest them. Their activities had therefore been transferred to Fort Davis. After their "run" upon that community they broke the agreement and returned to Fort Stockton. The townspeople at once became stirred up and a posse led by Francis Rooney had captured Charlie Davis and placed him in the jail at Fort Stockton. The rest of the gang were supposed to be somewhere in the Davis Mountains. Ryan offered to get into communciation with them if Caruthers desired it. As this seemed likely to lead to some valuable developments, Caruthers assented to the proposal.

A few days later Sheriff Ryan returned with the report that he had met George Davis and Jesse Evans and found them very eager to bring about somehow the release of Charlie Davis.

In the meantime the citizens of Fort Stockton had appealed for Rangers and a detachment under Ed Seiker had arrived. As Caruthers outranked Seiker and had been longer on the ground, he assumed direction of the ruse that was to be used.

The next news was that Jesse Evans and his companions, after hearing what had taken place in Fort Davis, had pulled out for Old Mexico in alarm. Rumor had it that they were at Presidio del Norte, whence they might easily cross over the Rio Grande. Caruthers made up his mind that he would carry the pursuit into Old Mexico, though doing so ran the risk of international complications. In view of the ticklish character of the expedition the pursuing squad was made up of volunteers: Ed Seiker, George Bingham, Tom Carson, Dick Russell, and Blub Thomas. Thomas changed his mind as the party was about to start and his place was filled by Sam Henry. As guide, the party took along Olito Herredia, a Mexican deputy sheriff of Presidio County.

After nightfall on July 1, 1880, the party left Fort Davis and rode steadily all night and all the next day. On the second night they camped on Alamito Creek, near the Victoriano Hernández ranch. Early the next morning they were in the saddle for the next day's ride which would take them into Presidio del Norte, only about eighteen miles away. There they expected either to find and capture the Evans gang or to carry the pursuit across the Rio Grande. As they started out, Bingham voiced their general uncertainty about what the day might bring forth by remarking to Caruthers, "Sergeant, I guess I'll be in Mexico or hell before night."

As the party were watering their horses in Alamito Creek a few miles below the Hernández ranch, Sam Henry caught sight of four men in the distance riding toward a rough section of the mountain and called out to Caruthers, "Some men have just come out of the creek above you!" Caruthers ordered his men to follow them. When the Rangers got closer, Caruthers called, "Halt!" but the four men put their horses to the run and at the same time began firing. The Rangers gave chase, returning the fire. A running fight ensued for a mile or more until the four men turned off into a trail leading toward the top of a small mountain. The Rangers did not hesitate to follow, Bingham leading; Carson, Russell, Seiker, and Caruthers following.

When the Rangers reached the top of the mountain, the four men had dismounted and concealed themselves behind a natural breastwork formed by the rocks. The Rangers dropped from their horses and in the face of sharp volleys charged the stronghold. Carson's rifle sent a bullet into the hip of George Davis, but he crawled to an opening in the rim of rocks and continued to fire until a bullet from Seiker's gun killed him. This casualty caused a panic among the other three, who broke and ran. The Rangers followed, pressing them so hard that they were glad to make terms and surrender.

Sergeant Ed Seiker transmitted the following official account of the fight to Ranger headquarters:

> A solid volley was shot at our little band, there being but three or four of us up at the time. Before we dismounted, a bullet cut Carson's hatbrim and one passed under his leg and his stirrup leather, wounding his horse on the side, under the saddle blanket. They shot volley after volley at us at forty yards range, we in open view and they behind rocks.
>
> One of the party fired at us, and Carson shot him in the side; he was evidently determined to sell out and shoot after Carson shot him, and was shooting around our heads very closely when I saw him stick his head out to get a shot. I shot him between the eyes, the bullet coming out at the back of his head.
>
> George Bingham was at my left and about 35 yards in the rear, when he was shot through the heart. We charged the party and took their stronghold; then we had the advantage for the first time, and they surrendered. Had I known that Bingham was

killed at this time, I should have killed all of them; but we had disarmed them before we knew of his death and then they prayed for mercy.

Bingham must have been killed in the first volley when we came up the hill; so that left Carson, Russell and myself to do the work. It was a dreary sight on the night of the 3rd; we were a mile and a half from the road, on top of a mountain a hundred feet above the level of the road and in the morning a heavy rain fell upon us. The bodies were covered with blankets, and the prisoners tied with ropes and lying by a little brush fire to keep warm.

The fight commenced about 1 o'clock and lasted about an hour. As soon as it was over we got a Mexican and started him on a horse of one of the prisoners to Del Norte to summon a coroner, who arrived the next morning. But then we could not move Bingham to Fort Davis, as his remains would not keep. So we buried him on the side of the road, and our little band showed him all the honor in our power. We formed and fired three volleys over his grave; then, with subdued hearts, we wended our ways through the mountain passes towards Fort Davis, where we arrived safely with our prisoners.

Bingham died at his post, fighting bravely. He was in the act of loading his gun when the fatal shot struck him, but none of us saw him fall. Carson and Russell deserve great credit for coming up so bravely in the fight.

The Ranger detachment had difficulties in keeping this batch of notable prisoners in custody. In his Lincoln County period Jesse Evans had on two occasions escaped jail, first from custody in Lincoln and then from the Fort Stanton guardhouse. His present predicament was different; he could now count on no friends among those guarding him. It became clear to Evans that the only hope of escape lay in help from the outside. He had no friends in the area capable of so daring an exploit even if so inclined.

His thoughts turned to Billy the Kid. During the months they had fought on opposing sides of the Lincoln County War he had come to have a healthy respect for the courage and daring of William Bonney. The two enemies had patched up a truce just before the Chapman killing in February, 1879, and both were now on the proscription list issued by Governor Wallace in the clean-up of Lincoln County that followed. Some inkling of the nature of the appeal of the letter to Billy the Kid may be had from Lieutenant Nevill's report to Ranger headquarters under date of August 26, 1880, when Jesse Evans and his associates had been in the Fort Davis jail for some six weeks:

The prisoners are getting very restless. I have a letter they wrote to a friend of Evans in New Mexico calling himself Billy Antram [Antrim] to come to their rescue, and to use his words, he "was in a damned tight place. Only 14 rangers here at any time, 10 on a scout and only 4 in camp now," and that Antram and a few men could take them out very easy, and if he could not do it now to meet him on the road to Huntsville, as he was certain to go. I understand that this man Antram is a fugitive from somewhere and a noted desperado. If he comes down, and I expect he will, I will enlist him for a while and put him in the same mess with Evans & Co. They offered Lewis Latham, a negro deputy, $1,000 to go in with two others (white) and capture the four men I left here, and turn them out. I don't think the jail is safe with five men long at a time. I don't think there is more than two or three men here that could be counted on in case a mob should attack, and these fellows have several sympathizers and two very influential friends. One of them is a very prominent candidate for sheriff [Wilcox], the other is Fairchild, a bar-keeper. Between them, if disposed to, could command a pretty good mob of negroes and Mexicans. They have, however, shown no disposition to help these, as yet, that I have been able to discover, but they may be playing it very sly. At least the prisoners bank heavily on them as evidenced by their notes they thought they were slipping by without my knowledge.

A week or so later Lieutenant Nevill reported the frustration of an attempt to escape by the time-honored method of digging out. John Gunter had contributed to the diversion of his Ranger captors:

The prisoners have been trying to dig out with a spoon. Corporal Harris caught them after they had a hole about the depth of a man's arm. There is one corner of the jail that they can dig through in half a night if they get anything to work with, and unfortunately they put a negro in who helped to build it and knew its weakness. Since then August Gross (alias John Gunter) played being stricken with paralysis in one leg and arm. Said he would die if he did not get to stay out in the air. I thought I would try him last Sunday, and he forgot himself on several occasions during the day while he was being watched. He would cross the paralyzed leg, and once, when the violin was being played and on change suddenly from waltz to jig, he went to patting his foot pretty lively, when I had him locked up again. Since he tried to get the doctor to say he had to have fresh air. He is not dead yet but getting well very fast.

Toward the end of September Lieutenant Nevill made an extended report of the precautions he had taken with these prisoners. He also boasted that he was prepared for "Captain Kid" should the redoubtable young fellow appear on rescue bent. The jail was of the Mexican type; that is, it was virtually a dungeon underneath an adobe building surrounded by a courtyard.

> I keep five men there all the time. There is only one entrance to the whole building and I have it bolted at night on the inside, which prevents any ingress from without at night, except it be over the walls, which are 12 feet high. The guard inside is directly over the prisoners, and in full view of both walls a lamp is suspended from floor of guard room to shine on the prisoners all night so they can be seen all the time. Five men in this position I think will be more effective than nine of us before as we had to keep our horses on the outside and necessitated the guard, or one of them, being on the outside and also of having one of the doors open at all hours of the night.
>
> Besides, I have an arrangement by which I will receive notice as soon as anything happens or suspicious parties come around, and also have been promised to be notified if Captain Kidd should start down this way by a party who would be almost certain to find out. But I fear more danger on the road than I do here now, but I shall try to be as soon as they are if I should have to escort them down the road. Captain Graham is on his way here; guess he will be in in two or three days. Gunter is to have his brother-in-law here from Alabama and an attorney from Lampasas by the name of White.

The trials came up in the October term of court. The Davis brothers, being of the influential Graham family in Williamson County, Texas, managed to secure bail and to have their cases continued from term to term until they passed into the limbo of dead issue. John Gunter (Selman) was convicted of manslaughter in connection with Bingham's death and served three or four years in the penitentiary. Jesse Evans was convicted and sentenced to twenty years, ten years for robbery in connection with the Fort Davis store and ten years for manslaughter in connection with the Bingham killing. After about a year and a half in the Texas penitentiary he effected a "break" and became lost to history. A faint tradition has it that he turned his back on outlawry and returned to the section of the country from which he had come into the Southwest.

46. Capture of Billy the Kid

A SHORT TIME AFTER the killing of Grant at Fort Sumner in January, 1880, the Kid and John Chisum happened to meet at Fort Sumner and the Kid took the opportunity to make demand for $500 in payment for services to the Tunstall-McSween-Chisum party's interests. Just as the mantle of leadership had fallen to McSween after Tunstall's murder, so Chisum, following McSween's death, had been recognized as the guiding head. Since Tunstall's death Billy had received no wages, though he had continued to serve, first under McSween and then (so he understood) under the sponsorship of Chisum. Further, he had helped in the elimination of some of the old Jesse Evans gang which had been stealing Chisum's cattle. Chisum declined to pay even when the Kid threatened him with a pistol. Chisum showed no loss of composure even though he was looking into the muzzle of a revolver and that, too, in the hands of a dangerous young desperado. Coolly reaching into his pocket for pipe and tobacco, Chisum said in his slow drawling speech, "Let me get a smoke, Billy, for then I can talk better. Now, Billy, listen. If you talked about that money until your hair was as white as mine, you could not convince me that I owed it to you." The Kid kept his finger on the trigger but Chisum went on, "Billy, you couldn't shoot an honest man, could you, while he was looking you square in the eye? You have killed several men, I know, but they needed killing."

By this time the Kid had begun to yield to the adroit attack, and Chisum pressed home the advantage by a reminder of how during the

Lincoln County War the McSween party hid out in the vicinity of South Spring River and he had let them have whatever they needed from his store on credit. At this juncture the Kid lowered his pistol into the holster, but he did not relinquish his claim. "All right, Mr. Chisum," he said, "but only for the present. If you won't pay me that $500 in money I'll steal from your cattle until I get it." In this interview Chisum vindicated his confidence in his persuasiveness. An often-made remark was that if he could talk two minutes to a man, no matter how angry or quarrelsome, he could pacify the boisterous one; but it had been as close a call as Chisum perhaps had ever had, and he realized that. Henceforth the Kid would bear a grudge.

Billy the Kid became the scourge of the cattlemen. By the spring of 1880 the Kid's gang had been enlarged by new recruits, not participants in the Lincoln County War. One was an unsavory character named Dave Rudabaugh, wanted for murder and sundry lesser crimes. Of an entirely different stripe was a young man who signed his name Billie Wilson but whose true name was David L. Anderson, who very briefly sought refuge with the Kid's party to avoid arrest on what he considered unjust charges. The gang's membership had always been fluid. The nucleus, however, remained always Billy the Kid, with Bowdre and O'Folliard as right and left bowers, no matter who else might be associated for a longer or shorter period. All that spring of 1880 they were busy raiding different ranches and ranges, not neglecting even the Mescalero Indians. They would take their booty to Las Vegas or some other place to the eastward and there dispose of it. Things went very smoothly until in the fall of 1880 they began to afflict the town of White Oaks with their presence and their activities.

WHITE OAKS RESISTS BILLY

White Oaks was determined to show no patience toward Billy the Kid. A thriving town forty miles northwest of Lincoln, it had come into being in the early part of 1880 when news of the discovery of gold in the Baxter mountains spread abroad. As a settlement that was rapidly outstripping all others in the county in growth and business, it might have become congenial soil for the Kid and his associates; but it did not turn out to be a haven for them. The people of White Oaks mostly came from an eastern environment that had made them sensible and law-abiding. Saloons, gambling halls, and other means of recreation and stimulation such as a frontier town deemed essential they would tolerate; but they did not intend to let White Oaks become a rendezvous for those whom Colonel Dudley used to characterize as "murderers, horse and cattle thieves, and escaped convicts." The residents of White Oaks were determined to keep out that sort of lawlessness even though the place was a mining camp growing rapidly into a town of two or three thousand. Consequently, it was never hospitable toward the Kid.

At the slightest hint of the Kid's being in the vicinity, Will Hudgens, the deputy sheriff, could easily gather a posse to drive him away. One of these efforts, when a White Oaks posse had surrounded the Kid and his band at Greathouse and Kuch's ranch on the road to Las Vegas, resulted in Jimmie Carlyle, a young blacksmith very popular with all White Oaks, being killed. The circumstances are confused but the story seems to run as follows. There was an exchange of hostages while the topic of surrender was under discussion. Greathouse became the hostage of those "forted up" in the ranch house; Carlyle played a corresponding role for the White Oaks posse. For some reason Carlyle decided to leave the ranch house. The Kid's crowd tried to prevent this, and when Carlyle leaped through a window, he was killed. White Oaks regarded this killing as a mortal offence. Naturally it was laid on the shoulders of Billy the Kid. So strong was the feeling that when a later posse came in pursuit of the Kid they burned the ranch house to the ground. It had become a place of infamy that must be wiped out. Not the least foothold for that crowd in the vicinity of White Oaks was to be allowed, such was the popular feeling.

In the latter part of 1880 the law-abiding element in Lincoln County asserted itself by electing Pat Garrett sheriff in the November voting. Garrett had lived in Fort Sumner during the height of the feud and had taken no active part in it. His coming into New Mexico from the buffalo grounds of West Texas had coincided almost exactly with the beginning of overt warfare in Lincoln County. As he had married and settled himself into a job at Fort Sumner, he felt no inclination to thrust himself into the troubles of ninety miles away. When these grew less virulent, he moved to Roswell and took up a valuable piece of land close to that of Captain J. C. Lea, who now owned not only the buildings that were Roswell but a good deal of land adjoining. He did not, of course, trespass on the domain of John Chisum, for that shrewd old cow king was still the power to be reckoned with in the Pecos Valley. Now that the Chisums had withdrawn from the dangers incident to Lincoln County and were established, temporarily at least, on the Canadian, Captain Lea had stepped into John Chisum's shoes and become the outstanding citizen of that section. The Civil War disturbances in Missouri had given Captain Lea a detestation of lawlessness so strong that he was energetically endeavoring to stamp it out in Lincoln County. In his new neighbor, Pat Garrett, he saw the type

White Oaks, a mining town 40 miles northwest of Lincoln, was a late comer among Lincoln County settlements and set out to be law-abiding. When a young blacksmith was killed some forty miles north of there by the cohorts of Billy the Kid, White Oaks added to Lincoln County's growing zeal for order.

of man needed for the law enforcing agencies and became active in procuring his nomination and election to the sheriffship.

Even before he was inducted into office, Pat Garrett took the field. Ordinarily he would have been sworn in in January, but in November such an emergency arose near White Oaks that Garrett had to start upon his special task of curbing the depredations of Billy the Kid, although he could only do so as deputy sheriff. Everybody understood that Garrett and the Kid had developed an acquaintance at Fort Sumner and that possibly some degree of friendship existed between them. Garrett would not let this hinder him in the performance of his sworn duty. None who knew the man felt that his previous association with the young outlaw would lead to his showing the least partiality.

Luck played into Garrett's hands at the start. He had the Kid his prisoner in a little less than a month. Considering the obstacles Garrett had to encounter, it is remarkable that by the close of December he lodged the Kid in jail at Santa Fe. Billy the Kid had the whole country terrified. Friends were ready to give him the timely warning as well as aid and comfort; enemies dared not deny him provisions or concealment. No one would give out information concerning him even when called upon by officers of the law. As a consequence of this condition Garrett could make so little headway at first that it looked as if he would fail. The pursuit, however, took on a different complexion when Frank Stewart with a posse of Panhandle cowboys joined forces with Garrett. Billy the Kid's gang had stolen cattle from a ranch on the Canadian River and disposed of it to Pat Coghlan at Tularosa. The cattlemen's association in that section of the Texas Panhandle had in Frank Stewart a very energetic "agent," a cross between a private detective and a deputy sheriff. To him was delegated the task of locating the cattle carried away into Lincoln County. Stewart and Garrett had a conference at Las Vegas the outcome of which was that Stewart gave over to Garrett six of the Panhandle cowboys. With Lon Chambers, Lee Hall, Jim East, "Poker Tom," "the Animal," and "Tenderfoot Bob," as reinforcements, Garrett, who had no one with him at the time except Barney Mason, felt equipped with a posse adequate enough to carry the pursuit into the rough Las Canaditas region east of Fort Sumner. Learning that the Kid's crowd had re-appeared at Fort Sumner, Garrett altered his course promptly. The Kid knew that Garrett was active now but did not perhaps realize that his posse had been so greatly strengthened by the six men from the Panhandle.

Garrett laid a trap at Fort Sumner for the Kid's crowd but caught only O'Folliard. Mischance had it that this young man should be at the head of the party when it rode into the ambush Garrett had prepared

384 Sparks are Extinguished

in the vicinity of the old Indian Hospital building northeast of the
Post proper, where Charlie Bowdre's wife was living. Tom Pickett,
a new member of the band, though riding beside O'Folliard, escaped
all the bullets that Garrett and Lon Chambers fired at the head of
the group. Those that turned and escaped, Billy the Kid, Rudabaugh,
Bowdre, and Billie Wilson, felt that O'Folliard's death was the beginning of the end but prepared to sell out dearly. They betook themselves to an old unused rock house at Stinking Spring, about twenty-
five miles from Fort Summer, and awaited Garrett's next move.
During the night of December 20 Garrett with his posse slipped in and
surrounded the stronghold which was sturdily built of rock with a minimum allowance of doors and windows. Before full daylight the
struggle began between the five men "holed up" in the house and the
seven in Garrett's posse. Bowdre was picked off when he came outside,
apparently to feed his horse. In the dim light Garrett mistook him for
the Kid himself and give the signal to his men for a volley. The siege
lasted until four o'clock in the afternoon, interspersed with sharp fighting, sometimes with words as well as rifles. The intensely cold weather
was trying on both the besieged and the besiegers. Those in the house
suffered extremely from scanty provisions and lack of wood for a fire.
They concluded the best course was to surrender.

With these three important prisoners Garrett hastened toward
Santa Fe. He reached Las Vegas on the afternoon of December 26 and
lodged them for the night in the jail. The next morning, when he proposed to go on by train to Santa Fe, he found strong objection from
the Las Vegas Mexicans to his taking away Rudabaugh. They did not
care about the other prisoners, but Rudabaugh must be left so that
they might mete out, in all probability, vengeance for his killing the
Mexican jailer when he had made his "break" from the Las Vegas jail
some weeks before. Garrett, however, was determined to make good
his promise of safe conduct to all four. Rudabaugh in particular had
been apprehensive and had gained from Garrett a special promise of
protection. The situation grew very tense as the time approached for the
train to leave. A noisy mob gathered at the station and threatened to
take Rudabaugh by force from Garrett's custody. Garrett's firmness,
aided by a mollifying speech by Miguel I. Otero, prevented any clash
and the train pulled out with the prisoners on it, guarded by Garrett,
Stewart, Mason, and Mike Cosgrove. The latter had been impressed
into service at Las Vegas when Jim East and "Poker Tom," who had
been among the guards at first, had to be released from duty.

On December 27 Garrett turned his prisoners over to Charles
Conklin, deputy United States marshal at Santa Fe. The Santa Fe

New Mexican in its issue for December 28 recorded as follows the arrival of Garrett with his batch of notable prisoners.

The most important arrivals on the last night's train were Billy the Kid, Rudabaugh, and Billie Wilson, whom it is unnecessary to introduce to the readers of the *New Mexican*. Everybody in the territory has probably heard of the famous outlaws who have so long infested the country and filled the papers with accounts of crime; and every law-abiding man will be delighted to hear that they were safely landed in the Santa Fe jail. For this great boon Sheriff Pat Garrett and his posse of brave men are to be thanked.

Since the Kid was now in the custody of the United States authorities and lodged in the Santa Fe jail there seemed small chance of getting out of confinement. The Kid did come close to turning the trick as the *New Mexican* for March 1, 1881, relates:

Yesterday it was discovered that the Kid and his gang had concocted and were stealthily carrying out a plan by which they hoped to gain their freedom and escape the fate that was awaiting them. And very fortunate it was that the discovery was made just when it was, for a night or two more would have sufficed for the completion of the well-laid scheme.

It appears that Sheriff Rómulo Martínez, fearing that the four desperate men, the Kid, Rudabaugh, Billie Wilson, and Kelly, would ere long make a desperate effort to get out, had promised to pay one of his prisoners if he would assist in helping one of the guards keep watch; and yesterday the fellow informed him that the men were trying to escape. Sheriff Martínez, accompanied by Deputy United States Marshal Neis at once proceeded to the jail, and entering the cell, found the men at supper. They examined the room and found the bed ticking was filled with stones and earth, and, removing the mattress, they found a deep hole.

Further investigation showed that the men had dug themselves nearly out, and, by concealing the loose earth in the bed and covering the hole with it, had almost reached the street without awakening the suspicion of the guard. Last night they were closely guarded and heavily ironed, and today further precautions will be taken.

Though checked in this attempt at regaining freedom, the Kid tried to play a trump card by an appeal direct to Governor Wallace. Overlooking or ignoring the fact that for nearly two years he had been leading a life of cattle stealing interspersed with killing and that such a career might cancel any previous offer of clemency from the Governor,

the Kid sent the following note written in some devil-may-care mood
that led to indulgence in a threat which was, to put it mildly, a daring
audacity.

Santa Fe, New Mex.,
March 2nd. 1881

Gov. Lew Wallace,

    Dear Sir: I wish you would come down to the jail and see me.
It will be to your interest to come and see me. I have some letters
which date back two years, and there are parties very anxious to
get them; but I will not dispose of them until I see you. That is,
if you will come immediately.

Yours respect,
Wm. H. Bonney

    Perhaps the appeal was not made earlier because the Governor
had been absent from Santa Fe almost continuously since the Kid was
placed in jail. On December 26 he had left for a trip to Washington,
from which he returned on February 8. Three days later, that is on
February 11, he had left again, this time for the Black Range in the
western part of the territory where he had mining interests. Billy the
Kid had therefore invoked his help at the first opportunity.

    The course followed by Governor Wallace, as described by him-
self in later years, was: "I knew what the papers were, and I proceeded
to forestall any move on his part by giving them to the newspapers
myself with an account of just how I had come to make the promises
contained therein. When this material appeared in print, I sent a
copy to the Kid. I heard nothing further from him, and I presume he
understood that the door of my clemency was shut."

47. The Kid's Trial and Conviction

On March 28, 1881, Billy the Kid was taken from Santa Fe to Mesilla where he was to be tried under the change of venue to Doña Ana County that had been standing for two years. Billie Wilson, one of those who was captured by Garrett at Stinking Springs the previous December, was also taken, to be tried for passing a counterfeit $100 bill. The Kid was to be tried for murder upon one or more of the several indictments hanging over him. In charge of the prisoners were Tony Neis, deputy United States marshal, and Francisco Chávez, chief of police at Santa Fe. Every precaution was taken to forestall any interference with getting the two prisoners to Mesilla, whether it came in the form of rescue by friends or lynching from enemies. All went well on the trip until Rincon was reached, where it was necessary to leave the railroad and go overland to Mesilla. According to the Santa Fe *New Mexican* there was a demonstration at that point, although it is an open question whether it was friendly or hostile. Neis was in such general uneasiness that he was likely to misjudge the event. As given in the newspaper, this happened:

> In the light of after events it appears that it was a fortunate thing for Billy the Kid, and perhaps for Billie Wilson, that they did not go south on Sunday, the day which had been fixed for their departure. They were prevented from doing so by some business obligations of Chief of Police Frank Chávez, who went with Deputy Sheriff United States Marshall Neis as guard and who could not get off on the appointed day. If they had gotten off on that day as was anticipated, they would have found at Rincon a

body of perhaps thirty men who were determined and prepared to get away with them even it were found necessary to dispose of the officials in order to carry out their plans. Judge Thornton was on the train which the crowd thought would bring the Kid, and he was questioned by them as to the day upon which the wanted men would arrive. He was not posted and prudently said that he had heard nothing of their proposed removal, from which it was inferred that the party would not come for a day or two. Nevertheless a close watch was kept for them, and when at last they did reach Rincon, there were some six or seven roughs on hand, who showed a very bristling front. Deputy Marshall Tony Neis hurried the prisoners from the train into a saloon in order to get them out of the way as soon as possible and having done so hired a back room for them. One of the men said so that the officers could hear the remark, "Let's take them fellows anyhow," whereupon Neis replied, "You don't get them without somebody being killed," and then the party entered the house.

The men on the outside then endeavored to organize, while the officers and prisoners awaited anxiously in the room. Neis had a double-barreled gun and a six-shooter, and Chávez a rifle. The Kid and Wilson were evidently very uneasy, and Neis not being acquainted with the intentions of the mob and suspecting that their object was to release the prisoners, told them that if it came to the scratch he would turn his guns loose on both of them before they should be taken. The Kid was badly frightened as the marshal's words carried conviction with them, and he and Wilson kept still enough. Some disinterested men finally succeeded in dispersing the mob, whom they assured that if any attempt was made to rescue the men they would have a hard fight for it, and the project was abandoned.

The officers with their charges took the coach at Rincon for Mesilla, to which place they proceeded unmolested; on arriving at Mesilla the Kid was badly frightened again. The sight of a large number of Lincoln County men was too much for his nerves, and the man who is said to have taken the lives of twenty-odd men trembled in his boots, he said, "See all those fellows here waiting for me? Not a damn one of them had to attend court, and here they are just to get away with me. They'll take me out of jail and hang me." The presence of the men annoyed the Kid again because he was well aware that among them were many who could be summoned as witnesses against him in the trial for the murder of Al Roberts, and whose evidence would be a dead setback to his case. No demonstration was made at Mesilla, however, and as there is a good jail there and a strong guard, the Kid is probably safe from the mob. From all accounts Neis bore himself well throughout the trip, but he says he doesn't want to undertake the job again, very much. Chávez behaved well also; and but for the bold front which the officers put on, Uncle Sam might have been spared the expense of one murder trial at least.

On April 6 the trial started in the old adobe building that did duty both as a school and as a courthouse at Mesilla. Against the rear wall of the room was a low platform on which sat Judge Bristol, who had presided over enough trials growing out of the Lincoln County disturbances and by now was quite obviously sick and tired of the whole affair. In front of the judge's desk was a small space kept clear for the lawyers. A little to the side of the judge's desk was Billy the Kid, handcuffed and closely guarded. Across one side of the room was the jury, all Mexicans. The rest of the room contained rough wooden benches which afforded seats for the spectators, a motley crowd representative of all the elements composing the southwestern segment of New Mexico. There were the law-abiding settlers, cattlemen and farmers chiefly; there were the roughs and riffraff that came and went; there were officers and men from Fort Stanton; and there were even a few Mescalero Indians.

The general expectation was that the Kid would be tried for one of the killings that made it possible to lodge a federal charge against him. The prosecution of federal cases was considered much more substantial and thoroughgoing than was that of territorial cases. The prosecution thought a conviction much more likely on one of the federal charges, of which there were two, one for killing Roberts and another for killing Bernstein. As there was grave doubt whether it could be proved that the Kid was responsible for the Bernstein killing, that charge was eliminated. The choice fell upon the one connected with the killing of Roberts. Judge Leonard, whom the court had appointed as counsel for the Kid, raised at once the question of jurisdiction. The killing had occurred on land belonging to Dr. Blazer, which was not under government control although it was inside the Mescalero reservation. Judge Bristol promptly accepted this contention and quashed the indictment. At the same time, however, he ordered the United States Marshal to deliver the Kid to the territorial authorities so that he might be tried under some other indictment.

The trial in the territorial court began on April 8, the basis for it being the killing of Sheriff Brady. The prosecution was conducted by S. B. Newcomb, a Las Cruces attorney who had succeeded Rynerson as district attorney. By court appointment the defense was in charge of Fountain & Bail, prominent attorneys in Mesilla. Only two days were needed for the trial. The first of them was largely occupied with selecting the jury; on the second day began the taking of testimony, which was quickly completed. Then came the speeches by the lawyers and the charge from Judge Bristol which practically demanded a conviction for murder in the first degree, the penalty for which would have been hanging. After a short deliberation the jury presented a verdict — guilty. The remaining steps were over in a few days more. On April 13 Judge Bristol formally sentenced the Kid to be hanged at Lincoln on May 13 between nine and three o'clock in conformity to the New Mexico law that put the execution date thirty days after the sentence.

While there is little or nothing to show how the Kid accepted the situation, yet he does not appear to have lost his *sang-froid*. Certainly he did not "crack up" or denounce the judge and court, although there is a legend to that effect. In an interview with one of the newspaper men there seems to be an indication that he was still buoyed up by hope of executive clemency from Governor Wallace.

Shortly after sentence was passed upon the Kid, a reporter of the Mesilla *News* interviewed him with the following effect. Said the Kid, after considerable delay:

"Well, I had intended at one time not to say a word in my own behalf, because persons would say, 'Oh, he lied.' Newman, editor of *Semi-Weekly* gave me a rough deal; has created prejudice against me, and is trying to incite a mob to lynch me. He sent me a paper which shows it; I think it is a dirty mean advantage to take of me, considering my situation and knowing I could not defend myself by word or act. But I suppose he thought he would give me a kick down hill. Newman came to see me the other day. I refused to talk to him or tell him anything. But I believe the *News* is always willing to give its readers both sides of a question.

"If mob law is going to rule, better dismiss judge, sheriff, etc. and let all take chances alike. I expect to be lynched in going to Lincoln. Advise persons never to engage in killing."

Editor — Think you will be taken through safe? Do you expect a pardon from the governor?

"Considering the active part Governor Wallace took on our side and the friendly relations that existed between him and me, and the promise he made me, I think he ought to pardon me. Don't know that he will do it. When I was arrested for that murder, he let me out and gave me my freedom of the town, and let me go about with my arms. When I got ready to go, I left. Think it hard I should be the only one to suffer the extreme penalties of the law."

Here the sheriff led us away and said we had talked long enough.

Another glimpse of the Kid at this juncture comes from a letter to Edgar Caypless, an attorney at Santa Fe who had befriended him when he was confined in jail there. Caypless was in reality attorney for

Rudabaugh but in his visits to the jail he had become acquainted with the Kid. Possibly he would have become his attorney if the Kid had had money to employ him. The Kid had allowed Caypless to start a replevin suit to get back from W. Scott Moore of Las Vegas his favorite bay mare. When the Kid surrendered to Garrett at Stinking Springs, he had let Frank Stewart take the mare, perhaps realizing that she would go to him anyhow as booty. As Garrett's account has it, "At Fort Summer, the Kid made Stewart a present of his mare, remarking in his usual joking way that he expected his business would be so confining for the next few months that he could hardly find time for horseback exercise." At Las Vegas Stewart transferred the animal to W. Scott Moore, who gave a $60 revolver in exchange. The Kid finally decided to try to get the animal back and let Caypless start suit to that end.

Two days after being sentenced he wrote Caypless urging him to finish the matter in order that he might have money for an appeal. Incidentally, he presents incisively the situation after his trial:

Mesilla, N.M.
April 15, 1881

Mr. Edgar Caypless,
  Santa Fe, N.M.

Dear Sir: I would have written before this but could get no paper. My United States case was thrown out of court and I was rushed to trial on my territorial charge. Was convicted of murder in the first degree and am to be hanged on the 13th of May. Mr. A. J. Fountain was appointed to defend me and had done the best he could for me. He is willing to carry the case further if I can raise the money to bear his expense. The mare is about all I can depend on at present, so I hope you will settle the case right away and give him the money. Please do as he wished about the matter. I know you will do the best you can for me in this. I shall be taken to Lincoln tomorrow. Please write and direct care of Garrett, sheriff. Excuse bad writing. I have my handcuffs on.

I remain as ever,
Yours respectfully,
William Bonney.

This letter does not exhibit the least whine or grumble at his lot. What the young fellow was concerned about was the next move. His active brain was turned toward the future. He is to go the next day back to Lincoln to live a month under the shadow of the gallows, but he is in no funk over his plight. Resourcefulness, courage — two qualities that had stood him in good stead during his career, were still with him.

48. The Kid's Daring Getaway

The journey back to Lincoln was into familiar ground. Until Billy the Kid reached the Fort where he was to be turned over to Garrett he was in the custody of Doña Ana officials. How closely he was guarded and with what spirit he left Mesilla may be seen by the following extract from one of the New Mexico newspapers.

Deputy U.S. Marshal Robt. Olinger and Deputy Sheriff Dave Wood of Doña Ana county, and a posse of five other brave men left Las Cruces on Saturday evening, April 16th at 10 o'clock, with Billy the Kid for Lincoln where they arrived safe on the Wednesday following. Kid was informed before starting that if his friends attempted to rescue him he would be shot first and the rescuing party attended to afterwards. He is now in Sheriff Garrett's hands and will be closely guarded by him and his deputies until the execution, May 13th. Kid maintains his usual good spirits. We take a short extract upon the subject from Newman's *Semi-Weekly:*

He appeared quite cheerful and remarked that he wanted to stay with the boys until the whisky gave out anyway. Said he was sure his guard would not hurt him unless a rescue should be attempted, and he was certain that would not be done, "unless perhaps those fellows over at White Oaks come to take me," meaning to kill him. It was, he said, about a stand-off whether he was hanged or killed in the wagon. The Mesilla jail was the worst he had ever struck. The sheriff wanted him to say something good about it when he left, but he had not done so. He wanted to say something about John Chisum, and it would be some satisfaction to him to know that some men would be punished after he had been hung.

He was handcuffed and shackled and chained to the back seat of the ambulance. Kinney sat beside him. Olinger on the seat facing him. Mathews facing Kinney, Lockhart driving, and Reade, Woods, and Williams riding along on horseback on each side and behind. The whole party were armed to the teeth, and any one who knows the men of whom it was composed, will admit that a rescue would be a hazardous undertaking.

As there was no secure jail at Lincoln, Garrett confined the prisoner in a room in the northeast corner of the second floor of the Dolan store, which the county had accommodatingly taken off Catron's hands for use as a courthouse. The only access to this room was through the sheriff's office. As a further precaution the prisoner was not only kept handcuffed at all times, but heavy leg irons were riveted about his ankles. Robert Olinger, whose hatred of Billy was well known, was assigned as guard. He and another guard, J. W. Bell, were instructed that one or the other must remain at the prisoner's side constantly, day and night, to make escape impossible.

Exactly six days after he was locked up at Lincoln, on April 28, Billy the Kid killed both guards and escaped.

Many theories have been advanced as to how Billy accomplished this small miracle. Some of the stories may have been encouraged by the Kid himself, intentionally misleading to protect his friends. In the escape the crucial factor was the obtaining of a pistol. One story has it that during a card game Billy slipped his hands out of the handcuffs, seized Bell's pistol and shot him when he tried to escape. The pistol-snatching story, however, was later exploded by Judge Lucius Dills, whose investigations revealed that Bell's pistol was still in its holster fully loaded when his body was removed from where he had fallen in the yard. The Santa Fe *New Mexican* withdrew this theory but it was too late to check its popular acceptance. It had captivated the folk imagination and so embedded itself that after more than three quarters of a century it is still the most widely used means of accounting for the Kid's action.

The second theory was one supported by Garrett. On the day of the escape he had been over at White Oaks and therefore did not have firsthand knowledge of what had happened in Lincoln. The Kid's escape was such a setback to his prestige as sheriff that he naturally instituted a thorough investigation. In the *Authentic Life of Billy the Kid*, written by Ash Upson but based in great measure on information furnished by Garrett, the following version was adopted. Bell had taken the Kid downstairs and out into the yard where there was a privy. As they were returning the Kid got considerably ahead of his guard, reaching the armory closet where weapons and ammunition were locked in a room at the head of the stairs, with Bell lagging so far behind at to be near the foot of the stairway. The Kid procured a pistol and then awaited Bell's ascent of the stairs. When Bell realized that his prisoner had the upper hand, he turned and started back toward the doorway. Billy, instinctively realizing that Bell would shout for help if he reached the door, fired. The Kid and Bell had been on friendly terms and only as a last resort, in self-protection, would the Kid have shot him.

Though this account has its puzzling features, it stands today as the official one. The thing which makes Garrett's theory hard to accept is his supposition as to how Billy obtained the pistol. It seems incredible that Bell, a conscientious and experienced officer, would have lagged so far behind his prisoner that the latter, handicapped by leg irons, had time to hobble up the stairs, enter the room at his right, cross to the armory closet in the far corner over the stairwell, break through the locked closet door, secure a pistol, and then return to the head of the stairs while Bell was still near the foot of the stairway.

There is a better key for unlocking the mystery of the pistol. Although Billy the Kid himself gave out to several persons accounts of how he secured the weapon, he probably never revealed the true story. His loyalty to the persons who had aided him would lead him to adopt a version which would throw people off the scent. The most credible account is one which has been handed down from generation to generation in the families of native New Mexican residents of Lincoln. It is treated as a jealously guarded secret, seldom divulged, but going back quite as close to the event itself as the other two. The pistol was planted in the privy in the courthouse yard by a boy who lived nearby and who, though said to be related to the Baca family, was nevertheless a devoted admirer of William Bonney. His name was José M. Aguayo according to Florencio Chávez and others, including Saturnino Baca's son-in-law, Frank Salazar, though in the whispered re-tellings the spelling of his name is somewhat varied. Use of the outhouse was not confined to people in the court building and the young man with a newspaper in his hand, sauntering thither, attracted no particular attention.

Billy's loyal friend Sam Corbet had paid him a visit each day and was permitted to chat briefly with him at the door of the room where the prisoner was confined. On this Thursday morning Corbet contrived to slip a piece of paper into the Kid's hand without being observed by Olinger or Bell. It bore but one word, "privy," but Billy understood the message. Some other prisoners were being held in the west wing of the second floor of the building and it was customary for either Olinger or Bell to escort these across the road at mealtime to Wortley's eating place. The Kid waited until Olinger and his prisoners were well occupied with their meal before he asked Bell to take him down to the yard. There, concealed in an old newspaper in the outhouse, was a pistol!

On the way back toward the room where he was confined the Kid naturally walked in advance. The turn at the foot of the stairs gave him opportunity to take the pistol from its place of concealment in his clothing without detection. When he reached the head of the stairs his drawn gun made him master of the situation. Obviously, here Bell made his fatal mistake; instead of throwing up his hands in surrender, he turned and ran.

There is little divergence in the accounts of what occurred after Bell staggered from the stairway and fell in the courthouse yard. The Kid hopped to the east window of the room where he had been confined, picking up Olinger's buckshot-loaded shotgun as he passed through the sheriff's office. This window overlooked the pathway which Olinger would naturally follow leaving the Wortley place to investigate the sound of the two shots at the courthouse. As he passed through the gate of the courthouse yard, he heard his name called from the window above. He was looking up when he was blasted with a charge from his own shotgun.

Making his way to the hall window at the rear of the building, the Kid spied the courthouse handyman, Godfrey Gauss, in the yard below. At the sight of Billy, Gauss dashed for the protection of the new building back of the courthouse where he shared sleeping quarters with Sam Wortley. The Kid, however, called out reassuringly and asked the handyman for some tool he might use to remove his shackles. As Gauss himself later wrote the story:

> With a little prospecting pick I had thrown him through the window he was working for at least an hour, and could not accomplish more than to free one leg, and he came to the conclusion to await a better chance, tied one shackle to his waistbelt, and start. Meanwhile I had saddled a small skittish pony belonging to Billy Bert, [sic] as there were no other horses available, and had also, at Billy's command, tied a pair of red blankets behind the saddle. I came near to forgetting to say that whilst I was busy saddling, and Mr. Billy the Kid trying hard to get his shackles off, my

partner, Mr. Sam Wortley, appeared in the door leading from the garden where he had been at work, into the yard, and that when he saw the two sheriffs lying dead he did not know whether to go in or retreat, but on the assurance of Billy the Kid that he would not hurt him, he went in and made himself generally useful.

When Billy the Kid went down the stairs at last, on passing the body of Bell, he said "I'm sorry I had to kill him, but couldn't help it." On passing the body of Olinger he gave him a tip with his boot, saying, "You are not going to round me up again."

We went out together where I had tied up the pony, and he told me to tell the owner of same, Billy Burt, that he would send him back the next day. I, for my part, didn't much believe in this promise, but sure enough, the pony arrived safe and sound, trailing a long lariat, at the court house in Lincoln.

And so, Billy the Kid started out that evening, after he had shaken hands with everybody around having had a little difficulty in mounting on account of the shackle on his leg, he went on his way rejoicing.

The spectacular feat of regaining his freedom accomplished the apotheosis of Billy the Kid. To some he had been a hero, to many others a desperate character, but now the dramatic story of his escape caught the popular imagination and won a kind of grudging admiration even from those who decried the fact that two more names were added to the long list of those who had lost their lives in both factions of the Lincoln County War. Even the Santa Fe *New Mexican*, always anti-McSween and therefore disparaging to the Kid, felt compelled to bow after this exploit. The issue of May 4, 1881, had this to say:

> The above is a record of as bold a deed as those versed in the annals of crime can recall. It surpasses anything of which the Kid has been guilty so far that his past offenses lose much of heinousness in comparison with it, and it effectually settles the question whether the Kid is a cowardly cut-throat or a thoroughly reckless and fearless man. Never before has he faced boldly or run any great risk in the perpetration of his bloody deeds. Bob Olinger used to say that he was a cur and that every man he had killed had been murdered in cold blood without the slightest chance of defending himself. The Kid displayed no disposition to correct this until this last act of his when he taught Olinger by bitter experience that his theory was anything but correct.

49. The End of Billy the Kid

BILLY'S DEPARTURE from Lincoln was unhampered. The great majority of the townspeople were sympathetic with the young fellow. Those otherwise disposed had too much respect for the Kid's prowess to interfere. A short ride brought him to the nearby Capitán foothills where he spent the night at the goat-ranch home of his friend, schoolmaster José Córdova. Here he released his mount, knowing that the pony would instinctively find its way home, and the next morning Billy set to work to rid himself of the remaining leg iron. He borrowed another horse and saddle, this time with the owner's willing consent, and headed for Fort Sumner.

For almost three months the Kid led the life of a fugitive. Fearing that his presence in Fort Sumner might bring down trouble on the Maxwells and his other friends, he spent most of his time among the sheep camps scattered over the mesas to the east, slipping into Fort Sumner only occasionally to participate in a baile at some friendly Mexican house.

Garrett's efforts to locate the fugitive were frustrated by an almost complete lack of help from the citizenry, but he took new hope with the arrival of John W. Poe, who had succeeded Frank Stewart as agent for the Canadian River Cattle Association. Poe heard that Billy the Kid was in the Fort Sumner neighborhood, but when he reported this to Garrett, the latter was inclined to reject the idea. At Poe's insistence, however, the sheriff-elect consented to investigate, taking Poe and T. L. McKinney as deputies.

After a day or two of rather fruitless scouting around, Garrett became more convinced than ever that they were on a cold trail. Poe still urged him to continue and suggested that as a last measure they go to Pete Maxwell and pry out what information they could from him. They reached Maxwell's about midnight on July 13, and Garrett, who was perfectly at home about the place through his former residence there, entered the corner room where Maxwell was sleeping, while his deputies seated themselves on the edge of the porch. As they sat there in the darkness a man coatless and shoeless passed by and entered the room close behind Garrett. Garrett has seated himself on the bed and was beginning to question Pete Maxwell when this man sprang into the room, looking back out the doorway and calling out excitedly, "Quién es? Quién es?" At the same moment Maxwell whispered to Garrett, "That's him." The man backed across the room, instinctively trying to reach a corner of the room whence he might command the two sources of danger he was instinctively sensing — the two men outside, the third man inside. Still he asked, "Quién es?" as though doubtful of identity. Garrett could take no chance nor risk further delay. His revolver was jerked from holster and aimed. A shot startled the two deputies outside. Garrett dropped to the floor beside the bed and fired a second time. It was, however, needless to do so. At the first shot the Kid had fallen and in one or two more ticks of a watch was dead. Garrett rushed outside making the announcement to his companions, "That was the Kid came in there onto me, and I think I have got him."

The cautiously undertaken investigation showed that it was really the body of William Bonney, alias Billy the Kid. The next day he was buried by the side of Bowdre and O'Folliard in what had formerly been the military cemetery at Fort Sumner. The problems connected with the Kid's appearance in Pete Maxwell's on that fateful night became resolved into a rather simple sequence of homespun events. In the earlier part of the night he had accompanied Ramón Trujillo from a sheep camp a few miles away to the García home at Fort Sumner, where a dance was being held. When the dance closed, about eleven o'clock, he had gone back with Trujillo to the camp but had almost immediately set out again for Fort Sumner. What motive prompted him to do this remains in uncertainty. A choice ranges all the way from a tryst with some *querida* to a business meeting with a cowboy from Montgomery Bell, a prominent ranchman who was to send $150 to the Kid by messenger.

On reaching Fort Sumner he went to a long adobe building to the south of the Maxwell dwelling house and entered the room occupied by Celsa Gutiérrez and her husband, who was one of the Maxwell

Pat Garrett was elected sheriff of Lincoln County in 1880 with the backing of John Chisum and certain other law-abiding citizens but even before being sworn in he had to begin upon his special task of curbing Billy the Kid. In July, 1881, he finally closed in on the Kid and killed him in Pete Maxwell's bedroom at Ft. Sumner.

employees. From there he went to another room occupied by his friend
Bob Campbell. To make himself comfortable he removed shoes and
coat and seated himself in a chair outside of Campbell's room. Growing
hungry, he asked about food. On being told that a freshly killed quarter
of beef hung on the north porch of the Maxwell house, he walked
across the intervening yard, butcher knife in hand. His route took him
past Poe and McKinney, seated at the eastern end of the south porch.
He moved on past the two strangers a few paces but grew suspicious or
at least uncertain about them. Instead of continuing on around the end
of the house and reaching the north porch, he changed course and
dodged into the doorway of Pete Maxwell's bedroom, there to have his
fatal rendezvous with Pat Garrett.

Garrett's report to the governor of the territory gives an unvarnished report of the affair.

Fort Sumner, N.M., July 15, 1881

To His Excellency, the Governor of New Mexico:

I have the honor to inform your Excellency that I received
several communications from persons in and about Fort Sumner
that William Bonney alias the Kid had been there or in that
vicinity for some time.

In view of these reports I deemed it my duty to go there and
ascertain if there was any truth in them or not, all the time doubting their accuracy; but on Monday, July 11, I left home taking
with me John W. Poe and T. L. McKinney, men in whose
courage and sagacity I relied implicitly, and arrived just below
Fort Sumner on Wednesday, the 13th. I remained concealed near
the houses until night, and then entered the Fort about midnight,
and went to Mr. P. Maxwell's room. I found him in bed, and had
just commenced talking to him about the object of my visit at
such an unusual hour, when a man entered the room in his stock-
ing feet, with a pistol in one hand and a knife in the other. He
came and placed his hand on the bed just beside me, and in a low
whisper he asked of Mr. Maxwell, "Who is it?" and repeated the
question.

I at once recognized the man and knew he was the Kid, and
reached behind for my pistol, feeling almost certain of receiving
a ball from his at the moment of doing so, as I felt sure he now
recognized me; but fortunately he drew back from the bed at
noticing my movement, and although he had his pistol pointing
at my breast, he delayed to fire, and asked in Spanish, "Quién es?
Quién es?" This gave me time to bring mine to bear on him, and
the moment I did so, I pulled the trigger, and he received his

death wound, for the ball struck him in the left breast and pierced his heart. He never spoke, but died in a minute. It was my desire to have been able to take him alive, but his coming upon me so suddenly and unexpectedly led me to believe that he had seen me enter the room or had been informed by some one of the fact, and that he came there, armed with pistol and knife, expressly to kill me if he could. Under that impression I had no alternative but to kill him or suffer death at his hand.

A few days later when Garrett was in Santa Fe pressing his claim for the $500 reward, a reporter of the Santa Fe *New Mexican* plied him with questions about his "capture by killing" of the Kid. That paper carried an account of the interview:

"How did the Kid happen to stop at Maxwell's house?" asked the reporter.

"He didn't stop there," replied Garrett. "He had only made three visits to Sumner since his escape and just came in unexpectedly while I was there. You see, I went in to see Maxwell and ask him where the Kid was. I asked him as soon as I got in whether the Kid was in the country, and he became agitated and answered that he was. Just then a man came in at the door and spoke to my men outside in Spanish, supposing them to be Mexicans. I didn't recognize him. He then came in and approached the bed and after speaking to Maxwell, asked who were those outside. I had not had time to fix my revolver, and had not expected to see him there. I therefore reached around and adjusted, and Maxwell started up in the bed. The Kid pulled down on me, and asked "Who is it?" He must have then recognized me, as I had him, for he went backward with a cat-like movement, and I jerked my gun and fired. The flash of the pistol blinded me, and I fired in the same direction again, and was ready to shoot the third time; but I heard him groan and knew that he was struck. All this, however, has been told. What I want you to say is that Maxwell was not guilty of harboring the Kid."

"I shall do that, but I want to ask you a few questions first. How do you account for the Kid not shooting as soon as he recognized you?"

"I think he was surprised and thrown off his guard. Almost any man would have been. Kid was as cool under trying circumstances as any man I ever saw. But he was so surprised and startled that for a second he could not collect himself. Some men cannot recover their faculties for some time after such a shock. I think the Kid would have done so in a second more, if he had time."

"It is said by some people that the Kid was cowardly and never gave a man a chance," remarked the reporter.

"No, he was game. I saw him give a man one once. I have seen him tried. He would fight any way. I have known him to turn loose in a crowd of Mexicans, and get away with them. He would lick Mexicans that would weigh twenty-five or fifty pounds more than he did. He was quick as a flash."

"Was he a good shot?"

"Yes, but he was no better than the majority of men who are constantly handling and using six-shooters. He shot well though, and he shot well under all circumstances, whether in danger or not."

"Why do you suppose he hung around Lincoln County instead of leaving the country?"

"Oh, he thought that was his safest plan. In fact, he said so. He said he was safer out on the plains, and could always get something to eat among the sheep herders. So he decided to take his chances out there where he was hard to get at."

After some further conversation into which Mr. Garrett entered more freely than was his wont, and another reference to the Maxwell affair, the reporter left.

From the statements of all who knew Pete Maxwell it would appear that Garrett's idea was the correct one and that he was guilty of nothing except being abjectly afraid of the Kid.

Every detail of the Kid's death was seized upon and read most avidly. Since the decimation and dispersal of the McSween party in July, 1878, when Billy's role had changed from one of partisan fighting man to that of a hunted outlaw, his name and fame had spread throughout the territory. To some, particularly to many of the native New Mexicans, he was a hero and the victim of circumstance. In the eyes of others he was a bloodthirsty villain. He had become a legend in his own time and now would pass into the permanent folklore of the frontier.

PART VI

The Ashes

50. The Killing of Juan Patrón

THE STRUGGLE WHICH has come to be known as the Lincoln County War may be said to have begun with the murder of John Tunstall and closed with the death of Alexander McSween. Actually the conflict covered a period of years. The first spark had been kindled five years before, in clashes between the interests of the House of Murphy and those of small ranchers and farmers, including many native New Mexicans. More significantly, it had its roots in the competition for political-economic power between the Murphy organization and its rivals, notably John Chisum. Nor did the climactic five days fight at Lincoln end the hatreds and antagonisms between the surviving partisans of the two factions.

The year 1884 brought on the deaths of two who had played important roles in the Lincoln County affairs. One of these was Juan Patrón; the other was John Chisum. Death came to the first in the violent fashion so characteristic of the section; it came to the second through the inroads of insidious disease.

After the disaster to the McSween party in July, 1878, Juan Patrón had found life in his native Lincoln Plaza increasingly uncomfortable. He had, in fact, reason to fear for his life and for the safety of his family. Eventually seeking peace and safety, he determined to make a new home for himself and his family at Puerto de Luna, far from Lincoln and near the homes of relatives of his wife, Beatriz Labadie, whom he had married at Las Vegas. He proposed to establish a mercantile business in association with his wife's uncle, Guillermo

Giddings, son of John Giddings, one of the pioneer settlers of that section. Leaving his wife at the home of Lorenzo Labadie in Santa Rosa, Patrón established temporary living quarters in an old house opposite the site of the proposed new store.

On the night of April 9 Patrón and his brother-in-law, Crescencio Gallegos, dropped into the saloon connected with the store of "Governor" Moore at Puerto de Luna. It was about ten o'clock and several Texas cowboys and natives were drinking and gambling in the saloon. After talking to some of those present Patrón said to Gallegos, "Let's go home. That glass of beer has made me sleepy. Besides, it is time for us to get to bed." Hardly had the words been uttered when a stranger to those in the place spoke out. The heavily-armed newcomer later identified as one Mitch Maney, addressed Patrón: "Hold on. Don't go yet." With that he threw his arms around Gallegos' shoulders; at the same time he drew his gun and pointed it at Patrón who was standing in front of Gallegos. He fired and the bullet, passing through the heart, killed Patrón instantly. The cowboy continued firing and wounded Gregorio Barros. Then having exhausted his supply of cartridges in the chambers of his revolver, he decided to be on his way. Out of the saloon he walked, mounted his horse, and rode away.

Patrón's friends took up his body and carried it to his home. Puerto de Luna seethed with excitement. A leading citizen, not only of that community but of the territory of New Mexico, had been shot down by the hand of an assassin. In a few hours fifty or more men on horseback were in pursuit of the murderer. Nicolas Griego acted upon a feeling that the most likely place to look for Mitch Maney was George V. Davidson's place in the canyon of Cañada de Juan de Dios and thither he went. Waiting near the house until daylight, his vigil was rewarded by a sight of the fugitive entering the house. Griego then went to the house, told Davidson what had occurred at Puerto de Luna, and secured Davidson's assistance in arresting Maney. The two started for Puerto de Luna with the prisoner, and on their arrival, just when the inquest was about to be held, a lynching seemed imminent. However, Pablo Analla, the justice of the peace, and other citizens prevailed upon the more vindictive ones to hold themselves in check and let the law take its course.

At the preliminary hearing Mitch Maney was bound over to the August term of court at Las Vegas without bail. The prisoner was forwarded to Las Vegas under an escort of twenty heavily-armed citizens. In due course the case came to trial in the following December. The prosecution was in charge of a formidable array of lawyers; no

Juan B. Patrón. This remarkable young man, a native of the area, educated at Notre Dame University in Indiana, was the recognized *Guia* (leader) of the Mexican-American citizenry in Lincoln County. Except for Dolan and McSween themselves, he was perhaps the most notable of the leaders actively engaged in the Lincoln County War and its aftermath. His killing in 1884 was attributed by many to the bitter enmities engendered by the War.

less persons than William Breeden, the attorney general of the territory, and Thomas B. Catron. The defense counsel consisted of Sydney M. Barnes and Lee & Fort. The outcome of the trial was a hung jury, but in its deliberations, so one of the Las Vegas papers was pleased to note, the "jury stood evenly divided, six for conviction and six for acquittal. It was indeed gratifying to learn that there was no race division in the jury. Three natives and three Anglos stood for guilty and four natives and two Anglos stood for not guilty."

A re-trial was set for the March term of court and the prisoner allowed bail. It was claimed that some of Maney's witnesses had failed to appear because they were afraid to come to Las Vegas, where they were under indictment for gambling. Breeden, the attorney general, however, promised them all immunity if they appeared at the spring term of court; his motive was to have all the facts on both sides brought to light. As the case never came to trial again, these were never determined in a conclusive way.

At once there was an effort among Patrón's friends to associate this killing with the Lincoln County troubles. They were confident that Maney had been hired to commit the murder by someone who feared that Patron knew too much about rascality and evil deeds in that section of the country or who had nursed some grudge against Patron for the part he had taken in county affairs. The other motive that might be ascribed for the killing was less sensational. As one of Maney's friends, George Peacock, told it to a Las Vegas paper, it had happened as the result of a quarrel incident to gambling. "I have known Mitch Maney since boyhood," said Peacock,

> His father is a prominent lawyer in Texas and his family is of high standing. I never saw Mitch drunk in my life. It was I who sent him to Puerto de Luna to get a check cashed. I understand that both Patrón and Gallegos were under the influence of liquor and that they both insulted Mitch Maney, which brought on the shooting. Mitch is not a quarrelsome boy, and this is the first time I ever heard of his getting into trouble, and I am inclined to believe he shot in self-defense.

Mr. Peacock's theory was ridiculed by those who had been actual witnesses but, whatever the circumstances and the motives back of the killing, Patrón's passage was in keeping with the turbulence of the times. In fact it might be described as hereditary, for Patrón's father, Isidro Patrón, had come to his end on that night in December 1873 when the Harrell clan descended upon Lincoln and shot up the danceroom. Juan Patrón had received overtures from the Murphy outfit when in the fall of 1876 they felt that they needed a vigilance committee to enable them to get rid of obnoxious persons, but he had refused to side with them. His affiliation was so strong with the opposite faction that, when he was in Santa Fe attending the session of the legislature and there arose the question of his returning to Lincoln to give some assistance to McSween, he received a telegram from Rynerson, the district attorney, warning him not to come back. After his return Rynerson had explained that Jesse Evans stood ready to kill him. In the subsequent developments Patrón had consistently supported the McSween cause; it was largely his influence that gave that faction the large following it had among the native New Mexican element.

Patrón's career was remarkable and he well deserved the eulogistic paragraph that the Las Vegas *Gazette* of April 9 used as an introduction to the account of his death:

The untimely ending of the life of Juan B. Patrón will cause many sad hearts, not only in San Miguel County, but in the entire territory of New Mexico. Few men had a more extensive or better acquaintance throughout the territory than Juan B. Patrón. He was respected and beloved by our American citizens as much as he was by our native citizens, and few young men in New Mexico had more friends. He was twenty-nine years of age on his last birthday, and was, perhaps, the best informed native resident in New Mexico; and his life's work showed that he was not only intelligent, but honest, studious, and industrious. He was a native New Mexican, and early in life was taken in charge by the Rt. Rev. Archbishop Lamy of Santa Fe, who gave him a superior education, both in the Catholic schools of New Mexico and at Notre Dame, Indiana. He was married to the daughter of Hon. Lorenzo Labadie and a sister of Tranquilino Labadie, recently city clerk of Las Vegas. He was elected to the house of representatives from Lincoln County, New Mexico, and when the legislature assembled in Santa Fe in January, 1878, he was elected speaker of the house, and while a member of that body displayed marked ability for one so young.

51. Exit John Chisum

TOWARD THE LATTER PART of 1884 the news came to New Mexico of the death of John Chisum at Eureka Springs, Arkansas. After Lincoln County had begun to improve in peacefulness and respect for law and order, the Chisum herd had been brought back from the Panhandle and the South Spring River ranch began to undergo development on a scale elaborate for that locality and period. The original ranch house, which had been on the place when Chisum moved to it in 1875, and which had won scars in fights that had taken place there prior to and during the Lincoln County War, gave place to the so-called "long house." Like its predecessor it was of adobe but was simply a series of eight rooms in a row. Shrubbery and flowers were planted all around the house. Orchard planting was undertaken on a large scale. Farming activities came to the front and the cattle king of the Pecos country centered his interest on alfalfa and other agricultural possibilities.

In the summer of 1884 Chisum felt it necessary to make a trip east in the interest of his health. For some time a tumor had been developing on his neck and now it had become so large and uncomfortable that something had to be done. In July he started on his trip but with a premonition that he might never return. At Kansas City he underwent an operation which was supposed to be successful. After remaining a few weeks for recuperation, he started back to New Mexico but by the time he reached Las Vegas on the return trip he discovered that the old trouble was reappearing. At once he returned to Kansas City for further treatment but the physicians were unwilling to operate again until he had undergone a course of treatment. As Eureka Springs in Arkansas were then in high favor on account of the medicinal baths, John Chisum went thither. More and more he realized the seriousness of his case, even though for a time there was hope that he was getting better. He sent for his brother Jim Chisum and turned over to him the Chisum interests in New Mexico. About the middle of December he grew rapidly worse, and on the twentieth he died. In fulfillment of his request, Jim Chisum carried the body to Paris, Texas, for burial in the Chisum lot.

The death of Chisum removed the man who had built up the large cattle business associated with the Chisum name. None of the brothers who survived him proved equal to the task of holding the business together. The corporate name became the Jinglebob Land & Cattle Company, the stockholders being Jim Chisum, his two sons, Walter and William, his daughter, Sallie Chisum Robert, and her husband, William Robert. John Chisum, it is said, felt that his nephew-in-law would be the mainstay of the management of the Chisum affairs after his death, but family friction forced him off the scene. The Jinglebob Land & Cattle Company procured a loan from a bank in Danville, Kentucky; finally the bank had to foreclose and the Jinglebob Company was closed out in 1891.

Though no one can successfully dispute the fact that John Chisum was the dominating figure in the early development of the Pecos Valley, there is food for endless discussion as to the extent he was involved in the Lincoln County War. In his efforts to monopolize the best portions of the range along the Pecos and in his efforts to retaliate upon Indians and cattle rustlers, he occasionally resorted for forcible measures or, at least, winked at the efforts of his employees to make reprisals. During the Lincoln County War he was able to keep his men from becoming directly involved, although there were men who had been in his employ fighting in both factions. His friendship for Tunstall and McSween caused many to associate him directly with their affairs; naturally they considered him the powerful supporter of the McSween faction, filling much the same position that Catron did for the Dolan faction. Chisum himself, so it is said, liked to boast that his efforts won Governor Wallace's support for Mrs. McSween when she was carrying on the struggle. How his influence was exerted no one can say now. Possibly there is significance in the fact that in all the mass of documentary material few, if any, documents appear bearing the signature "John S. Chisum." Shrewdness and caution were cardinal endowments of the old style Texas cattleman, and John Chisum possessed both in high degree. The seal of secrecy was upon many of his actions;

transactions were conducted by word of mouth rather than by written communications. John Chisum was notably absent from scenes of trouble when the Lincoln County War was at its height, yet this absence did not bring about any lessening of the popular understanding that he was an associate of the McSween faction. He probably breathed more easily when the news reached him at Santa Fe from Las Vegas that Pat Garrett had killed Billy the Kid. The latter had labored under the impression that Chisum had assumed responsibility for the upkeep of the small group which endeavored to protect the interests of the McSween and Tunstall estates. Billy had made no secret of his resentment that Chisum had reneged on this obligation. As long as that young man was alive John Chisum had remained uneasy.

52. James J. Dolan – The Last Years

THE FIVE DAY BATTLE at Lincoln in July, 1878, though it resulted in the death of Alex McSween and the dispersal of his supporters, was for Jimmy Dolan at best a Pyrrhic victory. The J. J. Dolan & Co. store had been lost by mortgage foreclosure to T. B. Catron and Dolan's fortunes appeared to be indeed at low ebb. He was, however, still comparatively young (he was just thirty years of age at the time of the Five Day Battle) and he still had the advantage of powerful political allies at the territorial capital. He was, furthermore, a clever, resourceful, and practical man.

On July 13, 1879, just a year after the July fight at Lincoln, he married Caroline, daughter and heir of Charles Fritz who owned the Spring Ranch on the Bonito. Two years after the death of his first wife in 1886 he wed Maria Eva Whitlock at Lincoln, but long before this time he had re-established himself politically and financially. He had taken over the Tunstall property at Lincoln and re-entered the mercantile business for a time before selling the store to Rosenthal & Co. He had also taken over the Tunstall ranch on the Feliz, which became the family home. In 1882 cattle belonging to Rynerson and Dolan were moved here from Ranchería, east of Tularosa. In 1887 the ranch was incorporated as the Feliz Cattle Co., forerunner of the Flying H ranch.

The days of violence were over, but politics continued to be Dolan's special field. He served as county treasurer from 1883 until 1888 when he was elected to the territorial senate. The following year he secured appointment to the Federal Land Office at Las Cruces, a post he held for some two years.

Death came to James Joseph Dolan February 26, 1898. He was buried at the Spring ranch below Lincoln in the Fritz family cemetery near the Bonito, the little stream which on past occasions had been so turbulent but now flowed quietly on its mission bringing water to the farms in the peaceful valley.

53. John H. Riley, Businessman

AFTER THE FIVE DAY FIGHT in July, 1878, Johnny Riley was seen at Lincoln infrequently, if at all. Early the following year he settled at Las Cruces where he was associated with W. L. Rynerson in various cattle ventures and homesteaded land east of Las Cruces at what later became the community of Organ. November 9, 1882, he married Miss Annie Cuniffe at Las Cruces.

In 1885 and for a time thereafter he was in Colorado in the employ of contractor James Carlyle in construction work for the Colorado Central Railroad. Returning to the Mesilla Valley, he was again associated with the Catron-Rynerson interests in business and political activities. Supported by his old "Ring" friends, he was elected Doña Ana County tax assessor in 1889.

Riley was aligned with the Good faction in the Tularosa Basin's bloody Good-Cooper range feud in which Walter Good, Charles Dawson, George McDonald and others lost their lives; it was, in fact, claimed that many of the cattle in John Good's herds were in reality the property of Riley and Rynerson. In this conflict, as in the Lincoln County War and as later in the Tularosa "Water War," John Riley's role was that of strategist rather than front-line fighter.

In 1894 Riley purchased the 500-head cattle herd of that remarkable hermit, "Frenchy of Dog Canyon." He prudently excluded from the purchase any claim to the fresh water spring in Dog Canyon so avidly coveted by Frenchy's neighbors; Frenchy's retention of his home at the spring cost the old man his life before the year was out.

It was shortly thereafter that Riley separated from his family, making his home thence forth in Colorado. With the help of J. D. Isaacks and others he drove his herd to a 1,000 acre range near Fowler, some thirty-five miles east of Pueblo.

A clipping in the family scrapbook from an unidentified newspaper published in June, 1898, says:

> Hon. John H. Riley of Colorado Springs has sold his fine La Cueva ranch property to J. D. Isaacs of Las Cruces. The ranch was sold for $5,000 & 300 head of cattle.

Becoming a citizen of Colorado did not immediately end Riley's involvement in New Mexico politics. Around the turn of the century he was reported as "lobbying" at the territorial capital at Santa Fe. After his move to Colorado he remained active in the Tularosa Canyon water controversy. Riley and Rynerson had acquired a substantial tract of land including, most importantly, the water rights along the river above the village of Tularosa. The villagers were at the mercy of the holders of such water rights; their community could be cut off without water if they failed to come to terms with the landholders above the town. The conflict had resulted in some bloodletting from time to time before it was finally settled by legal negotiation. Under this agreement the town was able to retain its needed water supply while Riley and his then-partner, T. B. Catron, retained ownership of their ranch nearby. Riley and Catron acquired the land and the water rights of the other landholders in the canyon above the town and assigned these to the village group, receiving in exchange fifty water rights in the Tularosa Irrigation District. For Riley, who personally negotiated the settlement, it was a highly satisfactory deal.

The Colorado ranch, operated by Riley and his partner, Harry Leonard, prospered. It seems to have been eventually converted from cattle raising, as Mr. Riley's obituary in the Colorado Springs *Gazette* referred to it as "one of the finest hog ranches in the state of Colorado." For the last eighteen years of his life Riley divided his time between the ranch and Colorado Springs, where he maintained rooms, first on Weber Street and then for twelve years at the El Paso Club.

John Henry Riley died of pneumonia at Colorado Springs on February 10, 1916, at the age of sixty-five.

54. J. B. Mathews–
After Violence, Peace

ALTHOUGH HE HAD BEEN in personal charge of the expedition which killed John Tunstall and had always loyally followed the leadership of his senior partner, Jimmy Dolan, in the Lincoln County War, Billy Mathews was not by nature a man of violence. As hostilities subsided he quickly disassociated himself from his connection with the feud and moved to the Peñasco Valley where he engaged in the cattle business on a modest scale.

Well thought of in the community, Mathews was named postmaster at the newly established Lower Peñasco post office in November, 1884. Three months later he relinquished the office to his wife, the former Miss Dora Bates, whom he had married in 1883, and associated himself with James F. Hinkle in the formation of the Peñasco Cattle Co., an organization soon to be known as a successful and highly ethical operation. In 1893 he became manager of the Pecos Irrigation & Improvement Co., a large-scale project in the development of farm lands on and near what had once been John Chisum's South Spring River ranch.

Active in civic and Masonic affairs, Jacob Basil Mathews had been postmaster at Roswell for six years prior to his death there, June 3, 1904.

Sue McSween, widow of Alexander McSween, braved
the dangers of the Lincoln County War at her husband's side and struggled for years afterward to right
the wrongs against her late husband and his estate.

55. Sue McSween–Remarkable Woman of a Remarkable Age

THE KILLING OF HER attorney, Chapman, and the threats against her own personal safety did not dampen the courage of Alex McSween's widow. Robert Widenmann had completely neglected his duties as administrator of the Tunstall estate, had not even been seen in Lincoln County since June, 1878, and by October had left New Mexico. Mrs. McSween and Isaac Ellis did what they could to conserve the assets of the estate even before she was officially confirmed as administratrix in November, 1879.

As executrix for her late husband's estate, Mrs. McSween presented her belief that McSween had owned some interest in the Tunstall store, but this proved to be in error. On the other hand, when she informed Dick Brewer's parents in Wisconsin that, at the time of his death, she held his note dated October 13, 1877, for $682 plus accrued interest at 2% per month, the elder Brewers acceded to her suggestion that they deed her the Brewer ranch in payment. With the money realized from her sale of Brewer's 640 acres of fine farm and grazing land on the Ruidoso and with funds salvaged from the assets of the McSween estate, she was presently able to launch a ranching venture of her own, well away from Lincoln, in the Three Rivers area west of the Sierra Blanca range. It has been said that the gift of a small herd of cattle from John Chisum assisted the widow in making her new start but, whether or not this is true, the fact is that this courageous woman was presently a successful rancher in her own right.

In June of 1884 the widow McSween married thirty-four year old, Virginia-born George Barber, who had been educated in Milwaukee, Wisconsin, and had spent nine years surveying government lands in the Dakotas before moving to New Mexico for reasons of health in 1875. Arriving at Lincoln from Colfax County in the winter of 1876-77, he had been friendly with the Tunstall-McSween group but had taken no active part in the factional feuding. Under the tutelage of Ira E. Leonard he had "read law," and after McSween's death he purchased from the estate the 402 volume library and furniture of McSween's law office. When the ex-Mrs. McSween obtained a divorce from Barber in 1891, she testified that he had never supported her at any time during their marriage. In any event, it appears that while Mr. Barber devoted his principal attention to his professional activities, management of the ranch was left in the hands of Mrs. Barber.

Again a single woman, Mrs. Barber's life continued unchanged. William A. Keleher has called attention to two articles which appeared during 1892 in the Lincoln County newspaper, the *Old Abe Eagle*. One, in the April 21 issue, noted that Mrs. Barber had driven 700 to 800 head of cattle from her ranch to the railroad at Engle. The September 1 issue quotes from an article appearing in the New York *Commercial Advertiser:*

> Near the town of White Oaks, N.M., lives one of the most remarkable women of this remarkable age, at the present time a visitor in this city. The house in which she lives, a low, white-walled adobe building, is covered with green vines and fitted out with rich carpets, artistic hangings, books and pictures, exquisite china and silver, and all the dainty belongings with which a refined woman loves to surround herself. The house was built with her own hands. The huge ranch on which it is located with its 8,000 cattle, is managed entirely by her. It is she who buys or takes up the land, selects and controls the men, buys, sells and transfers the cattle. She is also a skilled and intelligent prospector, and found the valuable silver mine on her territory in which she now owns a half interest. She sings charmingly, accompanying herself as dexterously as she uses an adze or jack plane. She entertains delightfully at her home, whist parties, little dances, and even an occasional german. Her name is Mrs. Susan E. Barber. A woman who can run a ranch, build a house, manage a mine and engineer a successful german, deserves a prominent place in the ranks of women of genius.

As the years began to take their toll, Mrs. Barber was gradually forced to relinquish her responsibilities in the rugged life of a ranch-woman. However, it was not until 1917 that she sold her famous Tres Ríos ranch to Albert Bacon Fall and retired to a quiet life at White Oaks, now an almost-deserted hamlet but one rich in the memories of the great mining boom and the days of violence.

Still active in mind and spirit at the age of eighty-six, Sue McSween Barber died at her White Oaks home in 1931, one of the last survivors among those who had played leading roles in the Lincoln County War.

Index

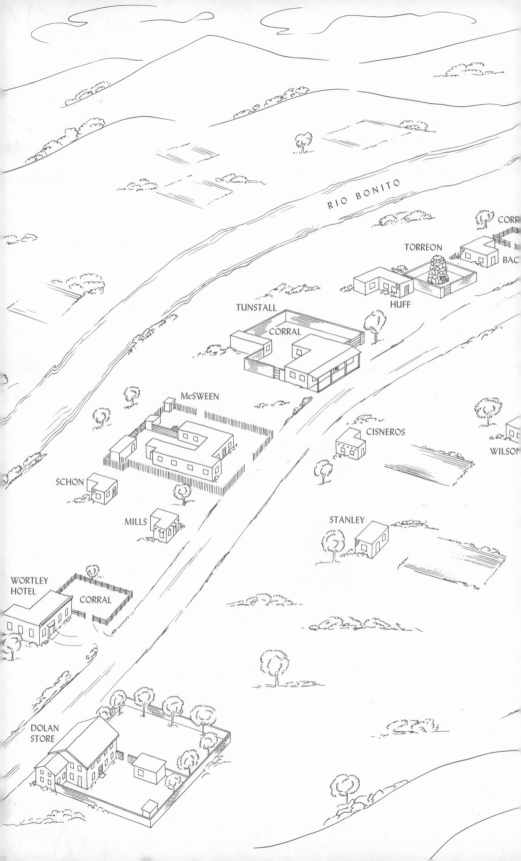

RIO BONITO

CORR

TORREON

BAC

HUFF

TUNSTALL

CORRAL

McSWEEN

CISNEROS

WILSON

SCHON

MILLS

STANLEY

WORTLEY
HOTEL

CORRAL

DOLAN
STORE

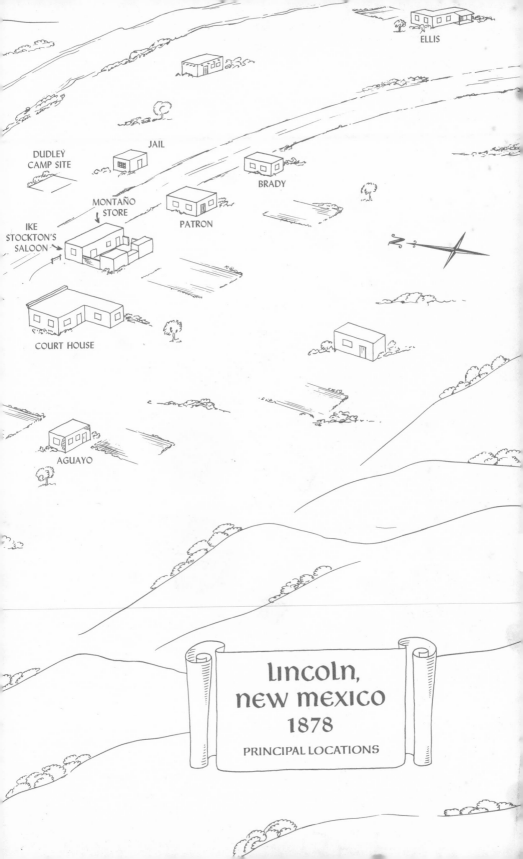

ELLIS

DUDLEY
CAMP SITE

JAIL

BRADY

MONTAÑO
STORE

PATRON

IKE
STOCKTON'S
SALOON

COURT HOUSE

AGUAYO

lincoln,
new mexico
1878
PRINCIPAL LOCATIONS